Tenth Edition

MANAGEMENT OF ORGANIZATIONAL BEHAVIOR

LEADING HUMAN RESOURCES

Paul Hersey
Center for Leadership Studies
Escondido, California

Kenneth H. Blanchard
The Ken Blanchard Companies, Inc.
Escondido, California

Dewey E. Johnson
Sid Craig School of Business
California State University, Fresno

PEARSON

Original edition, entitled MANAGEMENT OF ORGANIZATIONAL BEHAVIOR, 10th Edition, by HERSEY, PAUL; BLANCHARD, KENNETH H.; JOHNSON, DEWEY E., published by Pearson Education, Inc, publishing as Prentice Hall, Copyright © 2013 by Pearson Education, Inc.

Indian edition published by Pearson India Education Services Pvt. Ltd. Copyright © 2015.

ISBN 978-93-3254-985-2

First Impression, 2015

This edition is manufactured in India and is authorized for sale only in India, Bangladesh, Bhutan, Pakistan, Nepal, Sri Lanka and the Maldives. Circulation of this edition outside of these territories is UNAUTHORIZED.

Published by Pearson India Education Services Pvt.Ltd,CIN:U72200TN2005PTC057128.
Formerly known as TutorVista Global Pvt Ltd, licensees of Pearson Education in South Asia

Head Office: 7th Floor, knowledge Boulevard, A-8(A) Sector-62, Noida (U.P) 201309, India

Registered Office: 4th floor, Software Block, Elnet Software City, TS 140 Block 2 & 9, Rajiv Gandhi Salai, Taramani, Chennai - 600 113, Tamil Nadu, Fax: 080-30461003, Phone: 080-30461060, www.pearson.co.in Email: companysecretary.india@pearson.com

Digitally printed in India by CMS IT Services Private Limited, New Delhi in the year of 2017.

Dedication:

To

RALPH E. HERSEY, SR., a retired telephone pioneer with more than 50 patents for Bell Laboratories, whose work made direct dialing a reality. In looking back over his 39 years of work with the telephone industry, he once commented that of all his contributions, the most rewarding aspect to him personally was that he became known as a developer of people.

and

the REAR ADMIRAL THEODORE BLANCHARD, USNR, former naval officer who was decorated with two Silver Stars, the Bronze Star, the Presidential Citation, and a Navy Unit Commendation for his courageous and competent World War II leadership in the Pacific. People who worked for him over the years always described him as an inspirational, dedicated, and caring leader who always fought for his people and the "underdog," whether in peace or war.

and

DEWEY EMANUAEL JOHNSON, entrepreneur, small-business owner, farmer, and community leader. He was known for his selfless dedication to others. He could always be counted on to give personal leadership and financial support to business and civic organizations.

CONTENTS

PREFACE

The 10th Edition of *Management of Organizational Behavior* truly reflects and integrates 50 years of the most significant theory and research developed by thought leaders in behavioral science. Our purpose is to share with you the special insights we have developed through our research and its practical application during that time with our clients in more than 40 countries throughout the world. The acceptance of our approach to leadership in these countries demonstrates that because it is *situation-based*, it is easily adaptable to organizations, small groups, individuals, and families, regardless of their culture. Simply stated, our focus is on the interaction of people, motivation, and leadership.

It seems appropriate to pause and look back, as well as forward, as we release this milestone edition.

LOOKING BACK: HOW DID SITUATIONAL LEADERSHIP® GET STARTED?

Some years ago, Dr. Paul Hersey was working as a Human Resources Director when he observed that leaders were effective in one situation. However, when they were assigned to different jobs, they were ineffective. Why? Because the situations they were facing were different. Their new jobs required different behaviors adapted to the tasks and relationships now involved. Paul shared his findings with Dr. Ken Blanchard and together they developed the initial foundation of Situational Leadership® that was first published in 1969. Since then, Situational Leadership® has been refined through the previous nine editions of *Management of Organizational Behavior*. This current edition reflects not only the most relevant research findings from the behavioral sciences, but insights gained through working with clients around the world. The adoption of Situational Leadership® by these clients is strong evidence that it works and assists them in building sustainable, high-performance organizations—whether they are businesses, educational institutions, hospitals, political or military organizations, or even families.

LOOKING FORWARD: WHERE IS LEADERSHIP GOING?

While we cannot say exactly where, we do know that leaders of the future will need to cope with velocity, complexity, and the unknown trajectory of technology. While the knowledge we gain about effective leadership practices may be shared virally, virtually, and stored "in the cloud," the need for leaders to adapt their situations may be one of the few things unlikely to change. Follow us on . . .

WHAT'S NEW IN THE TENTH EDITION?

Think of this edition as a tapestry, woven with threads as colorful, diverse, and well-worn as Freud, Machiavelli, and Maslow, and as newly spun as Google statistics and complexity science. You will be challenged to think about how you can apply ideas that have stood the test of time, as well as adapt to emergent trends that are transforming our workplaces as rapidly as our technologies.

Since we first published this book, management theory has certainly grown and evolved, and leadership practices have changed to tackle the turbulence of organizational life in the 21st century. Even the way we conducted our research for this edition demonstrates just how much change has taken place. Our updates are not the outcome of months spent in the card catalogs and stacks of academic libraries. Instead, we could access digital archives of the most recent journal archives, blog posts, and streaming video within seconds of starting a search.

Our goal in this 10th edition has been to add fresh mortar to the foundation we first laid half a century ago. Yes, the classic models and frameworks are still here, but you will also find new (we can no longer say "hot off the presses") content on key topics, including:

- Motivation: Emergence of the progress motive, renewal of the purpose motive (2-37)
- Emotional intelligence: Cultivating your self-awareness as a leader (11-189, 15-264)
- Teams: Building the collective EQ of your team (13-238)
- Communication: Gender and generational differences; when conversations falter (12-228)
- Decision Making: How brain structure and contexts impact decisions (15-264)
- Performance Management: Balanced scorecard metrics, feedforward (14-256)
- Leadership: Strengths and myths (4-82)

In addition, we have punctuated the text with illustrative stories, questions, and quotes (look for the Beatles and Bernie Madoff, the Miracle on the Hudson, and the Arab spring, to name a few).

INSTRUCTOR SUPPLEMENT

The Instructor Manual and case studies are available for download at the resource center. Please contact your Pearson Sales Representive to obtain an access code.

ACKNOWLEDGMENTS

We owe much to colleagues and associates, without whose guidance, encouragement, and inspiration the first edition of this book—much less the ninth—would never have been written. In particular, we are indebted to Harry Evarts, Ted Hellebrandt, Norman Martin, Don McCarty, Bob Melendes, Walter Pauk, Warren Ramshaw, and Franklin Williams.

We wish to make special mention to Chris Argyris, William J. Reddin, Peter Drucker, and Edgar A. Schein. Their contributions to the field of applied behavioral science have been most valuable to us in the course of preparing this book, and we hereby express our appreciation to them.

We also want to express our gratitude and appreciation for the tremendous contributions of Ron Campbell, President, Center for Leadership Studies, to the preparation of this book and for his thoughtful review of the manuscript.

Our thanks and appreciation also go to the following colleagues:

- Tom Weise, Professor of Communication, College of the Sequoias, Visalia, California, for major contributions to "Effective Communications"
- Gustav Pansegrouw, President, Center for Leadership and Organization Studies, Johannesburg, South Africa
- Bo Gyllenpalm, Founder and President, Situational Management Services, AB, Stockholm, Sweden
- Nima Faqihinezd, Managing Director of family business, Dubai, United Arab Emerates
- Nguyen Thanh Quang Huy, Business Planning and Performance Management Manager, Prudential, Ho Chi Minh City, Vietnam.
- Mary Moir, Executive Editor, Wendell, Minnesota
- Elizabeth Cordero, Pediatric Educator, Renown Hospita, Reno, NV
- John Lattin, MD, Pediatrician, Northwest Medical Group, Fresno, CA
- Dr. Walter Natemeyer and Brandy Archambeault for updates and edits.

The comments and suggestions provided by students, managers, teachers, researchers, consultants, and reviewers have been particularly important to us as we have prepared this and previous editions. We thank them for their insightful suggestions and comments.

Reviewers for Pearson

Kathy Benton,
Colorado Christian University

Dan Hallock,
University of North Alabama

Diane Huber,
University of Iowa

Marcus Flores,
Colorado Christian University

Liliana Meneses,
University of Maryland University College

Morgan Milner,
Eastern Michigan University

Dean Ridings,
Colorado Christian University

Scott Wednger,
Missouri State University – Springfield

Alan Whitlatch,
South Dakota State University

Our appreciation goes to Stephanie Wall, Ashley Santora, Lynn Savino, and Tom Benfatti of Pearson Education for their dedication to the development, design, and production of this 10th edition.

Finally, special thanks are due to Suzanne, Margie, and Joan, our wives, for their continued patience, support, and interest in the progress of our work. You have always been and continue to be the inspirational force in our lives.

Paul Hersey
Kenneth H. Blanchard
Dewey E. Johnson

ABOUT THE AUTHORS

Paul Hersey, Ed.D., is chairman of the board and professor of Organizational Behavior and Management, California American University, Graduate School of Applied Behavioral Sciences. Paul is also founder and chairman of the board of the Center for Leadership Studies, Inc.

Paul has helped develop well more than 10 million managers and salespeople from more than 1,000 businesses and other organizations. He has made presentations in more than 125 countries and is an internationally known behavioral scientist and highly successful entrepreneur. He has been recognized by the Academy of Management and *Training and Development* magazine as one of the world's outstanding authorities on training and development in leadership, management, and selling.

Paul has authored or coauthored more than 50 books, monographs, and articles, including three Prentice Hall books: *Management of Organizational Behavior: Utilizing Human Resources* (with Ken Blanchard), *Organizational Change through Effective Leadership* (with Ken Blanchard and Robert Guest), and *Selling: A Behavioral Science Approach*. He has also coauthored *The Family Game: A Situational Approach to Effective Parenting* (with Ken Blanchard). His recent books include *The Situational Leader, Situational Selling: An Approach to Increasing Sales Effectiveness,* and *Situational Parenting* (with Ron Campbell).

Kenneth H. Blanchard, Ph.D., is the chief spiritual officer of The Ken Blanchard Companies, a full-service global management training and consulting company that he and his wife, Dr. Marjorie Blanchard, founded in 1979 in San Diego, California. Ken is also a visiting lecturer at his alma mater, Cornell University, where he is a trustee emeritus on the board of trustees. He teaches a master of science in the Executive Leadership Degree Program, jointly sponsored by the University of San Diego and The Ken Blanchard Companies. Ken is also cofounder of Lead Like Jesus, a nonprofit organization dedicated to inspiring and equipping people to walk their faith in the marketplace.

Ken's best-selling book, *The One Minute Manager®*, coauthored with Spencer Johnson, has sold more than 13 million copies worldwide, is still on best-seller lists, and has been translated into more than 25 languages. Among his many other books are *The Power of Ethical Management* with Norman Vincent Peale and *Managing by Values,* coauthored with Michael O'Connor. *Raving Fans®* and *Gung Ho!TM,* coauthored with Sheldon Bowles, continue to appear on best-seller charts. Ken's latest book, *Leading at a Higher Level,* translates 25 years of research and global experience into one volume of practical strategies for leaders.

Dewey E. Johnson, Ph.D., is Professor of Management Emeritus, California State University, Fresno.

Elected to more than a dozen offices in national and regional professional associations, Dewey is a cofounder and former chair of the Management Education and Development Division, Academy of Management; past National President and Fellow, Small Business Institute Director's Association; and recipient of the Provost's Outstanding Professor Award for Service from his university.

Prior to entering the academic community, Dewey served with the U.S. Air Force as a pilot, commander, and staff officer, retiring with the rank of colonel. He was awarded the Legion of Merit with one oak leaf cluster and many other decorations.

Dewey has published many articles and has been a presenter at more than 170 domestic and international conferences in the areas of leadership, small business, and performance management. He has made more than 36 consulting and teaching trips to the Peoples Republic of China.

1

Leadership and Management
An Applied Behavioral Sciences Approach

THE LEADERSHIP DIFFERENCE

Every country has many examples, past and present, of courageous men and women who have stepped forward and accomplished great things under extremely challenging conditions. Some are widely known, like Nelson Mandela, who fought apartheid in South Africa, or Aung San Suu Kyi, who continues to struggle for human rights in Burma. Mark Zuckerberg, founder of Facebook, harnessed the Internet so that millions can "friend" each other. Luis Urzua, the shift commander, organized and calmed the Chilean miners trapped underground for 69 days until they were rescued. Still others may live in your neighborhood or work in a nearby school but have never made headlines. All these men and women saw the need for action, believed in what they were doing, inspired others and, with them, changed their worlds. This is the essence of leadership—recognizing the need for action, motivating and inspiring others, and making things happen.

Effective leadership rarely happens by accident. Nor is it passed along through DNA. Rather, it is the result of relevant, proven skills that can be learned and applied by almost anyone in any organization who is trying to influence others. We can readily see what a difference leadership makes in the business world from research about retention. What is the number one reason people stay with an organization? They work with a good leader. This is the good news. But the source of the bad news is the same. The number one reason people leave an organization is that they work for a bad leader. Data show clearly that "managers trump companies."[1] In other words, alluring benefit packages and profit sharing cannot make up for the day-to-day damage that can be done by a manager who is insecure or unclear, overinvolved or unavailable. High-performing employees will seek out other opportunities if their leaders inhibit their talents. And with a workforce increasingly populated by younger "Gen X" and "Gen Y" employees who are more mobile and more loyal to their immediate leader than to an organization, the costs and consequences of losing people are high: team disruption, lower productivity, and managerial time diverted to selection and hiring. In fact, it costs 10 times more to recruit and train a follower than to provide the leadership environment to retain them. So learning to be an effective leader benefits you, your people, and your organization—now and in the future.

THE IMPACT OF GLOBALIZATION ON LEADERSHIP AND MANAGEMENT

Whether you live in the United States or in the United Kingdom, Laos or Latvia, we all know that the pace of technical, social, economic, and potential change has accelerated exponentially in the past few decades. Not only has the pace of our lives quickened, but so have the interrelated impacts of these changes. For example, the ability to instantly message or tweet a piece of information played an important communication role in the political uprisings known as the "Arab spring" of 2011. Technology touches politics, which then transforms the social and economic landscape, which in a country like Egypt, occurred within two weeks.

In the midst of this ongoing turbulence, organizations are breathlessly trying to both keep up and anticipate what is coming next. They outsource, downsize, and rebrand. The tools and technology alone are dizzying to keep up with. Today we have high-speed wireless Internet service that is accessible to millions. We have smart phones from which we can send e-mail to our customers and access satellite maps to locate their stores. We can e-mail a digital design to an overseas supplier today who can manufacture, ship, and have that product on the shelves of a store in less than a week.

Technology Is Making Your Competition One Click Away

It is a fact that in a few short years, e-commerce has transformed the global market place. And with this change, perhaps the most significant challenge facing organizations is that the power has shifted from sellers to buyers. With just one click, online buyers can search for the best quality, service, terms, flexibility, and innovation. If you are not pleased with one firm's products or services, another's Web site is just one more click away. Now that over 2 billion of us across the world use the Internet,[2] it is easier than ever for people to buy goods and services that they want rather than what suppliers think the buyers need.

Michael Hammer, coauthor with James Champy of the influential book *Reengineering the Corporation,* describes this shift:

> [P]owerful modern customers—whether consumers or corporations—want one thing: *more.* They want more products for less money, more quality and service, more flexibility and convenience, and more innovation. The guilty party in the morality play that is modern business is not the rapacious capitalist or the manipulative manager; it is you and I, every consumer who looks carefully at price and quality, who shops around, who abandons yesterday's product for today's better one. It is the powerful customer who has forced radical changes on the reluctant managers of organizations in every industry.[3]

In fact, as Andrew S. Grove, cofounder of Intel, knows, adaptability is the key to business survival in the face of runaway change:

> There are two options: Adapt or die. The new environment dictates two rules: First, everything happens faster; second, anything that can be done will be done, if not by you, then by someone else, somewhere. Let there be no misunderstanding. These changes lead to a less kind, less gentle and less predictable workplace.[4]

Faced with a radical need to continually adapt, successful organizations rely on a deep sense of purpose to both steady the course and chart new directions. That purpose helps clarify their responsibilities toward customers, employees, owners, society, and the environment—aii of the key stakeholders who are affected by their performance.

The Domain of Leadership and Management Has Become Worldwide

Given the sharp impacts of globalization, what separates the leaders who feel overwhelmed by the tsunami of change from those who can ride the waves? Is it creativity or connections, moxie or optimism? Michael Porter sums it up this way:

> Real . . . leaders believe in change. They possess an insight into how to alter competition, and do not accept constraints in carrying it out. Leaders energize their organizations to meet competitive challenges, to serve demanding needs, and above all, to keep progressing . . . . Leaders also think in international terms, not only in measuring their true competitive advantage, but in setting strategy to enhance and extend it.[5]

But strategy can no longer take the form of a five-year plan. Effective leaders are those who can mobilize their people to accomplish results with strategic speed. *Agility, change, execution,* and *results*: These are the operative words for leaders in the new world order.

Technology is enabling faster performance of many processes; it is also giving organizations the systems and tools to be relentless cost cutters. Traditional layers of management are being stripped away as the Internet reduces the need for middlemen, brokers, and distributors. These managers, who are fewer in number, must have sharper business acumen and better people skills to get the job done. They must increasingly accomplish their goals through virtual teams since the geographic distance between leader and follower is increasing. Managers need employees to become self-directed faster than ever anticipated, which requires high levels of confidence, commitment, and motivation. The era of the knowledge worker is here, and it has already changed the way organizations function, lead, hire, and promote.

PEOPLE PROVIDE THE ADVANTAGE

From a historical perspective, we can see that the sources of competitive advantage have varied over time. According to Ed Lawler, organizations once focused primarily on the control of natural resources, but then had to progressively compete through economic and financial expertise, improved marketing ability, control of technology, and now the improved use of human resources.[6] Vincent Omachonu and Joel Ross, authorities on quality management, support Lawler's conclusion:

> Historically, productivity improvement has focused on technology and capital equipment to reduce the input of labor cost. Improved output was generally thought to be subject to obtaining more production by applying industrial engineering techniques such as methods analysis, work flow, etc. Both of these approaches are still appropriate, *but the current trend is toward better use of the potential available through human resources* [emphasis added].[7]

People are now the primary source of competitive advantage. That is why companies now view retention, talent management, and being seen as an "employer of choice" as key concerns in the age of the knowledge worker.[8]

DISTINCTIONS BETWEEN MANAGEMENT AND LEADERSHIP

Management Defined

Any review of the literature will quickly show that there are almost as many definitions of management as there are writers in the field. A common thread that appears in these definitions is that the manager is required to *accomplish organizational goals or objectives*. We define *management* as the process of working with and through individuals and groups and allocating other resources (such as equipment, capital, and technology) to accomplish organizational goals. This definition applies to organizations, whether they are businesses, educational or religious institutions, hospitals, political or military organizations, or even families. Everyone is a manager in at least certain activities.

Leadership Defined

In essence, leadership is a broader concept than management. Management is a special kind of leadership in which the achievement of organizational goals is paramount. The important distinction between the two, therefore, lies in the term *organizational goals*. Our definition of leadership is that leadership occurs whenever one person attempts to **influence the behavior of an individual or group**, regardless of the reason. It may be for one's own goals or for the goals of others, and these goals may or may not be congruent with those of the organization.

WARREN BENNIS   Warren Bennis, a highly regarded leadership scholar, has differentiated the roles of the leader from that of the manager through a number of provocative contrasts:

> Leaders conquer the context—the volatile, turbulent, ambiguous surroundings that sometimes seem to conspire against us and will surely suffocate us if we let them—while managers surrender to it. The manager administrates; the leader innovates. The manager is a copy; the leader is an original. The manager maintains; the leader develops. The manager focuses on systems and structure; the leader focuses on people. The manager relies on control; the leader inspires trust. The manager has a short-range view; the leader has a long-range perspective. The manager asks how and when; the leader asks what and why. The manager has an eye on the bottom line; the leader has his eye on the horizon. The manager imitates; the leader originates. The manager accepts the status quo; the leader challenges it. Managers do things right; leaders do the right things.[9]

While these polarities point to key differences in the roles, it is important to realize that leadership and management are complementary activities. John Kotter, an authority on leadership and change, has asserted that leaders must cope with setting direction, as well as aligning and inspiring others to follow, while managers need to focus on the complexity of implementation.[10] Both are necessary for an organization to achieve its goals.

The Impact of Management and Leadership—For Better or Worse

Let us look at one study in which 500 respondents in a variety of organizations were asked to rank their concerns. The results are listed in Table 1–1.

Every concern listed is the result of ineffective leadership and management and can be corrected by enlightened leadership and management. As we will see, theories about effective leadership and management practices abound, but reliable metrics are often in shorter supply. But this is not the case at the statistical powerhouse known as Google. Google recently conducted an in-depth investigation, called Project Oxygen, into what makes its own best managers effective.[11] Its analysis was based on over 10,000 observations about managers across more than 100 variables and yielded the following list of behaviors, based on the order of importance (see Table 1–2).

What may be most interesting about the Google findings is that there are so few surprises. It seems that while the context in which managers operate today is fast and fluid, what makes them effective remains fairly consistent. As the list reveals, effective management of people in organizations comes down to the one-on-one or one-on-a-group influence process. Performance

TABLE 1–1 Top Ten Leadership and Management Concerns

Concern	Rank
Ineffective communication	9.0
Crisis management for most situations	8.0
Lack of feedback on performance	7.0
No or inappropriate goal setting	6.2
Not enough training	5.7
Lack of opportunity for advancement	5.6
Rewards not related to performance	4.9
Unreasonable workloads	3.9
Boss will not let me do my job	3.2
Lack of challenging work	1.8

Source: Top Ten Leadership and Management Concerns from Richard I. Lester, Ph.D., Educational Advisor, Ira C. Eaker College for Professional Development, Maxwell AFB, AL, January 1995.
Note: 10 = most important: 1 = least important.

TABLE 1–2 Best Manager Behaviors

Google's Project Oxygen found the following 8 behaviors make managers most effective:

1. Be a good coach
2. Empower your team and don't micro-manage
3. Express interest in employees' success and well-being
4. Be productive and results-oriented
5. Be a good communicator and listen to your team
6. Help your employees with career development
7. Have a clear vision and strategy for the team
8. Have key technical skills, so you can help advise the team

Source: Adam Bryant, "Google's Quest to Build a Better Boss," *New York Times*, March 12, 2011.

starts with this essential building block. Peter Drucker, one of the most influential and respected observers of management, confirms our view:

> The center of a modern society is the managed institution. The managed institution is society's way of getting things done these days. In addition, management is the specific tool, the specific function, and the specific instrument, to make institutions capable of producing results. The institution, in short, does not simply exist within and react to society. It exists to produce results on and in society.[12]

THREE COMPETENCIES OF LEADERSHIP

Leading or influencing requires three competencies:

1. *Diagnosing*—understanding the situation you are trying to influence,
2. *Adapting*—altering your behavior and the other resources you have available to meet the contingencies of the situation, and
3. *Communicating*—interacting with others in a way that people can easily understand and accept.

We will discuss each of these competencies in greater detail in subsequent chapters, but for now here is a brief summary of each competency:

- *Diagnosing is a cognitive—or cerebral—competency.* It is understanding what the situation is now and knowing what you can reasonably expect to see in the future.
- *Adapting is a behavioral competency.* It involves changing behaviors—yours and theirs—and redirecting other resources in a way that helps close the gap between the current situation and what you want to achieve.
- *Communicating is a process competency.* Even if you are able to understand and adapt to meet the situation, you still need to communicate effectively. If you cannot communicate in a way that people can understand and accept, you will be unlikely to meet your goal.[13]

KEY MANAGEMENT FUNCTIONS

Many authors consider the functions of *planning, organizing, motivating,* and *controlling* to be central to any discussion of management. These functions are relevant regardless of the type of organization or level of management being discussed. As Harold Koontz and Cyril O'Donnell have said:

> Acting in their managerial capacity, presidents, department heads, foremen, supervisors, college deans, bishops, and heads of governmental agencies all do the same thing. As managers they are all engaged, in part, in getting things done with and through people. As a manager, each must, at one time or another, carry out all the duties characteristic of managers.[14]

In today's world, even a well-run household uses these managerial functions.

Planning involves setting goals and objectives for the organization. Once plans have been made, *organizing* becomes meaningful. This step involves bringing together resources—people, capital, and equipment—in the most effective way to accomplish the goals. Organizing is essentially about integrating of resources.

Along with planning and organizing, *motivating* plays a large part in determining the level of performance of employees, which in turn influences how effectively the organizational goals will be met. In his research on motivation more than a century ago, psychologist William James of Harvard University found that hourly employees could maintain their jobs (i.e., not be fired) by working at approximately 20 to 30 percent of their ability. His study also showed that highly

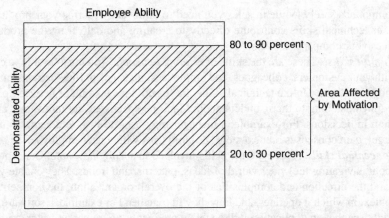

FIGURE 1–1   The Potential Influence of Motivation on Performance

motivated employees work at close to 80 to 90 percent of their ability.[15] Figure 1–1 illustrates that if motivation is low, employees' performance will suffer as much as if their ability were low. While today's work environments undoubtedly require more from people who want to keep their jobs, there is an area of discretionary performance affected by motivation that managers can and need to influence if they want to achieve results and remain competitive.

Another function of management is *controlling*. This involves feedback of results and follow-up to compare accomplishments with plans and to make appropriate adjustments where outcomes have deviated from expectations.

Although these management functions are described separately and as if they have a specific sequence, they are actually interrelated, as illustrated in Figure 1–2. At any one time, however, one or more functions may be of primary importance.

SKILLS OF A MANAGER

In a classic analysis, Robert Katz was among the first to conclude that effective management depends more on using skills that you can learn and develop than exhibiting personality traits you were born with. He classified these skills into three major areas: technical, human, and conceptual.[16]

- *Technical skills.* These are the skills of *doing your job*. You must be able to use the specific knowledge, methods, techniques, and equipment necessary in order to perform key tasks and activities. For example, in a research laboratory, you might need to handle chemical

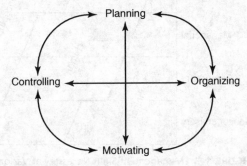

FIGURE 1–2   Interrelated Management Functions

compounds safely, while in sales you need to know and describe your product's benefits. Your technical skills contribute directly to creating and delivering the products and services your company delivers.

- **Human skills.** These are the skills of *relating to people*. You must be able to communicate with your customers, colleagues, and employees; manage conflict; demonstrate teamwork; and lead others. Unlike technical skills, these activities take place between people, which requires listening to them, understanding their perspectives, and motivating and involving them in decisions. For example, a manager may need to inspire a team to meet a stretch target, gain consensus on next steps, or build trust with a new employee.

- **Conceptual skills.** These are the skills involved in *seeing the whole*. Conceptual skills are about navigating the wider world of ideas, patterns, and trends. They enable you to understand the direction and complexities of the overall organization, the competitive or social context in which it operates, and how they fit together. For example, a software programmer might see that an application will enable a product to go to market faster, a manager could recognize the disconnection between customer demand and manufacturing capability, or an executive could envision how new governmental regulations will affect pricing. This systems knowledge permits an individual to act according to the objectives of the total organization rather than only on the basis of the goals and needs of one's own immediate group.[17]

The appropriate mix and time spent using these skills vary as people advance from supervisory to top management positions, as illustrated in Figure 1–3.

Technical skills become less important as you advance from lower to higher levels in the organization, but more conceptual skill is necessary. Supervisors at lower levels need considerable technical skill because they are often required to train and develop their employees. At the other extreme, executives in a business organization do not need to know how to perform all the specific tasks at the operational level. They should, however, be able to see how all these functions are interrelated in accomplishing the goals of the total organization. These conceptual skills are particularly important at the higher organizational levels because executives must increasingly focus on external trends and global competition.

Notice, though, that human skills are crucial at all levels. In recent years, a number of these skills have become part of what is now widely known as "emotional intelligence"—awareness

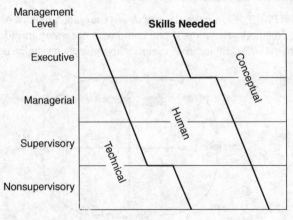

FIGURE 1–3 Management Skills Necessary at Various Levels of an Organization

of your emotions and those of others, and the ability to read and influence other people in social and work settings. In his pivotal work on the topic, Daniel Goleman has asserted that emotional intelligence is critical to leadership effectiveness, particularly building relationships.[18] It is so critical, in fact, that career derailment—being fired, forced out, or intentionally marginalized—could occur if you rely too heavily on a single skill set over time or lack the interpersonal skills necessary to lead people at different levels.

ORGANIZATIONS AS SOCIAL SYSTEMS

Although the emphasis in this text will be on developing human skills, most managers operate in organizations that are complex social systems. The human/social subsystem is only one of several subsystems. Others include an administrative/structural subsystem, an informational/decision-making subsystem, and an economic/technological subsystem.[19]

The focus of the administrative/structural subsystem is on authority, structure, and responsibility within the organization: "who, what, how, when, where, and why." The informational/decision-making subsystem emphasizes key decisions and the information needed to keep the system operating. The main concern of the economic/technological subsystem is the work to be done and its cost-effectiveness within the specific goals of the organization.

Within a systems approach, changes in one subsystem affect changes in other parts of the total system. As illustrated in Figure 1–4, if the total system is healthy and functioning well, each

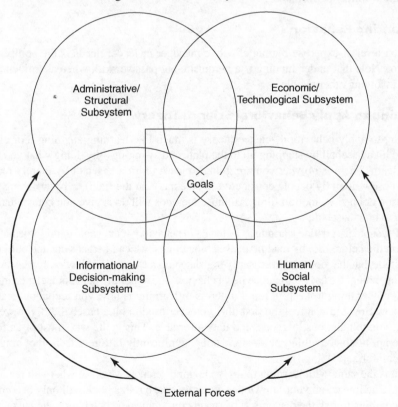

FIGURE 1–4   The Interrelated Subsystems of an Organization

of its parts or subsystems is effectively interacting with the others. Therefore, an organization cannot overemphasize the importance of one subsystem at the expense of the others over a sustained period of time without problems arising. At the same time, the internal management of the organization cannot ignore the needs and pressures from the external environment.

INGREDIENTS FOR EFFECTIVE HUMAN SKILLS

If you accept the fact that human skill development is important, you may ask what kind of expertise managers and leaders must have in order to influence the behavior of other people. Simply put, they must understand past and current behavior, then use it to direct, change, and influence behavior.

Understanding Behavior

First, to get things done through other people, managers need to understand why people behave as they do. What motivates people? What produces the patterns of behavior that are characteristic of an individual or group? Motivation and its causes are the areas on which most of the literature in the behavioral sciences focuses. In this book, we will explore motivation in considerable depth, particularly how different levels of willingness—which includes confidence, commitment, and motivation—affect performance.

Influencing Behavior

The next level of expertise that an effective manager or leader needs is the ability to influence behavior. Note that understanding is a perquisite but passive skill, whereas influencing requires action involving other people.

Learning to Apply Behavioral Science Theory

Learning to apply behavioral science theory is much like learning anything. For example, you learn to hit a baseball by stepping up to the plate and swinging—by doing what you are attempting to learn. There is no way you are going to learn to hit a baseball by merely reading books (even those written by people considered to be experts in the field) or by watching great hitters (in person or on slow-motion film). All those methods will do is give you conceptual knowledge of how to hit a baseball.

Psychologists define learning as a change in behavior—being able to do something differently than you did before. So, by reading or watching others, we can perhaps change our knowledge or our attitude, but that does not necessarily translate into a change in behavior. If we want to actually learn something, we have to practice new behaviors and hopefully gain competence in doing them.

Another thing to keep in mind in terms of learning is how you feel about learning something new. How did you feel the first time you ever tried to hit a baseball? If you were like most people, you felt anxious, nervous, and uncomfortable. This is the way most of us feel any time we attempt to do something new—something significantly different from the things we are already comfortable doing.

It is the same with learning to use behavioral science. Much of what you read in this book may have an impact on your knowledge and attitudes, but this book will only become relevant if you are willing to risk the discomfort of "trying on" some new behaviors. We have to go through a period of "unfreezing" if we want to learn.

http://www.infed.org/thinkers/et-lewin.htm

Another caution is to be patient with yourself—give the new behavior time to work. After all, how likely is it that you will get a base hit the very first time you try to hit a baseball? The probability is low. It is no different when you try to learn and apply behavioral science theory. Initially you will probably be less effective than you would have been had you used your old style of behavior. People who go through a training experience in which they gain knowledge and shift attitudes often find that when they try on a new behavior for the first time, it may not work. As a result, they begin to question the value of the whole training experience, claiming that it does not work in the "real world." It is this kind of response that has hindered managers from attempting to make behavioral science theory an integral part of managing more effectively. All of us have to recognize that, just like hitting a baseball, applying behavioral science theory takes practice. The first few times up, the probability of success is quite low, but the more we practice and the more we attempt to get relevant feedback, the more the probability of success will increase.

Our intention in this book is to help you understand apply behavioral science concepts that can have an impact on making you more effective as a leader—whether you are an executive, supervisor, teacher, or parent. But remember that applied behavioral science is not an exact science such as physics, chemistry, and biology. There are no universal truths when it comes to leadership and management. People are difficult to predict. But behavioral sciences can give you ways to increase your behavioral batting average.

Notes

1. Marcus Buckingham, *First Break All the Rules: What the World's Greatest Managers Do Differently* (New York: Simon & Shuster, 1999), 34–36.
2. "World Internet Usage Statistics News and World Population Stats," *Internet World Stats—Usage and Population Statistics*. Accessed June 1, 2011, www.internetworldstats.com/stats.htm.
3. Michael Hammer, "Is Work Bad for You?" *Atlantic Monthly*, August 1999, 87–93.
4. Andrew S. Grove, "A High Tech CEO Updates His Views on Managing and Careers," *Fortune*, September 18, 1995.
5. Michael Porter, "New Strategies for Competitive Advantage," *Planning Review*, May/June 1990, 14.
6. Ed Lawler III, *The Ultimate Advantage: Creating the High Involvement Organization* (San Francisco: Jossey-Bass, 1992), 3–24.
7. Joel E. Ross, *Total Quality Management*, 3rd ed. (Delray Beach, FL: St. Lucie Press, 1999), 335.
8. Sharon S. McGowan, "Engaged Employees: Going the Extra Mile," *Hudson Critical Thinking: Thought Leadership Series*, 3.
9. Warren Bennis, quoted in Cherie Carter-Scott, "The Differences between Leadership and Management," *Manage*, November 1994, 12. Also see Tom Payner, "Go Forth and Manage Wisely," *Supervision Magazine*, August 1994, and Bernard M. Bass and Ralph M. Stogdill, *Bass and Stogdill's Handbook of Leadership* (New York: The Free Press, 1990).
10. John Kotter, "What Leaders Really Do," *Harvard Business Review*, December 2001, 3.
11. Adam Bryant, "Google's Quest to Build a Better Boss," *New York Times*, March 12, 2011.
12. Peter F. Drucker, "Management's New Paradigms," *Forbes*, October 5, 1998, 176.
13. Harold Koontz and Cyril O'Donnell, *Principles of Management*, 5th ed. (New York: McGraw-Hill, 1972), 20.

14. William James, *The Principles of Psychology*, 1 (London: Macmillan and Co., Ltd., 1890).

15. Paul Hersey, *Situational Selling* (Escondido, CA: Center for Leadership Studies, 1985), 8.

16. These descriptions were adapted from a classification developed by Robert L. Katz, "Skills of an Effective Administrator," *Harvard Business Review*, January-February 1955, 33–42. See also Robert S. Dreyer, "Do Good Bosses Make Lousy Leaders?" *Supervision*, March 1995, 19–20.

17. Tim O. Peterson and David D. Van Fleet, "The Ongoing Legacy of R. L. Katz: An Updated Typology of Management Skills," *Management Decision* 42, no. 10 (2004): 1297–1308.

18. Daniel Goleman, *Working with Emotional Intelligence* (New York: Bantam Books, 1998), 198–205. See also Daniel Goleman, Richard Boyatzis, and Annie McKee, "Primal Leadership: The Hidden Driver of Great Performance." *Harvard Business Review,* December 2001, 42–51, and Jennifer M. George, "Emotions and Leadership: The Role of Emotional Intelligence," *Human Resources* 53 (2000): 1031.

19. Paul Hersey and Douglas Scott identify these components of an internal social system in "A Systems Approach to Educational Organizations: Do We Manage or Administer?" *OCLEA* (a publication of the Ontario Council for Leadership in Educational Administration, Toronto, Canada), September 1974, 3–5. Much of the material for that article was adapted from lectures given by Boris Yavitz, Dean, School of Business Administration, Columbia University.

2

Motivation and Behavior

O ften we hear our clients say, "One of the biggest challenges I face is keeping my people motivated." Managers facing today's global competition are highly pressured to produce results, and quickly. It is not enough to just set ambitious goals and objectives and assume people will want to achieve them. This is where leadership comes in. We need to influence people to produce by understanding what makes them tick. Psychologists and philosophers, brokers and business gurus alike have tried to understand how motivation affects behavior. Researchers have conducted hundreds of studies in order to define and measure motivational factors. Our goal is to first help you understand some of the most significant concepts and theories about the "whys" of behavior, as well as how to better predict and influence future behavior. This is part of developing the leadership competency of diagnosing introduced in Chapter 1. You can then adapt your leadership style to harness each person's individual motivation and dramatically improve the likelihood of reaching organizational goals.

THEORIES OF MOTIVATION

Motives Defined

Our behavior is basically goal-oriented; that is, motivated by a desire to attain some specific result. The basic unit of behavior is an *activity*. In fact, all behavior is a series of activities. As human beings, we are always doing something: walking, talking, eating, sleeping, working, thinking. In many instances, we are doing more than one activity at a time, such as talking with someone as we walk or drive to work. At any given moment, we may decide to change from one activity to another. This aspect of human nature raises some important questions. Why do people engage in one activity and not another? Why do they change activities? How can we as managers understand, predict, and influence a person to engage in a high-value activity rather than a lower priority one? To predict behavior, managers must know which individual motives or needs have the potential to evoke a particular action at a particular time.

Motives are the "whys" of behavior. They arouse our attention, determine the general direction of our behavior, and then sustain or diminish our interest in continuing an activity. In essence, motives or felt needs are the mainsprings of action in human behavior. In our discussions, we shall use these two terms—*motives* and *needs*—interchangeably. In this context, the term need not be associated with urgency or any pressing desire for something. It simply means something within that prompts a person to action.

Sources of Motivation: Inside, Outside, or Unknown?

FREUD AND THE SUBCONSCIOUS   All of us at one time or another may have wondered, "Why did I do that?" Sigmund Freud was one of the first to recognize that the reasons for our actions are not always apparent to the conscious mind. He further described specific drives that motivate distinctive individual behavioral patterns ("personality") that are to a considerable degree subconscious and, therefore, not easily accessible for examination and evaluation.

Freud contended that an analogy can be drawn between the motivation of most people and the structure of an iceberg. In Freud's view, a significant segment of human motivation appears below the surface of the conscious mind, as indicated in Figure 2–1. Therefore, one usually is aware of only a small portion of one's own motivation.[1] Some individuals may make little or no effort to gain self-insight. Even those who seek professional help—for example, psychotherapy—may only end up gaining a slight understanding of what truly motivates their own behavior

---

ASSIGNMENT

Two frequent pieces of advice for being a good leader are: Good leaders are consistent! and Good leaders are flexible! How would these concepts integrate into the notion of being Situational?

"Although people object when a scientific analyses traces their behavior to external conditions and thus deprives them of credit and the chance to be admired, they seldom object when the same analyses absolves them of blame."

—B.F. Skinner

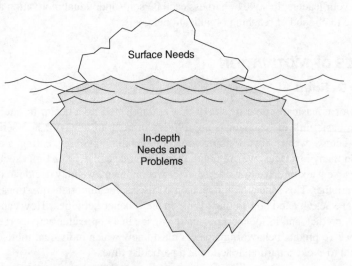

FIGURE 2–1   Freud's Iceberg Analogy

Intrinsic versus Extrinsic Motivation

Intrinsic motivation comes from within the person. Examples include meaningful work, increasing responsibility, professional growth, or autonomy. By contrast, extrinsic motivation comes from outside the person, such as money, the work environment, or quality of management. In David McLelland's enduring investigations of motivation, he identified three primary motivators: the need for achievement, the need for power, and the need for affiliation. People whose intrinsic need for achievement is strong can actually increase their productivity and capacity if that need is met, for example, through stretch goals and new opportunities.[2] We will look at the significance of McLelland's work later in this chapter and the next chapter.

Organizations have long pondered whether the "carrot" (rewards) or the "stick" (punishment) is the most powerful way to motivate employees. This dilemma is based on the belief that extrinsic motivators matter most. However, Daniel Pink, in his recent investigation of motivation in the workplace, asserts that businesses rely on short-term incentives and compensation practices that underestimate what many behavioral scientists have concluded for decades—that intrinsic motives are stronger and longer lasting than extrinsic ones.[3]

It Depends on the Situation

In a recent study, employees expressed the need for achievement in a way that perhaps reflects the pressured pace within today's work environments. In an analysis of more than 12,000 diary entries made by knowledge workers over three years, neither recognition nor incentives topped the list of motivational factors. Instead, making progress in their work, an intrinsic motivator, proved to be number one. Given that knowledge workers are navigating between applications and e-mails on their computers 37 times per hour, making progress may indeed seem more and more elusive. However, the satisfaction of making progress was affected by the manager relationship. Recognition without real progress was experienced as shallow and could even prompt cynicism. On the other hand, progress without praise from the manager was also demotivating. The combination of feeling that they had accomplished work and genuine appreciation from managers provided the greatest motivation for employees.[4]

This example demonstrates the complex interaction between intrinsic and extrinsic motivators. It also validates what psychologist Kurt Lewin described long ago as a fundamental equation of human behavior[5]:

$$B = f(P \Leftrightarrow S)$$

where B represents individual behavior, f represents "a function of" or "is caused by," P is the person, and S is the situation. Lewin's equation implies that B is a function of something both *inside* the *Person* and *outside* the *Person* in the *Situation*.[6] For instance, the way individuals feel about things occurs *inside* a person in that their motives and needs are reflected in their attitudes, whereas it is an individual's personality that can be seen *outside* that person by virtue of their actions.[7] Note that P and S are not independent, but rather are interdependent. *Persons* are influenced by the *Situations* in which they find themselves, and *Situations* are influenced by *Persons*. These are important ideas in the context of "situational," or "contingency," leadership, in which the appropriate leader behavior is determined by the situation. This significant point lies at the heart of our Situational Leadership® approach.

How Motive Strength Changes

We have said that motives, or needs, are the reasons "why" underlying our observable behavior. All of us have hundreds of needs, many of them competing for a response. This begs the

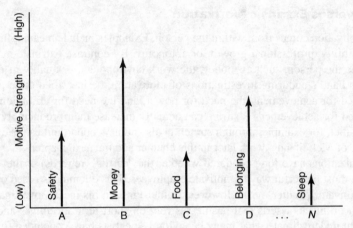

FIGURE 2–2 The Strongest Motive Determines Behavior (Motive B in this Illustration

question: Which of these competing motives will you attempt to satisfy? The answer: The need with the greatest strength at a particular moment leads to activity. As illustrated in Figure 2–2, motive B has the highest motive strength, and therefore it is the need that determines behavior. A motive tends to decrease in strength if it is either satisfied or blocked from satisfaction. Satisfied or blocked needs normally do not motivate individuals to further immediate action.

NEED SATISFACTION When a need is satisfied, according to Abraham Maslow, it is no longer a motivator of behavior.[8] High-strength needs are considered "satisfied" when a competing need becomes more potent. For instance, if a high-strength need is thirst, drinking tends to lower the strength of this need, and other needs may now become more potent. Or in the workplace, if an employee has a strong need for recognition, praising his or her results publicly in a team meeting will satisfy that need for the time being.

BLOCKED NEED SATISFACTION The satisfaction of a need may be blocked. If so, a reduction in need strength sometimes follows, but it does not always occur initially. Instead, there may be a tendency for the person to engage in coping behavior. This is an attempt to overcome the obstacle by trial-and-error problem solving. The person may try a variety of behaviors to find one that will accomplish the goal or will reduce the tension created by blockage, as illustrated in Figure 2–3.

Initially, this coping behavior may be quite rational. Let us again consider an employee with a high need for recognition, seen in the behavioral form of seeking a promotion. He may begin by telling his manager that he is interested in a promotion and why he believes he is qualified for a next-level position and an interview for an opening. If that attempt does not work, he may undertake additional, relevant skills training for the position. Still thwarted, he may even begin a campaign of networking and high-visibility stretch assignments. Individuals often continue one attempt after another until some degree of perceived success and goal attainment is finally achieved.

If people continue to strive for something without success, they may substitute goals that can satisfy the need. For example, if Mary has a strong desire to be a CPA but continually receives average grades in accounting, she may be willing eventually to settle for another type of business career.

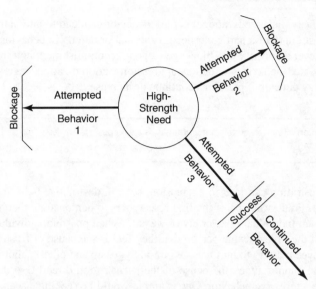

FIGURE 2–3   Coping Behavior when Blockage Occurs in Attempting to Accomplish a Particular Goal

COGNITIVE DISSONANCE   If continually unsuccessful rational coping behavior does not satisfy the need, it may lead to forms of irrational coping behavior. Leon Festinger analyzed this phenomenon.[9] His theory of cognitive dissonance deals primarily with the relationships that exist between perceptions people have about themselves and their environment. When individual perceptions have nothing to do with each other, they are considered irrelevant to each other. If one supports the other, they are said to be in a consonant relationship. Dissonance is created when two perceptions that are relevant to each other are in conflict. This situation creates tension, which is psychologically uncomfortable and causes the individual to try to modify one of the incompatible perceptions so as to reduce the tension or dissonance. In a sense, that person engages in coping behavior to regain a condition of consonance or equilibrium. For example, Festinger's research showed "heavy smokers are less likely to believe that there is a relationship between smoking and lung cancer than nonsmokers."[10] In other words, if they cannot give up smoking, they can at least remain skeptical about research that reports harmful effects. The same phenomenon is at work when a person's successive promotion attempts result in a belief that the organization selects people primarily based on politics rather than job qualifications.

> "For every person who's a manager and want to know how to manage people, there are 10 people who are being managed and would like to figure out how to make it stop."
>
> —Scott Adams, creator of the *Dilbert* cartoon

FRUSTRATION   People experience the blocking of goal attainment as frustration. It is an individual and internal condition, rather than a result of the external environment. A person may be frustrated by an imaginary barrier—the impact of organizational politics—yet fail to be frustrated by a real barrier—limited promotional opportunities—during an economic downturn.

As previously discussed, rational coping behavior can lead to alternative goal setting or a decrease in the strength of a particular need. Irrational or defensive behavior, on the other hand, may occur in several forms when blockage to goal accomplishment continues and frustration develops. Frustrated behaviors—such as aggression, rationalization, regression, fixation, and resignation—may develop if pressures continue or increase.

> "Frustration, although quite painful at times, is a very positive and essential part of success."
> —Bo Bennett

Strong frustration can lead to aggression, seen in destructive behaviors such as hostility and striking out. Freud was one of the first researchers to demonstrate that hostility or rage can be exhibited by an individual in a variety of ways.[11] When possible, individuals will direct their hostility against the object or the person that they feel is the cause of frustration. For example, an angry employee may try to hurt her boss through gossip and other malicious behavior. Often, however, people cannot attack the cause of their frustration directly, so they may engage instead in passive aggressive behavior. One example would be seeking a scapegoat as a target for their hostility; scapegoats could be other colleagues, family members, or even innocent pets. As Norman R. F. Maier said, aggression is only one way in which frustration can be shown.[12]

> "Aggression unopposed becomes a contagious disease."
> — Jimmy Carter

> "The tendency to aggression is an innate, independent, instinctual disposition of man . . . it constitutes the powerful obstacle to culture."
> — Sigmund Freud

> "The fate of our times is characterized by rationalization and intellectualization and, above all, by the disenchantment of the world."
> —Max Weber

Rationalization, which simply means making excuses, can be another expression of frustration. For example, an individual might blame someone else for an inability to accomplish a given goal: "It was my boss's fault that I didn't get a raise." Or, the person may downgrade the desirability of that particular goal: "I didn't want to do that anyway."

Regression is essentially not acting one's age. Roger G. Barker, Tamara Dembo, and Kurt Lewin showed experimentally that when children are exposed to mild frustration, their play may resemble that of a child two or more years younger.[13] Maier found the same behavioral pattern in working adults, noting that "frustrated people tend to give up constructive attempts at solving their problems and regress to more primitive and childish behavior."[14] Both a person who cannot start the car and proceeds to kick it and the manager who throws a temper tantrum when annoyed are demonstrating regressive behavior.

> "If you act like an ass, don't get insulted if people ride you."
> —Yiddish proverb

Fixation occurs when a person continues to exhibit the same behavior pattern over and over again, even though experience has shown that it can accomplish nothing. Unfortunately, "frustration can freeze old and habitual responses and prevent the use of new and more effectual ones."[15] Maier showed that although habits are normally broken when they bring no satisfaction or lead to punishment, a fixation actually becomes stronger under those circumstances.[16] In fact, he argued that it is possible to change a habit into a fixation by too much punishment. This phenomenon is seen in children who blindly continue to behave in an objectionable manner after being severely punished. Maier concluded that punishment could have two effects on behavior: It may either eliminate the undesirable behavior or lead to fixation and other symptoms of frustration as well. It follows that punishment may be a dangerous management tool, since its effects are difficult to predict. According to James A. C. Brown, common symptoms of fixation in organizational settings are "the inability to accept change, the blind and stubborn refusal to accept new facts when experience has shown the old ones to be untenable, and the type of behavior exemplified by the manager who continues to increase penalties" even when doing so is only making conditions worse.[17]

> "We first make our habits, and then our habits make us."
> —John Dryden

> "Habits are formed by the repetition of particular acts. They are strengthened by an increase in the number of repeated acts."
> —Mortimer J. Adler

Resignation or apathy occurs after prolonged frustration, when people lose hope of accomplishing their goal in a particular situation, and so withdraw from reality and the source of their frustration. We see this behavior in people performing boring, routine jobs, where they often resign themselves to the fact that there is little hope for improvement within their environments.

> "Most men lead lives of quiet desperation and go to the grave with the song still in them. What is called resignation is confirmed desperation."
> —Henry David Thoreau

As a manager developing your diagnostic skills, it is important to remember that aggression, rationalization, regression, fixation, and resignation are all symptoms of frustration and may be indications that problems exist.

INCREASING MOTIVE STRENGTH   Behavior may change if an existing need increases to the point that it is now the highest strength motive. The strength of some needs tends to appear in a cyclical pattern. For example, the need for food tends to recur regardless of how well it has been previously satisfied. We all get hungry again. You can increase or delay the speed of this cyclical pattern by affecting the environment. For example, your need for food may not be high-strength unless the immediate environment is changed so that you see and smell a plate of tempting food. Even then, you may be just fine with having fruit for dessert until you smell the cookies baking. The point is that people may have a variety of needs at any given time. You may be hungry, thirsty, and tired. You may want to be part of a team, earn the highest individual bonus for sales, and be ready for a more prestigious job. In either case, the need with the highest strength will determine what you do.[18]

> "What we call happiness in the strictest sense comes from the (preferably sudden) satisfaction of needs which have been damned up to a high degree."
> —Sigmund Freud

> "A man is successful if he gets up in the morning, gets to bed at night, and in between he does what he wants to do!"
> —Bob Dylan

Goals

Goals are outside an individual; they are sometimes referred to as "hoped for" rewards toward which motives are directed. These goals are often called incentives by psychologists. However, we prefer not to use that term because many people in our society tend to equate incentives with tangible financial rewards, such as increased pay. There are, however, many intangible rewards, such as praise or power, that are just as important and effective for use as incentives when endeavoring to evoke a particular behavior. Managers who are successful in motivating employees are often providing an environment in which appropriate goals (incentives) are available to satisfy needs.

> "Confusion of goals and perfection of means seems, in my opinion, to characterize our age."
> —Albert Einstein

> "Establishing goals is all right if you don't let them deprive you of interesting detours."
> —Doug Larson

GOALS

Activities resulting from high-strength needs can generally be classified into two categories—*goal-directed activity* and *goal activity*. These concepts are important in understanding human behavior because they influence the strength of our needs differently.

Goal-directed activity, in essence, is motivated behavior that leads to reaching a goal, while goal activity is satisfying the goal itself. If your strongest need at a given moment is hunger, food is the goal, your goal-directed activities might include looking for a place to eat or cooking, and eating is the goal activity.

An important distinction between these two classes of activities is their effect on the strength of the need. In goal-directed activity, the strength of the need tends to increase as you engage in the activity until the goal is reached or frustration sets in. As discussed earlier, frustration develops when you are continually blocked from reaching a goal. If the frustration becomes intense enough, the strength of the need may decrease until it is no longer potent enough to affect your behavior—you give up.

> "Rowing harder does not help if the boat is headed in the wrong direction."
> –Kenichi Ohmae

Conversely, once goal activity begins, the strength of the need tends to decrease as you engage in it. For example, as you eat more and more, the strength of the hunger need declines at that particular time. At the point when another need becomes more potent than the present need, behavior changes.

As an example, think of a day-long strategy meeting with a catered lunch. As the day begins, everyone is focused on the agenda and enthusiastically discusses topics. As the clock approaches lunch time, and the wait staff begins setting up food in the back of the room (goal-directed activity), the aromas of the food start to distract everyone. The need for food soon increases to the point where it takes a conscious effort not only to stay on task but also to wait until the lunch is completely set up before devouring what is offered. As everyone begins to eat (goal activity), however, the strength of this need for food diminishes to the point where other needs become more important. Participants are then able to focus their energies on the issues presented at the meeting, and their activity changes accordingly. In essence, the desire to get back to the agenda and finish discussions—the need for achievement—has become more potent than the previous need for food. After an hour or so, however, it is likely that another need may increase in strength and become more potent than the meeting agenda. Perhaps it is the physical need for a nap, a short walk for fresh air, or a cookie. Note that being full from lunch is a transitory state because it is likely that the need to have something to snack on will become stronger over time. So needs are never completely satiated; we simply satisfy them for a limited period of time.

FROM MOTIVES TO GOALS

The relationship between motives, goals, and behavior can be shown in a simplified fashion, as illustrated in Figure 2–4. The strongest motive produces behavior that is either goal-directed or goal activity. Because not all goals are attainable, individuals do not always reach goal activity,

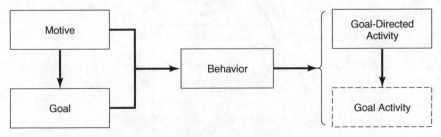

FIGURE 2–4   Relationship among Motives, Goals, and Activities

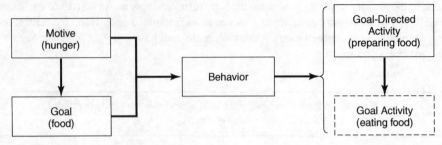

FIGURE 2–5   Use of a Tangible Goal

regardless of the strength of the motive. Thus, goal activity is indicated by a dashed line. An example of the use of a tangible goal to influence behavior is illustrated in Figure 2–5.

Food is a broad goal, and the type of food that will satisfy the hunger motive will vary from situation to situation. The same is true for any broad goal. If you are starving, you may eat anything; at other times, you may realign your goals in such a way that only a steak will satisfy your hunger. The same holds true for intangible goals, such as the need for recognition. If it is strong enough, praise from a manager may be an effective incentive in influencing people to continue to do good work. In other circumstances, only a promotion will do. Remember that, as a manager, if you want to influence another person's behavior, you must first understand what motives or needs are most important to that person at that time. A goal, to be effective, must be aligned with the highest-strength need of the person involved.

Is it better to engage in goal-directed activity or in goal activity? Actually, staying at either level exclusively creates problems. If one stays at goal-directed activity too long, frustration will occur to the extent that the person may give up or may display other patterns of irrational behavior. On the other hand, if one engages exclusively in goal activity and the goal is not challenging, a lack of interest and apathy will develop, with motivation again tending to decrease. A more satisfying and effective pattern might be a continuous cycling between goal-directed activity and goal activity, as shown in Figure 2–6.

For instance, a goal that is appropriate for a six-year-old may not be a meaningful goal for the same child at seven. Once the child becomes proficient in attaining a particular goal, it becomes appropriate for the parent to provide an opportunity for the child to identify and set new goals. In the same light, what is an appropriate goal for a new employee may not be meaningful for an employee who has been with an organization for a year or longer.

This cycling process between goal-directed activity and goal activity is a continuous challenge for the parent or manager. As employees increase in their ability to accomplish goals, it is

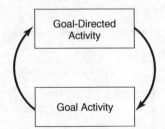

FIGURE 2–6   Cycling Function of
Goal-Directed Activity and Goal
Activity

appropriate that the manager re-evaluate them and provide an environment that allows for continual realignment of goals with the employee's current highest-strength needs through appropriate growth and development opportunities. The learning and developing process should not be confined to only one stage of a person's life. In this process, the role of managers is not always that of setting goals for their workers. Instead, a manager's effectiveness may be increased by providing an environment in which their direct reports can participate in setting their own goals. When people are involved in their own goal setting, it not only enhances employee performance and productivity, but also increases their commitment. Why? Because they will tend to engage in much more goal-directed activity before they become frustrated and give up. On the other hand, if their manager sets the goals for them, they are likely to give up more easily because they perceive the goals to be their manager's and not their own.

Goals: How High Is High Enough?

Goals should be set high enough so that a person has to stretch to reach them, but low enough so that they can be attained. As J. Sterling-Livingston so aptly stated:

> Subordinates will not be motivated to reach high levels of productivity unless they consider the boss's high expectations realistic and achievable. If they are encouraged to strive for unattainable goals, they eventually give up trying and settle for results that are lower than they are capable of achieving. The experience of a large electrical manufacturing company demonstrates this; the company discovered that production actually declined if production quotas were set too high, because the workers simply stopped trying to meet them. In other words, the practice of "dangling the carrot just beyond the donkey's reach," endorsed by many managers, is not a good motivational device.[19]

David C. McClelland and John W. Atkinson demonstrated in their research that the degree of motivation and effort increases until the probability of success reaches 50 percent; then it begins to fall even though the probability of success continues to increase.[20] People are not highly motivated if a goal is seen as almost impossible or virtually certain to achieve.

Another issue regarding goals is that a final goal is often set and the person is judged only in terms of success in reaching that final goal. For example, suppose a team has four months to finalize a new marketing plan. After the first month, the project is only 5 percent completed. If the vice president for marketing starts "micromanaging"— that is, watching and criticizing their every move—there is a high probability that the team will stop trying. Progress on the marketing plan may even get worse instead of accelerating. A better alternative would be for the vice president to set shorter, interim goals that are realistic for the team to accomplish. This moderate change in behavior would allow the team to receive positive reinforcement that builds confidence and commitment toward reaching the final goal.

EXPECTANCY THEORY

What additional factors affect the strength of needs? Victor Vroom's expectancy theory of motivation attempts to answer that question.[21] His theory is also consistent with our previous assertion that felt needs cause human behavior.

 http://mba.yale.edu/news_events/CMS/Articles/5791.shtml

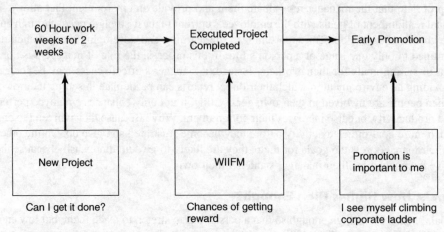

FIGURE 2–7   An Expectancy Model for Motivation

In simplified form, Vroom suggests that felt needs cause behavior, and this motivated behavior in a work setting is increased if a person perceives a positive relationship between effort and performance. Motivated behavior is further increased if there is a positive relationship between good performance and outcomes or rewards, particularly if the outcomes or rewards are valued. In fact, he identified three relationships that have the capacity to either enhance motivated behavior or hamper it:

- A positive relationship between effort and performance
- A positive relationship between good performance and rewards
- The achievement of valued outcomes or rewards—intrinsic, extrinsic, or both.

Let us look at an example. A new manager perceives that she will need to put in several 60-hour workweeks on a major new project. Furthermore, the manager also perceives that good job performance will probably result in an early promotion that carries with it a badly needed 10 percent pay raise (see Figure 2–7). If this sequence of events happens, both the manager's willingness to work hard and confidence in the behavior pattern will be reinforced. However, should one or more steps in the sequence prove wrong—for example, performance does not improve, promotion is denied, or pay raise falls short of expectations—motivation, willingness, and confidence will decline.

> "Success breeds success."
> —Mia Hamm, American Gold Medal Soccer Player

This linkage between effort and performance and between performance and valued outcomes is important not only to our understanding of motivation but also to our understanding of a number of leadership theories, especially the Path-Goal theory discussed in Chapter 5.[22]

AVAILABILITY THEORY

Another important factor that affects need strength is availability. Although expectancy and availability are related, expectancy tends to affect motives, or needs, and availability tends to affect the perception of goals.

Expectancy is the perceived probability of satisfying a particular need of an individual on the basis of experience. Although *expectancy* is the technical term used by psychologists, it refers directly to the sum of the past experience. Experience can be either actual or vicarious. Vicarious experience comes from sources the person considers legitimate, such as parents, peer groups, teachers, and books or periodicals.

> "It has been my experience that folks who have no vices have very few virtues."
> —Abraham Lincoln

To illustrate the effect that experience can have on behavior, let us look at an example. Suppose a boy's father is a basketball star and the boy wants to follow in his footsteps. Initially, his expectancy may be high, and, therefore, the strength of the need is high. If he is cut from the eighth-grade team, the boy might continue to try. A single failure usually is not enough to discourage a person (in fact, it sometimes results in increased activity) and will not significantly affect his expectancy. But if he continues to get cut from a team year after year, eventually this motive will weaken or decrease in priority. In fact, after enough unsuccessful experiences, he may give up completely. Also suppose that this same boy's mother is a brilliant surgeon and that the boy at times envisions himself following in her footsteps and saving lives one day too. Initially, both his expectancy and need may be high. What happens when he gets high marks in biology and chemistry? What happens when year after year he continues to excel and receive awards for his performance? When expectancy and availability are aligned, we tend not to spend much time on analyzing the "why" behind those successes but rather bask in the joy of the match between what we expected and what we were able to attain. As a leader, the ability to distinguish between what is expected and what is actually available and achievable can mean the difference between being able to motivate others or being the cause of their frustration.

Availability reflects the perceived limitations of the environment. It is determined by how accessible the goals that can satisfy a given need are perceived to be by an individual. For example, if the electricity goes off in a storm, you cannot watch television. That goal activity is no longer possible because of the limitations of the environment. You may have a high desire to watch television, but since you cannot satisfy that desire, you will settle for something else, such as sleeping.

Consequently, availability is an environmental variable. Yet it should be stressed that it is not important whether the goals to satisfy a need are really available. It is the perception of availability, or the interpretation of reality, that affects one's actual behavior. In other words, reality is what a person perceives.

> "Reality is merely an illusion, albeit a very persistent one."
> —Albert Einstein

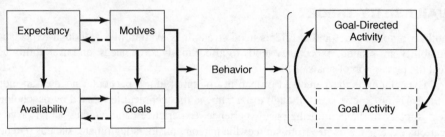

FIGURE 2–8 Expanded Diagram of a Motivating Situation

An example of how perception and expectation can affect behavior was dramatically il-lustrated in an experiment with a fish. A pike was placed in an aquarium with many minnows swimming around it. After the fish became accustomed to the plentiful supply of food (expecta-tion), a sheet of glass was placed between the pike and the minnows. When the pike became hungry, it tried to reach the minnows, but it continually hit its head on the glass (thwarted ex-pectation). At first, the strength of the need for food increased, and the pike tried harder than ever to get the minnows. But finally its repeated failure of goal attainment resulted in enough frustration that the fish no longer attempted to eat the minnows. In fact, when the glass partition was finally removed, the minnows again swam all around the pike, but no further goal-directed activity took place. Eventually, the pike died of starvation while in the midst of plenty of food. In both cases, the fish operated according to the way it perceived reality and not on the basis of reality itself.

An expanded diagram of a motivating situation including expectancy and availability is presented in Figure 2–8. Motives, needs within an individual, are directed toward goals that are aspirations in the environment. These are interpreted by the individual as being available or unavailable. This interpretation affects expectancy. If expectancy is high, motive strength will increase. The pattern tends to be cyclical, moving in the direction of the solid arrows; but to some extent, these are interacting variables indicated by the dashed arrows. For example, experience may affect the way we perceive availability, and the presence of goals in the environment may affect the strength of motives. Unlike some of the other motivational theories, expectancy and availability are based more on choices related to the present and future, which may be more read-ily subject to influence than drives related primarily to past learning.

HIERARCHY OF NEEDS

From the range of motivational theories presented so far, you can see why managers would ben-efit from having some understanding about the needs that are often most important to people. A classic framework that helps explain the strength of certain needs was developed by Abraham Maslow.[23] According to Maslow, human needs arrange themselves into a hierarchy, as illustrated in Figure 2–9. As each level of needs is satisfied, the next higher level of needs begins to mo-tivate and dominate the behavior of the individual, ascending upward through the hierarchy as each level gains in strength.

The physiological needs are shown at the top of the hierarchy because they tend to have the highest strength until they are met for the moment or satisfied. These are the basics

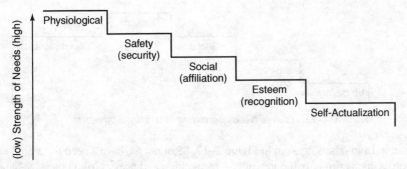

FIGURE 2–9 Maslow's Hierarchy of Needs

needed to sustain human life—food, clothing, shelter. The majority of a person's activity will probably be at this level until your body can function, and the other needs will provide little motivation.

Once physiological needs become satisfied, the safety, or security, needs become predominant, as illustrated in Figure 2–10. These needs comprise the need to be free of the fear of physical danger and deprivation of the basic physiological needs. In other words, this is a need for self-preservation. In addition to the here and now, there is a concern for the future. Will people be able to keep their jobs or their properties? Can they provide food and shelter tomorrow and the next day? If an individual's safety or security is in danger, other things seem relatively unimportant. In a period when layoffs are occurring, we often see safety needs escalate.

Once physiological and safety needs are fairly well satisfied, social needs will emerge as dominant, as illustrated in Figure 2–11. Because people are social beings, they have a need to belong to and be accepted by various groups. When social needs become dominant, a person will strive for meaningful relations with others. This level corresponds to what McClelland described as the need for affiliation.[24]

After individuals begin to satisfy their need to belong, they generally want to be more than just a member of their group. They then feel the need for esteem—both self-esteem and

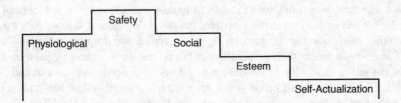

FIGURE 2–10 Safety Needs Dominant in the Need Structure

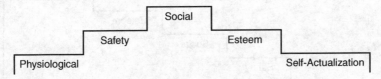

FIGURE 2–11 Social Needs Dominant in the Need Structure

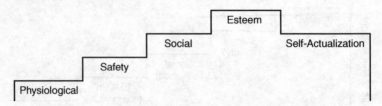

FIGURE 2–12   Esteem Needs Dominant in the Need Structure

recognition from others, as seen in Figure 2–12. Most people have a need for a high evaluation of themselves that is firmly based in reality—recognition and respect from others. Satisfaction of esteem needs produces feelings of self-confidence, prestige, power, and control. People begin to feel that they are useful and have some positive impact on their relationships and environment. There are other occasions, though, when persons are unable to satisfy their need for esteem through constructive behavior. An individual may resort to disruptive or immature behavior—irrational coping responses described earlier in this chapter—to satisfy the desire for attention. Employees may withhold their best work efforts, argue with other team members, or undermine their manager. In fact, some of the social problems we have today may have their roots in the frustration of esteem needs.

Once esteem needs begin to be adequately satisfied, the self-actualization needs emerge as dominant, as shown in Figure 2–13. Self-actualization is the need to maximize one's potential, whatever it may be. A musician must play music, a poet must write, a general must win battles, and a professor must teach. As Maslow expressed it, "What a man can be, he must be." Thus, self-actualization is to become what one is capable of becoming. Individuals satisfy this need in different ways. In one person, it may be expressed in the desire to be an ideal mother; in another, it may be expressed in managing an organization; in another, it may be expressed athletically; in still another, by playing the piano.

The way self-actualization is expressed can change over the life cycle. For example, a self-actualized athlete may eventually look for other areas in which to maximize potential as physical attributes change over time or as horizons broaden. In addition, the hierarchy does not necessarily follow the pattern described by Maslow. It was not his intent to say that this hierarchy applies universally. Maslow felt this was a typical pattern that operates most of the time. He realized, however, that there were numerous exceptions to this general tendency. For example, the Indian leader Mahatma Gandhi frequently sacrificed his physiological and safety needs for the satisfaction of other needs when India was striving for independence from Great Britain. In his historic fasts, Gandhi went weeks without nourishment to protest governmental injustices. He was operating at the self-actualization level while some of his other needs went unsatisfied.

Maslow's hierarchy of needs is not intended to be an all-or-nothing framework in which one level of needs has to be completely satisfied before the next level emerges as the most

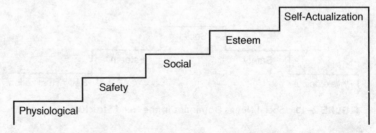

FIGURE 2–13   Self-Actualization Needs Dominant in the Need Structure

FIGURE 2–14 Need Structure When Physiological and Safety Are High-Strength Needs

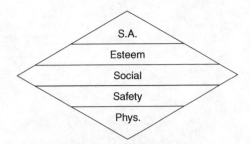

FIGURE 2–15 Need Structure When Social Needs Are High-Strength and Self-Actualization and Physiological Needs Are Much Less Important

important. It may be more useful in predicting behavior on the basis of a high or a low probability. For instance, Figure 2–14 attempts to portray need structure in an emerging nation. In contrast, Figure 2–15 shows the need structure in a developed society.

Many people in our society today might be characterized by very strong social or affiliation needs, relatively strong esteem and safety needs, with self-actualization and physiological needs much less important. Some people, however, can be characterized as having satisfied to a large extent the physiological, safety, and social needs, and their behavior tends to be dominated by esteem and self-actualizing activities, as shown in Figure 2–16. This structure will tend to become more characteristic if standards of living and levels of education continue to rise. These are intended only as examples. For different individuals, varying configurations may be appropriate. In reality, they would fluctuate tremendously from one individual or group to another.

Alderfer's ERG Theory

A revised and realigned version of Maslow's hierarchy of needs, ERG theory, was developed by Clayton Alderfer of Yale University.[25] Alderfer suggested that there are three core needs: *Existence*, *Relatedness*, and *Growth*. Alderfer's existence grouping generally corresponds to Maslow's basic physiological and safety needs, relatedness corresponds to social needs, and growth corresponds to esteem and self-actualization. Table 2–1 illustrates these relationships.

What does Alderfer's ERG theory add to our understanding of needs? Stephen Robbins, author of *Organizational Behavior*, suggests that it is a more valid description of the need hierarchy than is Maslow's theory for two principal reasons:

1. Maslow's step-by-step hierarchy assumes that only one of the five categories of needs will be predominant at a given time. ERG theory allows for more than one need—for example, safety and social—to be operating more or less equally at one time.
2. Maslow's theory asserted that a person will remain at a need level until it is adequately satisfied. ERG theory suggests that a person frustrated or blocked at a need level will regress to a lower level.[26]

TABLE 2–1	Comparison of Maslow's and Alderfer's Categories of Needs	
Maslow		**Alderfer**
Self-Actualization/Esteem		Growth
Social		Relatedness
Safety/Physiological		Existence

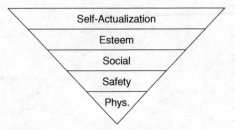

FIGURE 2–16   Need Structure When Esteem and Self-Actualization Needs Are High-Strength Needs

Having discussed Maslow's hierarchy of needs, we can now examine what researchers say about some of our motives and the incentives that tend to satisfy them.

Physiological Needs

The satisfaction of physiological needs (shelter, food, or clothing) is usually associated in our society with money. According to Saul W. Gellerman, author of *Motivation and Productivity,* the most subtle yet most important characteristic of money is its power as a symbol. Its most obvious symbolic power is its market value. It is what money can buy, not money itself, that gives it value. But money's symbolic power is not limited to its market value. Because money has no intrinsic meaning of its own, it can symbolize whatever people want it to mean.[27] Most people are not interested in dollars as such, but only as a means to be used to satisfy other motives. It is what money can buy—for example, groceries—not money itself, which can satisfy your physiological needs. Of course, money can play a role in the satisfaction of needs at every level.

Extensive studies have found that money is a very complicated incentive that is entangled with all kinds of needs besides physiological ones, and its importance is difficult to ascertain. It is clear that money's ability to satisfy seems to diminish as you surpass physiological and safety needs. In many cases, money can buy the satisfaction of social needs if, for example, it provides entry into a desired group, such as a country club. But as you become concerned about esteem and eventually self-actualization, money becomes a less effective tool for meeting needs. The stronger your esteem and self-actualization needs, the more you will have to find other means of satisfaction other than through money.

> "Money is not required to buy one necessity of the soul."
> —Henry David Thoreau

> "Money has never made man happy, nor will it, there is nothing in its nature to produce happiness. The more of it one has the more one wants."
> —Benjamin Franklin

Safety Needs

The biggest Ponzi scheme in history, devised by American investment advisor Bernie Madoff, reveals a complex collision of different motives. Madoff relied on money to meet his apparent needs for power, status, and esteem and ultimately lost it all—for himself and many of those he had drawn in. Diana B. Henriques, who led the *New York Times'* coverage of the Madoff scandal, recognized the unique way that Madoff played on the needs of his investors:

> A Madoff scheme is different. It exploits not investors' greed but investors' fear—their fear of volatility, their fear of losing what they have. In fact, through many of the years of Madoff's fraud, investors could have made a lot more money even in some of the very prominent mutual funds. . . . But they were willing to give up those greater returns in exchange for the consistency of Madoff's returns. He made them feel safe.[28]

Madoff was able to exploit the investors' needs for safety during a chaotic economic downturn, all the while failing to recognize that no matter how large his fund became or how often he duped the regulators, his need for power would never be satisfied.

Were Madoff's investors consciously aware of their needs for safety? As mentioned earlier, some motives appear above the surface, while others are largely subconscious and not obvious or easy to identify. According to Gellerman, safety, or security, needs appear in both forms.[29] Conscious security needs are quite evident and very common among most people.

We all have a desire to remain free from the hazards of life we cannot control—accidents, wars, diseases, and economic instability. Many of us seek to minimize the potential impact of such catastrophes and diminish the strength of our security needs through purchasing insurance. Gellerman suggested that many organizations tend to overemphasize the security motive by providing elaborate programs of fringe benefits, such as health, accident, and life insurance and retirement plans. The emphasis on security may make people more docile and predictable, but it does not necessarily make them more productive. In fact, if creativity or initiative is necessary in their jobs, an overemphasis on security can thwart desired behavior.

Although concern for security can affect major decisions, such as remaining in or leaving an organization, Gellerman indicated it is not likely to be an individual's dominant motive. Conscious security needs usually play a background role, often inhibiting or restraining impulses rather than initiating outward behavior. For example, if a particular course of action, such as disregarding a rule or expressing an unpopular opinion, might endanger one's job, then security considerations motivate a person not to take that course of action. Organizations can influence security needs either positively—through pension plans, insurance programs, and the like—or negatively by arousing fears of being fired or laid off, demoted, or passed over. In both cases, the effect can be to make behavior too cautious and conservative.

Peter F. Drucker suggested that one's attitude toward security is important to consider when choosing a job.[30] He raised some interesting questions:

- Do you belong in a job calling primarily for faithfulness in the performance of routine work and promising security?
- Do you find real satisfaction in the precision, order, and system of a clearly defined job?
- Do you prefer knowing what your work is today and what it is going to be tomorrow, that your job is secure, and what your relationship is to the people above, below, and next to you?
- Do you belong in a job that is less predictable, which offers a challenge to imagination and ingenuity—with the attendant penalty for failure?
- Do you tend to grow impatient with anything that looks like a "routine" job?

The answers to these questions are not always easy even though we all understand ourselves to some degree. But the answers are involved with how important the security motive is for a particular individual.

A strong subconscious orientation toward security is often developed early in childhood. Gellerman discussed several ways in which it can be implanted. A common way is through identification with security-minded parents who are willing to accept whatever fate comes along. This mindset often develops in depressed economic areas where the prospects for improvement are poor.[31] The world in which they interact seems uncertain and uncontrollable to people raised in a security-minded home. As a result, they may not feel able to influence their environment.

The security-minded people we have been describing are often very likable and pleasant to have around. They are not overly competitive and tend not to put people on the defensive. Others tend to expect little of them and thus are seldom critical of their work. Such people often are able to obtain secure, non-threatening positions in an organization.

Subconscious security motives may also develop in children through interaction with overprotective parents. Such parents are constantly trying to shield their children from heartache, disappointment, or failure. The supportive attitude of these parents in many instances permits their children to have their own way. Conflict is avoided at all costs. As a result, these children are given a distorted picture of reality and gain little insight into what they can expect of other people and what others will expect of them. In some cases, they become unrealistic in their optimism about life; that is, they have a false sense of security. Even in the face of disaster, when they should feel threatened, they seem to believe that all is well until it is too late.

When such people leave home after high school to seek their way in the world, they quickly wake up to reality. Often they find themselves unequipped to handle the hardships of life because they have not been permitted the opportunity to develop the capacity to handle frustration, tension, and anxiety. As a result, even a minor setback may throw them for a loop. Peter Drucker suggests that getting fired from their first job might be the best thing that could happen to such young people. This experience, while upsetting, is the least painful and least damaging way to learn how to cope with a setback, and that is a lesson worth learning.

> "Teach a highly educated person that it is a disgrace to fail and that he must analyze every failure to find its cause. He must learn how to fail intelligently, for failing is one of the greatest arts in the world."
> —Charles Kettering

If people learn how to recover from failure when they are young, they will be better equipped to handle worse problems as they get older.

Many people regard a strong need for security as a weakness or fault, and frown upon it as if it were less respectable than other motives. This attitude seems unjustified, since nearly everyone has some conscious and subconscious security motives. Tom Rath and Barry Conchie, using data gathered over 30 years by the Gallup Organization, found that in fact stability—which is highly related to security—is one of four basic needs that followers have.[32] Life is never so simple or clear-cut that each of us does not maintain some concern for security.

Social Needs

After the physiological and safety needs have become somewhat satisfied, the social, or affiliation, needs may become predominant. Since people are social animals, most individuals like to interact with others in situations where they feel they belong and are accepted. Although this is a common need, it tends to be stronger for some people than for others and stronger in certain situations than others.

Statistic

40% of workers feel disconnected from their employers.

—The Conference Board

In working toward a better understanding of our complex need to belong, Stanley Schachter of the University of Minnesota made a significant contribution.[33] His efforts were directed, in particular, toward studying the desire to socialize as an end in itself—that is, when people interact simply because they enjoy it. In some of these situations, no apparent reward such as money or protection was gained from this affiliation.

Schachter found that it is not always simply good fellowship that motivates affiliation. In many instances, people seek affiliation because they desire to have their beliefs confirmed. People who have similar beliefs tend to seek each other out, especially if a strongly held belief has been shattered. In this case, they tend to assemble and try to reach some common understanding about what happened and what they should believe (even if it is the same as before). In this instance, the need for affiliation is prompted by a desire to make one's life seem more under control. When a person feels alone, the world may seem "out of whack," but finding others who hold the same beliefs somehow makes order out of chaos.

In pursuing this question further, Schachter found that when people are excited, confused, or unhappy, they do not seek out just anyone—they tend to want to be with others "in the same boat." Misery does not love just any company; it loves other miserable company. These conclusions suggest that the strong informal work groups that Elton Mayo found during his experiments on human behavior in the factory system (see Chapter 3) might have been a reaction to the boredom, insignificance, and lack of competence that the workers felt.[34] As a result, workers congregated because of mutual feelings of being beaten by the system.

> "Only the mediocre are always at their best."
> —Jean Giraudoux

On the other hand, informal groups can be a tremendous asset to management if their internal organization is understood and fully utilized. The productivity of a work group seems to depend on how the group members see their own goals in relation to the goals of the organization. For example, if they perceive their own goals as being in conflict with the goals of the organization, then productivity will tend to be low. However, if these workers see their own goals as being the same as the goals of the organization or as being satisfied as a direct result of accomplishing organizational goals, then productivity will tend to be high.

Teams can provide those with a strong need for affiliation an organizationally sanctioned way to connect with others around a common work goal. Organizations are increasingly turning to teams as part of their competitive strategy, but there are many obstacles to both leading and participating in effective teams. We will talk about both of these issues in more detail in Chapter 13.

Esteem Needs

The need for esteem or recognition appears in a number of forms. In this section, we will discuss two motives related to esteem—prestige and power.

PRESTIGE   What exactly is prestige? Gellerman described it as "a sort of unwritten definition of the kinds of conduct that other people are expected to show in one's presence; what degree of respect or disrespect, formality or informality, reserve or frankness."[35] Prestige includes your image, your reputation, and your personal brand. It is the sum of impressions about your identity held by others.

People seek prestige throughout their lives in various ways. Many tend to seek only the material symbols of status, such as a bigger office, while others strive for personal achievement or self-actualization, which may command prestige in itself. Regardless of the way it is expressed, there seems to be a widespread need for people to have their importance validated and, in fact, set at a level that they feel is deserved. As discussed earlier, people normally want to have a high evaluation of themselves that is firmly based in reality as shown by the recognition and respect accorded to them by others.

POWER   The resource that enables a person to influence or induce compliance from others is power. It is a person's influence potential. There tends to be two kinds of power—position and personal. Individuals who are able to induce compliance from others because of their position in the organization have position power; individuals who derive their influence from their personality and behavior have personal power. Some people are endowed with both position and personal power. Others seem to have no power at all.

When it comes to personal power, Maggie Craddock points out that we first learn about the give and take of power from our early experiences in our families. After all, the people who took care of us as children are our first models for how to use authority, shaping both the emotional and behavioral style of power we later use in the workplace.[36] We will discuss power in greater detail in Chapter 8.

Self-Actualization Needs

Of all the needs discussed by Maslow, the one that social and behavioral scientists know least about is self-actualization. Perhaps because people satisfy this need in different ways, self-actualization is a difficult need to pin down and identify. Although little research has been done on the concept of self-actualization, extensive research has been done on three motives that we feel are related to it—competence, achievement, and purpose.

COMPETENCE   According to Robert W. White, one of the mainsprings of action in a human being is a desire for competence.[37] Competence implies control over environmental factors— both physical and social. People with this motive do not wish to wait passively for things to happen. They want to be able to control their environment and make things happen.

The competence motive can be identified in young children as they move from the early stage of wanting to touch and handle everything in reach to the later stage of wanting not only to touch but to take things apart and put them back together again. That is how children begin to learn their way around their world. They become aware of what they can and cannot do—not in terms of what they are allowed or permitted to do but in terms of what they are able to do. During these early years, children develop a feeling of competence.

This feeling of competence is closely related to the concept of expectancy discussed earlier in this chapter. Whether children have a strong or weak sense of competency often depends on their past successes and failures. If their successes overshadow their failures, then their feeling of competence will tend to be high. They will have a positive outlook toward life, seeing almost every new situation as an interesting challenge that they can overcome. If, however, their failures rule the day, their outlook will be more negative and their expectancy for satisfying various needs may become low. Since expectancy tends to influence motives, people with low feelings of competence are often less motivated to seek new challenges or take risks. These people would rather let their environment control them than attempt to change it. According to White, the competence motive reveals itself in adults as a desire for job mastery and professional growth. The job is one arena in which people can use their ability and skills within a work environment that is challenging, but not overwhelming. In the best organizations, the competence motive in an individual can be expressed freely, and significant personal rewards can be gained. But in routine, closely supervised jobs, this is often impossible. Such situations make the worker dependent on the system and, therefore, completely frustrate people with high competence needs.[38]

ACHIEVEMENT   Over the years, behavioral scientists have observed that some people have an intense need to achieve. In recent research conducted by Sirota, Mischkind, and Meltzer, the three goals most commonly sought by employees have been identified as, once again, achievement (esteem), camaraderie (social/belonging), and equity (fair pay and job security).[39] As mentioned earlier, David McClelland and his associates at Harvard University have been studying the need for achievement for more than 40 years. Their research has concluded that the need for achievement is a distinct human motive that can be distinguished from other needs, one that can be isolated and assessed in any group.[40]

Statistic

25% of employees are just showing up to work to collect a paycheck.

—The Conference Board

McClelland illustrated some of these characteristics of people with a high need for achievement in describing a laboratory experiment. Participants were asked to throw rings over a peg from any distance they chose. Most people tended to throw at random—now close, now far away; but individuals with a high need for achievement seemed to measure carefully where they were most likely to get a sense of mastery—not too close to make the task ridiculously easy or too far away to make it impossible. They set moderately difficult, but potentially achievable goals. In biology, this approach is known as the overload principle. In weight lifting, for example, strength cannot be increased by tasks that can be performed easily or that will injure the organism. Strength can only be increased by lifting weights that are difficult enough to stretch the muscles but not enough to cause injury.

Many people tend to be extreme in their attitude toward risks in that they either favor wild speculative gambling or minimize their exposure to losses. Gamblers seem to choose big risks because the outcome is beyond their power and, therefore, they can easily rationalize away their personal responsibility if they lose. The conservative individual chooses tiny risks where the gain is small but secure, perhaps because there is little danger of anything going wrong for which that person might be blamed.

The high need for achievement surfaces only when people believe they can influence the outcome. Achievement-motivated people are not gamblers. They prefer to work on a problem that has a challenging degree of risk rather than leave the outcome to chance. In business, this aggressive realism is the mark of the successful entrepreneur. As a manager, working with your employees to set moderately difficult but potentially achievable goals can translate into a positive attitude toward risks that can both lead to professional growth and contribute to organizational success.

Another characteristic of achievement-motivated people is that they seem to be more concerned with personal achievement than with the rewards of success. They do not reject rewards, but the rewards are not as essential as the accomplishment itself. They get a bigger kick out of winning or solving a difficult problem than they get from any money or praise they receive. To achievement-motivated people, money is valuable primarily as a measurement of their performance. It provides them with a means of assessing their progress and comparing their achievements with those of other people. They normally do not seek money for status or economic security.

A desire by people with a high need for achievement to seek situations in which they get concrete feedback on how well they are doing is closely related to this concern for personal accomplishment. Consequently, achievement-motivated people are often found in sales jobs or as owners and managers of their own businesses. In addition to concrete feedback, the nature of the feedback is important to achievement-motivated people. They respond favorably to information about their work (i.e., task-relevant feedback). They are not interested in comments about their personal characteristics, such as how cooperative or helpful they are. Affiliation-motivated people, however, might want social or attitudinal feedback.

> "Appreciation is a wonderful thing; it makes what is excellent in others belong to us as well."
> —Voltaire

Achievement-motivated people behave as they do, according to McClelland, because they habitually spend time thinking about doing things better. In fact, he has found that whenever people start to think in achievement terms, things start to happen. College students with a high need for achievement will generally get better grades than equally bright students with weaker achievement needs. Achievement-motivated people tend to get more raises and are promoted faster because they are constantly trying to think of better ways of doing things. Companies with many such people grow faster and are more profitable.

Neal Gilbert and Charles Whiting warn, however, that if professionals are not afforded the opportunity to self-actualize (increase their competence and achievement) in their organization, "their only recourse [will be] to leave the organization."[41] Employees who are not empowered will look elsewhere to empower themselves, perhaps placing their considerable talent in the hands of a competitor. This is a formidable threat in knowledge-based organizations where the departure of two or three key individuals may mean the death of the company.

Achievement-motivated people can be the backbone of most organizations, but what about their potential as managers? As we know, people with a high need for achievement get ahead because as individuals they are producers—they get things done. But when they are promoted—when their success depends not only on their own work but on the activities of others—they may be less effective. Because they are highly task-oriented and work to their capacity, they tend to expect others to do the same. As a result, they sometimes lack the human skills and patience necessary for effectively managing people who are competent but have a higher need for affiliation or some other need than they do. In this situation, their overemphasis on results often frustrates other people and prevents them from maximizing their own potential.

Interestingly, McLelland and Burnham found that among managers, those motivated by power were most effective. These managers recognized that getting results depends on building power through influencing others, rather than relying on their own achievements.[42] Achievement-motivated people do not always make the best managers unless they develop their human skills. As we pointed out in Chapter 1, being a good producer is not sufficient to being an effective manager.

Sirota, Mischkind, and Meltzer further point out, importantly, that while managers must recognize the needs of their people, they first need to stop demotivating them. How? By instilling an inspiring purpose, providing regular recognition, and acting as an expediter for them, among other practices.[43] Managers may need to shift their mindset from thinking of motivating as something they do to employees. Instead, work with them to discover, understand, and unleash their key motivations through communicating, appreciating, listening, and removing barriers.

> "Better than half of the leaders I have met don't need to learn what to do – they need to learn what to stop."
> —Peter Drucker

PURPOSE AND VALUES   At the pinnacle of Maslow's hierarchy, self-actualization also comprises a profound search for and commitment to your sense of purpose, your core values, and how well they align to those of the organization.

In reflecting on his experiences of surviving a World War II concentration camp, Viktor Frankl, an Austrian psychiatrist, asserted in his book *Man's Search for Meaning* that "the striving to find a meaning in one's life is the primary motivational force in man."[44] This was the same theme Tom Peters and Robert Waterman used in their best-selling book *In Search of Excellence*. They observed, "The dominating need of human beings is to find meaning, . . . to control one's destiny, . . . to be an expert in the promotion and protection of values."[45]

Having a profound sense of purpose is, for many, the ultimate need. Daniel Pink's research has shown that once the need for reasonable pay is met, people seek three things: autonomy, mastery, and purpose. He now sees a rise in the purpose motive, evidenced by the fact that people with sophisticated technical skills are volunteering significant amounts of their time outside of work and giving away what they develop for free![46] Consider, for example, that all Linux programmers and contributors to Wikipedia contribute their time and ideas simply because they believe in the purpose—whether it is open source code or collaborative information sharing.

In today's pressured work environments, effective leaders recognize that purpose is a powerful, motivating force, but only when people internalize it. Justin Menkes describes that when leaders are able to infuse purpose into the work, to define it in a way that allows employees to understand it in a larger context, people start to see their efforts as making a meaningful positive difference in the world.[47] For example, Herb Kelleher, founder of Southwest Airlines, helped reframe the work of baggage handlers from moving bags to ensuring that a passenger has his insulin, or a grandmother has the gift she chose for her first grandchild upon arrival. In essence, purpose drives passion.

Many for-profit and nonprofit businesses, too, are not only declaring their values but modifying their business models to expressly achieve a noncommercial purpose. The TOMS shoes company is a current case in point. For every pair of shoes it sells, it gives a pair away to a child in need. In so doing, TOMS involves its customers in making a contribution as part of its overarching "One for One" purpose. It seems that organizations as well as individuals are energized by a clear purpose, a high-level intrinsic need.

Summary

People have many needs, all of which we try to satisfy in a number of ways and settings. No one person has exactly the same mixture or strength of these needs as another. Some people are driven mainly by achievement, others are concerned primarily with security, still others by power. Theories of motivation have identified both intrinsic and extrinsic motives, explored the complex interactions between them, and described their impact on behavior. Although we must recognize individual differences, as managers we cannot presume to decide which motives are most important to our employees. If we are to understand, predict, and influence behavior, we must know what our employees really want from their jobs. Only then can we appeal to their strongest motivations and increase the probability of meeting both professional and organizational goals.

Notes

1. Sigmund Freud, *The Ego and the Id* (New York: Norton, 1923). See also Freud, *New Introductory Lectures on Psychoanalysis* (New York: Norton, 1933).

2. David C. McClelland, John W. Atkinson, R. A. Clark, and E. L. Lowell, *The Achievement Motive* (New York: Appleton-Century-Crofts, 1953); McClelland, *The Achieving Society* (Princeton, NJ: D. Van Nostrand, 1961); John William Atkinson, *Motivation and Achievement* (New York: Halsted Press, 1974). See also Craig Pinder, "Concerning the Application of Human Motivation Theories in Organizational Settings," *Academy of Management Review* 21 (1977): 384–397.

3. Daniel Pink, *Drive: The Surprising Truth about What Motivates Us* (New York: Penguin Group, 2009), 8.

4. Teresa M. Amabile and Steve J. Kramer, "What Really Motivates Workers," in "The HBR List: Breakthrough Ideas for 2010," *Harvard Business Review*, January 1, 2010, 1–2; Amabile and Kramer, "Inner Work Life: Understanding the Subtext of Business Performance," *Harvard Business Review*, May 1, 2007, 5; Amabile and Kramer, *The Progress Principle: Using Small Wins to Ignite Joy, Engagement, and Creativity at Work* (Boston: Harvard Business School Press, 2011).

5. Kurt Lewin, "Behavior and Development as a Function of the Total Situation," in *Field Theory in Social Science*: Selected Theoretical Papers, Dorwin Cartwright, ed. (New York: Harper & Row, 1951), 239–240. See also Gregory B. Northcraft and Margaret A. Neale, *Organizational Behavior: A Management Challenge*, 2nd ed. (Fort Worth: Dryden Press, 1994), 66.

6. Lewin used the expression E = Environment, whereas we have used S = Situation in keeping with the context of this book.

7. Lewin, "Behavior and Development as a Function of the Total Situation," 239.

8. Abraham H. Maslow, *Motivation and Personality* (New York: Harper & Row, 1954). See also Maslow, *Motivation and Personality*, 2nd ed. (New York: Harper & Row, 1970).

9. Leon Festinger, *A Theory of Cognitive Dissonance* (Stanford, CA: Stanford University Press, 1957); Stephen Kaplan, *Cognition and*

Environment: Functioning in an Uncertain World (New York: Praeger, 1982).

10. Festinger, *A Theory of Cognitive Dissonance*, 155.

11. Freud, *The Ego and the Id.*

12. Norman R. F. Maier, "Psychology in Industry," *The Academy of Management Review* 14 (1989): 83–91.

13. Roger Barker, Tamara Dembo, and Kurt Lewin, *Frustration and Aggression* (Iowa City: University of Iowa Press, 1942).

15. Maier, "Psychology in Industry," 253.

16. Maier, "Psychology in Industry," 88–90.

17. John A. C. Brown, *The Social Psychology of Industry* (Baltimore: Penguin Books, 1954), 252.

18. Dewey E. Johnson, *Concepts of Air Force Leadership* (Washington, D.C.: Air Force ROTC, 1970), 209.

19. J. Sterling-Livingston, "Pygmalion in Management," *Harvard Business Review*, September/October, 1988, 81–89.

20. See John W. Atkinson, "Motivational Determinants of Risk-Taking Behavior," *Psychological Review* 64, no. 6 (1957): 365.

21. Victor H. Vroom, "Leader," in *Handbook of Industrial and Organizational Psychology,* ed. Marvin D. Dunnette (Chicago: Rand McNally, 1976), 1527–1551

22. Martin L. Maehr and Larry A. Braskampt, *The Motivation Factor: A Theory of Personal Investment* (Lexington, MA: Health, 1986).

23. Maslow, *Motivation and Personality.*

24. David C. McClelland, John W. Atkinson, R. A. Clark, and E. L. Lowell, *The Achievement Motive* (New York: Appleton-Century-Crofts, 1953); McClelland, *The Achieving Society* (Princeton, NJ: D. Van Nostrand, 1961); John William Atkinson, *Motivation and Achievement* (New York: Halsted Press, 1974). See also Craig Pinder, "Concerning the Application of Human Motivation Theories in Organizational Settings," *Academy of Management Review*, 21 (1977): 384–397.

25. Clayton P. Alderfer, *Human Needs in Organizational Settings* (New York: The Free Press of Glenco, 1972).

26. Stephen Robbins, *Organizational Behavior, Concepts, Controversies and Applications* (Englewood Cliffs, NJ: Prentice Hall, 1979).

27. Saul W. Gellerman, *Motivation and Productivity* (New York: American Management Association, 1963).

28. Diana B. Henriques, "Examining Bernie Madoff, 'The Wizard of Lies'" Interview by Terry Gross. *Fresh Air*. NPR. WHYY, Philadelphia, PA, April 26, 2011. See also Henriques, *The Wizard of Lies: Bernie Madoff and the Death of Trust* (New York: Times Books/Henry Holt and Company, 2011), 56.

29. Gellerman, *Motivation and Productivity*, 154–55.

30. Peter Drucker, "How to Be an Employee," *Psychology Today* (March 1968), a reprint from *Fortune* magazine.

31. Gellerman, *Motivation and Productivity*, 151.

32. Tom Rath and Barry Conchie, *Strengths Based Leadership* (New York: Gallup Press), 82.

33. Stanley Schachter, *The Psychology of Affiliation* (Stanford, CA: Stanford University Press, 1959).

34. Elton Mayo, *The Social Problems of an Industrial Civilization* (Boston: Harvard Business School, 1945); see also Mayo, *The Human Problems of an Industrial Civilization* (New York: Macmillan, 1933).

35. Gellerman, *Motivation and Productivity*, 151.

36. Maggie Craddock, *Power Genes: Understanding Your Power Persona and How to Wield It at Work* (Boston: Harvard Business Review Press, 2011), 5.

37. Robert W. White, "Motivation Reconsidered: The Concept of Competence," *Psychological Review* 66 no. 5 (1959): 297–330.

38. *Ibid.*

39. David Sirota, Louis A. Mischkind, and Michael Irwin Meltzer, "Stop Demotivating Your Employees!" *Harvard Management Update* (July 2008): 3–5.

40. David C. McClelland, John W. Atkinson, R. A. Clark, and E. L. Lowell, *The Achievement Motive* (New York: Appleton-Century-Crofts, 1953); McClelland, *The Achieving Society* (Princeton, NJ: D. Van Nostrand, 1961); John William Atkinson, *Motivation and Achievement* (New York: Halsted Press, 1974); McLelland and David H. Burnham, "Power Is the Great Motivator," *Harvard Business Review* 73, January/February 1995, 126–130. See also Craig Pinder, "Concerning the Application of Human Motivation Theories in Organizational Settings," *Academy of Management Review* 21 (1977): 384–397.

41. Charles E. Whiting and E. Neal Gilbert, "Empowering Professionals," *Management Review* 82, no. 6 (June 1993): 57.

42. McLelland and David H. Burnham, "Power Is the Great Motivator," *Harvard Business Review* 73, January/February 1995, 126–130.

43. David Sirota, Louis A. Mischkind, and Michael Irwin Meltzer, "Stop Demotivating Your Employees!" *Harvard Management Update* (July 2008): 3–5.

44. Viktor E. Frankl, *Man's Search for Meaning* (New York: Washington Square Press, 1963),

154. See also Jerry L. Fletcher, *Patterns of High Performance: Discovering the Way People Work Best* (San Francisco: Berret-Koehler, 1993).

45. Tom Peters and Robert H. Watermann, Jr., *In Search of Excellence: Lessons from America's Best Run Companies* (New York: Harper & Row, 1982), 76, 80, 86.

46. Pink, *Drive,* 14.

47. Justin Mendes, *Better Under Pressure: How Great Leaders Bring Out the Best in Themselves and Others* (Boston: Harvard Business Review Press, 2011), 43–46.

3

Classic Motivational Theories

Behavioral science pioneers such as Elton Mayo, Douglas McGregor, Chris Argyris, George Homans, Frederick Herzberg, and Abraham Maslow have made such important contributions that their work continues to shape our understanding of human behavior. Maslow's theory of a hierarchy of needs was discussed in some detail in Chapter 2. So this chapter will be devoted to highlighting significant theories developed by others in this corps of important researchers in our discussion of what motivates people. We can easily hear the echoes, even in our hyper, cyber-driven work worlds, where a blog entry in a recent issue of *Fast Company* laments that most managers still hold Theory X assumptions about their employees.[1] Their relevance lives on.

> "Do not go where the path may lead, go instead where there is no path and leave a trail."
> —Ralph Waldo Emerson

THE HAWTHORNE STUDIES

Elton Mayo

In 1924, efficiency experts at the Hawthorne, Illinois, plant of the Western Electric Company designed a research program to study the effects of illumination in the work environment on productivity. At first, nothing about this program seemed exceptional enough to arouse any unusual interest. After all, efficiency experts had long been trying to find the ideal mix of physical conditions, working hours, and working methods that stimulate workers to produce at maximum capacity. Yet, by the time these studies were completed (over a decade later), there was little doubt that the work at Hawthorne would stand the test of time as one of the most exciting and important research projects ever conducted in an industrial setting. It was at Western Electric's Hawthorne plant that the Human Relations movement began to gather momentum, and one of its early advocates, Elton Mayo of the Harvard Graduate School of Business Administration, gained recognition.

Telephone Relay from Western Electric, Elton Mayo's Hawthorne Study.

Presented to: Dr. Paul Hersey

In the initial phases of the study, efficiency experts assumed that more light would result in higher output by workers. Two groups of employees were selected: a test group, which worked under varying degrees of light, and a control group, which worked under normal illumination conditions in the plant. As lighting power was increased, the output of the test group went up as anticipated. Unexpectedly, however, the output of the control group went up also—without any increase in light. When illumination was decreased to the level of moonlight with one test group, output increased even further. What was happening? When the illumination test ended in April 1927, the researchers concluded that something other than illumination was affecting productivity.

Determined to explain these and other surprising test results, the efficiency experts decided to expand their research at Hawthorne. They felt that in addition to technical and physical changes, they should explore employee behavior as well.

The next phase of experiments started later in 1927 with a group of women who assembled telephone relays. For more than a year and a half during this experiment, the researchers improved the working conditions of the women by implementing such innovations as scheduled rest periods, company lunches, and shorter workweeks. Work output increased. Baffled by the results, the researchers then decided to take everything away from the women, returning the working conditions to exactly the way they had been at the beginning of the experiment. This radical change was expected to have a negative psychological impact on the women and to reduce their output. Instead, their output increased to a new all-time high. Why?

The answers were found not in the production aspects of the experiment (changes in plant and physical working conditions) but in the human aspects. Because of the attention given to them by experimenters, the women felt that they were an important part of the company. They no longer viewed themselves as isolated individuals, working together only in the sense that they were physically close to each other. Instead, they had become participating members of a congenial, cohesive work group. They felt closer to each other, more capable, and more driven to produce. These needs, which had long gone unsatisfied at the workplace, were now being fulfilled. The women worked harder and more effectively than previously. Pay was also an important factor. The women, paid on a piecework basis, were able to keep the pay benefits of increased productivity. Without realizing it, the study had tapped both their intrinsic and extrinsic sources of motivation.

Elton Mayo wanted to test this finding further. He set up two different studies, one in 1928 and one in 1929, and identified an interesting phenomenon. He got the researchers to extend their study by interviewing more than 20,000 employees from every department in the company. Interviews were designed to help researchers find out what the workers thought about their jobs, their working conditions, their supervisors, their company, and anything that bothered them, and how those feelings might be related to their productivity. After several interview sessions, the researchers found that a structured question-and-answer-type interview was useless for getting the information they wanted. Instead, the workers wanted to talk freely about what they thought was important.

Statistic

25% of employees find employee benefits an important reason for joining an organization while 42% of employees reported their organization's benefits as an important reason to stay.

— The MetLife Study of Employee Benefit Trends (New York: MetLife, 2003)

So the predetermined questions were discarded, and the interviewer allowed the workers to say what they wanted to say.

The interviews proved valuable in a number of ways. First, they were therapeutic; the workers were given an opportunity to express themselves. Many felt this was the best thing the company had ever done. The result was a wholesale change in their attitudes. Since many of their suggestions were being implemented, the workers began to feel that management viewed them as important contributors, both as individuals and as a group. They were now participating in the operation and future of the company and not just performing unchallenging, unappreciated tasks.

Second, the implications of the Hawthorne studies signaled the need for management to study and understand relationships among people. In these studies, as well as in the many that followed, the most significant factor affecting organizational productivity was found to be the interpersonal relationships that develop on the job, not just pay and working conditions. The researchers found that when informal groups aligned with management, as they did at Hawthorne through the interview program, productivity rose. The increased productivity seemed to reflect the workers' feelings of competence—a sense of mastery over the job and work environment. The researchers also discovered that when the group felt that their own goals were in opposition to those of management, productivity remained at or dropped to low levels.

These findings were important because they helped answer many of the questions that had puzzled management about why some groups seemed to be high producers while others hovered at a minimal level of output.

> "Motivation will almost always beat mere talent."
> —Norman R. Augustine

The findings also encouraged management to involve workers in planning, organizing, and controlling their own work, which helped secure their positive cooperation.

Mayo saw his findings about informal work groups as an indictment of a society that had been treating human beings as insensitive machines concerned only with economic self-interest. As a result, workers had been expected to look at work merely as an impersonal exchange of money for labor. Work in American industry, according to Mayo, meant humiliation—the performance of routine, tedious, and oversimplified tasks in an environment over which one had no control. This environment denied satisfaction of esteem and self-actualization needs on the job. He went on to map his conclusions to Maslow's hierarchy of needs and found that only physiological and safety needs were satisfied. In this environment, the lack of avenues for satisfying other higher-level needs led employees to feel tense, anxious, and frustrated. Mayo called such feelings of helplessness *anomie*—a condition characterized by workers' feeling unimportant, confused, and unattached—victims of their own environment.

Although anomie was a creation of the total society, Mayo felt it was particularly evident in industrial settings where too many managers assumed that people were primarily dominated by physiological and safety needs, wanting to make as much money as they could for as little work as possible. As a result, management organized work on the basic assumption that workers, on the whole, were contemptible and self-serving. Mayo called this assumption the Rabble Hypothesis. He deplored the authoritarian, task-oriented management practices that it created.

THEORY X AND THEORY Y

Douglas McGregor

Mayo's research paved the way for the development of the now classic Theory X–Theory Y framework developed by Douglas McGregor in 1957.[2] McGregor believed that the traditional organization—with its centralized decision making, hierarchical pyramid, and external control of work—assumes that most people prefer to be directed, are not in having responsibility, and want safety above all. In that case, money, fringe benefits, and the threat of punishment are what motivate people. He called these assumptions Theory X (see Theory X, Table 3–1). The Theory X view of human nature and motivation is then very similar to Mayo's Rabble Hypothesis.

Managers who accept Theory X assumptions attempt to structure, control, and closely supervise their employees. They believe that external control is clearly appropriate for dealing with unreliable and irresponsible people.

> "Remember the difference between a boss and a leader: a boss says 'Go!' – a leader says 'Let's go'!"
> —E. M. Kelly

TABLE 3–1	Assumptions About Human Nature That Underlie McGregor's Theory X and Theory Y	
Theory X		**Theory Y**
1. Work is inherently distasteful to most people.		1. Work is as natural as play, if the conditions are favorable.
2. Most people are not ambitious, have little desire for responsibility, and prefer to be directed.		2. Self-control is often indispensable in achieving organizational goals.
3. Most people have little capacity for creativity in solving organizational problems.		3. The capacity for creativity in solving organizational problems is widely distributed in the population.
4. Motivation occurs only at the physiological and security levels.		4. Motivation occurs at the social, esteem, and self-actualization levels, as well as at the physiological and security levels.
5. Most people must be closely controlled and often coerced to achieve organizational objectives.		5. People can be self-directed and creative at work if properly motivated.

After describing Theory X, McGregor questioned whether this view of human nature was correct and if management practices based on it would really work in many situations. How could Theory X prevail among people in a democratic society, with its increasing level of education and standard of living? Weren't people capable of more responsible behavior?

> "Opportunity is missed by most people because it is dressed in overalls and looks like work."
> —Thomas Edison

Drawing heavily on Maslow's hierarchy of needs, McGregor concluded that Theory X assumptions about human nature, when universally applied, are often inaccurate. Furthermore, management approaches that develop from these assumptions may fail to motivate many individuals to work toward organizational goals. Why? Because management by direction and control is a questionable method for motivating people whose physiological and safety needs are reasonably satisfied and whose social, esteem, and self-actualization needs are becoming predominant.

According to McGregor, work could be as natural and satisfying for people as play, provided that they have enough money to satisfy their physiological and safety needs. But Theory X management undermines that possibility by assuming that people cannot satisfy their esteem and self-actualization needs at work because they do not—and should not—have control over their jobs. Under Theory X management, most employees would consider work a necessary evil rather than a source of personal challenge and satisfaction.

McGregor felt that management needed to develop practices based on a more accurate understanding of human nature and motivation. He therefore developed an alternative theory of human behavior called Theory Y. This theory assumes that people are not, by nature, lazy and unreliable. Instead, people can be self-directed and creative at work if properly motivated. Based on that premise, McGregor contended that it should be an essential task of management to unleash this potential in individuals.

In practice, high-performing Theory Y organizations have engaged employees and cohesive work teams whose goals parallel and support the achievement of organizational goals. There is both high productivity and people come to work gladly because work is inherently satisfying.

From this discussion of Theory X and Theory Y, it is tempting to conclude that managers who accept Theory X assumptions about human nature usually direct, control, and closely supervise people, while Theory Y managers are supportive and facilitating.

"If there is anything I would like to be remembered for it is that I helped people understand that leadership is helping other people grow and succeed. To repeat myself, leadership is not about you. It's about them."
—Jack Welch

We want to caution against drawing this conclusion. It could lead to the trap of thinking that Theory X is "bad" and Theory Y is "good" and that everyone is independent and self-motivated. For McGregor, Theory Y implied only that most people have the potential to be independent and self-motivated. To understand the difference, we need to look more closely at the difference between attitude and behavior.

Theory X and Theory Y are attitudes, or mindsets, about people. While the "best" assumptions for a manager to have may be Theory Y, it may not be appropriate to behave consistently with those assumptions all the time. Managers may have Theory Y assumptions about human nature yet find it necessary to behave in a very directive, controlling manner (as if they had Theory X assumptions) with some people in the short run to help them grow and develop. In other words, not everyone is ready to be independent on the job right away. Effective managers know when to behave in ways that look like Theory X or Theory Y is at work, even if that is not their prevailing mindset.

WORK GROUPS

George C. Homans

Management has long recognized that work groups, whether formal or informal, have the potential to control the behavior of their members and, as a result, the level of productivity. How do groups control behavior? George C. Homans (1950) developed an early model of social systems that began to address this important question.[3]

According to Homans, there are three elements in a social system. *Activities* are the tasks that people perform. *Interactions* are the behaviors that occur between people in performing those tasks. And *sentiments* are the attitudes and feelings that develop between individuals and within groups. Homans argued that while these concepts are separate, they are closely related. In

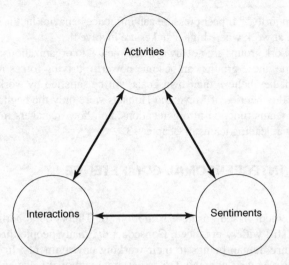

FIGURE 3–1 The Mutual Dependency of Activities, Interactions, and Sentiments

fact, as Figure 3–1 illustrates, they are mutually dependent. A change in any one of these three elements will produce some change in the other two.

In an organization, certain activities, interactions, and sentiments are essential, or required from its members if it is to survive. In other words, jobs (activities) have to be done that require people to work together (interactions). These jobs must be sufficiently satisfying (sentiments) for people to continue doing them. As people interact on their jobs, they develop sentiments toward each other. The more positive the sentiments, the more people will tend to interact productively with each other.

Over time, groups tend to develop expectations or norms that specify how people in the group should behave under specific circumstances. For example, a group of workers might have a norm that "you should not talk to Mary or help her any more than necessary." If the group is cohesive enough—people benefit from being in it and would be reluctant to leave it— members will readily conform. On the other hand, people who deviate significantly from the norms usually incur negative sanctions from the group. As Athos and Coffey have described, "The group has at its disposal a variety of penalties, ranging from gentle kidding to harsh ostracism, for pressuring deviant members into line."[4] In the face of sanctions, members can either choose to conform to the group's expectations or decide to continue deviating from them. If the resulting pressure from their peers becomes too great for doing so, they may leave the group.

The influence that group pressure can have in achieving conformity in the perceptions and behavior of people is well documented. For example, Solomon E. Asch (1958) conducted a classic experiment in which groups of eight college men were each asked to match the length of a line with one of three unequal lines.[5] Seven members of each group were privately told to give the same incorrect answer. The uninstructed member was the last one asked to give his answer and was thus confronted with the dilemma of either reporting what he saw as being correct or reporting what all the others had said in order to be congruent with the group. Asch reported that "one-third of all the estimates were errors identical with or in the direction of the distorted estimates of the majority."[6] If peer pressure can influence behavior in this kind of exercise, imagine what it can do at work where higher stakes are involved!

But strong work groups are not always detrimental to organizations. In fact, as Mayo identified at Hawthorne, these groups can become powerful driving forces in accomplishing organizational goals if they believe their own goals will be satisfied by working for organizational goals. Of course, the theories of Mayo and Homans were only the beginning of exploring how work groups and teams function in organizations, and how managers influence them. We will look more closely at leading teams in Chapter 13.

INCREASING INTERPERSONAL COMPETENCE

Chris Argyris

Although management based on the assumptions of Theory X is perhaps no longer widely appropriate, it is still widely practiced. Consequently, many people throughout the world are treated as immature human beings in their working environments. In attempting to analyze this dynamic, Chris Argyris compared different organizational value systems, as illustrated in Table 3–2.

According to Argyris, bureaucratic or pyramidal values (much like Theory X assumptions) lead to shallow, mistrustful relationships.[7] Since these relationships do not permit the natural and free expression of feelings, they are not authentic and result in decreased interpersonal competence. "Without interpersonal competence or a 'psychologically safe' environment, the organization is a breeding ground for mistrust, intergroup conflict, rigidity, and so on, which in turn lead to a decrease in organizational success in problem solving."[8]

If, on the other hand, humanistic or democratic values are adhered to in an organization, Argyris believed that trusting, authentic relationships will develop among people. This will result in increased interpersonal competence, intergroup cooperation, flexibility, and increases in organizational effectiveness. In this kind of environment, people are treated as whole human beings. Both organizational members and the organization itself are given an opportunity to develop to the fullest potential. There is an attempt to make work exciting and challenging.

TABLE 3–2 Argyris's Immaturity-Maturity Continuum	
Immaturity ⟶ Maturity	
Passive	Active
Dependent	Independent
Behave in a few ways	Capable of behaving in many ways
Erratic shallow interest	Deeper and stronger interests
Short-time perspective	Long-time perspective (past and future)
Subordinate position	Equal or superordinate position
Lack of awareness of self	Awareness and control over self

> "Constant development is the law of life, and a man who always tries to maintain his dogmas in order to appear consistent drives himself into a false position."
> —Mohandas Karamchand Gandhi

Implicit in living these values is "treating each human being as a person with a complex set of needs, all of which are important in his work and in his life . . . and providing opportunities for people in organizations to influence the way in which they relate to work, the organization, and the environment."[9]

ARGYRIS'S IMMATURITY-MATURITY THEORY

The fact that bureaucratic-pyramidal values still dominate most organizations has produced many of our current organizational problems. While at Yale in the 1950s, Argyris examined industrial organizations to determine what effect management practices have had on individual behavior and personal growth within the work environment.[10] According to Argyris, seven changes should take place in the personality of individuals if they are to develop into mature people.

First, individuals move from a passive state as infants to a state of increasing activity as adults. Second, individuals develop from a state of dependency upon others as infants to a state of relative independence as adults. Third, individuals behave in only a few ways as infants, but as adults they are capable of behaving in many ways. Fourth, individuals have erratic, casual, and shallow interests as infants, but develop deeper and stronger interests as adults. Fifth, the time perspective of children is very short, involving mostly the present, but as they mature, their time perspective increases to include the past and the future. Sixth, individuals as infants are subordinate to everyone, but they move to equal or superior positions with others as adults. Seventh, as children, individuals lack awareness of "self," but as adults, they are not only aware of, but they are able to control "self." Argyris suggested that these changes reside on a continuum and that the "healthy" personality develops along the continuum from "immaturity" to "maturity" (see Table 3–2).

> "The common wisdom is that . . . managers have to learn to motivate people. Nonsense. Employees bring their own motivation."
> —Chris Argyris

These changes are only general tendencies, but they can help us think more critically about the concept of maturity. Both an individual's culture and personality can inhibit and limit complete expression and growth toward adulthood. Yet the tendency is to move toward the "maturity" end of the continuum with age. Argyris would be the first to admit that few, if any, persons develop to full maturity.

In examining the widespread worker apathy and lack of effort in organizations, Argyris questioned whether these problems were simply the result of individual laziness. He suggests that they are not. Argyris contends that, in many cases, when people join the work force, they are kept from maturing by the management practices they experience. Given minimal control over their environment, they are encouraged to be passive, dependent, and subordinate, and as a result they behave immaturely. In fact, in many organizations the worker is not expected to act as a mature adult.

According to Argyris, keeping people immature is built into the very nature of organizations. He argues that because organizations are created to achieve goals that can best be met collectively, the organization often acts as the architect, determining how those objectives may be achieved. In this sense, the individual is fitted to the job. Management tries to increase and enhance organizational and administrative efficiency and productivity by making employees "interchangeable parts."

Basic to these concepts is the notion that power and authority should rest in the hands of a few at the top of the organization, and those at the lower end of the chain of command are strictly controlled by management or the system itself. Task specialization that results from such an environment lends itself to oversimplification of the job so that it becomes repetitive, routine, and unchallenging. Leadership is directive and task-oriented. Decisions about the work are made by the manager, and the employees only carry out those decisions. This type of leadership evokes managerial controls, such as budgets, some incentive systems, time-and-motion studies, and standard operating procedures, elaborate processes—all of which can restrict the initiative, creativity, and overall contributions of employees. Again, we can see Theory X assumptions at play and individuals restricted to satisfying lower levels of motivation.

MOTIVATION-HYGIENE THEORY

Frederick Herzberg

As Maslow noted, needs such as esteem and self-actualization seem to become more important as people develop. One of the most interesting series of studies that concentrated heavily on these areas was directed by Frederick Herzberg in the 1950s.[11] His research led to a theory of work motivation that has broad implications for management and its efforts toward effectively leading human resources.

In developing his motivation-hygiene theory, Herzberg seemed to sense that thought leaders such as McGregor and Argyris were contributing to knowledge about human nature, motives, and needs. And he recognized that it could be invaluable to organizations and individuals:

> To industry, the payoff for a study of job attitudes would be increased productivity, decreased absenteeism, and smoother working relations. To the individual, an understanding of the forces that lead to improved morale would bring greater happiness and greater self-realization.[12]

"[T]he things that people said positively about their job experiences were not the opposite of what they said negatively about their experiences . . . the factors that make people happy all are related to what people did: the job content . . . what made people unhappy was related to . . . job environment, . . . the way they're treated."
—Frederick Herzberg (From a 1971 interview in Management Review)

Herzberg set out to collect data on job attitudes from which assumptions about human behavior could be made. The motivation-hygiene theory resulted from the analysis of an initial study by Herzberg and his colleagues at the Psychological Service of Pittsburgh. This study involved extensive interviews with some 200 engineers and accountants from 11 industries in the Pittsburgh area. In the interviews, they were asked about what kinds of things on their job made them satisfied or dissatisfied.

TABLE 3–3 Motivation and Hygiene Factors	
Motivator	**Hygiene Factor**
The Job Itself	**Environment**
Achievement	Policies and administration
Recognition for accomplishment	Supervision
Challenging work	Working conditions
Increased responsibility	Interpersonal relations
Growth and development	Money, status, security

In analyzing the data from these interviews, Herzberg concluded that people have two different categories of needs—which he called hygiene factors and motivators—that are essentially independent of each other and affect behavior in different ways. He found that when people felt dissatisfied with their jobs, they were concerned about the environment in which they were working. On the other hand, when people felt good about their jobs, this feeling had to do with the work itself. Herzberg called the first category of needs hygiene, or maintenance, factors: *hygiene* because they describe people's environment and serve the primary function of preventing job dissatisfaction; *maintenance* because they are never completely satisfied—they have to continue to be maintained. He called the second category of needs *motivators* because they seemed to be effective in motivating people to superior performance. Table 3–3 presents a summary of motivation and hygiene factors.

Hygiene Factors

Company policies and administration, supervision, working conditions, interpersonal relations, money, status, and security were identified as maintenance factors. These are not an intrinsic part of a job but are related to the conditions under which a job is performed. Herzberg related his original use of the word *hygiene* to its medical meaning (preventive and environmental). He found that hygiene factors produced no increase in employee productivity; they only prevented losses in worker performance due to work restrictions. That is another reason why Herzberg called these maintenance factors.

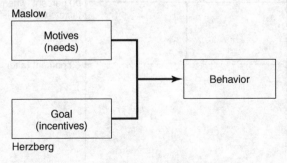

FIGURE 3–2 The Relationship of Maslow's and Herzberg's Theories to Motivation Situation

Motivators

Herzberg refers to factors that involve feelings of achievement, professional growth, and recognition that you can experience in a job that offers challenge as motivators. He used this term because these factors seemed capable of having a positive effect on job satisfaction, often resulting in an increase in total productivity.

> "I can charge a man's battery and then recharge it again. It is only when a person has his own generator that we can talk about motivation. He then needs no outside stimulation. He wants to do it."
>
> —Frederick Herzberg

Let us look at an example to further illustrate the difference between hygiene factors and motivators and help explain the reason Herzberg classified needs this way. Imagine that an employee is highly motivated and is working at 90 percent capacity. The person has a good working relationship with the supervisor, is well satisfied with pay and working conditions, and is part of a cohesive work group. Suppose the supervisor is suddenly transferred and replaced by a person who is difficult to work with, or suppose the employee finds out that someone whose work seems inferior is receiving more pay. How will these factors affect this individual's behavior? We know that performance or productivity depends on both ability and motivation. These unsatisfied hygiene needs (supervision and money) may lead to decreased productivity. This decline may be intentional, or the employee may not be consciously aware of holding back. In either case, productivity will be lowered. In this example, even if the employee's salary is adjusted well above expectations and the former supervisor returns, productivity will probably increase only to its original level.

Now take the same employee and assume that dissatisfaction has not occurred; work is at 90 percent capacity. Suppose the person is given an opportunity to develop and satisfy motivational needs in an environment where there is freedom to exercise some initiative and creativity, to make decisions, to handle problems, and to take responsibility. What effect will this situation have on this individual? If the employee is able to fulfill the supervisor's expectations in performing these new responsibilities, that person may still work at 90 percent capacity but may have developed and grown in ability and may be capable now of even greater productivity. Capacity has increased.

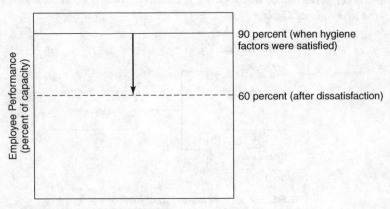

FIGURE 3–3 Effect of Dissatisfying Hygiene Factors

Hygiene factors, when satisfied, tend to eliminate dissatisfaction and work restriction, but they do little to motivate an individual to superior performance or increased capacity. Enhancement of the motivators, however, will permit an individual to grow and develop, often increasing ability. In essence, hygiene factors affect an individual's willingness, and motivators affect an individual's ability.

Pulse Check

Which of the following best describes your team?

- ☐ High Hygiene + High Motivation = Dream come true. Engaged, productive employees, few complaints
- ☐ High Hygiene + Low Motivation = Complacency. Few complaints, but low discretionary effort; job is seen as a paycheck
- ☐ Low Hygiene + High Motivation = Retention risk. Challenging work but complaints high; compensation and work conditions seen as not up to par
- ☐ Low Hygiene + Low Motivation = High toxicity! Low productivity and complaints abound.

Given your answer, how could you, as a manager, positively influence the hygiene and/or motivation your people are experiencing?

The Relationship of Herzberg's Theory to Maslow's Theory

Maslow's theory is helpful in identifying needs or motives, and Herzberg's theory provides us with insights into the goals and incentives that tend to satisfy those needs. So if you know the high-strength needs (Maslow) of the individuals you want to influence, then you should be able to determine what goals (Herzberg) you could provide to motivate those individuals. At the same time, if you know what goals these people want to satisfy, you can predict what their high-strength needs are. Why? Because money and benefits tend to satisfy needs at the physiological and security levels; interpersonal relations and supervision are examples of hygiene factors that tend to satisfy social needs; increased responsibility, challenging work, and growth and

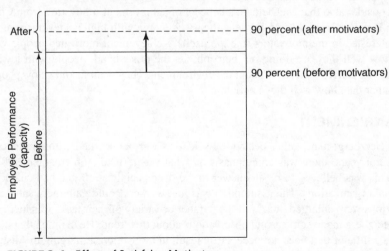

FIGURE 3–4 Effect of Satisfying Motivators

Job Enrichment	Broader Scope of responsibilities	Narrow, well defined task and outcomes
McClelland	Need for Achievement	Need for Affiliation
Herzberg	Motivators Achievement Challenging Work Increased Responsibilities	Hygiene Policies Working Conditions Pay Benefits
Maslow	Self-Actualized – Esteem – Social – Safety – Physiological	
Argyris	Mature ← – – – – – – – → Immature Active Passive Independent Dependent Aware Lack of Awareness	
McGregor	Believes: X – – – – – – – – – – – – – · Y Work is as natural as play	Work is distasteful to most people

FIGURE 3–5 Comparison of Five Theories of Motivation

Source: Based on Gregory B. Northcraft and Margaret A. Neal, *Organization Behavior: A Management Challenge*, 2nd ed., (Fort Worth: Dryden Press, 1994), p. 113.

development are motivators that tend to satisfy needs at the esteem and self-actualization levels. We believe that the physiological, safety, social, and part of the esteem needs are all hygiene factors. The esteem needs are divided because there are some distinct differences between status and recognition. Status tends to be a function of the position you occupy. A person could have gained a position through family ties, so it might not be a reflection of personal achievement or earned recognition. Recognition is gained through competence and achievement. It is earned and granted by others. Consequently, status is similar to physiological, safety, and social needs as a hygiene factor, while recognition is more similar to esteem as a motivator.

Consider also that McClelland's concept of achievement motivation from Chapter 2 is related to Herzberg's motivation-hygiene theory.[13] People with high achievement motivation tend to be interested in the motivators (the job itself). Achievement-motivated people want feedback about how well they are doing on their job. On the other hand, people with low achievement motivation are more concerned about the environment. They want to know how people feel about them rather than how well they are doing.

JOB ENRICHMENT

Before Herzberg, many other behavioral scientists were concerned with employee motivation. For several years, there was an emphasis on what was termed "job enlargement" or "job rotation." This was believed to be an answer to the overspecialization that had characterized many industrial organizations. The assumption was that workers could gain more satisfaction at work if their jobs were enlarged, that is, if the number or variety of their tasks was increased.

Herzberg made some astute observations about this trend. He claimed that doing a little of this and a little of that does not necessarily result in motivation. Enlarging the dish washer's job to include not only washing dishes but also pots and pans and utensils does no more to satisfy and provide an opportunity to grow than washing only dishes. What we really need to do with work, Herzberg suggested, is to enrich the job. Job enrichment means that you deliberately upgrade the responsibility, scope, and challenge involved in the work.

CASE STUDY

Example of Job Enrichment

Job enrichment may be illustrated by the experience an industrial relations superintendent had with a group of janitors. After a transfer to a new plant, the superintendent learned that the position responsibilities included supervising 15 janitors in a plant maintenance crew. There was no foreman over this crew. Reviewing the files one day, the superintendent noticed that there was a history of complaints about housekeeping around the plant. After talking to others and observing, it took the superintendent little time to confirm these reports. The janitors seemed to be lazy, unreliable, and generally unmotivated. They were walking examples of Theory X assumptions about human nature come to life.

Determined to do something about the behavior of the janitors, the superintendent called a group meeting, discussed some of the problems, and asked the janitors, since they were the experts, for ideas. "Does anyone have a suggestion?" There was dead silence. The superintendent sat down and said nothing. The silence lasted for almost 20 minutes. Finally, one janitor spoke up, related a problem, and made a suggestion. Soon others joined in and suddenly the janitors were involved in a lively discussion while the superintendent listened and jotted down their ideas. At the conclusion of the meeting, the suggestions were summarized with tacit acceptance by all, including the superintendent.

After the meeting, the superintendent referred any housekeeping problems to the janitors, individually or as a group. For example, when any cleaning equipment or material salespersons came to the plant, the superintendent did not talk to them—the janitors did. In fact, regular meetings continued to be held in which problems and ideas were discussed.

These changes had a tremendous influence on the behavior of the crew. They developed a cohesive productive team that took pride in their work. Even their appearance changed. They began appearing at work in clean, pressed work clothes. All over the plant, people were amazed at how clean and well kept everything had become. The superintendent was continually stopped by supervisors in the plant and asked, "What have you done to those lazy, good-for-nothing janitors, given them pep pills?" Even the superintendent could not believe what had happened. It was not uncommon to see one or two janitors running floor tests to see which wax or cleaner did the best job. Since they had to make all the decisions, including committing funds for their supplies, they wanted to know which ones were the best. Such activities, while taking time, did not detract from their work. In fact, the crew worked harder and more efficiently than ever before.

This example illustrates several positive aspects of job enrichment. The tasks were redesigned so that the janitors would be responsible for the housekeeping of the plant—what is called *horizontal job expansion*. In addition, the janitors were given responsibility for making decisions regarding equipment, supplies, and methods—what is called *vertical job expansion*—previously reserved to higher management. Both horizontal and vertical job expansion are required to gain the greatest improvement in motivation and satisfaction.[14]

This example also illustrates that even at low levels in an organization, people can respond in responsible and productive ways to a work environment in which they are given an opportunity to grow and mature. People begin to satisfy their esteem and self-actualization needs by participating in the planning, organizing, motivating, and controlling of their own tasks.

Summary

Two polar positions are evident in this chapter's discussion of motivating employees. At one extreme (and many people still think it is the most common extreme) are organizations that are dominated by Theory X assumptions about human nature and bureaucratic-pyramidal values. Managers in these organizations think and act as if people are motivated only by physiological and safety needs and the hygiene factors. Subordinates in these organizations tend to be passive, dependent, and childlike. At the other extreme are the "ideal" organizations in which Theory Y assumptions about human nature and humanistic-democratic values prevail. Managers in these organizations believe that people are motivated by affiliation, esteem, and self-actualization needs.

We can draw some general conclusions from this synthesis of theories.

1. **People seek security.** Certain security needs are fundamental to people's existence. If these needs are not addressed, people will not put their main focus on job performance. We will come back to this point in Chapter 8 when we discuss readiness dimension of Situational Leadership®.

2. **People seek social systems.** Whether we call this need relatedness, affiliation, interpersonal relations, or belongingness, humans are social beings in their work lives.

3. **People seek personal growth.** Whether we call this self-actualization, advancement, growth, or need for achievement, personal growth is a powerful need. An effective leadership model must endeavor to incorporate all three of these basic human need categories.

Notes

1. Paul Glover, "Has Extrinsic Motivation Left the Building?" Expert blog in *Fast Company*, March 3, 2010.

2. For detailed descriptions of this research, see *Reflections on the Hawthorne Studies, 75 Years Later: Symposium Presented for the Management History Division, 1999 Annual Academy of Management Meeting,* Chicago, IL., August 9, 1999. Fritz J. Roethlisberger and William J. Dickson, *Management and the Worker* (Cambridge: Harvard University Press, 1939); T. N. Whitehead, *The Industrial Worker*, 2 vols. (Cambridge: Harvard University Press, 1938); Elton Mayo, *The Human Problems of an Industrial Civilization* (Salem, NH: Ayer Company, 1977). See also R. E. Dutton, "On Alix Carev's Radical Criticism of the Hawthorne Studies: Comment," *Academy of Management Journal* 14 (September 1971): 394–396; Randolph M. Hale, "Managing Human Resources: Challenge for the Future," *Enterprise* (June 1985): 6–9.

3. Douglas McGregor, *The Human Side of Enterprise* (New York: McGraw-Hill, 1960). See also McGregor, *Leadership and Motivation* (Boston: MIT Press, 1966); Craig C. Pinder, *Work Motivation: Theory, Issues, and Applications* (Glenview, IL: Scott, Foresman, 1984).

4. George C. Homans, *The Human Group* (New York: Harcourt, Brace & World, 1950).

5. Anthony G. Athos and Robert E. Coffey, *Behavior in Organization: A Multidimensional View* (Englewood Cliffs, NJ: Prentice Hall, 1968), 101.

6. Solomon E. Asch, "Effects of Group Pressure Upon the Modification and Distortion of Judgments," in *Groups, Leadership and Men*, ed. Harold Guetzkow (New York: Russell and Russell, 1963), 177–190. Also in Dorwin Cartwright and Alvin Zander, *Group Dynamics*, 2nd ed. (Evanston, IL: Row, Peterson, 1960), 189–200.

7. Asch, "Effects of Group Pressure," p. 181.

8. Chris Argyris, *Interpersonal Competence and Organizational Effectiveness* (Homewood, IL: Irwin, Dorsey Press, 1962), 43.

9. *Ibid.*

10. *Ibid.*

11. Chris Argyris, *Personality and Organization* (New York: Harper & Row, 1957); Argyris, *Interpersonal Competence and Organizational Effectiveness*; Argyris, *Integrating the Individual and the Organization* (New York: Wiley, 1964).

12. Frederick Herzberg, Bernard Mausner, and Barbara Snyderman, *The Motivation to Work* (New York: Wiley, 1959); Herzberg, *Work and the Nature of Man* (New York: World Publishing, 1966). See also Richard M. Steers and Lyman W. Porter, *Motivation and Work Behavior*, 2nd ed. (New York: McGraw-Hill, 1979); Terence R. Mitchell, "Motivation: New Directions for Theory, Research and Practice," *Academy of Management Review* (January 1982): 80–88. See also Renato Tagiuri, "Managing People: Ten Essential Behaviors." *Harvard Business Review* 73, January–February 1995, 10–11.

13. Herzberg, Mausner, and Snyderman, *The Motivation to Work*, p. ix.

14. David C. McClelland, John W. Atkinson, R. A. Clark, and E. L. Lowell, *The Achievement Motive* (New York: Appleton-Century-Crofts, 1953); McClelland, *The Achieving Society* (Princeton, NJ: D. Van Nostrand, 1961). See also David McClelland and David H. Burnham, "Power Is the Great Motivator," *Harvard Business Review* 73, January/February 1995, 126–130.

4

Leadership

An Initial Perspective

hile we offered our working definition of leadership—the "what"—in Chapter 1, we will spend this and subsequent chapters exploring more about "why" and "how" of leadership. Effective leaders are continuously wrangling the hardest questions. As Peter F. Drucker pointed out, "Managers (business leaders) are the basic and scarcest resource of any business enterprise."[1]

LEADERSHIP AND VISION

Managers must know where they are going if they are to achieve their purposes. Today, just as thousands of years ago, without a vision, people and organizations perish.[2] Therefore, leaders must be vision creators. This is an immensely powerful and far-reaching idea. It is fundamental to the process of leading organizations.

> "I have vision, and the rest of the world wears bifocals."
> —Butch Cassidy

> "Every substantial organization I have ever seen had low performance standards. If you want superior performance, then you have got to set high standards."
> —Norman Schwarzkopf

Warren Bennis observed that "the single defining quality of leaders is their ability to create and realize a vision."[3] Marshall Loeb said, "All the leaders I know have a strongly defined sense of purpose. And when you have an organization where the people are aligned behind a clearly defined vision or purpose, you get a powerful organization."[4] And Jack Welch, former chief executive officer of General Electric, stated, "The effective leader leads through a vision, a shared set of values, a shared objective."[5]

It is the responsibility of top management to create a vision for the organization and to turn it into concrete strategies, solid management systems, and informed resource allocations that enable an organization to turn vision into performance.[6] However, as Conger has cautioned, every strength has its vulnerability. Leaders need to take care not to let the strength of their personal commitment to the visions result in dismissing alternative and competing approaches.[7]

THE VISION INTO PERFORMANCE MODEL

It is important to look at achieving results from a strategic perspective. Just as a tapestry has a pattern that defines it, so does success. The key words we hear most as drivers of tomorrow's success are:

- Vision
- Change
- Implementation
- Results

These four words are integral to the Vision into Performance (VIP) model developed in the following pages. It combines each of these characteristics in a process-oriented model composed of these key components.

- Vision
- Business idea–Organizational Environment
- Strategy–Culture
- Goal–Teams
- Task–People
- Results

Many variables affect organizational performance, so the VIP model focuses on those variables that empirical research and managerial practice have identified as the most critical. At the top left of the model (see Figure 4–1), we identify a strategic vision because every organization has a driving vision, whether articulated or not, that determines its direction. Vision is a core part of a person (or organization), the being and the becoming that reveals itself in thoughts, concepts, and dreams. Some may call this vision by different names, such as aspiration, purpose, charter, or goal. Whatever the name, it is a picture of the future painted by the organization's core values and desires.

Johnson & Johnson, the health care products company, describes its credo—the articulation of its core values—as both a "moral compass" and a "recipe for business success." Even the credo's first two sentences clearly capture who its customers are, and the standard to which the company aspires:

> We believe our first responsibility is to the doctors, nurses and patients, to mothers and fathers and all others who use our products and services. In meeting their needs, everything we do must be of high quality.[8]

The credo goes on to detail specifics around costs and communities, research and reserves. As one of its executives added, "Johnson & Johnson is a trustmark, not a trademark.[9]

Returning to the model, we see that in the lower right corner is the desired outcome of the vision—performance. This component tells us day by day how we are doing, in a tactical sense, to achieve the vision. Leadership turns visions into performance! (See Figure 4–1.)

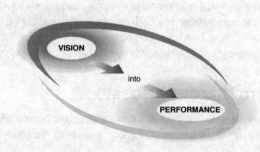

FIGURE 4–1   Vision into Performance

"Never tell people how to do things. Tell them what to do, and they will surprise you with their ingenuity."
—George Patton

The left side of the model focuses on planning and decision-making. Managers make decisions that spell out the business ideas, strategies, mission, key results or success factors, goals, objectives, and tasks required to move the organization in the desired direction.

No matter how eloquent the plans, they must be implemented. Leadership is more than creating plans; it is achieving those plans. Most organizations focus on "what to do" and forget about "doing it." When you look at their plans, they are mostly structure. The main reason they do not work is that these plans neglect the influence of an organization's environment, culture, teams, and people.

As we move diagonally from upper left to lower right, we see that from Vision into Performance moves through five levels. In level one (see Figure 4–2), implementing business ideas in the internal and external environment is affected by the stakeholders, those persons, key players, or factors whose helping or hindering roles determine success or failure to the organization. Level two finds strategic initiatives carried out within the corporate culture, the way we do things around here (see Figure 4–3). Level three (see Figure 4–4) communicates key results and success factors to

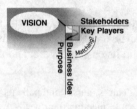

FIGURE 4–2   Vision into Performance: Level One

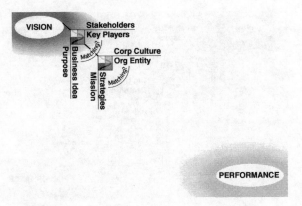

FIGURE 4–3   Vision into Performance: Level Two

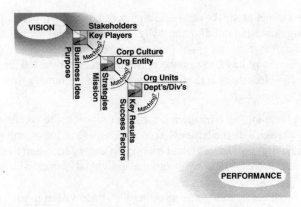

FIGURE 4–4   Vision into Performance: Level Three

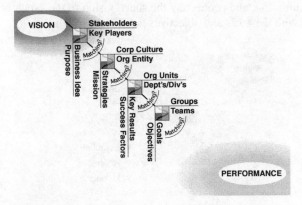

FIGURE 4–5   Vision into Performance: Level Four

the organizational units and department divisions. Level four (see Figure 4–5) suggests that goals are achieved by teams. In level five (see Figure 4–6), tasks are performed by people.

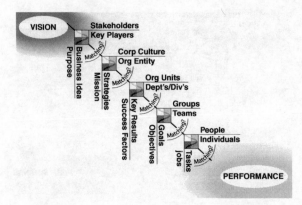

FIGURE 4–6   Vision into Performance: Level Five

The business issues along the right side represent a decision process spelling out the "what" and "how" looking down and defining the "why" and "what" looking up.

The human issues along the top of the figure represent the influence process of leading the organization, regardless of level, toward the accomplishment of the left side.

The leadership challenges at each level as we move diagonally from left (vision) to right, top to bottom performance are:

1. Establishing, refining, and monitoring the stated vision to the synchronization of stakeholders and key players with the business ideas and purpose of the organization (see Figure 4–7).
2. Defining, shaping (publicizing), and energizing the stated vision to the synchronization of the corporate culture and the organizational individual entities with the strategies and mission (see Figure 4–8).
3. Involving, facilitating, and communicating the stated vision to the synchronization of the organizational units and department divisions with the key results and success factors (see Figure 4–9).
4. Focusing, unifying, and connecting the stated vision to the synchronization of the groups and teams with the goals and objectives (see Figure 4–10).

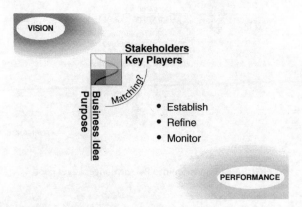

FIGURE 4–7   Vision into Performance: Leadership Challenges at Level One

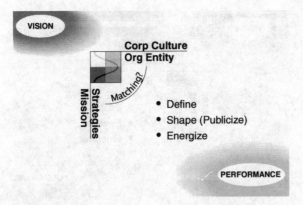

FIGURE 4–8   Vision into Performance: Leadership Challenges at Level Two

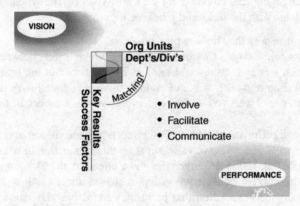

FIGURE 4–9   Vision into Performance: Leadership Challenges at Level Three

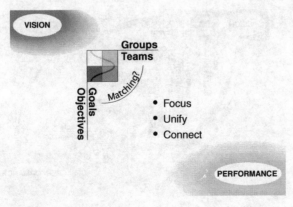

FIGURE 4–10   Vision into Performance: Leadership Challenges at Level Four

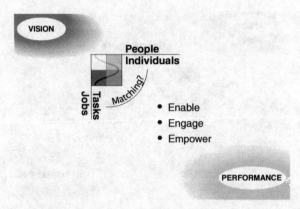

FIGURE 4–11 Vision into Performance: Leadership Challenges at Level Five

5. Enabling, engaging, and empowering the stated vision to the synchronization of the people and individuals with the tasks and jobs (see Figure 4–11).

This is illustrated by the "linking pin" boxes.

The leader's role today is that of a facilitating "linking pin" between the vision and performance, between strategic issues and tactical issues, between the transformational and the transactional (see Figure 4–12). It is not enough to simply watch over the decision-influence interface, no matter how well you do it. Leaders today must connect all the way from vision to performance.

Oren Harai, the University of San Francisco professor, management consultant, and frequent contributor to *Management Review,* sums up this connection in what he calls "three little words": inspire, shared, vision. He urges that to be effective, the 21st century organization must have a, " . . . coherent, comprehensive vision, a shared understanding and ownership of that vision, and an energy of inspiration that permeates and drives the vision."[10] How do effective leaders make this connection? It is through effective leadership, the primary topic of this and the next several chapters.

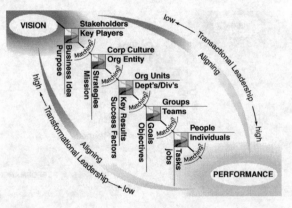

FIGURE 4–12 Vision into Performance with Transactional and Transformational Leadership

> "A manager is a person who directs the work of employees and is responsible for results. An effective manager brings a degree of order and consistency to tasks. A leader, by contrast, inspires employees with a vision and helps them cope with change."
> —D. Hellriegel, J. Slocum, Jr., R. Woodman

THE ACHIEVE MODEL

Background

A common problem that occurs in the management process is that many managers tend to be effective in letting followers know *what* performance problems exist, but they are not as effective in helping followers determine *why* those problems exist. In other words, many managers are strong in problem identification but are weaker in problem analysis, or diagnosis.

In order to be most effective in evaluating and solving performance problems, managers need to determine why problems have occurred. The ACHIEVE model was designed by Paul Hersey and Marshall Goldsmith to help managers determine why performance problems may have occurred and then develop change strategies aimed at solving those problems.[11]

In developing a model for analyzing human performance problems, Hersey and Goldsmith had two primary goals in mind: to determine the key factors that can influence staff members' performance and to present these factors in a way that can be used and remembered by practicing managers.

The first step in the development of the ACHIEVE model was to isolate the key factors that influence performance management. Earlier work by John W. Atkinson indicated that performance is a function of motivation and ability.[12] Put in simple terms, the follower has to have a certain degree of willingness to do the job and the skills necessary to complete the task. Lyman Porter and Edward Lawler explained this idea by including role perception, or job understanding. They noted that people can have all the willingness and skills needed to do the job but will still not be effective unless there is a clear understanding of what to do and how to do it.[13]

Jay Lorsch and Paul Lawrence approached the topic from a different perspective and concluded that performance was not merely a function of attributes possessed by the individual, but also depended on the organization and the environment.[14] Individuals can be highly motivated and have all the skills to do the job, but they will be effective only if they get needed organizational support and direction and their work fits the needs of their organizational environment.

The ACHIEVE model uses two more factors in the performance management equation. The first factor is *feedback*, which means that the followers need to know not just what to do but also how well they are doing it on an ongoing basis. Feedback includes day-to-day coaching and formal performance evaluation. The other performance management factor is *validity*. In today's environment, managers need to be able to document and justify decisions that affect people's careers. Valid personnel practices have become a legal necessity in the United States. In analyzing performance, managers need to continually check for validity in all personnel practices, such as job analyses, recruitment, appraisal, training, promotion, and dismissal.

Hersey and Goldsmith isolated seven variables related to effective performance management: (1) ability, (2) understanding, (3) organizational support, (4) motivation, (5) performance feedback, (6) validity, and (7) environment. Next, they put these factors together in a manner that managers could easily remember and use. One technique for making items on a list easy to remember is to make their first letters form a common word, an acronym. A seven-letter word that is synonymous with "to perform" is achieve. Substituting *clarity* for understanding, *help* for organizational support, *incentive* for the motivation factor, and *evaluation* for performance feedback gives the acronym **ACHIEVE**.

- ABILITY
- CLARITY
- HELP
- INCENTIVE
- EVALUATION
- VALIDITY
- ENVIRONMENT

USING THE ACHIEVE MODEL

In using the ACHIEVE model, the manager evaluates how each factor will affect the current or potential performance of followers for a given task. Then the manager should take the steps that "fit" the unique cause(s) of the performance problem. The seven factors in the ACHIEVE model, along with typical problem-solving alternatives, are listed next.

A—Ability (Knowledge and Skills)

In the ACHIEVE model, the term *ability* refers to the follower's knowledge, experience, and skill—the ability to complete the specific task successfully. It is important to remember that individuals are not universally competent. Key components of ability include task-relevant education (formal and informal training that facilitates the successful completion of the specific task), task-relevant experience (work experience that contributes to the successful completion of the task), and task-relevant skills (proficiencies that enhance the successful completion of the task). In analyzing follower performance, the manager should ask, "Does this follower have the knowledge, skill, and experience to complete this task successfully?"

If the person has an ability problem, solutions may include specific training, coaching, formal educational courses, or reassignment of specific duties or responsibilities. These alternatives should be considered from the viewpoint of cost-effectiveness.

C—Clarity (Understanding or Role Perception)

Clarity refers to an understanding and acceptance of what to do, when to do it, and how to do it. To have a thorough understanding of the job, the follower needs to understand clearly what the major goals and objectives are, how they should be accomplished, and their priority (which objectives are most important at what times).

If the follower has a problem in clarity, or understanding, there may well be a problem in the performance-planning phase. In many cases, oral agreement on objectives is not enough. The manager should ensure that all objectives are formally recorded. The follower should be encouraged to ask questions for further clarification.

H—Help (Organizational Support)

The term *help* refers to the organizational help, or support that the follower needs to effectively complete the task. Some organizational support factors include adequate budget and personnel, suitable equipment and facilities, and necessary support from other departments.

If there is a lack of help, or organizational support, managers should clearly identify where the problem exists. If the problem is the lack of money, human resources, equipment, or facilities, the manager should see whether the necessary resources can be acquired in a cost-effective manner. If the resources cannot be acquired, the manager may have to revise objectives to avoid holding followers responsible for circumstances beyond their control.

I—Incentive (Motivation or Willingness)

The term *incentive* refers to the follower's task-relevant incentive—the motivation to complete the specific task under analysis in a successful manner. In evaluating incentive, one must remember that people are not equally motivated to complete all tasks. Followers tend to be more motivated to successfully complete tasks that bring them either intrinsic or extrinsic rewards than to complete tasks that do not reward them personally.

If the follower has an incentive problem, the first step is to check the use of rewards and punishments. The follower should clearly understand that performance on this task is related to pay, promotion, recognition, and job security. Research indicates that managers sometimes hope that followers will engage in certain behaviors even if those behaviors go unrewarded. People have a natural tendency to pursue tasks that are rewarded and to avoid tasks that are not. Rewards can be tangible or intangible; feedback on performance, such as recognition or a pat on the back, can be an important part of the overall incentive system.

E—Evaluation (Coaching and Performance Feedback)

Evaluation refers to informal day-to-day performance feedback as well as formal periodic reviews. An effective feedback process lets followers know, on a regular basis, not only how well they are doing the job but also endeavors to assist and guide them in planning how to improve that performance. It is unrealistic to expect followers to improve performance if they are unaware that performance problems exist. Simply pointing out that performance problems exist is not necessarily enough to inspire improvement. People should know how they are being evaluated before their formal periodic evaluation occurs, and they should be given assistance in improving on deficiencies, (See the Developmental Cycle in Chapter 9 and the Regressive Cycle in Chapter 10.) Many performance problems can be caused by a lack of necessary coaching and performance feedback.

If there is an evaluation problem, it may be caused by a lack of day-to-day feedback on both effective and ineffective performance. Many managers tend to focus on the bad news and forget to recognize when things are going well. Recognition for a job well done is a vital part of the ongoing evaluation process. It can increase motivation, and it costs the organization very little.

One method that helps to highlight extremes in performance is the "significant incident" process, which includes formally documenting highly positive or negative performance. This practice ensures that the follower receives feedback that is part of the formal record.

V—Validity (Procedures, Practices, Rules, and Regulations)

The term *validity* refers to the appropriateness and legality of human resources decisions made by the manager. Managers need to make sure that decisions about people are appropriate in light of laws, regulations, and company policies. Managers should make sure that personnel practices do not discriminate against any specific group or individual, and they should also be aware that organizations need valid and legal performance evaluations, training, and promotion criteria.

If there is a validity problem, managers should know that personnel decisions need to be documented and justified on the basis of *performance-oriented* criteria. Managers uncertain about validity issues should discuss them with human resources or the organization's legal office. For example, shifting demographics of the modern workforce seem to indicate that current estimates of what constitutes "middle age" are much older than they were a decade ago. Lydia Bronte cautions managers to avoid the "tremendous age bias and the discounting of experience" of this increasingly able and older workforce.[15] Laws are continually changing to address this situation, and managers must constantly check the validity of their decisions, particularly in this age of corporate downsizing and workforce reduction.

E—Environment (Environmental Fit)

The term *environment* refers to the external factors that can influence performance even if the individual has all the ability, clarity, help, and incentive needed to do the job. Key elements of the environmental factors include competition, changing market conditions, government regulations, and suppliers.

If there is an environmental problem beyond their control, followers should not be rewarded or reprimanded for performance. In short, followers should be expected to perform at a level consistent with the limitations of their environment.

Legacies of the Past

Many distinguished authors and researchers have contributed to the rich legacy of leadership thought. Without the forward-looking visionaries of past generations (some of whom are listed in Table 4–1), we would not have some of the insights we have today. And, as we review the contributions of these visionaries from the past, we should not be too hasty to criticize their efforts and their different approaches. They probably were applicable in their time.

In this book, we will take these insights, these visions from the past, and develop a greater understanding of what is required to create and accomplish a productive future.

SCHOOLS OF ORGANIZATIONAL THEORY

We have defined leadership as the process of influencing the activities of an individual or a group in efforts toward goal achievement in a given situation. In essence, leadership involves accomplishing goals with and through people. Therefore, a leader must be concerned about tasks and human relationships. Although using different terminology, Chester I. Barnard identified these same leadership concerns in his classic work *The Functions of the Executive,* in the late 1930s.[16] These leadership concerns seem to be a reflection of two of the earliest schools of thought in organizational theory—scientific management and human relations.

Scientific Management Movement Frederick Winslow Taylor

In the early 1900s, one of the most widely read theorist on administration was Frederick Winslow Taylor. The basis for scientific management was the belief that the best way to increase output was to improve the techniques, or methods, used by workers. Consequently, he has been interpreted as considering people as instruments or machines to be manipulated by their leaders. Accepting this assumption, theorists of the scientific management movement proposed that organizations should be planned and developed to create more efficiency in work methods in order to increase production. Management was to be divorced from human affairs and emotions. The result was that the workers had to adjust to the management and not the management to the workers.

TABLE 4–1	Significant Motivation and Leadership Theories and Models	

Contributor	Theory or Model	Year of Publication of Significant Research
Taylor	Scientific Management	1911
Mayo	Hawthorne Studies	1933
Barnard	Executive Function	1938
Coch-French	Michigan Studies	1948
Stogdill	Ohio State Studies	1948
Homans	Human Group	1950
Maslow	Hierarchy of Needs	1954
McGregor	Theory X—Theory Y	1957
Tannenbaum-Schmidt	Continuum of Leader Behavior	1957
Blake-Mouton	Managerial Grid	1964
Argyris	Maturity-Immaturity	1964
McClelland	Achievement Theory	1965
Odiorne	Management by Objectives	1965
Herzberg	Motivation-Hygiene	1966
Likert	Systems 1–4	1967
Fiedler	Contingency Model	1967
Reddin	3-D Management Style	1967
Olsson	Management by Objectives	1968
Hersey-Blanchard	Situational Leadership®	1969
Vroom-Yetten	Contingency Model	1973
House-Mitchell	Path-Goal	1974
Vroom	Expectancy Theory	1976
House	Charismatic Leadership	1977
Burns	Transformational Leadership	1978
Kerr-Jermier	Substitutes for Leadership	1978
McCall-Lombardo	Fatal Leadership Flaws	1983

(continued)

TABLE 4–1 *(continued)*

Contributor	Theory or Model	Year of Publication of Significant Research
Greenleaf	Servant Leadership	1983
Bennis-Nanus	Leadership Competencies	1985
Tichy-Devanna	Transformational Leadership	1986
Manz	Super Leadership	1989
Yukl	Integrating Leadership Model	1989
Covey	Principle-Centered Leadership	1991
Fisher	Leading Self-Directed Work Teams	1993
Johnson	SOAR Model	1994
Pansegrouw	Transformational Model	1995
Gyllenpalm	Organizational Cone	1995
Whetter-Cameron	Empowerment	1995
Tichy	Leadership Engine	1997
Ball	DNA Leadership	1997
Byham-Cox	Empowerment	1998
Fairholm	Values-Based Leadership	1998
Cohen	8 Universal Laws of Leadership	1998
Ulrich, Zenger, Smallwood	Results-Based Leadership	1999
Wheatley	Leadership and the New Science	1999

To accomplish this plan, Taylor initiated time-and-motion studies to analyze work tasks to improve performance in every aspect of the organization. Once jobs had been reorganized with efficiency in mind, the economic self-interest of the workers could be satisfied through various incentive work plans (i.e., piece rates).

Scientific management stressed that a primary function of the leader was to set up and enforce performance criteria to meet organizational goals. The main focus of a leader, therefore, was on the needs of the organization and not on the needs of the individual.[17]

Human Relations Movement Elton Mayo

In the 1920s and early 1930s, the trend started by Taylor was replaced by the human relations movement, initiated by Elton Mayo and his associates. These theorists argued that in addition to finding the best technological methods to improve output, it was beneficial to management to look into human affairs. It was claimed that the real power centers within an organization were the interpersonal relations that developed within the working unit. The study of these human relations was the most important consideration for management and the analysis of organization. The organization was to be developed around the workers and had to take into consideration human feelings and attitudes.[18]

Under human relations theory, the function of the leader was to facilitate cooperative goal attainment among followers while providing opportunities for their personal growth and development. The main focus, contrary to scientific management theory, was on individual needs rather than the needs of the organization.

> "The key to being a good manager is keeping the people who hate me away from those
> who are still undecided."
> —Casey Stengal (1890–1975)

In summary, the scientific management movement emphasized a concern for task (output), while the human relations movement stressed a concern for relationships (people). These two concerns have characterized the writings on leadership ever since. Consequently, leadership concepts have evolved through three dominant phases: trait, attitudinal, and situational.

TRAIT APPROACHES TO LEADERSHIP

Before 1945, the most popular leadership approach focused on the study of leadership traits and suggested that certain physical or personality traits were essential for effective leadership. These inherent personal qualities were felt to be transferable from one situation to another. Since all individuals did not possess these qualities, only those who had them would be considered potential leaders. Consequently, this approach seemed to question the value of training individuals to assume leadership positions. It implied that if we could discover how to identify and measure these leadership qualities (which are inborn in the individual), we should be able to screen leaders from nonleaders. Leadership training would then only be helpful to those possessing the desirable leadership traits.

Reviews of research using this trait approach to leadership revealed few significant or consistent findings.[19] Eugene E. Jennings concluded that "50 years of study have failed to produce one personality trait or set of qualities that can be used to discriminate leaders and nonleaders."[20]

This is not to say that certain traits will not hinder or facilitate leadership; the key is that no set of traits has been identified that clearly predicts success or failure. As Gary Yukl, a professor at the University of California at Berkeley, has observed:

> In retrospect, it is apparent that many leadership researchers overreacted to the earlier pessimistic literature reviews by rejecting the relevance of traits entirely. Possession of particular traits increases the likelihood that a leader will be effective, but [it does] not guarantee effectiveness, and the relative importance of different traits is dependent upon the nature of the leadership situation.[21]

Trait research is still continuing. Warren Bennis completed a five-year study of 90 outstanding leaders and their followers. On the basis of this research, he identified four common traits, or areas of competence, shared by all 90 leaders.[22]

1. *Management of attention.* The ability to communicate a sense of outcome, goal, or direction that attracts followers
2. *Management of meaning.* The ability to create and communicate meaning with clarity and understanding

3. *Management of trust.* The ability to be reliable and consistent
4. *Management of self.* The ability to know one's self and to use one's skills within the limits of one's strengths and weaknesses

Bennis suggested that leaders empower their organizations to create an environment where people feel significant and are part of the community or team, where learning and competence matter, and where work is exciting. Leaders should also create an environment where quality matters and dedication to work energizes effort.[23]

Bennis updated these traits with seven characteristics of effective performance:

1. *Business literacy.* Does the manager know the business—the real feel of it?
2. *People skills.* Does the manager have the capacity to motivate and bring out the best in people?
3. *Conceptual skills.* Does the manager have the capacity to think systematically, creatively, and inventively?
4. *Track record.* Has the manager done it before and done it well?
5. *Taste.* Does the manager have the ability to pick the right people—not clones, but people who can make up deficiencies?
6. *Judgment.* Does the manager have the ability to make quick decisions with imperfect data?
7. *Character.* Does the manager have the necessary character traits? The core competency of leadership is character, but character and judgment are the qualities we know least about when trying to teach them to others.[24]

> "Most leaders don't need to learn what to do. They need to learn what to stop."
> —Peter Drucker

Negative Leadership Traits and Behaviors

While many researchers have attempted to describe and measure effective leadership styles, fewer have invested time in looking under the leadership rock. Fifty years ago, John Geier found three traits that kept group members from competing for a leadership role (in order of importance): the perception of being uninformed, of being nonparticipative, or of being extremely rigid.[25] Why were these traits so critical? Because the other group members believed that members who were uninformed, uninterested, or overly rigid would hinder the group's accomplishment of its goals.

Years later, McCall and Lombardo looked specifically at those already in leadership roles. They examined differences between executives who went all the way to the top and those who were expected to go to the top but were "derailed" just before reaching their goal. Both winners and losers had strengths and weaknesses, but those who fell short seemed to have one or more of what McCall and Lombardo called "fatal flaws."[26] The most frequent cause for derailment was insensitivity to others, but the most serious was untrustworthiness. Betrayal of trust—not following through on promises or double-dealing—was the one "unforgivable sin."[27] Similarly, Goldsmith has identified 20 "bad habits" too often seen in leaders.[28] In recent years, perhaps because numerous public officials (e.g., Elliott Spitzer, Anthony Weiner) have been exposed for lying, there has been growing interest in the "shadow" side of leadership.[29] One's shadow can remain in the dangerous realm of blind spots (see Chapter 11) without constructive feedback.

Shelley Kirkpatrick and Edwin Locke in the *Academy of Management Executive* reinforced the views of Bennis, Yukl, and others:

> Recent research, using a variety of methods, has made it clear that successful leaders are not like other people. The evidence indicates that there are certain core traits which contribute to business leaders' success . . . . Leaders do not have to be great men or women by being intellectual geniuses or omniscient prophets to succeed, but they do need to have the "right stuff" and this stuff is not equally present in all people.[30]

In summary, empirical research suggests that leadership is a dynamic process, varying from situation to situation with changes in the leader, the followers, and the situation. Therefore, although certain traits may help or hinder in a given situation, there is no universal set of traits that will ensure leadership success. The lack of validation of trait approaches led to other investigations of leadership, particularly attitudinal ones.

ATTITUDINAL APPROACHES

The main period of the attitudinal approaches to leadership occurred between 1945, with the Ohio State and Michigan studies, and the mid-1960s, with the development of the Managerial Grid®.[31]

By attitudinal approaches, we mean approaches that use paper-and-pencil instruments such as questionnaires to measure attitudes or predispositions toward leader behavior. For example, the dimensions of the Managerial Grid—concern for production and concern for people—are attitudinal. *Concern* may be defined as a predisposition or feeling toward or against production and people. In this section, we will look specifically at three attitudinal approaches to leadership: the Ohio State studies; the Michigan studies, including Rensis Likert's work; and the Managerial Grid.

Ohio State Leadership Studies

The leadership studies initiated in 1945 by the Bureau of Business Research at Ohio State University identified the key dimensions of leader behavior.[32] The researchers, directed by Ralph Stogdill, defined leadership as the behavior of an individual when directing the activities of a group toward goal attainment. Their research focused on two dimensions of leader behavior: initiating structure and consideration. *Initiating structure* refers to "a type of leader behavior that describes the extent to which a leader is task oriented and directs subordinates' work activities toward goal achievement."[33] On the other hand, *consideration* refers to "a type of leader behavior that describes the extent to which a leader is sensitive to subordinates, respects their ideas and feelings, and establishes mutual trust."[34]

To gather data about the behavior of leaders, the Ohio State staff developed the Leader Behavior Description Questionnaire (LBDQ), an instrument designed to describe how leaders carry out their activities. The LBDQ contains 15 items pertaining to consideration and 15 to initiating structure. Respondents judge the frequency with which their leader engages in each form of behavior by checking one of five descriptions—always, often, occasionally, seldom, or never. Thus, consideration and initiating structure are dimensions of observed behavior as perceived by others. Examples of items used in the LBDQ for both of these dimensions are shown in Table 4–2.

Although the major emphasis in the Ohio State Leadership studies was on observed behavior, the staff did develop the leader opinion questionnaire (LOQ) to gather data about leaders' self-perceptions of their leadership style. The LBDQ was completed by leaders' followers, supervisors, or associates (peers), but the LOQ was filled out by the leaders themselves.

TABLE 4–2 Examples of LBDQ Items

Consideration	Initiating Structure
The leader finds time to listen to group members.	The leader assigns group members to particular tasks.
The leader is willing to make changes.	The leader asks the group members to follow standard rules and regulations.
The leader is friendly and approachable.	The leader lets group members know what is expected of them.

In studying leader behavior, the Ohio State staff found that initiating structure and consideration were separate and distinct dimensions. A high score on one dimension does not necessitate a low score on the other. The behavior of a leader could be described as any mix of both dimensions. Thus, it was during these studies that leader behavior was first plotted on two separate axes rather than on a single continuum. Quadrants were developed to show various combinations of initiating structure and consideration, as illustrated in Figure 4–13.

Michigan Leadership Studies

Researchers at the University of Michigan conducted leadership studies beginning in 1945. In the early studies, there was an attempt to approach the study of leadership by locating clusters of characteristics that seemed to be related and by determining various indicators of effectiveness. The studies identified two concepts that the researchers called *employee orientation* and *production orientation*.[35]

Leaders who were described as employee-oriented emphasized the relationship aspect of their job. They felt that every employee is important and took interest in everyone, accepting their individuality and personal needs. Production-oriented leaders emphasized production and

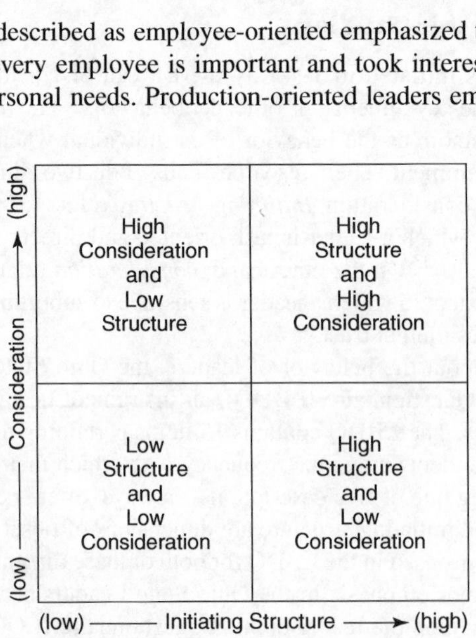

FIGURE 4–13 The Ohio State Leadership Quadrants

the technical aspects of the job; employees were seen as tools to accomplish the goals of the organization. These two orientations parallel the democratic (relationship) and authoritarian (task) concepts of the leader behavior continuum of the Tannenbaum-Schmidt model presented later in Chapter 5.

Group Dynamics Studies

Dorwin Cartwright and Alvin Zander, summarizing the findings of numerous studies at the Research Center for Group Dynamics, at the University of Michigan, claimed that group objectives fall into one of two categories: (1) the achievement of some specific group goal or (2) the maintenance or strengthening of the group itself.[36]

According to Cartwright and Zander, the type of behavior involved in goal achievement is illustrated by these examples: The manager "initiates action . . . keeps members' attention on the goal . . . clarifies the issue and develops a procedural plan."[37] On the other hand, typical behaviors for group maintenance are characterized by a manager who "keeps interpersonal relations pleasant . . . arbitrates disputes . . . provides encouragement . . . gives the minority a chance to be heard . . . stimulates self-direction . . . and increases the interdependence among members."[38] Goal achievement seems to coincide with the task concepts discussed earlier (production orientation), and group maintenance parallels the relationship concepts (employee orientation).

Research findings in recent years indicate that leadership styles vary considerably from leader to leader. Some leaders emphasize the task and can be described as authoritarian leaders; others stress interpersonal relationships and may be viewed as democratic leaders. Still others seem to be both task-oriented and relationship-oriented. There are even some individuals in leadership positions who do not focus on either.

Thus, task and relationship are not either-or leadership styles. They are separate and distinct dimensions that can be plotted on two separate axes.

> "There is nothing either good or bad, but thinking makes it so."
> —Hamlet by William Shakespeare

Rensis Likert's Management Systems

Using the earlier Michigan studies as a starting point, Rensis Likert conducted extensive research to discover the general pattern of management used by high-producing managers in contrast to the pattern used by the other managers. He found that "supervisors with the best records of performance focus their primary attention on the human aspects of their employees' problems and on endeavoring to build effective work groups with high performance goals."[39] These supervisors were called employee-centered. Other supervisors who kept constant pressure on production were called job-centered and were found more often to have low-producing sections. Figure 4–14 presents the findings from one study.

Likert also discovered that high-producing supervisors "make clear to their employees what the objectives are and what needs to be accomplished and then give them freedom to do the job."[40] He found that general rather than close supervision tended to be associated with high productivity. This relationship, found in a study of clerical workers, is illustrated in Figure 4–15. The figure shows that 9 out of 10 high-producing sections were led by first-line supervisors who used general supervision, whereas 8 out of 12 low-producing sections were led by supervisors who

Number of First-Line Supervisors Who Are

	Job Centered	Employee Centered
High-Producing Sections	1	6
Low-Producing Sections	7	3

FIGURE 4–14 Employee-Centered Supervisors Are Higher Producers Than Are Job-Centered Supervisors

Source: Rensis Likert, New Patterns of Management, Copyright © 1961, McGraw-Hill. Reprinted by permission of The McGraw-Hill Companies.

used close supervision. Note that general supervision did not always result in high production or close supervision in low production. But general supervision under the conditions described in this study had a higher probability of resulting in high production than did close supervision.

Likert and his colleagues' continuing research at the Institute for Social Research at the University of Michigan emphasized the need to consider both human resources and capital resources as assets requiring proper management attention. He found that most managers, when asked what they would do if they suddenly lost half of their plant, equipment, or capital resources, were quick to answer that they would depend on insurance or borrowed money to keep them in business. Yet when these same managers were asked what they would do if they suddenly lost half of their human resources—managers, supervisors, and hourly employees—they were at a loss for words. There is no insurance against outflows of human resources. Recruiting, training, and developing large numbers of new personnel into a working team take years. In a competitive environment, this task is almost impossible. Organizations are now realizing that their most important assets are human resources and that effectively managing them is one of their most crucial tasks.

As a result of behavioral research studies of numerous organizations, Likert implemented organizational change programs in various industrial settings. These programs were intended to help organizations move from Theory X to Theory Y assumptions, from fostering immature behavior to encouraging and developing mature behavior, from emphasizing only hygiene factors to recognizing and implementing motivators.

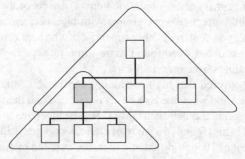

FIGURE 4–15 "Linking Pin" Role

In his studies, Likert found that the prevailing management styles of organizations can be depicted on a continuum from System 1 through System 4. These systems might be described as follows[41]:

System 1—the exploitive-authoritative system. Management has no confidence or trust in employees and seldom involves them in any aspect of the decision-making process. The bulk of the decisions and the goal setting of the organization are made at the top and issued down the chain of command. Employees are forced to work with fear, threats, punishment, and occasional rewards. Need satisfaction is at the physiological and safety levels. The limited management-employee interaction that does take place is usually with fear and mistrust. Although the control process is highly concentrated in top management, an informal organization generally develops in opposition to the goals of the formal organization.

System 2—the benevolent-authoritative system. Management has only condescending confidence and trust in employees, such as a master has toward the servants. The bulk of the decisions and goal setting of the organization are made at the top, but many decisions are made within a prescribed framework at lower levels. Rewards and some actual or potential punishment are used to motivate workers. Any interaction takes place with some condescension by management and fear and caution by employees. Although the control process is still concentrated in top management, some control is delegated to middle and lower levels. An informal organization usually develops, but it does not always resist formal organizational goals.

System 3—the consultative system. Management has substantial, but not complete confidence and trust in employees. Broad policy and general decisions are kept at the top, but employees are permitted to make more specific decisions at lower levels. Communication flows both up and down the hierarchy. Rewards, occasional punishment, and some involvement are used to motivate workers. There is a moderate amount of interaction, often with a fair amount of confidence and trust. Significant aspects of the control process are delegated downward, with a feeling of responsibility at both higher and lower levels. An informal organization may develop, but it may either support or partially resist goals of the organization.

System 4—participative-group system. Management has complete confidence and trust in employees. Decision making is widely dispersed throughout the organization, although well integrated. Communication flows not only up and down the hierarchy, but among peers. Workers are motivated by participation and involvement in developing economic rewards, setting goals, improving methods, and appraising progress toward goals. There is extensive and friendly management-employee interaction, with a high degree of confidence and trust. There is widespread responsibility for the control process, with the lower units fully involved. The informal and formal organizations are often one and the same. Thus, all social forces support efforts to achieve stated organizational goals.

In summary, System 1 is a task-oriented, highly structured authoritarian management style; System 4 is a relationship-oriented management style based on teamwork, mutual trust, and confidence. Systems 2 and 3 are intermediate stages between two extremes, which approximate closely Theory X and Theory Y assumptions.

To expedite the analysis of a company's present behavior, Likert's group developed a questionnaire that enables members to evaluate their organization in terms of its management system. This instrument is designed to gather data about a number of operating characteristics of an organization. These characteristics include leadership, motivation, communication, decision making, interaction and influence, goal setting, and the control process used by the organization. Sample items from this instrument are presented in Table 4–3. The complete instrument includes more than 20 such items.

In testing this instrument, Likert asked hundreds of managers from many different organizations to indicate where the most productive department, division, or organization they have known would fall between system 1 and system 4. Then these same managers were asked to repeat this process and indicate the position of the least productive department, division, or organization they have known. Although the ratings of the most and the least productive departments varied among managers, almost without exception each manager rated the high-producing unit closer to system 4 than the low-producing unit. In summary, Likert found that the closer the management style of an organization comes to system 4, the more likely it will be to have a continuous record of high productivity. Similarly, the closer a management style comes to system 1, the more likely it is to have a sustained record of low productivity.

Likert used this instrument not only to measure what individuals believe are the present characteristics of their organization but also to find out what they would like management characteristics to be. Data generated from this use of the instrument with managers of well-known companies indicated a large discrepancy between the management system their company was currently using and the management system they felt would be most appropriate. System 4 was seen as being most appropriate, but few saw their companies as utilizing this approach. These implications have led to attempts by some organizations to adapt their management system to approximate more closely system 4. Changes of this kind are not easy. They involve a massive reeducation of all concerned, from the top management to the hourly workers.

> "The better a man is, the more mistakes he will make, for the more new things he will try. I would never promote to a top-level job a man who was not making mistakes…otherwise he is sure to be mediocre."
> —Peter Drucker

Theory into Practice

One instance of a successful change in the management style of an organization occurred with a leading firm in the pajama industry.[42] After being unprofitable for several years, this company was purchased by another corporation. At the time of the transaction, the purchased company was using a management style falling between System 1 and System 2. Some major changes were soon implemented by the new owners. The changes that were put into effect included extensive modifications in how the work was organized, improved maintenance of machinery, and a training program involving managers and workers at every level. Managers and supervisors were exposed in depth to System 4 management. All of these changes were supported by the top management of the purchasing company.

Although productivity dropped in the first several months after the initiation of the change program, productivity increased by almost 30 percent within two years. It is not possible to calculate exactly how much of the increased productivity resulted from the change in management system, but it was apparent to the researchers that the impact was considerable. In addition to increases in productivity, manufacturing costs decreased 20 percent, turnover was cut almost in half, and morale rose considerably (reflecting a friendlier attitude of workers toward the organization). The company's image in the community was enhanced, and for the first time in years the company began to show a profit.

TABLE 4–3 Examples of Items from Likert's Table of Organizational and Performance Characteristics of Different Management Systems

Organizational Variable	System 1	System 2	System 3	System 4
Leadership processes used				
Extent to which superiors have confidence and trust in subordinates	Have no confidence and trust in subordinates	Have condescending confidence and trust, such as master has to servant	Substantial but not complete confidence and trust; still wishes to keep control of decisions	Complete confidence and trust in all matters
Character of motivational forces				
Manner in which motives are used	Fear, threats, punishment, and occasional rewards	Rewards and some actual or potential punishment	Rewards, occasional punishment, and some involvement	Economic rewards based on compensation system developed through participation; group participation and involvement in setting goals, improving methods, and appraising progress toward goals
Character of interaction-influence process				
Amount and character of interaction	Little interaction and always with fear and distrust	Little interaction and usually with some condescension by superiors; fear and caution by subordinates	Moderate interaction, often with fair amount of confidence and trust	Extensive, friendly interaction with high degree of confidence and trust

Source: Rensis Likert, The Human Organization. Copyright © 1967 McGraw-Hill. Reproduced with permission of The McGraw-Hill Companies.

The implication throughout Likert's writings is that the ideal and most productive leader behavior for industry is employee-centered or democratic. Yet, his own findings raise questions as to whether there can be an ideal or single normatively good style of leader behavior that applies in all leadership situations. Likert's findings indicated 1 of the 8 job-centered supervisors and 1 of the 9 supervisors using close supervision had high-producing sections; also, 3 of the 9 employee-centered supervisors and 4 of the 13 supervisors who used general supervision had low-producing sections. In other words, in almost 35 percent of the low-producing sections, the suggested ideal type of leader behavior produced undesirable results and almost 15 percent of the high-producing sections were supervised by the suggested "undesirable" style.

Similar findings and interpretations were made by Andrew Halpin and Ben Winer in a study of the relationship between aircraft commanders' leadership patterns and the proficiency rating of their crews.[43] Using the LBDQ, they found that 8 of 10 commanders with high-proficiency ratings were described as using above average consideration and initiating structure and that 6 of 7 commanders with low ratings were seen as below average in consideration and initiating structure. As Likert did, Halpin and Winer reported only that the leaders above average in both consideration and initiating structure are likely to be effective and did not discuss the two high-proficiency, high-consideration, high-initiating structure commanders and the one low-producing, low-initiating structure, low-consideration commander.

Evidence suggesting that a single ideal or normative style of leader behavior is unrealistic was provided by a study done in an industrial setting in Nigeria.[44] The results were almost the exact opposite of Likert's findings. In that country, the tendency was for job-centered supervisors who provide close supervision to have high-producing sections and for employee-centered supervisors who provide general supervision to have low-producing sections. Thus, a single normative leadership style does not take into consideration cultural differences, particularly customs and traditions as well as the level of education, the standard of living, or industrial experience. These are examples of cultural differences in the followers and the situations that are important in determining the appropriate leadership style to be used. Therefore, on the basis of the definition of the leadership process as a function of the leader, the followers, and other situational variables, a single ideal type of leader behavior seems unrealistic.

The Leadership Grid® Robert R. Blake and Anne Adams McCanse

In discussing the Ohio State, Michigan, and Likert leadership studies, we concentrated on two theoretical concepts—one emphasizing task accomplishment and the other stressing the development of personal relationships. Robert R. Blake and Anne Adams McCanse modified these concepts in their Leadership Grid (formerly the Managerial Grid by Robert R. Blake and Jane S. Mouton) and have used them extensively in organization and management development programs.[45]

In the Leadership Grid, five different types of leadership based on concern for production (task) and concern for people (relationship) are located in four quadrants (see Figure 4–16) similar to those identified by the Ohio State studies (Figure 4–13). Concern for production is illustrated on the horizontal axis. Production becomes more important to the leader as the rating advances on the horizontal scale. A leader with a rating of nine on the horizontal axis has a maximum concern for production. Concern for people is illustrated on the vertical axis. People become more important to leaders as their ratings progress up the vertical axis. A leader with a rating of nine on the vertical axis has maximum concern for people.

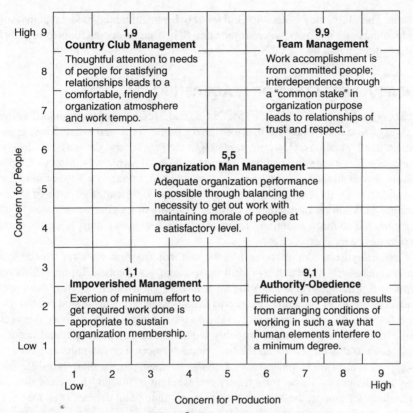

FIGURE 4–16 The Leadership Grid®

Source: The Leadership Grid figure for Leadership Dilemmas—Grid Solutions by Robert R. Blake and Anne Adams McCanse. (Formerly the Managerial Grid figure by Robert R. Blake and Jane S. Mouton) Houston: Gulf Publishing Company, p. 29. Copyright © 1991 by R. R. Blake, J. C. Mouton, and A. Jane. Reproduced by permission of the owners.

The five leadership styles are described as follows:

1,1 Impoverished Management. Exertion of minimum effort to get required work done is appropriate to sustain organization membership.

1,9 Country Club Management. Thoughtful attention to the needs of people for satisfying relationships leads to a comfortable, friendly organization atmosphere and work tempo.

9,1 Authority-Obedience Management. Efficiency in operations results from arranging conditions of work in such a way that human elements interfere to a minimum degree.

5,5 Organization Man Management. Adequate organization performance is possible through balancing the necessity to get work out while maintaining morale of people at a satisfactory level.

9,9 Team Management. Work accomplishment is from committed people; interdependence through a "common stake" in organization purpose leads to relationships of trust and respect.[46]

We want to point out one significant difference between the Leadership Grid and the Ohio State frameworks. "Concern for" is a predisposition about something, or an attitudinal dimension. Therefore, the Leadership Grid tends to be an attitudinal model that measures the values and feelings of a manager, whereas the Ohio State framework attempts to include behavioral as well as attitudinal items.

IS THERE A BEST STYLE OF LEADERSHIP?

Researchers such as Blake, Mouton, McCanse, and McGregor have argued that there is "one best" style of leadership—a style that maximizes productivity and satisfaction, growth and development in all situations. However, research in the past several decades has clearly supported the contention that there is no one best leadership style. Most recently, Marcus Buckingham has effectively debunked the myth of the well-rounded leader based on a 30-year landmark research study conducted by the Gallup organization. He asserts, instead, the value of strengths based leadership—building on your strengths instead of trying to fix your weaknesses.[47] Why has this finding garnered so much attention? To answer that question, we must place the current state of leadership theory into perspective.

First, many leadership theories, like the vast majority of behavioral science theories, have not been conclusively validated by scientific research. As Stephen Robbins observed, "Simple and universal principles [of organizational behavior] are avoided because there are no simple and universal truths or principles that consistently explain organizational behavior."[48] But just because research does not conclusively validate a behavioral science theory does not necessarily make it invalid. If it did, there probably would not be any organizational behavior theories or books such as this one based on the behavioral sciences. For example, as Robbins suggested in his appraisal of Maslow's hierarchy of needs, "Remember that there is a difference between finding 'insufficient evidence' for a theory and labeling it 'invalid.' It is clear that the available research does not support the Maslow theory to any significant degree. This does not imply that the theory is wrong, merely that it has not been supported."[49]

Solid "scientific" evidence supporting leadership theories may be lacking simply because leadership theories are, at this point, sets of empirical generalizations that by their very nature cannot be "scientifically" tested. In its strictest sense, scientific testing requires controlling variables, and few variables in an organization can be controlled over time. Likewise, anthropology and archaeology cannot be tested, but theories in those fields are nonetheless considered to be valid.

The primary reason why there is no one best way to be a leader is that leadership is basically situational, or contingent. As Robbins stated, "OB [organizational behavior] concepts are founded on situational conditions; that is, if X, then Y, but only under conditions specified in Z (the contingency variables)."[50] In other words, the effectiveness of a particular leadership style is contingent upon the situation in which it is used.

Effective managers must be able not only to determine the most appropriate leadership style but also to correctly apply that style. As James Owens observed:

> Managers expressed a virtual consensus that, based on their actual experience, each situation they handled demanded a different leadership style. No single style could suffice under the day-to-day, even minute-by-minute, varying conditions of different personalities and moods among their employees, routine process vs. changing or sudden deadlines, new and ever-changing government regulations and paperwork, ambiguous roles of workers, wide ranges in job complexity from simple to innovation-demanding, changes in organizational structure and markets and task technologies and so on. Contingency theory has come to mean, therefore, that the effective manager has, and knows how to use, many leadership styles as each is appropriate to a particular situation.[51]

Frances Hesselbein, past CEO of the Girl Scouts of America, put it quite eloquently, "Leadership is a matter of how to be, not how to do it. And the one indispensable quality of leadership is personal integrity with a sense of ethics that works full-time."[52] But perhaps Ralph Stogdill said it best: "The most effective leaders . . . exhibit a degree of versatility and flexibility that enables them to adapt their behavior to the changing and contradictory demands made on them."[53]

PREVIEW

What are some of these "changing and contradictory demands"? How do they influence leadership? How does a potential leader diagnose the situation to determine the high probability leadership style? These and many other important issues will be addressed in Chapter 5.

Notes

1. Peter F. Drucker, *The Practice of Management* (New York: Harper & Row, 1954). See also Allen L. Appell, *A Practical Approach to Human Behavior in Business* (Columbus, OH: Merrill, 1984).

2. Proverbs 29:18. See also Neil H. Snyder, "Leadership and Vision," *BusinessWeek*, 37, January/February 1994, 1–7.

3. Warren Bennis, *On Becoming a Leader* (Reading, MA: Addison-Wesley, 1989), 194. See also Marshall Loeb, "Where Leaders Come From," *Fortune*, September 19, 1994, 242; Gerald Egan, "A Clear Path to Peak Performance," *People Management*, v (May 18, 1995): 34–35; Gerald Kushel, *Reaching the Peak Performance Zone: How to Motivate Yourself and Others to Excel* (New York: AMACOM, 1994).

4. Marshall Loeb, "Where Leaders Come From," *Fortune*, September 19, 1994, 242.

5. Quoted in Bennis, *On Becoming a Leader*, 194.

6. Bennis, *On Becoming a Leader*, 194.

7. "Our Credo: Johnson & Johnson" *Johnson & Johnson-Health Care Products & Pharmaceuticals.*

8. Ronald Alsop, "Johnson & Johnson (Think Babies!) Turns Up Tops," *The Wall Street Journal*, September 23, 1999, p. B1.

9. Oren Harai, "Three Vital Little Words," *Management Review*, November 1995, 27.

10. This has been a primary research objective at the Center for Leadership Studies. This section on the ACHIEVE model is adapted from Paul Hersey and Marshall Goldsmith, "A Situational Approach to Performance Planning," *Training and Development* 34 (November 1980): 38–40.

11. John W. Atkinson, *An Introduction to Motivation* (New York: Van Nostrand, 1958).

12. Lyman Porter and Edward Lawler, *Managerial Attitudes and Performance* (Homewood, IL: Irwin, 1968). See also Charles R. Gowen, "Managing Work Group Performance by Individual Goals and Group Goals for an Interdependent Group Task," *Journal of Organizational Behavior* 7, no. 3 (Winter 1986): 5–27.

13. Jay Lorsch and Paul Lawrence, "Diagnosis of Organizational Problems." *In Organizational Development: Values, Processes, and Technology*, eds. Newton Margulies and Anthony P. Raia (New York: McGraw-Hill, 1972).

14. Steven Kerr, "On the Folly of Hoping for A While Rewarding B," *Academy of Management Journal* 4 (1975): 76–79. See also Thomas Kemper, "Motivation and Behavior, A Personal View," *Journal of General Management* 9, no. 3 (Fall 1983): 51–57; Martin Gevans, "Organizational Behavior: The Central Role of Motivation," *Journal of Management* 12, no. 2 (Summer 1986): 203–222.

15. Lydia Bronte, "Longevity and the Future of the Workplace," *Planning Forum Network* 7, no. 6 (Summer 1994): 7.

16. Chester I. Barnard, *The Functions of the Executive* (Cambridge, MA: Harvard University Press, 1938).

17. Frederick W. Taylor, *The Principles of Scientific Management* (New York: Harper & Brothers, 1911).

18. Elton Mayo, *The Social Problems of an Industrial Civilization* (Boston: Harvard Business School, 1945), 23.

19. Cecil A. Gibb, "Leadership." *In Handbook of Social Psychology*, ed. Gardner Lindzey (Cambridge, MA: Addison-Wesley, 1954). See also Ralph M. Stogdill, "Personal Factors Associated with Leadership: A Survey of Literature," *Journal of Psychology* 25 (1948): 35–71.

20. Eugene E. Jennings, "The Anatomy of Leadership," *Management of Personnel Quarterly* 1, no. 1 (Autumn 1961). See also Arthur G. Jago, "Leadership: Perspectives in Theory and Research," *Management Science* 28, no. 3 (March 1982): 315–336.

21. Gary A. Yukl, *Leadership in Organizations*, 3rd ed. (Englewood Cliffs, NJ: Prentice Hall, 1994), 255–256.

22. Warren Bennis, "The Four Competencies of Leadership," *Training and Development Journal* 38, no. 8 (August 1984): 15–19. See also Warren Bennis and Bert Nanus, *Leaders: The Strategies for Taking Charge* (New York: Harper & Row, 1986).

23. Bennis, "The Four Competencies of Leadership."

24. Adapted from Loeb, "Where Leaders Come From." 241–242.

25. John G. Geier, "A Trait Approach to the Study of Leadership in Small Groups," *Journal of Communications* 17 (December 1967): 316–323.

26. Morgan W. McCall, Jr., and Michael M. Lombardo, "What Makes a Top Executive?" *Psychology Today*, February 1983, 26–31. See also Morgan M. McCall, Jr., and Robert E. Kaplan, *Whatever It Takes: The Realities of Managerial Decision Making* (Englewood Cliffs, NJ: Prentice Hall, 1990).

27. *Ibid.*

28. Marshall Goldsmith, "Bad Habits," adapted from Goldsmith, *What Got You Here Won't Get You There* (New York: Hyperion Books, 2007), 40–41.

29. Scott W. Spreier, Mary H. Fontaine, and Ruth L. Malloy, "Leadership Run Amok: The Destructive Potential of Overachievers," *Harvard Business Review*, June 2006, 1–5. Online. See also Richard Bolden, "The Shadow Side of Leadership," *Effective Executive* 9 no. 2 (February 2007): 42–43, and Jay A. Conger, "The dark side of leadership," *Organizational Dynamics* 19 (1990): 44–45; Jay A. Conger and Rabindra N. Kanungo, *The Charismatic Side of Leadership* (Thousand Oaks, CA: Sage Publications, 1998).

30. Shelley A. Kirkpatrick and Edwin A. Locke, "Leadership: Do Traits Matter?" *Academy of Management Executive* 5, no. 2 (1991): 49, 59.

31. Robert R. Blake and Jane S. Mouton, *The Managerial Grid III*, 3rd ed. (Houston, TX: Gulf Publishing, 1984). See also Robert R. Blake and Jane S. Mouton, "The Managerial Grid III," *Personnel Psychology* 39 (Spring 1986): 238–240.

32. Ralph M. Stogdill and Alvin Coons, eds., *Leader Behavior: Its Description and Measurement, Research Monograph No. 88* (Columbus: Bureau of Business Research, Ohio State University, 1957). See also Fred E. Fiedler and Martin M. Chemers, "Improving Leadership Effectiveness," *Personnel Psychology* 38 (Spring 1985), 220–222.

33. Richard L. Daft, *Management,* 3rd ed. (Fort Worth: The Dryden Press, 1994), 484.

34. *Ibid.* See also Andrew W. Halpin, *The Leadership Behavior of School Superintendents* (Chicago: Midwest Administration Center, University of Chicago, 1959), 4.

35. Robert Kahn and Daniel Katz, "Leadership Practices in Relation to Productivity and Morale," in *Group Dynamics: Research and Theory*, 2nd ed., eds. Dorwin Cartwright and Alvin Zander (Evanston, IL: Row, Peterson, 1960). Many other studies are available from the University of Michigan, Ann Arbor, Mich., Institute for Social Research.

36. Dorwin Cartwright and Alvin Zander, eds., *Group Dynamics: Research and Theory,* 2nd ed. (Evanston, IL: Row, Peterson, 1960). See also Patrick R. Penland, *Group Dynamics and Individual Development* (New York: Dekker, 1974); Robert H. Guest, *Work Teams and Team Building* (New York: Pergamon, 1986).

37. Cartwright and Zander, *Group Dynamics*, p. 496. See also Shirley A. Olsen, ed., *Group Plannings and Problems—Solving Methods in Engineering Management*, (New York: Wiley, 1982).

38. Cartwright and Zander, *Group Dynamics*, p. 497.

39. Rensis Likert, *New Patterns of Management* (New York: McGraw-Hill, 1961), 7.

40. *Ibid.*, p. 9.

41. Adapted from Rensis Likert, *The Human Organization* (New York: McGraw-Hill, 1967), 197–211.

42. Lester Coch and John R. P. French, Jr., "Overcoming Resistance to Change," *Human Relations* 1, no. 4 (1948): 512–532.

43. Andrew W. Halpin and Ben J. Winer, *The Leadership Behavior of Airplane Commanders* (Columbus: Ohio State Research Foundation, 1952).

44. Paul Hersey, unpublished research project, 1965.

45. Robert R. Blake and Anne Adams McCanse, *Leadership Dilemmas—Grid Solutions* (Houston: Gulf Publishing Company, 1991). See also Robert R. Blake and Jane S. Mouton, *The Managerial Grid* (Houston, TX: Gulf Publishing, 1964); Blake and Mouton, "The Managerial Grid III," *Personnel Psychology*; Blake and Mouton, *The Versatile Manager:* *A Grid Profile* (Homewood, IL: Irwin, 1982); Blake and Mouton, *The Secretary Grid: A Program for Increasing Office Synergy* (New York: AMACOM, 1983).

46. Blake and McCanse, *Leadership Dilemmas—Grid Solutions*, p. 29.

47. Marcus Buckingham, *Now, Discover Your Strengths* (New York: Free Press, 2000).

48. Stephen P. Robbins, *Organizational Behavior: Concepts, Controversies, and Applications*, 4th ed. (Englewood Cliffs, NJ: Prentice Hall, 1989), 11–12.

49. *Ibid*, p. 136.

50. *Ibid*, p. 12.

51. James Owens, "A Reappraisal of Leadership Theory and Training," *Personnel Administrator* 26 (November 1981): 81.

52. Frances Hesselbein, "Driving Strategic Leadership through Mission, Vision, and Goals," *The Planning Forum Network* 7, no. 6 (Summer 1994): 4–5.

53. Ralph M. Stogdill, "Historical Trends in Leadership Theory and Research," *Journal of Contemporary Business* (Autumn 1974): 7.

5

Leadership

Situational Approaches

T he focus in situational approaches to leadership is on the observed behavior of leaders and their group members (followers) in various situations. This emphasis on behavior and environment allows for the possibility that individuals can be trained to adapt their style of leader behavior to varying situations. Therefore, it is believed that most people can increase their effectiveness in leadership roles through education, training, and development. Based on observations of the frequency (or infrequency) of certain leader behaviors in a variety of situations, models can be developed to help leaders make some predictions about the most appropriate leader behavior for their present situation. For these reasons, in this chapter we will talk in terms of leader *behavior* rather than leadership traits, thus emphasizing the situational approach to leadership.

> "The best way to predict your future is to create it."
> —Steven Covey

SITUATIONAL APPROACHES TO LEADERSHIP

As we noted in the last chapter, current organizational behavior theory views leadership as well as other organizational behavior concepts and theories as situational, or contingent in nature. The views of Stephen Robbins and others cited in Chapter 4 are not unique. Chester Schriesheim, James Tolliver, and Orlando Behling noted that "the literature supports the basic notion that a situational view is necessary to portray accurately the complexities of the leadership process."[1] Victor Vroom concurred, "I do not see any form of leadership as optimal for all situations. The contribution of a leader's actions to the effectiveness of his organization cannot be determined without considering the nature of the situation in which that behavior is displayed."[2]

Peter Drucker concluded that different people need to be led differently. There is no one right way to lead people, individually or in teams, organizations, or institutions. Drucker was influenced in this view by Abraham Maslow's work that we reviewed in Chapter 2.[3]

Earlier we identified the three main components of the leadership process as the leader, the follower, and the situation. Situational approaches to leadership examine the interplay among these variables in order to find causal relationships that will lead to predictability of behavior. You will find a common thread among the situational approaches in this and subsequent chapters: All situational approaches require the leader to behave in a flexible manner, to be able to diagnose the leadership style appropriate to the situation, and to be able to apply the appropriate style.

Although there are many situational models and theories, we will focus on four that have received wide attention in leadership research: the Tannenbaum-Schmidt Continuum of Leader Behavior, Fiedler's Contingency model, the House-Mitchell Path-Goal theory, and the Hersey-Blanchard Tridimensional Leader Effectiveness model.

Tannenbaum-Schmidt Continuum of Leader Behavior

Robert Tannenbaum and Warren H. Schmidt's 1957 *Harvard Business Review* article "How to Choose a Leadership Pattern" presented one of the most significant situational approaches to leadership.[4] In their model, the leader selects one of seven possible leader behaviors depending upon the forces among the leader, follower, and situation. As Figure 5–1 indicates, the range of choices is between democratic or relationship-oriented behaviors and authoritarian or task-oriented behaviors. You will remember that these are dimensions from the Michigan and Ohio State studies, respectively.

Previous writers felt that focus on the task tends to be represented by authoritarian leader behavior, while a concern for relationships or people is represented by democratic leader behavior. This feeling was popular because it was generally agreed that leaders influence their followers in either of two ways: (1) They can tell their followers what to do and how to do it, or (2) they can share their leadership responsibilities with their followers by involving them in the planning and execution of the task. The former is the traditional authoritarian style, which emphasizes task concerns. The latter is the more nondirective democratic style, which stresses the concern for human relationships.

The differences in these two styles of leader behavior are based on the assumptions that leaders make about the source of their power or authority and human nature. The authoritarian style of leader behavior is often based on the assumption that the power of leaders is derived from the position they occupy and that people are innately lazy and unreliable (Theory X). The democratic style assumes that the power of leaders is granted by the group they lead and that people can be self-directed and creative at work if properly motivated (Theory Y). As a result, in the authoritarian style, all policies are determined by the leader; whereas in the democratic style, policies are open for group discussion and shared decision-making.

There are a wide variety of styles of leader behavior between these two extremes. Tannenbaum and Schmidt depicted a broad range of styles as a continuum moving from authoritarian or manager-centered leader behavior at one end to democratic or follower-centered leader behavior at the other end (Figure 5–1). Tannenbaum and Schmidt now refer to these two extremes as manager power and influence and non-manager power and influence.

Leaders whose behavior is observed to be at the authoritarian end of the continuum tend to be task-oriented and use their power to influence their followers; leaders whose behavior appears

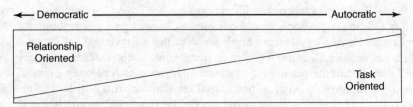

FIGURE 5–1   The Tannenbaum-Schmidt Continuum of Leader Behavior

Source: Based on *Harvard Business Review*, "How to Choose a Leadership Pattern" by Robert Tannenbaum and Warren H. Schmidt, May–June 1973. Copyright © 1973 by the President and Fellows of Harvard College. All rights reserved.

to be at the democratic end tend to be group-oriented and thus give their followers considerable freedom in their work. This continuum is often extended beyond democratic leader behavior to include a laissez-faire style.[5] This style of behavior permits the members of the group to do whatever they want to do. Because there is no leader behavior, the laissez-faire style is not included in the continuum illustrated in Figure 5–1. In reality, a laissez-faire atmosphere represents an absence of formal leadership. Any leadership that is being exhibited is informal and emergent.

In the 1973 reprint of their article in the *Harvard Business Review*, Tannenbaum and Schmidt commented that the interrelationships among leader, follower, and situation were becoming increasingly complex.[6] With this complexity, it becomes more difficult to identify causes and effects, particularly when more forces outside the traditional situation are exerting influence. As organizations become more international, as more stakeholders come into play, and as more traditional customs, practices, and authorities are eroded, the leadership process becomes more difficult. Warren Bennis's "Where Have All the Leaders Gone?" is one astute commentary on this phenomenon.[7]

> "In his decision making, today's leader is a multidirectional broker who must deal with four estates . . . his own management team, constituencies within his organization, forces outside his organization, and the media."
> —Warren Bennis

Fiedler's Contingency Model

Widely respected as the father of the contingency theory of leadership, Fred Fiedler developed the Leadership Contingency model. He suggested that three major situational variables determine whether a given situation is favorable to leaders: (1) their personal relations with the members of their group (leader-member relations), (2) the degree of structure in the task that their group has been assigned to perform (task structure), and (3) the power and authority that their position provides (position power).[8] Leader-member relations seem to parallel the relationship concepts discussed earlier. Task structure and position power seem to be associated with task concepts. Fiedler defined the favorableness of a situation as "the degree to which the situation enables the leader to exert influence over the group."[9]

The most favorable situation for leaders to influence their groups is one in which they are well liked by the members (good leader-member relations), have a powerful position (strong position power), and are directing a well-defined job (high task structure); for example, a well-liked general making an inspection in an army camp. On the other hand, the most unfavorable situation for leaders is one in which they are disliked, have little position power, and face an unstructured task—such as an unpopular head of a voluntary hospital fund-raising committee.

In a reexamination of old leadership studies and an analysis of new studies, Fiedler concluded that:

1. Task-oriented leaders tend to perform best in group situations that are either very favorable or very unfavorable to the leader.
2. Relationship-oriented leaders tend to perform best in situations that are intermediate in favorableness.[10]

These conclusions are summarized in Figure 5–2. Fiedler has made an important contribution to leadership theory, particularly in his focus on situational variables as moderating influences. Fiedler's model has research support, particularly in its general conclusions represented in Figure 5–2. He may, in his single continuum of leader behavior, be suggesting that there are only two basic leader behavior styles, task-oriented and relationship-oriented. Most evidence indicates that leader behavior must be plotted on two separate axes rather than on a single continuum. Thus, a leader who is high on task behavior is not necessarily high or low on relationship behavior. Any combination of the two dimensions may occur.

House-Mitchell Path-Goal Theory

The Path-Goal theory builds upon two concepts that we looked at earlier—the Ohio State Leadership studies and the Expectancy Model of Motivation. You will recall that the Expectancy model focused on the effort-performance and the performance-goal satisfaction (reward) linkages. You will also remember that the key dimensions of the Ohio State model are initiating structure and consideration, and that the model suggested that the most effective leaders would be high on both the initiating structure and the consideration dimensions.

Robert House, who did much of his early leadership research at Ohio State University, was interested in explaining the contradictions in the Ohio State model: for example, the situations in which initiating structure, consideration, or certain combinations of the two variables were not as effective as predicted. In other words, he was interested in explaining not only which style of leadership was effective but also why. He was interested in identifying those situations in which initiating structure was most appropriate as well as situations where consideration was most appropriate.

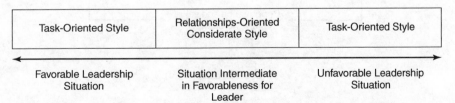

FIGURE 5–2 Leadership Styles Fiedler Concluded Are Appropriate for Various Group Situations

Source: Adapted from Fred E. Fiedler, *A Theory of Leadership Effectiveness* (New York: McGraw-Hill, 1967), p. 14.

Before we go further, it is important to state why this theory is called the Path-Goal theory. House and Mitchell explained it in this manner:

> According to this theory, leaders are effective because of their impact on [followers'] motivation, ability to perform effectively and satisfaction. The theory is called Path-Goal because its major concern is how the leader influences the [followers'] perceptions of their work goals, personal goals and paths to goal attainment. The theory suggests that a leader's behavior is motivating or satisfying to the degree that the behavior increases [followers'] goal attainment and clarifies the paths to those goals.[11]

The Path-Goal theory relates very well to the Expectancy model and the Ohio State Leadership model. The Expectancy model tells us that "people are satisfied with their job if they think it leads to things that are highly valued [goal], and they work hard if they believe that effort [path] leads to things that are highly valued."[12] The leadership model is related because "subordinates are motivated [path] by leader behavior to the extent that this behavior influences expectancies [goal]."[13] According to Path-Goal theory, leaders do this best when they supply what is missing from the situation. If clarification is missing, then the leader should provide structure. If intrinsic and/or extrinsic rewards are missing, then the leader should provide rewards. Richard Daft summarized this idea, "The leader's job is to increase personal payoffs to followers for goal attainment and to make the paths to these payoffs clear and easy to travel."[14]

"High expectations and belief in people leads to high performance . . . so very often belief creates fact."
—Paul Hersey

These relationships are shown in Figure 5–3. The leader can be seen as clarifying the path on the left side of this figure while increasing rewards on the right side. The end result of these

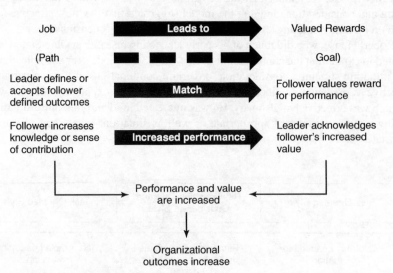

FIGURE 5–3 Leader Roles in the Path-Goal Model

Source: Based on MANAGEMENT by Richard Daft, copyright © 1994 by The Dryden Press, reprinted by permission of the publisher. Based on Bernard M. Bass, "Leadership: Good, Better, Best," *Organizational Dynamics,* 13 (Winter 1985), pp. 26–40.

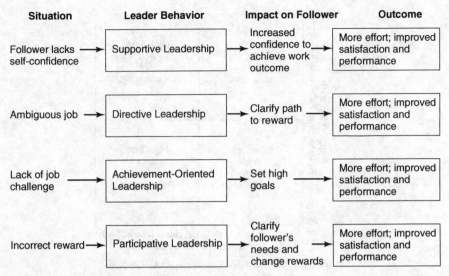

Situation	Leader Behavior	Impact on Follower	Outcome

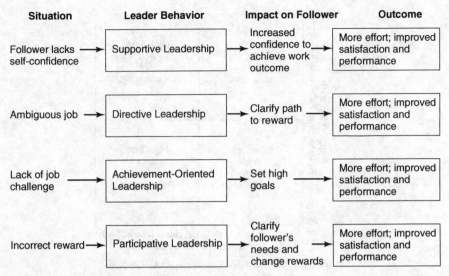

FIGURE 5–4   Path-Goal situations and Preferred Leader Behaviors

Source: Reprinted with permission from Richard L. Daft, *Management,* 3rd ed. (Fort Worth, TX: Dryden Press, 1993), p. 395. Adapted from Gary A. Yukl, *Leadership in Organizations* (Upper Saddle River, NJ: Prentice Hall, 1981), pp. 146–152.

leader actions is the follower increased effort and motivation, leading to greater accomplishment of organizational work outcomes.

We have identified Path-Goal as a situational approach because different situations call for different leader behaviors as shown in Figure 5–4. Let us start on the left side of this figure. Four situations are described calling for different leader behaviors. These behaviors, in turn, have a different impact on the follower and result in different outcomes. In situation 2, if the follower is not meeting performance expectations in an ambiguous job, directive leadership (spelling out who, what, when, and how) may serve to clarify work methods, procedures, and objectives. This clarification may lead to more effort, increased satisfaction, and improved job performance. Path-Goal theory is an excellent example of the need to diagnose a situation before attempting a leadership intervention.

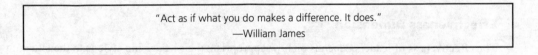

"Act as if what you do makes a difference. It does."
—William James

Hersey-Blanchard Tridimensional Leader Effectiveness Model

In this leadership model, the terms *task behavior* and *relationship behavior* are used to describe concepts similar to *initiating structure* and *consideration* in the Ohio State studies. The four basic leader behavior quadrants are labeled high task and low relationship, high task and high relationship, high relationship and low task, and low relationship and low task (see Figure 5–5).

These four quadrants represent four significantly different leadership styles. The leadership style of an individual is the behavior pattern, as perceived by others, that a person exhibits

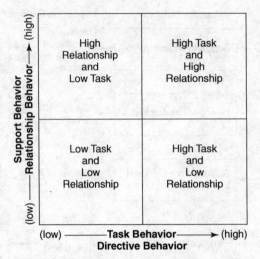

FIGURE 5–5 A Two-Dimensional Model: Basic Leader Behavior Styles Suggested by Hersey and Blanchard

when attempting to influence the activities of others. This may be very different from a person's own perception, which we define as *self-perception* rather than style. A person's leadership style involves some combination of task behavior and relationship behavior. The two types of behavior, which are central to the concept of leadership style, are defined as follows:

• *Task behavior.* The extent to which leaders are likely to organize and define the roles of the members of their group (followers) and to explain what activities each has to do and when, where, and how tasks are to be accomplished; characterized by endeavoring to establish well-defined patterns of organization, channels of communication, and ways of getting jobs accomplished.

• *Relationship behavior.* The extent to which leaders are likely to engage in dialogue between themselves and members of their group (followers) by opening up channels of communication and active listening; providing socioemotional support, "psychological strokes" such as praise and recognition, and facilitating behaviors; characterized by endeavoring to build independence and continuous high performance.[15]

Effectiveness Dimension

The effectiveness of leaders depends on how appropriate their leadership style is to the situation in which they operate. Therefore, an effectiveness dimension should be added to the two-dimensional model. This three-dimensional model is illustrated in Figure 5–6.

In his "3-D Management Style Theory," William J. Reddin was the first to add an effectiveness dimension to the task concern and relationship concern dimensions of earlier attitudinal models such as the Leadership Grid.[16] Reddin, whose pioneering work influenced us greatly in the development of the Tridimensional Leader Effectiveness model, felt that a useful theoretical model "must allow that a variety of styles may be effective or ineffective depending on the situation."[17]

By adding an effectiveness dimension to the task behavior and relationship behavior dimensions of the earlier Ohio State Leadership model, the Tridimensional Leader Effectiveness

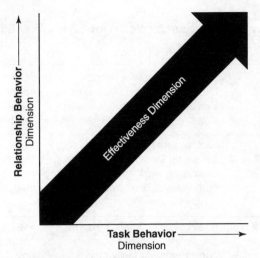

FIGURE 5–6 Adding an effectiveness Dimension to the Hersey-Blanchard Dimensions of Task and Relationship

model attempts to integrate the concepts of leader style with situational demands of a specific environment. When the style of a leader is appropriate to a given situation, it is termed *effective*; when the style is inappropriate to a given situation, it is termed *ineffective*.

If the effectiveness of a leader behavior style depends on the situation in which it is used, it follows that any of the basic styles may be effective or ineffective, depending on the situation. The difference between the effective and ineffective styles is often not the actual behavior of the leader, but the appropriateness of that behavior to the environment in which it is used. In reality, the third dimension is the environment. It is the interaction of the basic style with the environment that results in a degree of effectiveness or ineffectiveness. We call the third dimension effectiveness, because in most organizational settings various performance criteria are used to measure the degree of effectiveness or ineffectiveness of a manager or leader. But we feel it is important to keep in mind that the third dimension is the environment in which the leader is operating. One might think of the leader's basic style as a particular stimulus, and it is the response to this stimulus that can be considered effective or ineffective. This point is important because theorists and practitioners who argue that there is one best style of leadership are making value judgments about the stimulus, whereas those taking a situational approach to leadership are evaluating the response or the results rather than the stimulus.

Let us use an example. A department head has been given an important promotion from one department to another, much larger department. What would be his or her most effective leadership style? Would it be the one that earned him or her the valued promotion—in this case, a high relationship–low task style? Will this style be effective in the new situation? It could be extremely effective or extremely ineffective or somewhere in between. The effectiveness of a given leadership style will depend on its relevance to the situation as seen by the leader's followers, superiors, or associates. Table 5–1 describes one of the many different ways each style might be perceived as effective or ineffective by others.

A model such as the Tridimensional Leader Effectiveness model is distinctive because it does not depict a single ideal leader behavior style that is suggested as being appropriate in all

TABLE 5–1	How the Basic Leader Behavior Styles May Be Seen by Others	
Basic Style	**Effective**	**Ineffective**
High-task and low relationship behavior	Seen as having well-defined methods for accomplishing goals that are helpful to the followers	Seen as imposing methods on others: sometimes seen as unpleasant and interested only in short-run output
High-task and high relationship behavior	Seen as satisfying the needs of the group for setting goals and organizing work, but also providing high levels of socioemotional support	Seen as initiating more structure than is needed by the group and often appears not to be genuine in interpersonal relationships
High-relationship and low-task behavior	Seen as having implicit trust in people and as being primarily concerned with facilitating their goal accomplishment	Seen as primarily interested in harmony; sometimes seen as unwilling to accomplish a task if it risks disrupting a relationship or losing a "good person"' image
Low-relationship and low-task behavior	Seen as appropriately delegating to followers decisions about how the work should be done and providing little socioemotional support where little is needed by the group	Seen as providing little structure or socioemotional support when needed by members of the group

situations. For example, the high task and high relationship style is appropriate only in certain situations. In crisis-oriented organizations, such as the military or the fire department, there is considerable evidence that the most appropriate style would be high task and low relationship, because under combat, fire, or emergency conditions success often depends on immediate response to orders. Time demands do not permit talking things over or explaining decisions. But once the crisis is over, other styles might become appropriate. For example, although the fire chief may have to initiate a high level of structure at the scene of a fire, upon returning to the firehouse it may be appropriate for the chief to engage in other styles while the staff is participating in ancillary functions such as maintaining the equipment or studying new fire fighting techniques. Less structured behavior, or lower task behavior, may be much more effective for this situation.

Instrumentation

To gather data about the behavior of leaders, we developed two leader effectiveness and adaptability description (LEAD)[18] instruments: the LEAD Self and the LEAD Other. The LEAD Self contains 12 leadership situations in which respondents are asked to select from four alternative actions. The choices are: a high task–low relationship behavior, a high task–high relationship behavior, a high relationship–low task behavior, or a low relationship–low task behavior. They are to select the one they feel most closely describes their own behavior in that type of situation. An example of a situation-action combination used in the LEAD Self is shown in Table 5–2.

The LEAD Self was designed to measure self-perception of three aspects of leader behavior: (1) style, (2) style range, and (3) style adaptability. Style and style range are determined by

TABLE 5–2 Sample Item from LEAD Self Instrument	
Situation	**Alternative Actions**
Your employees, usually able to take responsibility, are not responding to your recent redefinition of standards.	A. Allow group involvement in redefining standards, but don't push. B. Redefine standards and supervise carefully. C. Avoid confrontation by not applying pressure. D. Incorporate group recommendations, but see that new standards are met.

four style scores, and the style adaptability (effectiveness score) is determined by one normative score. The LEAD Self was originally designed as a training instrument and should ideally be used only in training situations and not, as some researchers have done, as a research instrument. The length of the scale (12 items) and time required (10 minutes) clearly reflect the intended function.

The LEAD Self provides data in terms of the leader's self-perception. This information is helpful, but to really know your leadership style—how you influence others—you must collect data from those you attempt to lead. We developed the LEAD Other to gather this important leadership style information. The LEAD Self is filled out by leaders themselves, but the LEAD Other is completed by leaders' followers, superiors, or associates (peers). We will discuss both these instruments in more detail in Chapter 11.

What about Consistency?

Consistent leadership is not using the same leadership style all the time, but using the style appropriate for the followers' level of readiness in such a way that followers understand why they are getting a certain behavior, a certain style from the leader. Inconsistent leadership results from not using the appropriate style on a consistent basis. This means that inconsistent leadership could result from using the same style in every situation. Therefore, if a manager uses a supportive high relationship–low task style with a staff member when that person is performing well and also when that staff member is performing poorly, that manager would be inconsistent, not consistent. Managers are consistent if they direct their followers and even discipline them when they are performing poorly, but support and reward them when they are performing well. Managers are inconsistent if they smile and respond supportively all the time—whether their followers are doing their job well or not.

To be consistent (in our terms), managers must behave the same way in similar situations for all parties concerned. Their leadership style is driven by performance. Thus, a consistent manager would not discipline one follower when that person makes a costly mistake, and not discipline another staff member when they make a similar mistake, and vice versa. It is also important for managers to lead their followers the same way in similar circumstances even when it is inconvenient—when they do not have time or when they do not feel like it.

> "Leadership should be born out of the understanding of the needs of those who would be affected by it."
> —Marian Anderson

Some managers are consistent only when it is convenient. They may praise and support their people when they feel like it and redirect and supervise their activities when they have time. This behavior leads to problems. Parents are often guilty in this regard. For example, suppose Wendy and Walt get upset when their children argue with each other and are willing to clamp down on them when it happens. However, there are exceptions to their consistency in this area. If they are rushing off to a dinner party, they do not deal with the children's fighting. Or if they are in the supermarket with the kids, they will frequently permit behavior they would normally not allow because they are uncomfortable disciplining the children in public. Since children are continually testing the boundaries or limits of their behavior (they want to know what they can do and cannot do), Walt and Wendy's kids soon learn that they should not fight with each other except when Mom and Dad are in a hurry to go out or when they are in a store. Thus, unless parents and managers are willing to be consistent even when it is inconvenient, they may actually be encouraging misbehavior.

> "Good leaders make people feel that they're at the very heart of things, not at the periphery. Everyone feels that he or she makes a difference to the success of the organization. When that happens people feel centered and that gives their work meaning."
> —Warren Bennis

Another thing that frequently happens is that, instead of using appropriate leader behavior matched with individual readiness, performance, and demonstrated ability, leaders assign privileges on the basis of chronological age or gender. For example, a parent may permit an irresponsible 17-year-old son to stay out until 2:00 A.M. but make a very responsible 15-year-old daughter come home by midnight. Or a manager may assign a big project to his senior representative just because he or she been with the company the longest and not consider how well a recent college graduate might be able to contribute.

> "Effective leadership is not about making speeches or being liked; leadership is defined by results not attributes."
> —Peter Drucker

Attitude versus Behavior

One of the ideas behind the old definition of consistency was the belief that your behavior as a manager *must* be consistent with your attitudes. This idea bothered some people who were heavily involved with the human relations or the sensitivity-training movement. They believed that if you care about people and have positive assumptions about them, you should also treat them in high relationship ways and seldom in directive or controlling ways.

We feel that much of this problem stemmed from the failure of some theorists and practitioners to distinguish between an attitudinal model and a behavioral model. For example, in examining the dimensions of the Managerial Grid (concern for production and concern for people) and Reddin's 3-D Management Style theory (task orientation and relationship orientation), one can see that these dimensions appear to be attitudinal. Concern or orientation is a feeling or an emotion toward something. The same can be said about McGregor's Theory X and Theory Y assumptions about human nature. Theory X describes negative feelings about the nature of people, and Theory Y describes positive feelings. These are all models that describe attitudes and feelings.

On the other hand, the dimensions of the Hersey-Blanchard Tridimensional Leader Effectiveness model (task behavior and relationship behavior) are dimensions of observed behavior. Thus, the Tridimensional Leader Effectiveness model describes how people behave, whereas the Managerial Grid, the 3-D Management Style theory, and Theory X-Theory Y describe attitudes or predispositions toward production and people.[19]

Although attitudinal models and the Tridimensional Leader Effectiveness model examine different aspects of leadership, they are not incompatible. A conflict develops only when behavioral assumptions are drawn from the analysis of the attitudinal dimension of models such as the Managerial Grid and theories such as Theory X-Theory Y. First, it is very difficult to predict behavior from attitudes and values. In fact, it has been found that you can actually do a much better job of predicting values or attitudes from behavior. If you want to know what is in a person's heart, look at what that person does. Look at the person's behavior.

> "Nearly all men can stand adversity, but if you want to test a man's character, give him power."
> —Abraham Lincoln

For example, assume that a manager has a very high concern for product quality. Does that tell you what that manager is going to do about it? No. One manager who has a high concern for product quality may say the following: "Don't even talk to me about quality. I don't want to make any changes right now." In other words, the manager engages in avoidance or withdrawal behavior (low relationship behavior and low task behavior). Another manager who also has a high concern for product quality may meet with employees and tell them what to do, how to do it, when to do it, and where to do it (high task behavior and low relationship behavior). A third manager who has a high concern for product quality might visit a department saying, "Gee, I'm sorry you have problems. Do you want to talk to me about it? Let's discuss it. Gosh, I'm sympathetic" (high relationship behavior and low task behavior). Finally, another manager who has a high concern for product quality might try to provide high amounts of both task behavior and relationship behavior in helping the department form self-managed teams.

What we are suggesting is that the same value set can evoke a variety of behaviors. You cannot easily predict behaviors from values. A look at one of the simplest models in the behavioral sciences may help to emphasize our point of view. The model is S-O-R (a stimulus directed toward an organism produces a response). The trap that many humanistic trainers have fallen into is to suggest that we assess the effectiveness of management by looking at the stimulus, or the leadership style. In other words, they say there are good styles and bad styles. What we are saying is that if you are going to assess performance, you do not evaluate the stimulus, but you assess the response—the results. There is no best leadership style, or stimulus. Any leadership style can be effective or ineffective depending on the response that style gets in a particular situation. We also have to look at the impact the leaders have on the human resources. It is not enough to have a tremendous amount of productivity for the next six months. Your methods may upset your people, causing them to leave and join your competitors. You also have to be concerned about what impact you are having on your followers, on developing their competency and their commitment. So when we talk about response, or results, we are talking about the output and impact on the human resources.

There is another reason to be careful about making behavioral assumptions from attitudinal measures. Although high concern for both production and people in the Managerial Grid (9-9 attitude; see Figure 4–16) and positive Theory Y assumptions about human nature are basic ingredients for effective managers, it may be appropriate for managers to engage in a variety of behaviors as they face different problems in their environment. Therefore, the high task–high relationship style often associated with the Managerial Grid 9-9 "team management" style or the participative high relationship–low task behavior that is often argued as consistent with Theory Y may not always be appropriate.

For example, if a manager's employees can take responsibility for themselves, the appropriate style of leadership for working with them may be low task and low relationship. In this case, the manager delegates to those employees the responsibility for planning, organizing, and controlling their own operation. The manager plays a background role, providing socioemotional support only when necessary. In using this style appropriately, the manager would not be "impoverished" (low concern for both people and production) as the Managerial Grid suggests. In fact, delegating to competent and confident people is the best way a manager can demonstrate a 9-9 attitude and Theory Y assumptions about human nature. The same is true for using a directive high task–low relationship style. Sometimes the best way you can show your concern for people and production (9-9) is to direct, control, and closely supervise their behavior when they are insecure and do not have the skills yet to perform their job.

> "The challenge is not to manage time, but to manage ourselves."
> —Steven Covey

Summary

Empirical studies tend to show that there is no best style of leadership. Effective leaders adapt their leader behavior to meet the needs of their followers and the particular environment. If their followers are different, they must be treated differently. Therefore, effectiveness depends on the leader, the followers, and other situational variables. Anyone who is interested in effectiveness as a leader must give serious thought to both behavioral and environmental considerations.

Notes

1. Chester A. Schriesheim, James M. Tolliver, and Orlando C. Behling, "Leadership Theory: Some Implications for Managers," *MSU Business Topics* 22, no. 2 (Summer 1978): 34–40, in William E. Rosenbach and Robert L. Taylor, eds., *Contemporary Issues in Leadership* (Boulder, CO: Westview Press, 1984), 128.

2. Victor Vroom, "Can Leaders Learn to Lead?" *Organizational Dynamics* 4 (Winter 1976).

3. Peter F. Drucker, "Management's New Paradigms," *Forbes*, October 5, 1998, 152–530.

4. Robert Tannenbaum and Warren H. Schmidt, "How to Choose a Leadership Pattern," *Harvard Business Review*, May–June 1973. This is an update of their original 1957 article, one of the landmarks in leadership research.

5. Kurt Lewin, R. Lippitt, and R. White identified laissez-faire as a third form of leadership style. See Lewin, Lippitt, and White, "Leader Behavior and Member Reaction in Three 'Social Climates,'" in *Group Dynamics: Research and Theory,*

2nd ed., Dorwin Cartwright and Alvin Zander, eds. (Evanston, IL: Row, Peterson, 1960).

6. Tannenbaum and Schmidt, "How to Choose a Leadership Pattern."

7. Warren G. Bennis, "Where Have All the Leaders Gone?" *Technology Review* 758, no. 9 (March–April 1977): 3–12.

8. Fred E. Fiedler, *A Theory of Leadership Effectiveness* (New York: McGraw-Hill, 1967). See also Fred E. Fiedler and Martin M. Chemers, "Improving Leadership Effectiveness," *Personnel Psychology*, 38 (Spring 1985): 220–222; Fred E. Fiedler and Martin M. Chemers, *Improving Leadership Effectiveness: The Leader Match Concept* (New York: Wiley, 1984).

9. Fiedler, *A Theory of Leadership Effectiveness*, p. 13.

10. *Ibid.*, p. 14.

11. Robert J. House and Terence R. Mitchell, "Path-Goal Theory of Leadership," *Journal of Contemporary Business* 3 (Autumn 1974): 81. See also Mark J. Knoll and Charles D. Pringle, "Path-Goal Theory and the Task Design Literature: A Tenuous Linkage," *Akron Business and Economic Review* 17, no. 4 (Winter 1986): 75–83.

12. House and Mitchell, "Path-Goal Theory of Leadership," p. 81.

13. *Ibid.*

14. Richard L. Daft, *Management*, 3rd ed. (Fort Worth, TX: Dryden Press, 1993), 493.

15. Because the model is an outgrowth of the Ohio State leadership studies, these definitions have been adapted from their definitions of initiating structure (task) and consideration (relationship): Ralph M. Stogdill and Alvin E. Coons, eds., *Leader Behavior: Its Description and Measurement, Research Monograph No. 88* (Columbus: Bureau of Business Research, Ohio State University, 1957), 42–43.

16. William J. Reddin, "The 3-D Management Style Theory," *Training and Development Journal* 21 no. 4 (April 1967): 8–17. See also Reddin, *Managerial Effectiveness* (New York: McGraw-Hill, 1970).

17. Reddin, "The 3-D Management Style Theory," p. 13.

18. The LEAD (formerly known as the leader adaptability and style inventory, LASI), first appeared in Paul Hersey and Kenneth H. Blanchard, "So You Want to Know Your Leadership Style?" *Training and Development Journal* 28 (no. 2) (February 1974): 22–37. LEAD instruments are distributed through Center for Leadership Studies, 230 W. 3rd Ave., Escondido, CA, 92025.

19. Fiedler, in his contingency model of leadership effectiveness (Fiedler, *A Theory of Leadership Effectiveness*) also tends to make behavioral assumptions from data gathered from an attitudinal measure of leadership style. A leader is asked to evaluate his least preferred coworker (LPC) on a series of semantic differential type scales. Leaders are classified as high or low LPC depending on the favorableness with which they rate their LPC.

6

Determining Effectiveness

One of the most important issues facing the applied behavioral sciences is that of human productivity—the quality and quantity of work. Productivity involves both effectiveness (the attainment of goals) and efficiency (resource costs, including those human resource costs affecting the quality of life). Our focus in this chapter will be primarily on effectiveness because, as Peter Drucker, a founding father of management theory, wrote, "Effectiveness is the foundation of success—efficiency is a minimum condition for survival after success has been achieved. Efficiency is concerned with doing things right. Effectiveness is doing the right things."[1]

MANAGEMENT EFFECTIVENESS VERSUS LEADERSHIP EFFECTIVENESS

In discussing effectiveness, we must once again distinguish between management and leadership. As we discussed earlier, leadership is a broader concept than management. Management is thought of as a special kind of leadership in which the accomplishment of organizational goals is paramount.

> "The manager asks how and when; the leader asks what and why."
> —Warren Bennis

Leadership is an attempt to influence people, individually and in groups, for whatever reason. Influence and leadership may be used interchangeably. Not all leadership style is directed toward accomplishing organizational goals. In fact, many times when you are trying to influence someone else, you are not even part of an organization. For example, when you are trying to get some friends to go someplace with you, you are not engaging in management, but you are certainly attempting leadership. If they agree to go, you are an effective leader but not an effective manager. Even within an organizational setting, managers may engage in leadership rather than management if they are trying to accomplish personal goals, not organizational ones.

For example, a vice-president may have a strong personal goal to become the company president. In attempting to achieve this goal, this executive may not be concerned with organizational goals at all, but only with undermining the plans of the president and other executives who may be contenders for the job. The vice-president may accomplish this personal goal and, in that sense, be a successful leader. However, this individual cannot be considered an effective manager because these actions were probably disruptive to the effective operation of the firm.

> "Leadership is not magnetic personality—that can just as well be a glib tongue. It is not 'making friends and influencing people'—that is flattery. Leadership is lifting a person's vision to higher sights, the raising of a person's performance to a higher standard, the building of a personality beyond its normal limitations."
> —Peter Drucker

Parkinson's "law" suggests a clear example of a person's placing personal goals before organizational goals. His law states that in bureaucracies, managers often try to build up their own departments by adding unnecessary personnel, more equipment, or expanded facilities.[2] Although this tendency may increase the prestige and importance of the managers, it often leads to "an organizational environment that is not only inefficient but also stifling and frustrating to the individuals who must cope with [it]."[3] Thus, in discussing effectiveness, we must recognize the differences between individual goals, organizational goals, leadership, and management.

SUCCESSFUL LEADERSHIP VERSUS EFFECTIVE LEADERSHIP

An attempt by an individual to have some effect on the behavior of another is called *attempted* leadership. This attempted leadership can be successful or unsuccessful in producing the desired response. A basic responsibility of managers in any type of organization is to get work done, with and through people, so their success is measured by the output or productivity of the group they lead. With that thought in mind, Bernard M. Bass suggested a clear distinction between successful and effective leadership or management.[4]

Suppose manager A attempts to influence individual B to do a certain job. A's attempt will be considered successful or unsuccessful depending on the extent to which B accomplishes the job. It is not really an either/or situation. A's success could be depicted on a continuum (Figure 6–1) ranging from very successful to very unsuccessful, with gray areas in between that would be difficult to ascertain as either.

Let us assume that A's leadership is successful. In other words, B's response to A's leadership stimulus falls at the successful end of the continuum. We still do not know the whole story of effectiveness.

If A's leadership style is not compatible with the expectations of B, and if B is antagonized and does the job only because of A's position of authority, then we can say that A has been successful but not effective. B has responded as A intended because A has control of rewards and punishment—not because A motivated or inspired B to take action. The satisfaction of the goals of the manager or the organization also satisfies B's needs.

On the other hand, if A's attempted leadership leads to a successful response, and B does the job because it is personally rewarding, then we consider A as having not only authority, or

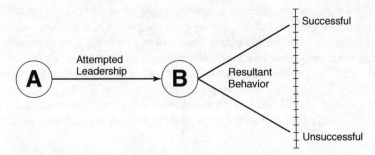

FIGURE 6–1 Bass's Successful Leadership Continuum

Source: Based on Bernard M. Bass, *Leadership, Psychology, and Organizational Behavior* (New York: Harper & Brothers, 1960), pp. 90, 448.

position power, but also respect, or personal power. B respects A and is willing to cooperate, realizing that A's request is consistent with some personal goals. In fact, B sees these personal goals as being accomplished by this activity. This is what is meant by effective leadership, keeping in mind that effectiveness also appears as a continuum that can range from very effective to very ineffective, as illustrated in Figure 6–2.

Success has to do with how the individual or the group behaves, performs, or reacts. On the other hand, effectiveness describes the internal state, or predisposition, of an individual or a group, and thus it is attitudinal in nature. There are two types of power that contribute to a leader's success and effectiveness. They are position power and personal power. Position power tends to be delegated down through the organization, determined by the authority or placement within the organization hierarchy. Personal power is generated upward from below through follower acceptance, admiration, and respect for leadership actions taken. Individuals who are interested only in success tend to emphasize their position power and use close supervision. Effective individuals, however, will also depend on personal power and use more general supervision.

Fred Luthans, a professor of management at the University of Nebraska, conducted a four-year observational study to determine the similarities and differences between successful managers (those who were rapidly promoted) and effective managers (those who had satisfied, committed employees and high-performing departments).[5] The study reported that successful managers

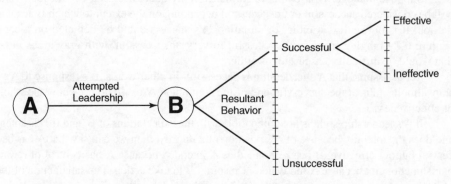

FIGURE 6–2 Bass's Successful and Effective Leadership Continuum

Source: Based on Bernard M. Bass, *Leadership, Psychology, and Organizational Behavior* (New York: Harper & Brothers, 1960), pp. 90, 448.

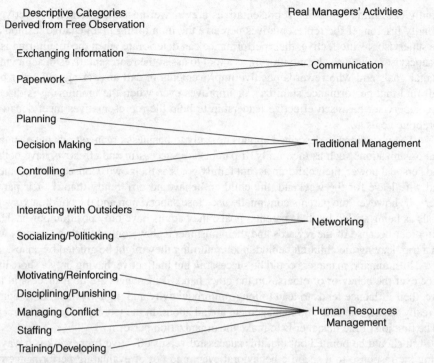

Descriptive Categories
Derived from Free Observation

Real Managers' Activities

Exchanging Information

Paperwork

Communication

Planning

Decision Making

Controlling

Traditional Management

Interacting with Outsiders

Socializing/Politicking

Networking

Motivating/Reinforcing

Disciplining/Punishing

Managing Conflict

Staffing

Training/Developing

Human Resources
Management

FIGURE 6–3 The Activities of Real Managers

Source: Academy of Management Executive, by A. Kirkpatrick and Edwin A. Locke. Copyright ©
1988 by Academy of Management (NY). Reproduced with permission of Academy of Management
(NY) in the format Textbook via Copyright Clearance Center.

spent more of their time and effort networking with others inside and outside the organization than did effective managers. Politicking and socializing occupied most of their time, with less time spent on the traditional activities of managing—planning, decision making, and controlling. In contrast, the effective managers spent most of their time on communication, that is, exchanging information and paperwork, and in human resource management (Figure 6–3). These activities contributed most to the quality and quantity of their high-performing departments.

Less than 10 percent of the managers in the study sample were in both the top third of successful managers and the top third of effective managers. These managers were able to achieve a balanced approach in their activities; they networked and got the right job done. The study concluded that more attention needs to be paid to designing systems to reward and support effective managers, not those with the most successful political and social skills. By rewarding effectiveness, organizations will increase their abilities to compete and excel in rapidly changing market and environmental conditions.

In the management of organizations, the difference between successful and effective often explains why many supervisors can get a satisfactory level of output only when they are right there looking over a worker's shoulder. But as soon as they leave, output declines and often such things as horseplay and less attention to detail increase while the overall quality output decreases.

This same phenomenon occurs in organizations that rely on phone conversations with service representatives for order placement. By monitoring incoming calls, the supervisor can rapidly determine if service representatives are answering calls quickly, correctly, and in a friendly fashion. If the representatives perceive the monitoring in a negative fashion and view the supervisor as ineffective, their performance can deteriorate when the monitoring is stopped. A supervisor who uses the monitoring as a tool to assist the representatives in achieving departmental goals and who rewards positive improvements in call answering and order placement will find that performance stabilizes or improves even when the monitoring is discontinued. The supervisor has used effective leadership to help the representatives meet department and corporate goals.

The phenomenon described applies not only to business organizations but also to less formal organizations such as the family. If parents are successful and effective, have both position and personal power, their children accept family goals as their own. Consequently, if the husband and wife leave for the weekend, the children behave no differently than if their parents were there. If, however, the parents continually use close supervision and the children view their own goals as being stifled by their parents' goals, the parents have only position power. They maintain order because of the rewards and the punishments they control. If these parents went away on a trip, leaving the children behind, upon returning they might be greeted by chaos.

In summary, managers could be successful, but ineffective, having only a short-lived influence over the behavior of others. On the other hand, if managers are both successful and effective, their influence tends to lead to long-run productivity and organizational development. This is really what leadership and management are all about. In the words of *The Wall Street Journal*, "The first job of the manager is to make the organization perform."[6]

It should be pointed out that this successful versus effective framework is a way of evaluating the response to a specific behavioral event and not of evaluating performance over time. Long-term evaluation is not a result of a single leadership event but a summation of many different leadership events. The evaluation of a leader or an organization over time will be discussed in the following section.

"Someone's sitting in the shade today because someone planted a tree a long time ago."
—Warren Buffett

WHAT DETERMINES ORGANIZATIONAL EFFECTIVENESS?

In discussing effectiveness, we have concentrated on evaluating the results of individual leaders or managers. These results are significant, but perhaps the most important aspect of effectiveness is its relationship to an entire organization. Here we are concerned with not only the outcome of a given leadership attempt but also with the effectiveness of the organizational unit over a period of time. Rensis Likert identified three variables—causal, intervening, and end result—that are useful in discussing effectiveness over time.[7]

Causal Variables

Causal variables are those factors that influence the course of developments within an organization and its results or accomplishments. These independent variables can be altered by the organization and its management; they are not beyond the control of the organization, as are general business conditions. Leadership strategies, skills, and behavior; management's decisions; and the policies and structure of the organization are examples of causal variables.

Intervening Variables

Leadership strategies, skills, behavior, and other causal variables affect the human resources or intervening variables in an organization. According to Likert, intervening variables represent the current condition of the internal state of the organization.[8] They are reflected in the commitment to objectives, motivation, and morale of members and their skills in leadership, communications, conflict resolution, decision making, and problem solving.

Output, or End Result, Variables

Output, or end result, variables are the dependent variables that reflect the achievements of the organization. In evaluating effectiveness, perhaps more than 90 percent of managers in organizations look at measures of output alone. Thus, the effectiveness of managers is often determined by net profits; the effectiveness of college professors may be determined by the number of articles and books they have published; and the effectiveness of basketball coaches may be determined by their win-loss records.

Many researchers talk about effectiveness by emphasizing similar output variables. Fred E. Fiedler, for example, in his studies evaluated "leader effectiveness in terms of group performance on the group's primary assigned task."[9] William J. Reddin, in discussing management styles, wrote in similar terms about effectiveness. He argued that the effectiveness of a manager should be measured "objectively by his profit center performance—maximum output, market share, or other similar criteria."[10]

There has been a move away from single-measure assessments of effectiveness. For example, Peter B. Vaill noted that organizational stakeholders are increasingly looking for "winning" in five categories of values.

- *Economic values.* Reflect what the firm's bottom line should be.
- *Technological values.* Reflect how the firm will do what it chooses to do.
- *Communal values.* Reflect the kind of "home" the firm will be for its employees.
- *Sociopolitical values.* Reflect the kind of neighbor the firm will be to its external constituencies.
- *Transcendental values.* Reflect what the firm means at a deeper level to its external constituencies.[11]

These five categories reflect a growing emphasis on organizational values.

A similar set was developed by professor Robert S. Kaplan and business consultant David P. Norton writing in the *Harvard Business Review*.[12] They suggested that businesses should concentrate on four perspectives in setting performance measures.

- *The customers' perspective.* How your customers see you
- *The internal operations perspective.* What you must excel at
- *The change perspective.* How you continue to improve and create value
- *The financial perspective.* How you look to shareholders

A third example is *Fortune* magazine's annual Corporate Reputations survey. The criteria *Fortune* uses are the quality of management; quality of product or services; financial soundness; value as a long-term investment; use of corporate assets; innovativeness; community or environmental responsibility; and ability to attract, develop, and keep talented people.[13]

Returning to the Likert model, we might visualize the relationship between the three classes of variables as stimuli (causal variables) acting upon the organism (intervening variables) and creating certain responses (output variables), as illustrated in Figure 6–4.[14]

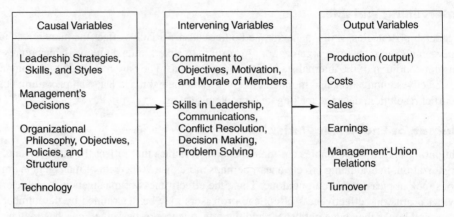

FIGURE 6–4   Relationship among Likert's Causal, intervening, and Output Variables

The causal variables largely produce the level or condition of the intervening variables, which in turn influence the end result variables. Attempts to improve the intervening variables directly will usually be much less effective than will attempts to improve them by changing the causal variables. The end result variables, also, can be improved most effectively by modifying the causal variables rather than the intervening variables.

Long-Term Goals versus Short-Term Goals

Intervening variables are concerned with building and developing the organization, and they tend to be long-term goals. This is the part of effectiveness that many managers overlook because it emphasizes long-term potential as well as short-term performance. This oversight is understandable because most managers tend to be promoted on the basis of short-term output variables, such as increased production and earnings, without concern for long-run potential and organizational development. This oversight creates an organizational dilemma.

Organizational Dilemma

One of the major problems in industry today is that there is a shortage of effective managers. Therefore, it is common for managers to be promoted in six months or a year if they are "producers." The basis on which top management promotes is often short-run output, so managers attempt to achieve high levels of productivity and often overemphasize tasks, placing extreme pressure on everyone, even when it is inappropriate.

> "Leaders grow; they are not made."
> —Peter Drucker

We probably all have had some experience with coming into an office or a home and raising the roof with people. The immediate or short-run effect is probably increased activity. We also know that if this style is often inappropriate for those concerned and if it continues over a long period of time, the morale of the organization will deteriorate. Some indications of deterioration of these intervening variables at work may be turnover, absenteeism, increased accidents, loss of resources, and the number and nature of grievances. Are grievances really significant problems, or do they reflect pent-up emotions due to anxieties and frustration? Are they settled at the complaint stage between the employee and the manager, or are they pushed up the hierarchy to be settled at higher levels or by arbitration? The organizational dilemma is that in many instances, a manager who places pressure on everyone and produces in the short run is promoted out of this situation before the disruptive aspects of the intervening variables catch up. In a sense, the manager is promoted or rewarded for his or her disruptive or ineffective behavior, and the next manager has to clean up the problems or deal with the end result variables that the leader did not cause.

> "Most things which are urgent are not important, and most things which are important are not urgent."
> —President Dwight Eisenhower

There tends to be a time lag between declining intervening variables and significant restriction of output by employees under such a management climate. Employees tend to feel that things will get better. Thus, when high-pressure managers are promoted rapidly, they often stay "one step ahead of the wolf."

The real problem is faced by the next manager. Although productivity records are high, this manager has inherited many problems. The introduction of a new manager may be enough to collapse the slowly deteriorating intervening variables. A tremendous drop in morale and motivation leading almost immediately to a significant decrease in output can occur. Change by its very nature is frightening; to a group whose intervening variables are declining, it can be devastating. Regardless of this new manager's style, the present expectations of the followers may be so distorted that much time and patience will be needed to close the now apparent "credibility gap" between the goals of the organization and the personal goals of the group. No matter how effective this manager may be in the long run, reviewing a productivity drop may cause senior management to give the manager only a few months to improve performance. But as Likert's studies indicate, rebuilding a group's intervening variables in a small organization may take one to three years, and in a large organization it may take up to seven years.

This dilemma is not restricted to business organizations. It is also common in school systems. Superintendents and other top administrators can be promoted to better, higher paying jobs in other systems if they are innovative and implement new programs in their systems. One such superintendent brought a small town national prominence by putting every new and innovative idea being discussed in education into a school. In this process, there was almost no involvement or participation by the teachers, or by community administrators, in the decision making that went into these programs. After two years, the superintendent, because of these innovations, was promoted to a larger system with a $15,000-a-year raise. A new superintendent was appointed in the "old" system, but, almost before the new superintendent unpacked, turmoil hit the system with tremendous teacher turnover, a faculty union, and a defeated bond issue. As things became unglued, people were heard saying that they wished the old superintendent was back. And yet, in reality, it was the old superintendent's style that had eroded the intervening variables and caused the current problems.

It should be clear that we do not think this is an either/or process. It is often a matter of determining how much to concentrate on each—output and intervening variables. Let us look at a basketball example. Suppose a women's team has good potential, with a large number of experienced senior players, but as the season progresses it does not look as if it is going to be an extremely good year. There comes a point in this season when the coach must make a basic decision. Will she continue to play her experienced seniors and hope to win a majority of her final games, or should she forget about concentrating on winning the last games and play her sophomores and juniors to give them experience, in hopes of developing and building a winning team for future years? The choice is between short-term and long-term goals. If the accepted goal is building the team for the future, then the coach should be evaluated on those terms and not entirely on the season's win-loss record. The art of achieving a balance is essential to effective leadership.

Although intervening variables do not appear on win-loss records, balance sheets, sales reports, or accounting ledgers, we feel that these long-term considerations are just as important to an organization as short-term output variables. Therefore, although difficult to measure, intervening variables should not be overlooked in determining organizational effectiveness. One of the instruments used by Likert to measure these variables was discussed in Chapter 4 (see Table 4–3).

In summary, we feel that effectiveness is actually determined by whatever the manager and the organization decide are their goals and objectives. They should remember that effectiveness is a function of:

1. Output variables (productivity/performance)
2. Intervening variables (the condition of the human resources)
3. Short-range goals
4. Long-range goals

PARTICIPATION AND EFFECTIVENESS

In an organizational setting, it is urged that the criteria for an individual's or a group's performance should be decided mutually in advance. In making these decisions, managers and their employees should consider output and intervening variables, short-range and long-range goals. This process has two advantages. First, it will permit employees to participate in determining the basis on which their efforts will be judged. Second, involving employees in the planning process will increase their commitment to the goals and objectives established. Research evidence supports this contention.

One of the classic studies in this area was done by Lester Coch and John French in an American factory.[15] They found that when managers and employees discussed proposed technological changes, productivity increased and resistance to change decreased when these procedures were initiated. Other studies have shown similar results.[16] These studies suggest that involving employees in decision making tends to be effective in our society. Once again, we must remember that the success of using participative management depends on the situation. Although this approach tends to be effective in many industrial settings in the United States, it may not be appropriate in other cultures.

This argument was illustrated clearly when French, Joachim Israel, and Dagfinn A–s attempted to replicate the original Coch and French experiment in a Norwegian factory.[17] In this setting, they found no significant difference in productivity between work groups in which participative management was used and those in which it was not used. In other words, increased participation in decision making did not have the same positive influence on factory workers in Norway as it did in the United States. Hersey's replication of one of Likert's studies in Nigeria came to the same conclusion. This Norwegian study suggests that cultural differences in the followers and the situation may be important in determining the appropriate leadership style.

MANAGEMENT BY OBJECTIVES

It is not an easy task to integrate the goals and objectives of all individuals with the goals of the organization. Yet, it is not an impossible task. A participative approach to this problem that has been used successfully in some organizations worldwide is a process called management by objectives (MBO). The concepts behind MBO were introduced by Peter Drucker in the early 1950s and have become popularized throughout the world, particularly through the efforts of George Odiorne and John Humble.[18–20] Through their work and the efforts of others, managers in all kinds of organizational settings, whether industrial, educational, governmental, or military, are attempting to run their organizations with the MBO process as a basic underlying management concept. [21]

> Management by objectives is basically a process whereby the senior and the junior managers of an enterprise jointly identify its common goals, define each individual's major areas of responsibility in terms of the results expected . . . and use these measures as guides for operating the unit and assessing the contribution of each of its members.[22]

In some cases, this process has been successfully carried beyond the managerial level to include hourly employees. The concept rests on a philosophy of management that emphasizes an integration between external control by managers and self-control by employees. It can apply to any manager or individual no matter what level or function, and to any organization, regardless of size.

The effective functioning of this system is an agreement between a manager and an employee about that employee's group's performance goals during a stated time period. These goals can emphasize either output variables or intervening variables or some combination of both. The important thing is that goals are jointly established and agreed upon in advance. At the end of the time period, performance is reviewed in relation to accepted goals. Both the employee and the manager participate in this review and in any other evaluation that takes place. It has been found that objectives that are formulated with each person participating seem to gain more acceptance than those imposed by an authority figure in the organization. Consultation and participation in this area tend to establish a personal stake in the attainment of the formulated objective by those who actually perform the task.

"There's nothing more demoralizing than a leader who can't clearly articulate why we're doing what we're doing."

—James Kouzes and Barry Posner

Before individual objectives are set, the common goals of the entire organization should be clarified. Also, any appropriate changes in the organizational structure should be made, such as changes in titles, duties, relationships, authority, responsibility, span of control, and so forth.

Throughout the time period, what is to be accomplished by the entire organization should be compared with what is actually being accomplished. Necessary adjustments should be made and inappropriate goals discarded. At the end of the time period, when the final mutual review of objectives and performance takes place, if there is a discrepancy between the two, efforts are initiated to determine what steps can be taken to overcome these problems. This step sets the stage for the determination of objectives for the next time period. The entire cycle of management by objectives is represented graphically in Figure 6–5.[23]

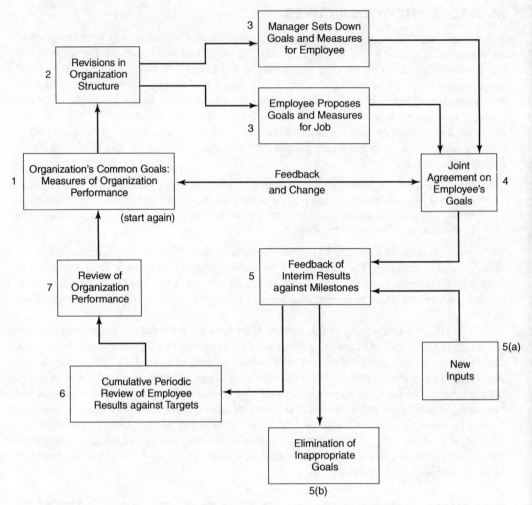

FIGURE 6–5 The Cycle of Management by Objectives

Many companies have found MBO to be a useful adjunct to achieving corporate effectiveness, but years of use have highlighted some of its shortcomings. Employees may react to the implementation of an MBO program with distrust and skepticism; they may question why managers are interested in their input after years of giving orders.

After it is implemented, the MBO system can generate excessive documentation and paperwork. Goals of improved communication and planning can be lost in the shuffle of papers. Related to this is the problem of overemphasizing the grading and evaluating the employee performance in achieving MBO goals. MBO needs to focus on helping employees assist each other to improve performance.

Another problem of the MBO system can develop when managers set meaningless or easily achieved goals. Goals must be carefully monitored with an eye on overall corporate goals and objectives. Problems can also develop when the feedback process is slow and managers are unable to change or adapt their goals to meet rapidly changing conditions.

Management by objectives can be a powerful tool in gaining mutual commitment and high productivity for an organization in which this type of employee involvement is appropriate. However, the system must be developed, implemented, and managed with an understanding of the problems it can generate.

STYLE AND EFFECTIVENESS

Abundant research supports the argument that all leader behavior styles can be effective or ineffective depending on the situation. Abraham K. Korman gathered some of the most convincing evidence to dispel the idea of a single best style of leader behavior.[24] Korman attempted to review all studies that examined the relationships between the Ohio State behavior dimensions of initiating structure (task) and consideration (relationship) and various measures of effectiveness, including group productivity, salary, performance under stress, administrative reputation, work group grievances, absenteeism, and turnover. In all, Korman reviewed more than 25 studies. In every case, the two dimensions were measured by either the leader opinion questionnaire (LOQ) or the leader behavior description questionnaire (LBDQ). The former is used to assess how leaders think they should behave in a given situation; the latter measures follower perceptions of leader behavior. Korman concluded that:

> [D]espite the fact that "Consideration" and "Initiating Structure" have become almost bywords in American industrial psychology, it seems apparent that very little is now known as to how these variables may predict work group performance and the conditions which affect such predictions. At the current time, we cannot even say whether they have any predictive significance at all.[25]

Thus, Korman found that consideration and initiating structure had no significant predictive value in terms of effectiveness. This finding suggests that since situations differ, so must leader style.

Fred Fiedler, in testing his contingency model of leadership in more than 50 studies covering a span of 16 years (1951–1967), concluded that both directive, task-oriented leaders and nondirective, human relations-oriented leaders are effective under some conditions. As Fiedler argued:

> While one can never say that something is impossible, and while someone may well discover the all-purpose leadership style or behavior at some future time, our own data and those which have come out of sound research by other investigators do not promise such miraculous cures.[26]

Summary

The evidence is clear that there is no single all-purpose leader behavior style that is effective in all situations. While our basic conclusion in this chapter is that the type of leader behavior needed depends on the situation, this conclusion leaves many questions unanswered for a specific individual in a leadership role. Such individuals may be personally interested in how leadership depends on the situation and how they can find some practical value in theory. To accommodate this type of concern, in Chapter 7 we will discuss the environmental variables that may help a leader or a manager to make effective decisions in a variety of leadership situations.

Notes

1. Peter F. Drucker, *Management: Tasks, Responsibilities, Practices* (New York: Harper & Row, 1973), 45.
2. C. Northcote Parkinson, *Parkinson's Law* (Boston: Houghton Mifflin, 1957).
3. Fred J. Carvell, *Human Relations in Business* (Toronto: Macmillan, 1970), 182.
4. Bernard M. Bass, *Leadership, Psychology, and Organizational Behavior* (New York: Harper & Brothers, 1960), 88–89.
5. Fred Luthans, "Successful vs. Effective Real Managers," *The Academy of Management Executive* 11, no. 2 (May 1988): 127–132.
6. *Wall Street Journal*, January 9, 1978, p. 12.
7. Rensis Likert, *The Human Organization* (New York: McGraw-Hill, 1967), 26–29.
8. Rensis Likert, *New Patterns of Management* (New York: McGraw-Hill, 1961), 2.
9. Fred E. Fiedler, *A Theory of Leadership Effectiveness* (New York: McGraw-Hill, 1967), 9.
10. William J. Reddin, "The 3-D Management Style Theory," *Training and Development Journal* (April 1967). This is one of the critical differences between Reddin's 3-D management style theory and the tridimensional leader effectiveness model. Reddin in his model seems to consider only output variables in determining effectiveness, whereas in the tridimensional leader effectiveness model both intervening variables and output variables are considered.
11. Peter B. Vaill, "Managing as a Performing Art." *The Manager's Bookshelf,* 3rd ed., eds. Jon Pierce and John Newstrom (New York: Harper Collins Publishers, 1993), 221.
12. Robert S. Kaplan and David P. Norton, "Putting the Balanced Scorecard to Work," *Harvard Business Review*, September–October 1993, p. 134.
13. Rahul Jacob, "Corporate Reputations," *Fortune*, March 6, 1995, pp. 54–64.
14. Adapted from Likert, *The Human Organization*, pp. 47–77.
15. Lester Coch and John R. P. French, Jr., "Overcoming Resistance to Change." in *Group Dynamics: Research and Theory*, 2nd ed., eds.

Dorwin Cartwright and Alvin Zander (Evanston, IL: Row, Peterson, 1960).
16. See Kurt Lewin, "Group Decision and Social Change." in *Readings in Social Psychology*, eds. G. Swanson, T. Newcomb, and E. Hartley (New York: Henry Holt, 1952), 459–473.
17. John R. P. French, Jr., Joachim Israel, and Dagfinn A–s, "An Experiment on Participation in a Norwegian Factory," *Human Relations* 13 (1960): 3–19.
18. Peter F. Drucker, *The Practice of Management* (New York: Harper & Row, 1964).
19. George S. Odiorne, *Management by Objectives: A System of Managerial Leadership* (New York: Pitman Publishing, 1965); Odiorne, *The Human Side of Management* (San Diego, CA: University Associates, 1987); Odiorne, *MBO II: A System of Managerial Leadership for the 80's* (Belmont, CA: Pitman, Learning, 1979); Odiorne, "The Managerial Bait-and-Switch Game," *Personnel* 63, no. 3 (March 1986): 32–37.
20. John W. Humble, *Management by Objectives* (London: Industrial Education and Research Foundation, 1967).
21. See also J. D. Batten, *Beyond Management by Objectives* (New York: American Management Association, 1966); Ernest C. Miller, *Objectives and Standards Approach to Planning and Control, AMA Research Study, '74* (New York: American Management Association, 1966); William J. Reddin, *Effective Management by Objectives: The 3-D Method of MBO* (New York: McGraw-Hill, 1971).
22. Odiorne, *Management by Objectives*, pp. 55–56.
23. *Ibid.*, p. 78.
24. Abraham K. Korman, "'Consideration,' 'Initiating Structure,' and Organizational Criteria—A Review," *Personnel Psychology: A Journal of Applied Research* 19, no. 4 (Winter 1966): 349–361.
25. *Ibid.*, p. 360.
26. Fiedler, *A Theory of Leadership Effectiveness*, p. 247.

7

Situational Leadership®

H ow is a good leader like a good doctor? This question may sound like the setup for delivery of a comic punch line. It is not. It points instead to one of the most important skills a leader can have. Edgar H. Schein captured it well 50 years ago when he said: "The successful manager must be a good diagnostician and must value a spirit of inquiry. The abilities and motives of the people under the manager vary, [so] managers must sense and appreciate the differences. He must have the personal flexibility and range of skills necessary to vary his own behavior."[1] Schein's words and thinking—*diagnosis, inquiry, flexibility*—have reverberated through some of the most seminal and lasting approaches to leadership to emerge since then, including ours.

Diagnosis is a highly important skill in Situational Leadership®, as you will learn in some detail in this and subsequent chapters. Stephen Covey later framed it as one of the "seven habits" of not only good leaders, but of highly effective people.[2] *Inquiry* is necessary in several of the leadership styles we will describe, and central to Chris Argyris' concepts of productive dialogue and the ladder of inference (introduced in Chapter 12).[3] *Flexibility* underlies the ability to adapt your leadership style, as described in our framework, and upon which emotional intelligence depends.

It is easy to tell managers that they *should* use behavioral science theory and research to develop the necessary diagnostic skills to maximize effectiveness. It is not easy to tell them *how* to use it. First, much of the research currently published in the field of applied behavioral sciences is not even understandable to many practicing managers; it often appears to be more an attempt to impress other researchers than to help managers to be more effective. Second, even if practitioners could understand the research, many would argue that it is impractical to consider every situational variable in every decision.

As a result, one of the major focuses of our work has been the development of a practical model that can be used by managers, salespeople, teachers, or parents to make the moment-by-moment decisions necessary to effectively influence other people. The result is Situational

Leadership®. This approach uses as its basic data the perceptions and observations made by managers—parents in the home or supervisors on the job—on a day-to-day basis in their own environments.

Situational Leadership® was developed by Paul Hersey and Kenneth H. Blanchard at the Center for Leadership Studies in the late 1960s.[4] Until 1982, Hersey and Blanchard worked together to continually refine Situational Leadership®. After that time, Blanchard and his colleagues at Blanchard Training and Development (BTD) began to modify the original Situational Leadership® Model and developed diagnostic instruments and training materials to support their approach (called SLII®) in training seminars and presentations. The best description of this approach to Situational Leadership® can be found in *Leadership and the One Minute Manager.*[5] The Situational Leadership® Model used in this book reflects the present thinking of Paul Hersey and the Center for Leadership Studies and does not include the changes to the model that Blanchard and his colleagues made in SLII®.

SITUATIONAL LEADERSHIP®

The Center for Leadership Studies

Situational Leadership® is based on an interplay among (1) the amount of guidance and direction (task behavior) a leader gives; (2) the amount of socioemotional support (relationship behavior) a leader provides; and (3) the Performance Readiness® Level that individuals or teams (followers) exhibit in performing a specific activity, task, or job. This concept was developed to help people attempting leadership, regardless of their role, to be more effective in their daily interactions with others. It provides leaders with some understanding of the relationship between an effective style of leadership and the level of Performance Readiness® of their people.

Although all the situational variables (leader, followers, senior management, associates, organization, job demands, and time) are important, the emphasis in Situational Leadership® is on the behavior of a leader in relation to followers on specific tasks. As Fillmore H. Sanford indicated, there is some justification for regarding the performers "as the most crucial factor in any leadership event."[6] Performers in any situation are vital, not only because individually they accept or reject the leader, but because as a group they actually determine whatever personal power the leader may have.

It may be appropriate at this point to note the difference between a model and a theory. A theory attempts to explain why things happen as they do. As such, it is not designed to recreate events. A model, on the other hand, is a pattern of already existing events that can be learned and therefore repeated. For example, in trying to imagine why Henry Ford was motivated to mass produce automobiles, you would be dealing with a theory. However, if you recorded the procedures and sequences necessary for mass production, you would have a model of the process. Situational Leadership® is a model, *not* a theory. Its concepts, procedures, actions, and outcomes are based on tested methodologies that are practical, easy to apply, and repeatable.

Chapter 4 emphasized that when discussing leader-follower relationships, we are not necessarily talking about a hierarchical relationship, that is, manager-employee. The same is true during our discussion of Situational Leadership®. *Any reference to leader(s) or follower(s) in this model should imply potential leader and potential follower.* Although our examples may suggest a hierarchical relationship, the concepts presented in Situational Leadership® are applicable whether you are attempting to influence the behavior of an employee, your supervisor, an associate, a friend, a relative, or a group.

Basic Concepts of Situational Leadership®

According to Situational Leadership®, there is no one best way to influence people. The leadership style a person should use with individuals or groups depends on the task-specific Performance Readiness® Level of the person the leader is attempting to influence. Before we look at the application of the Situational Leadership® Model, it is important that we understand leadership styles as they are used in the model and the idea of follower Performance Readiness®.

> "To think is easy. To act is hard. But the hardest thing in the world is to act in accordance with your thinking."
> —Goethe

Our earlier discussion of different leadership theories in Chapters 4 and 5 introduced us to our definition of *leadership style*—behavior by the leader as perceived by the followers. We also saw the ways that classifying leader behaviors developed, including the identification of task and relationship behavior.[7]

Task behavior is defined as the extent to which the leader engages in spelling out the duties and responsibilities of an individual or group. These behaviors include telling people what to do, how to do it, when to do it, where to do it, and who is to do it.

High amounts of task behavior might be required, for instance, when you ask someone for directions. The person probably very precisely and clearly tells you what streets to take and what turns to make. You are told where to start and where to finish. It is important to notice that being directive does not mean being nasty or short-tempered. The person helping you might be very pleasant toward you, but the actions and statements are aimed at completing the task—that of helping you find your way. Task behavior is characterized by one-way communication from the leader to the follower. The person is not so much concerned with your feelings, but with how to help you achieve your goal.

Relationship behavior is defined as the extent to which the leader engages in two-way or multi-party communication. The behaviors include listening, facilitating, and explaining the why's of something while offering supportive behaviors to others.[8]

High amounts of relationship behavior might be required when you reach an impasse with an assignment. You basically know how to do the assignment but need some encouragement to get you over the hump. The listening, encouraging, and facilitating a leader does in this example are an illustration of relationship behavior.

Task behavior and relationship behavior are separate and distinct dimensions. They can be placed on separate axes of a two-dimensional graph, and the four quadrants can be used to identify four basic leadership styles.[9] Figure 7–1 illustrates these styles. Plotting task behavior from low to high on the horizontal axis and relationship behavior from low to high on the vertical axis makes it possible to describe leader behavior in four ways, or styles. We feel it is important to note that both these axes begin at "low" not zero. A leader, whether effective or ineffective in his or her style, always engages in *some* amount of task and relationship behavior. On other words, "Low does not equal 'no.'"

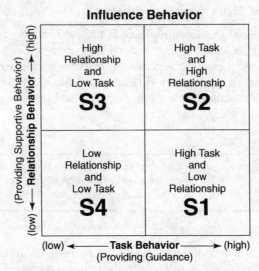

FIGURE 7–1 Leadership Styles

Source: Copyright © 1985, 2006, Leadership Studies, Inc.
All Rights Reserved.

As we discussed in Chapter 5, the four quadrants shown in Figure 7–1 can be used as the basis for assessing effective leader behavior. No one style is effective in all situations. Each style is appropriate and effective depending on the situation.

The following descriptions apply to the four styles:

- *Style 1 (S1)*. This leadership style is characterized by above-average amounts of task behavior and below-average amounts of relationship behavior.
- *Style 2 (S2)*. This leadership style is characterized by above-average amounts of both task and relationship behavior.
- *Style 3 (S3)*. This style is characterized by above-average amounts of relationship behavior and below-average amounts of task behavior.
- *Style 4 (S4)*. This style is characterized by below-average amounts of both relationship behavior and task behavior.

The important information presented by this model is in the operational definitions of task behavior and relationship behavior presented earlier. In leadership situations involving the family, schools, or other settings, different words may be more appropriate than *task* and *relationship*—for example, *guidance* and *supportive* behavior or *directive* behavior and *facilitating* behavior—but the underlying definitions remain the same.

Performance Readiness® of the Followers or Group

In Chapter 5, we looked at the situation—the complex pattern of conditions that exist within a given environment. We also noted that there is no one best style of leadership; it depends upon the situation within which the attempt to influence takes place. The more leaders can adapt their behaviors to the situation, the more effective their attempts to influence will be. The situation, in turn, is influenced by the various conditions present.

Some of the primary factors in the situation that influence leader effectiveness include the following:

- Leader
- Followers
- Supervisor
- Key associates
- Organization
- Job demands
- Decision time

These factors do not operate in isolation. They are interactive. For example, style S1 is often referred to as "crisis leadership" because it is appropriate in times of crisis. The important thing to remember is that we should use it to *respond* to crises, not to create them. If we treat an organization as if it is in crisis all the time, then that is what we get—crisis. If we treat people like children, they will often begin to behave like children. This is one of the most important concepts in the field of applied behavioral sciences—the concept of the *self-fulfilling prophecy*. In working with others and helping them develop, leaders should have positive assumptions about peoples' potential. Effective leaders believe that people have the potential to grow and that, given an opportunity, they can and will respond.[10]

We need to remind ourselves that the relationship between leaders and followers is the crucial variable in the leadership situation. If the followers decide not to follow, it does not matter what the supervisor or key associates think or what the job demands may be. *There is no leadership without someone following.*

In order to maximize the leader-follower relationship, the leader must first determine the task-specific outcomes the followers are to accomplish—on an individual and group basis. Without creating clarity on outcomes, objectives, subtasks, milestones, and so on, the leader has no basis for determining follower Performance Readiness® or the specific behavioral style to use for that level of Performance Readiness®.

"Leadership should be born out of the understanding of the needs of those who would be affected by it."
—Marian Anderson

Performance Readiness® Defined

Performance Readiness® in Situational Leadership® is defined as the extent to which a follower demonstrates the ability and willingness to accomplish a specific task.

People tend to be at different levels of Performance Readiness® depending on the task they are being asked to do. Performance Readiness® is not a personal characteristic; it is not an evaluation of a person's traits, values, age, and so on. Performance Readiness® is how ready a person is to perform a particular task. This concept of Performance Readiness® has to do with specific situations—not with any total sense of Performance Readiness®. All persons tend to be more or less ready in relation to a specific task, activity, or job that a leader is attempting to accomplish. Thus, a salesperson may be very responsible in securing new sales, but very casual about completing the paperwork necessary to close on a sale. As a result, it is appropriate for the manager to leave the salesperson alone in terms of closing on sales, but to supervise closely in terms of paperwork until the salesperson can start to do well in that area too.

In addition to assessing the level of Performance Readiness® of individuals within a group, a leader may have to assess the Performance Readiness® Level of the group as a group, particularly if the group interacts frequently in the same work area, as happens with students in the classroom. Thus, a teacher may find that a class as a group may be at one level of Performance Readiness® in a particular area, but a student within that group may be at a different level. When the teacher is one to one with that student, the teacher may have to behave very differently than when working with the class as a group. In reality, the teacher may find a number of students at various Performance Readiness® Levels. For example, the teacher may have one student who is not doing the assigned work regularly, and when the work is turned in, it is poorly organized and not very well done. The teacher may have to initiate some structure and supervise that student closely to get acceptable performance. Another student, however, may be doing good work but may be insecure and shy. With that student, the teacher may not have to engage in much task behavior in terms of schoolwork, but may need to be supportive, to engage in two-way communication, and to help facilitate the student's interaction with others in the class. Still another student may be competent and confident in the schoolwork and thus can be given minimum assistance. So leaders have to understand that they may have to behave differently one on one with members of their group from the way they behave with the group as a whole.

The two major components of Performance Readiness® are *ability* and *willingness*.[11]

Ability is the demonstrated knowledge, experience, and skill that an individual or group brings to a particular task or activity. They are defined as follows:

- *Knowledge* is demonstrated understanding of a task
- *Skill* is demonstrated proficiency in a task
- *Experience* is demonstrated ability gained from performing a task

When considering the ability level of others, one must be *task-specific*. A person who has a Ph.D. in music and 20 years of professional experience playing the piano may be of little help in the design of a new jet engine. It is essential to focus on the specific outcome desired and to consider the ability of the followers with respect to that outcome.

Willingness is the extent to which an individual or group has demonstrated confidence, commitment, and motivation to accomplish a specific task. They are defined as follows:

- *Confidence* is demonstrated self-assurance in the ability to perform a task
- *Commitment* is demonstrated dedication to perform a task
- *Motivation* is demonstrated desire to perform a task.

Willingness is only one word that describes this aspect of Performance Readiness®. Sometimes, it is not so much that people are really unwilling, it is just that they have never done a specific task before. Because they do not have any experience with it, they are insecure or afraid. In general, if it is an issue of never having done something, the problem is insecurity. The term *unwilling* might be most appropriate when, for some reason, the individuals have slipped, or lost some of their commitment and motivation to perform a specific task. It might imply that they are regressing.

Even though the concepts of ability and willingness are different, it is important to remember that they are an *interacting influence system*. This means that a significant change in one will affect the whole. The extent to which followers bring willingness into a specific situation affects

High	Moderate		Low
R4	R3	R2	R1
Able and Confident and Willing	Able but Insecure or Unwilling	Unable but Confident or Willing	Unable and Insecure or Unwilling

FIGURE 7–2 Performance Readiness®

Source: Copyright © 1985, 2006, Leadership Studies, Inc. All Rights Reserved.

the use of their present ability. And it affects the extent to which they will grow and develop competence and ability. Similarly, the amount of knowledge, experience, and skill brought to a specific task will often affect confidence, commitment, and motivation. Performance Readiness® Levels are the different combinations of ability and willingness that people bring to each task. (See Figure 7–2.)

The continuum of Performance Readiness® can be divided into four levels.[12] Each represents a different combination of follower ability and willingness or confidence:

- Performance Readiness® Level 1 (R1). Unable and insecure. The follower is unable and lacks confidence.
  or
  Unable and unwilling. The follower is unable and lacks commitment and motivation.
- Performance Readiness® Level 2 (R2). Unable but willing. The follower lacks ability, but is motivated and making an effort.
  or
  Unable but confident. The follower lacks ability, but is confident as long as the leader is there to provide guidance.
- Performance Readiness® Level 3 (R3). Able but insecure. The follower has the ability to perform the task, but is insecure or apprehensive about doing it alone.
  or
  Able but unwilling. The follower has the ability to perform the task, but is not willing or unmotivated.
- Performance Readiness® Level 4 (R4). Able and willing. The follower has the ability to perform and is committed.
  and
  Able and confident. The follower has the ability to perform and is confident about doing it.

Ron Campbell of the Center for Leadership Studies has expanded the continuum of follower Performance Readiness® (see Figure 7–2) to include behavioral indicators of the four Performance Readiness® Levels. Each level represents a different combination of follower ability and willingness or confidence. As shown in Figure 7–3, indicators of a person at R1 *for that specific task* would be such behaviors as not performing the task to an acceptable level or being intimidated by the task.

Because it is important to assess whether a person is insecure or unwilling, Campbell further refined these Performance Readiness® indicators to help differentiate between the two R1 Performance Readiness® states. We believe it is critical to note at this point that there can be

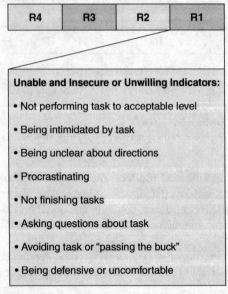

FIGURE 7–3   Performance Readiness® Level R1

significant differences in individual behavior when performance is driven by insecurity as compared to unwillingness. Most people have had years of behavioral conditioning not to show their insecurities, uncertainties, or anxiety. This often results in masked behavior, trying to cover up the real cause of their lack of performance.

> "Managers who are skilled communicators may also be good at covering up real problems."
> —Chris Argyris

In simple terms, we have been conditioned not to show our boss when we are unsure of things on the job. After all, if we are not totally confident, committed, and motivated, our boss might find someone who is and replace us. When it comes to applying the Situational Leadership® Model, we believe that the benefit of the doubt goes to the individual; they are insecure, or unsure, until they prove to the leader they are unwilling. Thus, we list "unable and insecure" before "unable and unwilling."

Specifically, an *unable and insecure R1* would exhibit:

• Body language expressing discomfort: furrowed brow, shoulders lowered, leaning back
• Confused, unclear behavior
• Concern over possible outcomes
• Fear of failure

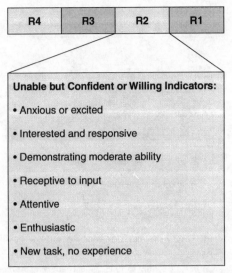

FIGURE 7–4   Performance Readiness® Level R2

An *unable and unwilling R1* would exhibit:

- Defensive, argumentative, complaining behaviors
- Late completion of tasks
- Performance only to exact request
- Intense frustration

The following paragraphs will present indicators for the three remaining Performance Readiness® levels. R2's indicators are illustrated in Figure 7–4. Specifically, an *unable but willing or confident R2* would:

- Speak quickly and intensely
- Seek clarity
- Nod head; make "yes, I know" type comments, seem eager
- Listen carefully
- Answer questions superficially
- Accept tasks
- Act quickly
- Be preoccupied with end results rather than incremental steps

R3's indicators are illustrated in Figure 7–5. Specifically, an *able but insecure R3* would:

- Question own ability
- Focus on potential problems
- Lack self-esteem
- Encourage leader to stay involved

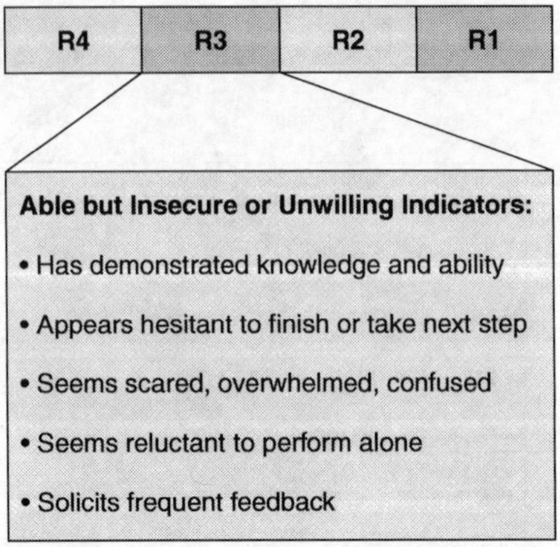

FIGURE 7–5 Performance Readiness® Level R3

Source: Copyright © 1985, 2006, Leadership Studies, Inc. All Rights Reserved.

An *able but unwilling R3* would

- Be hesitant or resistant
- Feel overobligated and overworked
- Seek reinforcement
- Be concerned performance is somehow punishing

R4's indicators are illustrated in Figure 7–6. Specifically, *an able and confident or willing R4* would do the following:

- Keep boss informed of task progress
- Make efficient use of resources
- Be responsible and results-oriented
- Be knowledgeable; share information to streamline operational tasks
- Be willing to help others
- Share creative ideas
- "Take charge" of tasks
- Complete responsibilities on time and perhaps early

These indicators are important clues to follower Performance Readiness®. Just as a physician must use clues in diagnosing patient illness, leaders must be alert for clues in follower behavior as a critical step to correctly diagnosing Performance Readiness®.

Going from R1 to R2 to R3

It is important to note that when it comes to developing Performance Readiness®, everyone is unique. Development is not a linear function. Everyone does not start at R1, progress to R2, R3, and then R4. Performance Readiness® is dynamic, and just as it changes depending on the task at hand, it can vary depending on the individual.

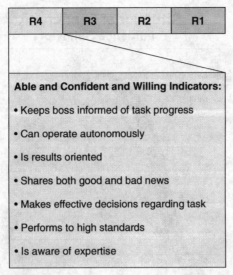

FIGURE 7–6 Performance Readiness® Level R4

Some readers have difficulty understanding the development of followers from R1 to R2 to R3. How can one go from being insecure to confident and then become insecure again? The important thing to remember is that at the lower levels of Performance Readiness® (R1 and R2), the leader is providing the direction—the what, where, when, and how. Therefore, the decisions are *leader-directed*. At the higher levels of Performance Readiness® (R3 and R4), followers become responsible for task direction, and the decisions are *follower-directed* (self-directed). This transition from leader-directed to self-directed may result in apprehension or insecurity.

As followers move from low levels of Performance Readiness® to higher levels, the combinations of task and relationship behavior appropriate to the situation begin to change. The curved line through the four leadership styles shown in Figure 7–7 represents the high probability combinations of task behavior and relationship behavior that correspond to the Performance Readiness® Levels directly below. To use the model, identify a point on the Performance Readiness® continuum that represents follower Performance Readiness® to perform a specific task. Then construct a perpendicular line from that point to a point where it intersects with the curved line representing leader behavior. This point indicates the most appropriate amount of task behavior and relationship behavior for that specific situation.

Note that the curved line never goes to either the lower left or the lower right corner. In both quadrants 1 and 4, there are combinations of both task and relationship behavior. Style S1 always has some relationship behavior, and style S4 always has some task behavior. It is not an option to have zero or no amount of task and/or relationship behavior demonstrated.

In selecting the combination of task behavior and relationship behavior with a high probability of success, you do not have to be exact. As you move away from the optimal combination, the probability of success gradually falls off, slowly at first and then more rapidly the farther away you move. Because of this, you do not need a direct hit—a close approximation keeps the probability of success high.

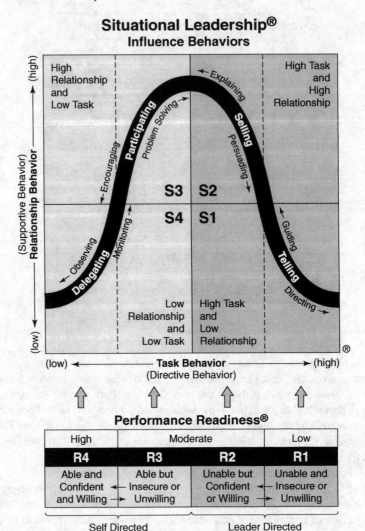

FIGURE 7–7 Situational Leadership® Model

Source: Situational Leadership® and Performance Readiness® are trademarks of Leadership Studies, Inc. Copyright © 1985, 2006, Leadership Studies, Inc. All Rights Reserved.

SELECTING APPROPRIATE STYLES

Matching Performance Readiness® Level 1 with Leadership Style S1—Telling

For a follower or group that is at Performance Readiness® Level 1 for a specific task, it is appropriate to provide high amounts of guidance but little supportive behavior. A word that describes this specific leadership style is *telling*—telling the followers what to do, where to do it, and how to do it. This style is appropriate when an individual or group is low in ability and willingness

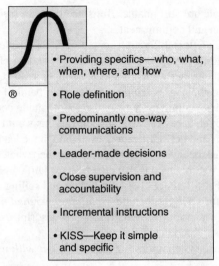

- Providing specifics—who, what, when, where, and how

- Role definition

- Predominantly one-way communications

- Leader-made decisions

- Close supervision and accountability

- Incremental instructions

- KISS—Keep it simple and specific

Effective	**Ineffective**
Telling	Demanding
Guiding	Demeaning
Directing	Dominating
Establishing	Attacking

FIGURE 7–8 Style S1: HT/LR

Source: Copyright © 1985, 2006, Leadership Studies, Inc. All Rights Reserved.

and needs direction. Other one-word descriptors for this leadership style include *guiding, directing*, or *structuring*. Figure 7–8 summarizes the telling style and presents one-word descriptors of effective and ineffective approaches at Performance Readiness® Level 1.[13]

The appropriate leader behaviors for an *unable and insecure R1*:

- Provide task information in digestible amounts
- Be sure not to overwhelm the follower
- Reduce fear of mistakes
- Help step by step
- Focus on instruction

For an *unable and unwilling R1* would be to:

- Directly state specific facts
- Positively reinforce small improvements
- Consider consequences for nonperformance
- Keep emotional level in check

Matching Performance Readiness® Level 2 with Leadership Style S2—Selling

The next range of Performance Readiness® is Performance Readiness® Level 2. This is an individual or group that is still unable, but they are willing or confident. The high probability styles are combinations of high amounts of both task and relationship behavior. The task behavior is appropriate because people are still unable. But since they are trying, it is important to be supportive of their motivation and commitment.

This S2 style is *selling*. It is different from telling in that the leader is not only providing the guidance but is also providing the opportunity for dialogue and for clarification in order to help the person "buy in" to what the leader wants. If a leader simply says, "Go stand by the door and keep people from coming through," that is *telling*. On the other hand, if the leader suggests, "I'd sure appreciate it if you would be willing to stand by the door to guide people around the classroom because people coming through here have been disruptive," this would be an example of *selling*. The follower can ask questions and get clarification, even though the leader has provided the guidance.

The definition of task behavior includes providing the "what, how, when, where, and who." The reason that "why" is not included is that efforts to explain why bridge both task and relationship behaviors. One of the differences between telling and selling is that selling answers "why" questions. Other words for style S2 include *explaining, persuading*, and *clarifying*. Figure 7–9 summarizes the selling style and presents one-word descriptors of effective and ineffective approaches at Performance Readiness® Level 2.

The appropriate leader behaviors for an *unable but willing* or *unable but confident R2* would be to:

- Seek "buy-in" through persuading
- Check understanding of the task
- Encourage questions
- Discuss details
- Explore related skills

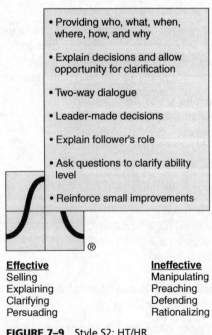

• Providing who, what, when, where, how, and why

• Explain decisions and allow opportunity for clarification

• Two-way dialogue

• Leader-made decisions

• Explain follower's role

• Ask questions to clarify ability level

• Reinforce small improvements

Effective	**Ineffective**
Selling	Manipulating
Explaining	Preaching
Clarifying	Defending
Persuading	Rationalizing

FIGURE 7–9   Style S2: HT/HR

Source: Copyright © 1985, 2006, Leadership Studies, Inc. All Rights Reserved.

- Explain "why"
- Give follower incremental steps (not "run with it")
- Emphasize "how to"

Matching Performance Readiness® Level 3 with Leadership Style S3—Participating

Performance Readiness® Level 3 would include a person or group that is able but has just developed ability and has not had an opportunity to gain confidence in doing it on their own. An example is the fledgling salesperson who goes out on a sales call for the first time without the sales manager.

Performance Readiness® Level 3 could also be a person or group that was able and willing, but for one reason or another is slipping in terms of motivation. Perhaps they are upset, mad at the supervisor, or just tired of performing this behavior and, therefore, are becoming unwilling.

In either case, the appropriate behavior would be high amounts of two-way communication and supportive behavior but low amounts of guidance. Because the group has already shown that they are able to perform the task, it is not necessary to provide high amounts of what to do, where to do it, or how to do it. Discussion, support, and facilitating behaviors would tend to be more appropriate for solving the problem or soothing the apprehension.

In *participating,* the leader's major role becomes encouraging and communicating. Other descriptors for this style of leadership include *collaborating, facilitating*, and *committing*. Each of these terms implies high relationship, low task behaviors. Figure 7–10 summarizes the participating style and presents one-word descriptors of effective and ineffective approaches at Performance Readiness® Level 3.

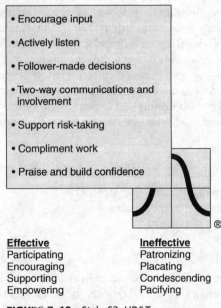

- Encourage input
- Actively listen
- Follower-made decisions
- Two-way communications and involvement
- Support risk-taking
- Compliment work
- Praise and build confidence

Effective	**Ineffective**
Participating	Patronizing
Encouraging	Placating
Supporting	Condescending
Empowering	Pacifying

FIGURE 7–10 Style S3: HR/LT

Source: Copyright © 1985, 2006, Leadership Studies, Inc. All Rights Reserved.

The appropriate leader behaviors for an *able but insecure R3*:

- Combine leader-follower decision making
- Determine next step
- Encourage and support
- Discuss apprehension

For an *able but unwilling R3* would be to:

- Share responsibility for decision making with the follower
- Feed the follower's "need to know"
- Focus on results
- Involve the follower in consequences of task to increase commitment and motivation

---

> Encouragement is a necessary part of supervision.
> —Thomas J. Watson

Matching Performance Readiness® Level 4 with Leadership Style S4—Delegating

Performance Readiness® Level 4 is where the individual or group is both able and willing or able and confident. They have had enough opportunity to practice, and they feel comfortable without the leader providing direction.

It is unnecessary to provide direction about where, what, when, or how because the followers already have the ability. Similarly, above-average amounts of encouraging and supportive behaviors are not necessary because the group is confident, committed, and motivated. The appropriate style involves giving them the ball and letting them run with it.

This style is called *delegating*. Other words for this leadership style include *observing* and *monitoring*. Remember—some relationship behavior is still needed, but it tends to be less than average. It is still appropriate to monitor what is going on, but it is important to give these followers an opportunity to take responsibility and implement on their own.

The appropriate leader behaviors for *an able and willing or confident R4* would be to:

- Listen to updates
- Resist overloading
- Encourage autonomy
- Practice overall hands-off management; observe
- Reinforce follower-led communications
- Provide support and resources
- Delegate activities
- Encourage freedom for risk taking

One point to remember is that when an individual or group is *developing*, the issue is usually one of insecurity; when they are *regressing*, the issue is usually one of unwillingness. We will go into these ideas in greater detail in subsequent chapters. Figure 7–11 summarizes the delegating style and presents one-word descriptors of effective and ineffective approaches at Performance Readiness® Level 4.

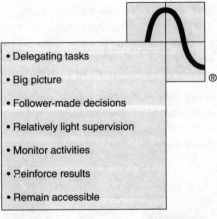

- Delegating tasks
- Big picture
- Follower-made decisions
- Relatively light supervision
- Monitor activities
- Reinforce results
- Remain accessible

Effective	**Ineffective**
Delegating	Abandoning
Observing	Dumping
Entrusting	Avoiding
Assigning	Withdrawing

FIGURE 7–11 Style S4: LR/LT

Source: Copyright © 1985, 2006, Leadership Studies, Inc. All Rights Reserved.

Appropriate Leadership Styles

The appropriate leadership styles for the four Performance Readiness® designations—low (R1), low to moderate (R2), moderate to high (R3), and high (R4)—are telling (S1), selling (S2), participating (S3), and delegating (S4), respectively. That is, low Performance Readiness® needs a telling style, low to moderate Performance Readiness® needs a selling style, and so on. These combinations are shown in Table 7–1.

TABLE 7–1	Leadership Styles Appropriate for Various Performance Readiness® Levels
Performance Readiness® Level	**Appropriate Style**
R1, Low Performance Readiness®	S1, Telling
Unable and unwilling or insecure	High task-low relationship
R2, Low to Moderate Performance Readiness®	S2, Selling
Unable but willing or confident	High task-high relationship
R3, Moderate to High Performance Readiness®	S3, Participating
Able but unwilling or insecure	High relationship-low task
R4, High Performance Readiness®	S4, Delegating
Able and willing or confident	Low relationship-low task

Situational Leadership® not only suggests the high probability leadership style for various Performance Readiness® Levels, but also indicates the probability of success of the other style configurations if a leader does not use the desired style. The probability of success of each style for the four Performance Readiness® Levels depends on how far the style deviates from the high probability style. The probability of success tends to be as follows:

- *R1*. S1 high, S2 moderate to high, S3 moderate to low, S4 low probability
- *R2*. S2 high, S1 moderate to high, S3 moderate to low, S4 low probability
- *R3*. S3 high, S2 moderate to high, S4 moderate to low, S1 low probability
- *R4*. S4 high, S3 moderate to high, S2 moderate to low, S1 low probability

When leaders use Situational Leadership® it is the *follower* who determines the appropriate leader behavior. The follower can get any behavior desired because it is the follower's behavior that determines the leader's behavior. And Situational Leadership® can be used at home, at the office, and in any kind of interpersonal situation. Think of how much easier parenting would be if children were to realize that Mom and Dad do not determine and control their behavior; *they* control both of their own behavior and that of Mom and Dad.

Why is it that a leadership style that may not be our "natural" style is frequently our most *effective* style? The reason is that we have worked at these learned styles, we have practiced and practiced those behaviors, and we have worked at them with some expert help. We have also paid attention to the details of applying these learned styles. We do not put the same amount of skill practice into our natural style as we do our learned styles. As a consequence, our natural styles may not be as effective.

Situational Leadership® is not a prescription with hard-and-fast rules. In the behavioral sciences, there are no absolute rules. Situational Leadership® attempts to improve the odds that managers will be able to become effective and successful leaders.

> "Leadership is much more an art, a belief, a condition of the heart, than a set of things to do. The visible signs of artful leadership are expressed, ultimately, in its practice."
> —Max DePree

APPLICATION OF SITUATIONAL LEADERSHIP®

In using Situational Leadership®, one should always keep in mind that there is no one best way to influence others. Rather, any leader behavior may be more or less effective depending on the Performance Readiness® Level of the person you are attempting to influence. Shown in Figure 7–12 is a comprehensive version of the Situational Leadership® Model that brings together our discussion of the past several pages. It will provide you with a quick reference to assist in (1) *diagnosing* the level of Performance Readiness®, (2) *adapting* by selecting high probability leadership styles, and (3) *communicating* these styles effectively to influence behavior. Implicit in Situational Leadership® is the idea that a leader should help followers grow in Performance Readiness® as far as they are able and willing to go. This development of followers should be done by adjusting leadership style through the four styles along the leadership curve in Figure 7–12.

Situational Leadership® contends that strong direction (task behavior) with followers with low Performance Readiness® is appropriate if they are to become productive. Similarly, it suggests that an increase in Performance Readiness® on the part of people who are somewhat

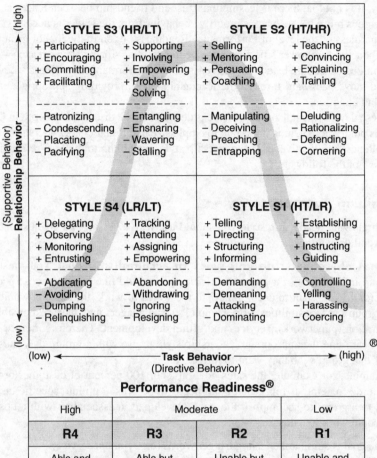

Situational Leadership®
Influence Behavior Descriptors

(high) ↑

(Supportive Behavior)
Relationship Behavior

STYLE S3 (HR/LT)

+ Participating   + Supporting
+ Encouraging   + Involving
+ Committing   + Empowering
+ Facilitating   + Problem
                     Solving

– Patronizing   – Entangling
– Condescending   – Ensnaring
– Placating   – Wavering
– Pacifying   – Stalling

STYLE S2 (HT/HR)

+ Selling   + Teaching
+ Mentoring   + Convincing
+ Persuading   + Explaining
+ Coaching   + Training

– Manipulating   – Deluding
– Deceiving   – Rationalizing
– Preaching   – Defending
– Entrapping   – Cornering

STYLE S4 (LR/LT)

+ Delegating   + Tracking
+ Observing   + Attending
+ Monitoring   + Assigning
+ Entrusting   + Empowering

– Abdicating   – Abandoning
– Avoiding   – Withdrawing
– Dumping   – Ignoring
– Relinquishing   – Resigning

STYLE S1 (HT/LR)

+ Telling   + Establishing
+ Directing   + Forming
+ Structuring   + Instructing
+ Informing   + Guiding

– Demanding   – Controlling
– Demeaning   – Yelling
– Attacking   – Harassing
– Dominating   – Coercing

(low) ↓

(low) ◄———— **Task Behavior** ————► (high)
(Directive Behavior)

®

Performance Readiness®

High	Moderate		Low
R4	**R3**	**R2**	**R1**
Able and Confident and Willing	Able but Insecure or Unwilling	Unable but Confident or Willing	Unable and Insecure or Unwilling

Self Directed   Leader Directed

+ When the leadership style is appropriately matched to the performance readiness® level and/or the leader's skill of delivering the style is effective.

– When the style is not a match with the performance readiness® level and/or the leader's skill of delivering the style is inadequate.

FIGURE 7–12 Expanded Situational Leadership® Model

Source: Situational Leadership® and Performance Readiness® are trademarks of Leadership Studies, Inc. Copyright © 1985, 2006, Leadership Studies, Inc. All Rights Reserved.

unready should be rewarded by increased positive reinforcement and socioemotional support (relationship behavior). Finally, as followers reach high levels of Performance Readiness®, the leader should respond not only by continuing to decrease control over their activities but also by continuing to decrease relationship behavior. People with high Performance Readiness® do not need socioemotional support as much as they need greater freedom. At this stage, one of the ways leaders can prove their confidence and trust in these people is to give them more and more autonomy. It is not that there is less mutual trust and friendship between leader and follower. In reality, there is more because less supportive behavior from the leader is needed.

Regardless of the level of Performance Readiness® of an individual or group, change may occur. Whenever a follower's performance begins to slip—for whatever reason—and ability or motivation decreases, the leader should reassess the Performance Readiness® Level of this follower and move backward through the leadership curve, providing appropriate socioemotional support and direction.

These developmental and regressive processes will be discussed in depth in Chapters 9 and 10. At this point, though, it is important to emphasize that Situational Leadership® focuses on the appropriateness or effectiveness of leadership styles according to the *task-relevant Performance Readiness®* of the followers.

Determining Appropriate Style

To determine what leadership style you should use with a person in a given situation, you must make several decisions.

What objective(s) do you want to accomplish? First, you must decide what areas of an individual's or a group's activities you would like to influence. Specifically, what objective(s) do you want to accomplish? In the world of work, those areas would vary according to a group's responsibilities. For example, sales managers may have responsibilities in sales, administration (paperwork), service, and group development. Therefore, before managers can begin to determine the appropriate leadership style to use with a group, they must decide what aspect of that group's job they want to influence.

Examine, for example, the sales goal "to ship 100 percent of customer orders within 24 hours of order receipt" is too general and needs to be broken up into specific tasks that can be assigned to a group to accomplish the goal. Developed in association with a customer service unit, it would work like this:

1. The goal is summarized using trigger words (e.g., *prompt service).*
2. Tasks to accomplish the goal are identified by the people involved.
   a. Answering the phone
   b. Completing the order form
   c. Completing the packing order
   d. Shipping the order
   e. Adjusting service problems

What is the Group's Performance Readiness®? The sales manager must then diagnose the Performance Readiness® of the group to accomplish these tasks. The key issue is how ready or receptive is the group to accomplish these tasks? If the group is at a high level of Performance Readiness®, only a low amount of leadership intervention will be required. If, on the other hand, the group is at a low level of Performance Readiness®, considerable leadership intervention may be required.

What Leadership Action Should be Taken? The next step is deciding which of the four leadership styles (see Table 7–1) would be appropriate for the group. Suppose the manager has determined that the group's Performance Readiness® Level is high in terms of accomplishing all of these tasks—that is, the group is able and willing (R4). Using Table 7–1, the manager would know that when working with this group, a delegating (S4) style (low task–low relationship behavior) should be used. Some members of the group may be lower in Performance Readiness® than the group as a whole with respect to specific tasks. For example, a team member may be R3 (able but insecure) with regard to responding to service problems on a new line of equipment. The manager should use an S3 (high relationship–low task) leadership style with that person to build confidence and self-esteem.

What was the Result of the Leadership Intervention? This step requires assessment to determine if results match expectations. As will be discussed in Chapter 10, individuals and groups learn a little bit at a time. Development involves positively reinforcing successive approximations as the individual or group approaches the desired level of performance. Therefore, after a leadership intervention, the manager must assess the result through rechecking the objectives, rediagnosing Performance Readiness®, and ascertaining if further leadership is indicated.

What Follow-up, If Any, is Required? If there is a gap between the present performance and desired performance of the individual or group, then follow-up is required in the form of additional leadership interventions, and the cycle starts again. In a dynamic leadership environment, follow-up is almost a certainty. Leadership under modern competitive conditions means hitting moving targets. Tasks, Performance Readiness®, and results are all continually changing; follow-up is a must. Leading is a full-time job that must be practiced every hour of every day.

Effective Task Statements

A well-formulated task statement contributes greatly toward the assessment of individual Performance Readiness®. In contrast, vague and weakly formulated task statements make it difficult to accurately assess task Performance Readiness®, and can lead to unnecessary friction and conflict. Gustav Pansegrouw, president of P-E Corporate Services, a management consulting firm, found the following technique for writing task statements very useful, particularly from the follower's perspective. A key task for a customer order clerk may be stated as follows:

To answer the phone promptly.

Using this task statement as a guide, the manager may assess the clerk's task Performance Readiness® Level as R2, willing but unable. Using the same task statement as a guide, the clerk may assess the task Performance Readiness® Level as R4, willing and able.

This difference in task Performance Readiness® assessment between the manager and clerk is usually the result of different meanings attached to the word *promptly*. If the task were formulated in the following way, the two persons would have a much clearer understanding of the task.

To answer the phone on the first ring.

With such a specific statement of the task as a guide, it becomes much easier to assess task-relevant Performance Readiness®. The probability of agreement between the two parties' assessments also increases.

The major difference between the two task statements just presented is that the second one contains a *clearly defined and measurable performance standard* for the task. The *expected performance* is thus an *integral part* of the task.

Of all the aspects of accomplishing tasks, individual Performance Readiness® is the most critical. At any given time, each person is at a variety of task-specific Performance Readiness® Levels, depending on the tasks that must be performed. It is not that an individual is high or low in Performance Readiness® since the level varies according to the specific task.

It should be remembered that, although Performance Readiness® is a useful concept for making diagnostic judgments, other situational variables—the supervisor's style (if close by), a crisis or time bind, the nature of the work—can be of equal or greater importance. Yet, the Performance Readiness® concept is a solid benchmark for choosing the appropriate style with an individual or group at a particular time.

Direction of Performance Readiness® Change

Recent research at the Center for Leadership Studies has indicated that it is useful to measure not only a follower's general level of Performance Readiness®, such as R1 or R2, but also the *direction* of this Performance Readiness®. The primary reason is that there are important differences in leader behavior if the follower's Performance Readiness® is increasing, decreasing, or static.

For example, place yourself in the role of leader in each of three situations. Recall that one aspect of your role as leader is to diagnose the follower's ability and willingness to respond to your efforts to implement a specific goal. In other words, how receptive is the follower in each of these situations to your leadership efforts?

- *Situation 1.* The follower's confidence, commitment, and motivation are low and are continuing to decline. Knowledge, experience, and skill remain marginal.
- *Situation 2.* The follower's knowledge, skill, and experience are increasing from an entry level, while confidence, commitment, and motivation remain low.
- *Situation 3.* Ability and willingness remain low; the follower is unable and insecure.

After reading the three situations, you can diagnose the appropriate Performance Readiness® Level by looking for the key elements of ability and willingness. Remember that ability has the three components of knowledge, experience, and skill, while willingness has the three components of confidence, commitment, and motivation. One convenient way of assessing these components is to use a scale from + + + for a high level of Performance Readiness® to − − − for a low level of Performance Readiness®.

Suppose you have made the correct diagnosis that the follower is R1—unable and insecure or unwilling regarding the task. You now want to diagnose the direction of the follower's Performance Readiness®. Does the information in each situation show any elements that seem to be increasing, decreasing, or remaining static?

In situation 1, the follower is declining in Performance Readiness®; in situation 2, the follower is increasing in Performance Readiness®; and in situation 3, the follower remains static or unchanged in Performance Readiness®.

What is the implication of this analysis to your leadership efforts? In each situation, the follower's general level of Performance Readiness® is R1. But does that mean that your leadership interventions should be the same? Probably not. Situation 1 suggests action to correct regressive behavior, situation 2 suggests continuing developmental behavior, and situation 3 suggests initiating developmental behavior. Each of these potential leadership interventions will be discussed further in Chapters 9 and 10.

Instruments to Measure Performance Readiness®

To help managers and their followers make valid judgments about follower Performance Readiness®, the Center for Leadership Studies has developed two Performance Readiness® scale instruments: *the manager rating scale* and *the staff rating scale.*[14] Both leadership instruments measure job Performance Readiness® (ability) and psychological Performance Readiness® (willingness) on five behavioral dimensions.

In the manager rating scale, for example, the manager selects one to five of the staff member's major objectives or responsibilities and writes them on the form. Then, with respect to each major objective or responsibility, the manager rates the staff member on five job Performance Readiness® dimensions and five psychological Performance Readiness® dimensions, basing the rating on observations of the staff member's behavior. Two of the five items from the job Performance Readiness® dimension and two of the five items from the psychological Performance Readiness® dimension are illustrated in Figure 7–13. The 10 items used on the instrument were selected after a pilot study from a pool of more than 30 indicators of each of the two dimensions. Note that behavioral indicators—e.g., "Has experience relevant to the job" and "Does not have experience relevant to the job"—are included. The staff rating scale instrument is designed the same way, but the staff member fills it out on their perception of their Performance Readiness®.

In more recent work, the Center for Leadership Studies developed a Performance Readiness® style match rating form that permits managers and their staff members to rate leadership style and Performance Readiness® on the same instrument. Figure 7–14 shows that integration. This instrument measures Performance Readiness® using only one scale for each dimension—one measuring *ability* and the other measuring *willingness.*[15] In this instrument, a person's ability (knowledge, skill, and experience) is thought of as a matter of degree. That is, an individual's ability does not change drastically from one moment to the next. At any given moment, an individual has a little, some, quite a bit, or a great deal of ability.

Your name _____ Today's date _____

Your staff member's name _____

		In performing the objective _____ this person							
Job Readiness Dimensions	1. Past job experience	Has experience relevant to the job				Does not have experience relevant to the job			
		8	7	6	5	4	3	2	1
	2. Job knowledge	Possesses necessary job knowledge				Does not have necessary job knowledge			
		8	7	6	5	4	3	2	1
Psychological Readiness Dimensions	1. Willingness to take responsibility	Is very eager							Is very reluctant
		8	7	6	5	4	3	2	1
	2. Achievement motivation	Has a high desire to achieve						Has little desire to achieve	
		8	7	6	5	4	3	2	1

FIGURE 7–13 Representative Sections from Performance Readiness® Scale: Manager Rating Scale

Source: Copyright © 1985, 2006, Leadership Studies, Inc. All Rights Reserved.

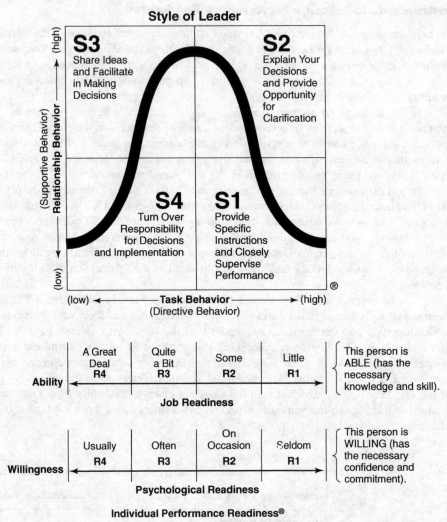

FIGURE 7–14   Defining Performance Readiness® and the Four Basic Leadership Styles

Source: Copyright © 1985, 2006, Leadership Studies, Inc. All Rights Reserved.

Willingness (confidence, commitment, and motivation), however, is different. A person's motivation can, and often does, fluctuate from one moment to another. Therefore, a person is seldom, on occasion, often, or usually willing to take responsibility in a particular area.

The use of both a *manager's rating scale* and a *staff member's scale* of the Performance Readiness® style match is necessary to initiate a program combining Situational Leadership® with *Contracting for Leadership Style.*[16] We will discuss that process in some detail in Chapter 11.

Components of Leadership Style

Once managers have identified the Performance Readiness® Level of the individual or group they are attempting to influence, the key to effective leadership is then to apply the appropriate leadership style. How can managers gain a greater understanding of the behaviors of each leadership style?

Instruments to Measure Leader Behavior   To help managers and their staff members make better judgments about leadership style, the Center for Leadership Studies has developed two leadership scale instruments: *Leadership Scale: Perception by Manager* and *Leadership Scale: Perception by Staff Member.*[17] Both leadership instruments measure task and relationship behavior on five behavioral dimensions. The five task behavior dimensions and five relationship behavior dimensions are listed in Table 7–2.

After the five dimensions were established for both leader behaviors, behavioral indicators of the extremes of each of these dimensions were identified to help managers and their staff members differentiate between high and low amounts of each leader behavior. For example, with the task behavior dimension "organizing" on the staff member form, the end points of a rating scale were chosen to be "organizes the work situation for me" and "lets me organize the work situation." For the relationship behavior dimension "providing feedback," the end points of the rating scale were chosen to be "frequently provides feedback on my accomplishments" and "leaves it up to me to evaluate accomplishments."

TABLE 7–2	Task Behavior and Relationship Behavior Dimensions and Their Behavioral Indicators

Task Behavior Dimension	Behavioral Indicator
	The extent to which a leader:
Goal setting	Specifies the goals people are to accomplish
Organizing	Organizes the work situation for people
Setting timelines	Sets timelines for people
Directing	Provides specific directions
Controlling	Specifies and requires regular reporting on progress

Relationship Behavior Dimension	Behavioral Indicator
	The extent to which a leader:
Giving support	Provides support and encouragement
Communicating	Involves people in "give and take" discussions about work activities
Facilitating interactions	Facilitates people's interactions with others
Active listening	Seeks out and listens to people's opinions and concerns
Providing feedback	Provides feedback on people's accomplishments

In the Performance Readiness® style match instrument, each of the four basic leadership styles is described as shown in Figure 7–14:

- *Telling (S1)*. Provide specific instructions and closely supervise performance
- *Selling (S2)*. Explain decisions and provide opportunity for clarification
- *Participating (S3)*. Share ideas and facilitate in making decisions
- *Delegating (S4)*. Turn over responsibility for decisions and implementation

Summary

Situational Leadership® is based on an interplay among (1) the amount of guidance and direction (task behavior) a leader gives; (2) the amount of socioemotional support (relationship behavior) a leader provides; and (3) the Performance Readiness® Level that followers exhibit in performing a specific task, function, or objective.

Performance Readiness® has two main components: ability and willingness.

Ability is the knowledge, experience, and skill that an individual or group brings to a particular task or activity.

Willingness is the extent to which an individual or group has the confidence, commitment, and motivation to accomplish a specific task.

According to Situational Leadership®, there is no one best way to influence people. The leadership style depends on the Performance Readiness® Level of the followers the leader is attempting to influence. The following chapters will help leaders select the highest probability style to use in different situations.

Notes

1. Edgar H. Schein, *Organizational Psychology* (Englewood Cliffs, NJ: Prentice Hall, 1965), 61.
2. Stephen R. Covey, *7 Habits of Highly Effective People* (New York: Free Press, 1989), 235–260.
3. Chris Argyris, *Overcoming Organizational Defenses: Facilitating Organizational Learning* (New York: Prentice-Hall, 1990); see also Peter Senge, *The Fifth Discipline*. New York: Doubleday, 1994.
4. Situational Leadership® was first published by Paul Hersey and Kenneth H. Blanchard as "Life Cycle Theory of Leadership" in *Training and Development Journal*, May 1969.
5. Kenneth Blanchard, Patricia Zigarmi, and Drea Zigarmi, *Leadership and the One Minute Manager* (New York: William Morrow, 1985). For further information on SLII®, contact Blanchard Training and Development, Inc., 125 State Place, Escondido, CA 92029. See

also Appendix A, an adaptation of an article by Paul Hersey and Ken Blanchard, "Life Cycle Theory of Leadership," published in the special 50th Anniversary Edition of *Training and Development*, January 1996.
6. Fillmore H. Sanford, *Authoritarianism and Leadership* (Philadelphia: Institute for Research in Human Relations, 1950).
7. The following section has been adopted from Paul Hersey, *Situational Selling* (Escondido, CA: Center for Leadership Studies, 1985), 19ff.
8. *Ibid.*
9. *Ibid.*
10. *Ibid.*, p. 22.
11. *Ibid.*, pp. 25–26.
12. A pocket guide to Situational Leadership® is available from the Center for Leadership Studies, Escondido, CA 92025.

13. These ideas were developed by Ron Campbell, Center for Leadership Studies, Escondido, CA.

14. These two instruments, originally using the term *maturity*, were developed by Ronald K. Hambleton, Kenneth H. Blanchard, and Paul Hersey through a grant from Xerox Corporation. We are grateful to Xerox Corporation not only for providing financial support for the instrument development project, but also for allowing us to involve many of their managers and employees in our development and validation work. In particular, we thank Audian Dunham, Warren Rothman, and Ray Gumpert for their assistance, encouragement, and constructive criticism of our work. The instruments are available through the Center for Leadership Studies, Escondido, CA.

15. These instruments, originally using the term *maturity*, were developed by Paul Hersey, Kenneth H. Blanchard, and Joseph Keilty. Information on these instruments is available through Center for Leadership Studies, Escondido, CA.

16. The integration of Situational Leadership® with Contracting for Leadership Styles was first published as Paul Hersey, Kenneth H. Blanchard, and Ronald K. Hambleton, "Contracting for Leadership Style: A Process and Instrumentation for Building Effective Work Relationships" in *The Proceedings of OD'78,* San Francisco, CA, sponsored by University Associates/LRC. This presentation is available through the Center for Leadership Studies, Escondido, CA.

17. The initial versions of these leadership scales were developed by Paul Hersey, Kenneth H. Blanchard, and Ronald K. Hambleton. Information on these instruments is available through the Center for Leadership Studies, Escondido, CA.

8

Situational Leadership®:

The Perception and Impact of Power

L eaders are often referred to as those "in power." Certainly power is closely related to leadership, since it is one of the means by which a leader influences the behavior of followers.[1] But it is not necessarily synonymous, as we will see in this chapter. An important part of developing your self-awareness as a leader is to understand not only how you actually influence other people, but also the extent to which you possess and use your power.[2]

> "Nearly all men can stand adversity but if you want to test a man's character, give him power."
> —Abraham Lincoln

POWER DEFINED

Earlier we defined leadership as any attempt to influence another individual or group. *Power is influence potential*—a resource that may enable a leader to gain compliance or commitment from others. Despite its critical importance, power is a subject that is often avoided, perhaps because it has been misunderstood and abused by some in leadership roles. But leaders who understand and know how to use power are more effective than those who either do not or will not use it. To successfully influence the behavior of others, the leader should understand the impact of power on the various leadership styles we have introduced in previous chapters. With the trend toward downsizing, outsourcing, and flatter organizations, many sources of power within organizations have been legislated, negotiated, or administered away. As Pfeiffer suggests, getting things done in more networked, less-hierarchical systems will require even more skilled influence efforts by managers.[3] Since you may have fewer types of power to draw from than in the past, it is even more important to effectively use the power bases that are available to enhance your effectiveness as a leader.

Despite the widespread usage of the term *power* in management literature, there are many definitions.[4] James Hillman reports that power's "rather innocent definition is simply the agency to act, to do, to be, coming from the Latin *potere*, to be able . . . power can be defined as sheer potency or potentiality, not the doing, but the capacity to do."[5] John B. Miner defined power as "the ability to induce a person to do something he or she would not otherwise have done." He goes on to add, "Influence is a broader concept, referring to anything a person does to alter the behavior, attitudes, values, feelings, and such of another person . . . . Power is thus one form of influence."[6] Stephen P. Robbins specifies three key aspects of power:

> Power refers to a capacity that A has to influence the behavior of B, so that B does something that he or she would not otherwise do. This definition implies (1) a *potential* that need not be actualized to be effective, (2) a *dependence relationship*, and (3) that B has some *discretion* over his or her own behavior.[7]

While each of these definitions has some validity, we agree with Rogers' simple definition of power as "the potential for influence."[8]

Power is, then, a resource that may or may not be used. The use of power resulting in a change in the probability that a person or group will adopt the desired behavioral change is defined as "influence." Therefore, leadership is any attempt to influence and power is a leader's *influence potential*. It is the resource that enables a leader to influence.

POSITION POWER AND PERSONAL POWER

"Power" has been further differentiated by numerous authors and practitioners. Amitai Etzioni was among the first to describe individuals who are able to induce other individuals to comply and take action because of their position in the organization as having position power; those who derive their power from their followers are considered to have personal power. Some are skilled enough to have both.[9]

Where do managers get the position power that is available to them? When you are hired or promoted into a higher level role, it may seem that you suddenly have more power. In reality, you may have more resources, a greater scope of responsibility, or more people who report to you. But the position itself does not have power in and of itself. Managers occupying positions in an organization may have more or less position power than their predecessor or a peer in a similar role in the same organization. *Position power* is the extent to which those people to whom managers report are willing to delegate authority and responsibility to them. So position power tends to flow down in an organization. This is not to say that leaders do not have any impact on how much position power they accrue. They certainly do. The confidence and trust they develop with the people around them will often determine the willingness of upper management to delegate to them. Remember, though, that whatever power is delegated downward can also be taken back. We have all seen this occur when managers still have the same responsibilities, but their authority (to distribute rewards and sanctions) to get the job done has been taken away.

> "Commitment is nice, but doses of compliance may be necessary."
> —Michael Beer, Harvard Business Review

Personal power is the extent to which followers respect, feel good about, and are committed to their leader. They believe that their own needs and goals will be recognized, supported, and facilitated by their leader. In other words, personal power is the extent to which people are willing to follow a leader. As a result, personal power in an organizational setting comes from below—from the followers—and so flows up in an organization. Thus, we must be careful when we say that some leaders are charismatic or have personal power that flows from them. Personal power is not inherent in the leader. If it were, managers with personal power could take over any department and have the same commitment and rapport they had in their last department. We know that they cannot. Although managers certainly can influence the amount of personal power they have by the way they treat their people, it is a subjective and volatile kind of power. It can be taken away rapidly by followers. Make a few dramatic mistakes and see how many people are willing to follow you. Personal power is a day-to-day phenomenon—it can be earned and it can be taken away. As McClelland and Burnham have noted, the personal power of a good manager can only be sustained when it is oriented toward the company and people he or she serves, and not personal aggrandizement.[10] In a compatible view, Janet Hagberg sees personal power in organizations as a result of both external power—the capacity for action (which includes influence)—with internal power—the capacity for reflection (awareness of self, others, and a greater purpose).[11] Personal power, by any definition, is a critical part of having and demonstrating emotional intelligence.

> "The first duty of a leader is to make himself be loved without courting love. To be loved without 'playing up' to anyone—even to himself."
> —Andre Malraux

> "Dignity does not come in possessing honors, but in deserving them."
> —Aristotle

Etzioni suggested that leaders should have both personal power and position power. But in some cases it is not possible to build a relationship on both. The question then becomes whether it is more important to have personal power or position power. Happiness and human relations have been culturally reinforced over the past several decades. With this emphasis, most people would pick personal power as being the most important, but there is another side of this coin.

In his sixteenth-century treatise *The Prince*, Machiavelli presented an interesting viewpoint when he raised the question of whether it is better to have a relationship based on love (personal power) or fear (position power).[12] Machiavelli contended, as did Etzioni, that it is best to be both loved and feared. If, however, one cannot have both, he suggested that a relationship based on love alone tends to be volatile, short-lived, and easily terminated when there is no fear of retaliation. On the other hand, a relationship based on fear tends to be longer-lasting, because the individual must be ready to incur the sanction (pay the price) before terminating the relationship. This is a difficult concept for many people to accept. One of the most difficult roles for leaders—whether they be a supervisor, teacher, or parent—is disciplining someone they care about. Yet, to be effective at enhancing others' growth and development, leaders sometimes have to sacrifice short-term friendship for long-term respect. Machiavelli warned, however, that one should be careful that this fear (amount of position power) does not lead to hatred. Hatred often evokes overt behavior in terms of retaliation, undermining, and attempts to overthrow.

In summary, position power can be thought of as the authority, which is delegated down, to use rewards and sanctions. Personal power is the cohesiveness, commitment, and rapport between leaders and followers. It is also affected by the extent to which followers see their own goals as being the same, similar to, or at least dependent upon the accomplishment of the leader's goals.

Although personal and position power are distinct, they are an interacting influence system. Often, followers are affected by their perceptions of both the leader's ability to provide rewards, punishments, and sanctions and the leader's ability to influence up the organization. As Pfeiffer has pointed out, although money can provide leverage it is not the only source of power; access to information or influential people can be even more valuable.[13] The extent to which people above you in the organization are willing to delegate position power is often dependent on their perception of the followers' commitment to you. So it is not sufficient to have either position or personal power alone—a leader needs to work at gaining both.

Selling within Your Own Organization

It is important to keep in mind that no matter where you are within your organization, you are trying to influence people.[14] If you are managing, you can use both position power and personal power to influence the people who report directly to you. When attempting to influence your supervisor, senior executives, and associates, however, you must depend almost exclusively on personal power. Therefore, you are selling. When you have little or no position power, you must learn to develop rapport through personal power, because it is through this trust and confidence that an effective relationship can be built. Figure 8–1 illustrates this important idea. Keep in mind that power is a real-world issue. People who understand and know how to use power are more effective than those who do not or will not. Recognition of the fact that all managers are in the business of selling is an important aspect of this understanding.

Supervisor/Associates

Selling

Leadership = Influence

Managing

Staff Members/Employees

FIGURE 8–1 Selling Up/ Managing Down

Source: Copyright © 1985, 2006, Leadership Studies, Inc. All Rights Reserved.

Additional Bases of Power

Although position power and personal power are important and useful concepts in examining power, they are limited because they force you to divide "the pie" into just two pieces. R. L. Peabody named four categories of power on the basis of statements of questionnaire respondents in a police department, a welfare office, and an elementary school: power of legitimacy (laws, rules, policies); of position; of competence (professional and technical expertise); and of person.[15]

A study by A. C. Filley and A. J. Grimes identified 11 reasons why an individual would seek a decision from another on various work-related matters in a professional organization.[16] These reasons, from most frequently to least frequently mentioned, were: responsibility and function (the person is responsible for the particular matter); formal authority (the person is in a position to make decisions generally); control of resources (the person controls money, information, and so on); collegial (a group of peers has the right to be consulted); manipulation (the person can get the decision made in the manner desired); default or avoidance (the person is available and will deal with the problem); bureaucratic rules (the rules specify the person to consult); traditional rules (custom, tradition, or seniority specify the person to consult); equity (the person is a fair decision maker); friendship (the person is personally liked); and expertise (the person has superior knowledge of the subject).

Many other power base classification systems have been developed,[17] but the framework devised by J. R. P. French and B. Raven[18] appears to be the most widely accepted. They proposed that there are five bases of power: coercive power, expert power, legitimate power, referent power, and reward power. Later, Raven, collaborating with W. Kruglanski,[19] identified a sixth power base—information power. Hersey and Walt Natemeyer modified some of the definitions of French, Raven, and Kruglanski and proposed a seventh base of power—connection power.[20] We will define each of these seven power bases later in this chapter.

The Perception of Power

In the following discussion of power bases, we use the word *perceived* in such instances as "coercive power—the perceived ability to provide sanctions." We do this because the key issue in the concept of power is that it is not based on the reality of how much power the manager has but rather on the followers' perception of that power. Truth and reality evoke no behavior. All behavior is based on people's perception and interpretation of truth and reality. For example, when a couple has a fight, it does not matter whether the cause was real or imagined—it was just as much of a fight. In a similar fashion, it is the perception others hold about power that gives people the ability to influence.

We operate using psychological maps. No matter how hard we work or how detailed our psychological map, no matter how much information and specificity it contains, the map is not the actual territory. It is a mere representation. However, the closer we match our psychological map to the territory, the higher the probability that we will be able to operate effectively within that territory.

Get the Information Out

People must not only perceive you as having power, they must also see you as able and willing to use it. It is not enough to have access to power; you have to let people know you are willing to use it. Information has value only when you get it out to the end user in a fashion that can be understood and accepted.

Consider a father examining his son's report card and suffering heart palpitations as he sees a solid column of Ds. Outraged that a product of his genes could so disgrace the family, he confronts his son: "Dave, this just won't do. I can't tolerate these grades, and if you don't show me an immediate turnaround, you're going to be grounded!" Six weeks later, Dave brings home another report card. This time the Ds are written in red ink with exclamation points. The father says, "David, get in here! I'm really upset, and now you have no choice at all. Hit those books hard or you're definitely going to be grounded!"

Next time it is the same except that the teacher has added some pointed remarks about Dave's inattentive behavior in class. Dave's father turns crimson, puts down the remote control, and shouts, "David Ralph, this is it . . . last chance city . . . you're in real trouble with the old man now!" What has Dave learned? He has learned that his father, who has the ability to ground him, will not use the power! Because of his father's reluctance to follow through with his threatened punishments, Dave knows that all he has to do is take heat for six minutes and he is off the hook for six weeks!

Power is a matter of perception—use it or lose it!

Performance Readiness®, Styles, and Power Bases

The relationship between Performance Readiness®, leadership style, and the power base that drives that style will now be explained.

Coercive Power—The Perceived Ability to Provide Sanctions, Punishment, or Consequences for Not Performing

Followers at Performance Readiness® Level R1 need guidance and direction. Too much supportive behavior with people at this level who are not currently performing may be perceived as permissive or as rewarding the lack of performance. Without some coercive power to drive the telling style (S1), attempts to influence will most likely be ineffective. Followers who do not perform need to know that if they do not respond appropriately, there may be some costs, sanctions, or other consequences. These may take the form of a reprimand, cut in pay, transfer, demotion, or even termination.

Managers often erode their coercive power by not following through. They may, for instance, have the ability to impose sanctions but for one reason or another be unwilling to do so. This reluctance to use sanctions can result in a loss of power. Another way to erode coercive power is by not differentiating in the use of sanctions on the basis of performance. If people feel that they will be punished regardless of performance, coercive power has little impact on a leader's ability to influence them.

It is even possible to "talk" coercive power away. Let us say that a manager begins a performance appraisal interview with a low performer by saying, "Now, look, both of us know that you've been here over 20 years and I can't fire you." In those few words, the manager has stripped away any coercive power the follower might have perceived.

Connection Power—The Perceived Association of the Leader with Influential Persons or Organizations

Connection power is an important driver for telling (S1) and selling (S2) leadership styles. Usually, followers at R1 and R2 want to avoid the sanctions or gain the favor they associate with powerful connections. The important issue is not whether there is a real connection, but whether there is a perception of a real connection.

For example, a first-level supervisor may be regarded as having limited power. But, if that supervisor is married to a relative of the company president, the perceived connection may provide added influence with others in the organization.

Reward Power—The Perceived Ability to Provide Things That People Would Like to Have

Reward power is enhanced if managers are seen as having the ability to give appropriate rewards. Followers who are unable to currently perform a certain task but willing to make an effort (R2) are most likely to try on new behaviors if they feel increases in performance will be rewarded. Rewards may include raises, bonuses, promotions, or transfers to more desirable positions. They may also include intangibles such as a pat on the back or feedback on accomplishment. In the final analysis, managers get what they reward. Therefore, it not only matters that the reward be offered in a timely manner but also that the reward be perceived as such by the receiver. More pointedly, what constitutes a reward is indeed in the eye of the beholder.

A significant amount of reward power has been legislated, negotiated, and administered away over the last few decades. This has resulted from companies endeavoring to avoid costly litigation when they are forced to downsize, restructure, and cut costs in response to the increasingly competitive global environment. Consequently, we often have to remind managers that reward power is not only tied to monetary rewards. This may require some creative thinking, but discovering what intangibles actually motivate followers can have an enormous impact on a leader's reward power. Managers, however, often erode what little reward power they have by making promises they do not keep. For example:

> SALESPERSON: I did it! I made the 15 percent over quota with room to spare. When am I going to get that 10 percent bonus?

> SALES MANAGER: I'm sorry, but economic conditions are such that we'll have to postpone it for a while. But don't worry, if you keep up the good work, I promise I will make it up to you.

Other managers erode their reward power by "hoping for A but rewarding B."[21] An example might be an organization that gives all salespeople a 10 percent cost-of-living adjustment and yet the difference between reward for average sales and outstanding sales is only 1 or 2 percent. In this case, "hanging around" for another year is significantly rewarded. This practice often results in high performers losing their motivation and commitment or looking outside the company for opportunities. A problem with power derived from rewards is that rewards will often run their course. The manager will be left with an employee who is no longer motivated through the use of rewards and an organization that can no longer provide rewards.

Legitimate Power—The Perception That It Is Appropriate for the Leader to Make Decisions Because of Title, Role, or Position in the Organization

Legitimate power can be a useful driver for both the selling and participating leadership styles but ineffective for followers who are both unable and unwilling or insecure (R1) who generally do not care whether someone's title is manager, regional manager, or vice president. Similarly, followers high in Performance Readiness® (R4) are far less impressed with title or position than they are with expertise or information. However, followers in the moderate ranges of Performance

Readiness® (R2 or R3) can often be influenced if they feel it is appropriate for a person in that position with that title to make that decision. For example, a salesperson might comment to a peer about the department's recent reorganization: "Pat should be making those kinds of decisions . . . that's what the sales manager gets paid to do."

Referent Power—The Perceived Attractiveness of Interacting with the Leader

In attempting to influence people who are able but insecure or unwilling (R3), high relationship behavior is necessary. If people have a confidence problem, the manager needs to provide encouragement. If they have a motivation problem, the manager needs to discuss and solve problem. In either case, if the manager has not taken time to build rapport, attempts to participate may be perceived as adversarial rather than helpful. Confidence, trust, and rapport are important ingredients necessary for influencing people. If a follower feels that the manager will provide encouragement and help when it is needed, referent power can make an important difference in the success of the influence attempt. Referent power is based on the manager's personal traits like those of integrity and honesty. A manager high in referent power is generally liked and admired by others because of personality. It is liking for, admiration for, and identification with the manager that influences others.

> "Men are more often bribed by their loyalties and ambitions than by money."
> —Robert H. Jackson, U.S. Supreme Court Justice

Information Power—The Perceived Access to, or Possession of, Useful Information

The styles that tend to effectively influence followers at above-average Performance Readiness® Levels (R3 and R4) are participating (S3) and delegating (S4). Information power is most helpful in driving these styles. The utilization of this power source has grown significantly since the inception of the Internet. In fact, it has continued to grow in importance as more data become available and accessible. Those who know how to access information needed in a timely manner tend to be the ones that others seek out, and sharing that information provides an opportunity for those knowledge holders to influence the behaviors of others.

Information power is based on perceived access to data. This is different from expert power, which is the understanding of or ability to use data. For example, one study found that secretaries in a major corporate office had a significant amount of information power but little expert power in some technical areas. They were able to help gain or prevent access to information, but with the exception of a few technical areas they had little expertise themselves.

Expert Power—The Perception That the Leader Has Relevant Education, Experience, and Expertise

Followers who are competent and confident require little direction or supportive behavior. They are able and willing to perform on their own. The driver for influencing these followers is expert power. With followers who are able and confidently willing (R4), leaders are more effective if they possess the expertise, skill, and knowledge that followers respect and regard as important.

An apt example is Al Smith, former governor of New York State. When he was a freshman legislator, he spent his nights studying the New York State budget instead of attending the many social events. As Tom Peters, well-known author and commentator on the management scene, described it, "His matchless command of the fine print [of the budget] launched an extraordinary career."[22]

IS THERE A BEST TYPE OF POWER?

The French and Raven initial classification system motivated a number of scholars to try to answer the following question: Given the wide variety of power bases available to the leader, which type of power should be emphasized in order to maximize effectiveness? In any attempt to answer this question, it is important to remember the definition of effectiveness. As stated in Chapter 6, both organizational and leadership effectiveness are a function of both output variables and intervening variables.

K. R. Student studied 40 production groups in two plants of a company that manufactured home appliances.[23] Employees rated the extent to which they complied with their foremen because of each of the five French and Raven power bases. Legitimate power was found to be the strongest reason for compliance, followed by expert power, reward power, referent power, and last, coercive power.

Student also related the foremen's power base utilization (as perceived by the workers) to a number of measures of performance. He found that legitimate power, while most important among the reasons for compliance, was not related to the performance of the work groups. Reward and coercive power were positively related to some performance measures (suggestions submitted, supply cost performance) but negatively related to others (average earnings, maintenance cost performance). Expert and referent power were significantly and positively related to four and five measures of performance, respectively, and thus emerged as the two most effective bases of supervisory power. Student explained these results by suggesting that expert and referent power are qualitatively different from legitimate, reward, and coercive power. Expert and referent power are considered idiosyncratic in character and dependent on an individual's unique role behavior, whereas legitimate, reward, and coercive power are organizationally determined and designed to be equal for supervisors at the same hierarchical level. Implicit in Student's conclusions is the contention that followers are more responsive to and satisfied with a leader whose influence attempts are not based entirely on position-based power (i.e., legitimate, reward, and coercive).

Similar results were obtained in a study by J. G. Bachman, C. G. Smith, and J. A. Slesinger.[24] Data were obtained from 36 branch offices of a national sales organization. Each office was managed by a single office supervisor. Employees were asked to rank each of the five power bases according to the extent to which it was a reason for compliance. These results were then correlated with satisfaction and performance measures. Legitimate and expert power again emerged as first and second in importance, followed by referent, reward, and coercive power, in that order.

In those offices in which referent and expert power predominated, performance and satisfaction were high. In those offices in which reward power was high, performance tended to be poor and there was marked dissatisfaction. Coercive and legitimate bases of power were associated with dissatisfaction, but they were unrelated to performance.

The findings of Student and Bachman and others were included in a comparative study of five organizations by Bachman, D. G. Bowers, and P. M. Marcus.[25] In addition to the appliance firm and the sales organization, other organizations examined were 12 liberal arts colleges, 40 agencies of a life insurance company, and 21 work groups of a large mid-western utility company. A ranking procedure was used to ascertain the strength of the supervisors' power bases in the colleges and the utility company, while an independent rating procedure for each power base was used with the life insurance agencies.

Expert and legitimate power were again the most important reasons for complying with supervisors in all three organizations. Expert power was most important, and legitimate power, second, in the colleges and insurance agencies. The order was reversed in the utility company. Referent power was third in importance in the colleges, fourth in the insurance agencies, and fifth in the utility companies. Reward power was third in importance in the utility company and the agencies and fourth in the colleges. Finally, coercive power was least important in the colleges and the insurance agencies and fourth in the utility company.

Expert and referent power were again strongly and positively related to satisfaction in these three additional organizations, whereas reward and legitimate power were not strongly related to the satisfaction measures. Coercive power was consistently related to dissatisfaction. Performance data were obtained from the insurance agencies but not from the colleges or utility company. Expert and reward power were positively related to insurance agency performance measures, and coercive, legitimate, and referent power yielded insignificant correlations.

J. M. Ivancevich and J. H. Donnelly studied salespersons' perceptions of their managers' power bases in 31 branches of a large firm that produces food products.[26] The employees were asked to rank the power bases in order of importance for compliance. Expert power was most important, followed by legitimate, reward, referent, and coercive power. Referent and expert power were positively related to performance; reward, legitimate, and coercive power showed no relationship.

R. J. Burke and D. S. Wilcox conducted a study of leader power bases and follower satisfaction in six offices of a large public utility company.[27] A 1-to-5 ranking method was used. Expert power emerged as most important, followed by legitimate, coercive, referent, and reward power. Referent and expert power were associated with greatest satisfaction; legitimate and reward power were intermediate; and coercive power was associated with least satisfaction.

In summarizing a review of the most important research relating supervisory power bases to follower satisfaction and performance, Walter Natemeyer made the following general conclusion: Although expert and legitimate power bases appear to be the most important reason for compliance, and expert and referent power bases tend to be often strongly and consistently related to follower performance and satisfaction measures, the results are not clear enough to generalize about a best power base.[28] In fact, the results suggest that the appropriate power base is largely affected by situational variables. In other words, leaders may need various power bases, depending on the situation.

Power Bases and Performance Readiness® Level

Hersey and Natemeyer suggest that there is a direct relationship between the level of Performance Readiness® of individuals and groups and the kind of power bases that have a high probability of gaining compliance from those people.[29] Situational Leadership® views Performance Readiness® as the ability and willingness of individuals or groups to take responsibility for directing their own behavior in a particular situation. Thus, it must be reemphasized that Performance Readiness® is a task-specific concept and depends on what the leader is attempting to accomplish.

As people move from lower to higher levels of Performance Readiness®, their competence and confidence to do things increase. The seven power bases appear to have significant impact on the behavior of people at various levels of Performance Readiness®, as seen in Figure 8–2.

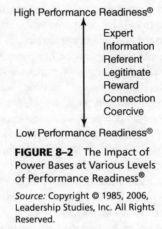

High Performance Readiness®

Expert
Information
Referent
Legitimate
Reward
Connection
Coercive

Low Performance Readiness®

FIGURE 8–2   The Impact of
Power Bases at Various Levels
of Performance Readiness®

Source: Copyright © 1985, 2006,
Leadership Studies, Inc. All Rights
Reserved.

INTEGRATING POWER BASES, PERFORMANCE READINESS® LEVEL, AND LEADERSHIP STYLE THROUGH SITUATIONAL LEADERSHIP®

Situational Leadership® provides the context for understanding the potential impact of each power base. It is our contention that the Performance Readiness® of the follower not only dictates which style of leadership will have the highest probability of success but also determines the power base that the leader should use in order to induce compliance or influence behavior to maximize performance.

The Situational Use of Power

Even if the leader is using the appropriate leadership style for a given Performance Readiness® Level, that style may not be maximizing the leader's probability of success if it does not reflect the appropriate power base. Therefore, just as an effective leader should vary leadership style according to the Performance Readiness® Level of the follower, it is appropriate to vary the use of power in a similar manner. The power bases that may influence people's behavior at various levels of Performance Readiness® are pictured in Figure 8–3.

Figure 8–3 shows a relationship only between power bases and Performance Readiness® Level. However, there also appears to be a direct relationship between the kind of power bases a person has and the corresponding leadership style that will be effective for that person in influencing the behavior of others at various Performance Readiness® Levels.

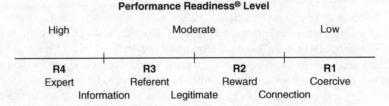

Performance Readiness® Level

High	Moderate	Low
R4	**R3**	**R2**	**R1**
Expert	Referent	Reward	Coercive
Information	Legitimate	Connection	

FIGURE 8–3   Power Bases Necessary to Influence People's Behavior at Various Levels of Performance Readiness®

Source: Copyright © 1985, 2006, Leadership Studies, Inc. All Rights Reserved.

Coercive Power   A follower low in Performance Readiness® generally needs strong directive behavior in order to become productive. To engage effectively in this telling style (S1), the leader may have to use coercive power. The behavior of people at low levels of Performance Readiness® (R1) seems to be generally influenced by the awareness that costs will be incurred if they do not learn and follow the rules of the game. Thus, sanctions—the perceived power to fire, transfer, demote, and so on—may be an important way that a leader can induce compliance from people who are unable and unwilling. The leader's coercive power may motivate the followers to avoid the punishment or "cost" by doing what the leader tells them to do.

Connection Power   As a follower begins to move from Performance Readiness® Level R1 to R2, directive behavior is still needed, but increases in supportive behavior are also important at this juncture. The telling (S1) and selling (S2) leadership styles appropriate for these levels of Performance Readiness® may become more effective if the leader has connection power. The possession of this power base may induce compliance because a follower at these Performance Readiness® Levels tends to engage in behaviors geared toward avoiding punishments or gaining rewards that are perceived to be available through the powerful connection.

Reward Power   A follower at a low to moderate level of Performance Readiness® often needs high amounts of supportive behavior and directive behavior (S2). This selling style is often enhanced by reward power. Since individuals at this Performance Readiness® Level are willing to try on new behavior, the leader needs to be perceived as having access to rewards in order to gain compliance and to reinforce growth in the desired direction.

Legitimate Power   The leadership styles that tend to influence effectively those at both moderate levels of Performance Readiness® (R2 and R3) are selling (S2) and participating (S3). Legitimate power seems to be helpful in the effective use of these styles. By the time a follower reaches these moderate levels of Performance Readiness®, the power of the leader has become legitimized. That is, the leader is able to induce compliance or influence behavior by virtue of the leader's position in the organizational hierarchy.

Referent Power   A follower at a moderate to high level of Performance Readiness® (R3) tends to need little direction but still requires a high level of communication and support from the leader. This participating style (S3) may be more effectively utilized if the leader has referent power. This source of power is based on good personal relations with the follower. With people who are able but insecure or unwilling, this power base tends to be an important means of instilling confidence and providing encouragement, recognition, and other supportive behavior. When that occurs, followers will generally respond in a positive way, permitting the leader to influence them because they like, admire, or identify with the leader.

Information Power   The leadership styles that tend to motivate followers effectively at above-average Performance Readiness® Levels (R3 and R4) are participating (S3) and delegating (S4). Information power seems to be particularly helpful in using these two styles in that people at these levels of Performance Readiness® look to the leader for information to maintain or improve performance. The transition from moderate to high Performance Readiness® may in fact be facilitated if the follower knows that the leader is available to clarify or explain issues and provide access to pertinent data, reports, and correspondence when needed. Through this information power, the leader is able to influence people who are both willing and able.

Expert Power   A follower who develops to a high level of Performance Readiness® often requires little direction or support. This follower is able and willing (R4) to perform the

Performance Readiness® Level

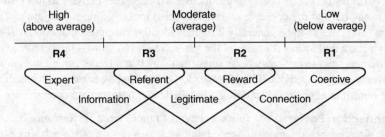

FIGURE 8–4   Power Bases Necessary to Influence People at Various Readiness Levels

Source: Copyright © 1985, 2006, Leadership Studies, Inc. All Rights Reserved.

tasks required and tends to respond most readily to a delegating leadership style (S4) and through the leader's judicious use of expert power. Thus, a leader may gain respect from and influence most readily a person who has both competence and confidence by possessing expertise, skill, and knowledge that this follower recognizes as important.

Power bases can be very subjective. We can draw conclusions about which power base tends to be most effective with each Performance Readiness® Level. However, there may be more than one power base driving the influence behavior. An easy way to think about sources of power in terms of making diagnostic judgments is to draw a triangle, as shown in Figure 8–4, around the three power bases necessary to influence below-average, average, and above-average levels of Performance Readiness®.

A way to examine the high probability power base for a specific Performance Readiness® Level is to draw inverted triangles, as shown in Figure 8–5. Note that R1 and R4, the extreme Performance Readiness® Levels, include only two power bases instead of three.

Developing Sources of Power

Although these seven power bases are potentially available to any leader as a means of influencing the behavior of others, it is important to note that there is a significant variance in the powers that leaders may actually possess. Some leaders have a great deal of power; others have very little. Part of the variance in actual power is due to the organization and the leader's position in the organization (position power), and part is due to individual differences among the leaders themselves (personal power), as shown in Figure 8–6.

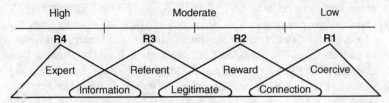

FIGURE 8–5   Power Bases Necessary to Influence People's Behavior at Specific Levels of Performance Readiness®

Source: Copyright © 1985, 2006, Leadership Studies, Inc. All Rights Reserved.

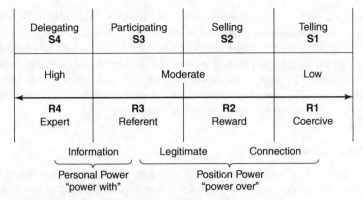

FIGURE 8–6 Summary of Relationships among Power Bases, Performance Readiness® Level, and Leadership Style

Source: Copyright © 1985, 2006, Leadership Studies, Inc. All Rights Reserved.

The power bases that are most relevant at the below-average levels of Performance Readiness® tend to be those that the organization or others can bestow upon the leader. The power bases that influence people who are above average in Performance Readiness® must, to a large degree, be earned from the people the leader is attempting to influence. Therefore, we suggest that position power and the phrase "power over" are most descriptive with coercive, connection, reward, and legitimate power bases; and we suggest that personal power and the phrase "power with" more accurately describe the effect on behavior from referent, information, and expert power.

Sources of Power

Just as some leaders start off with little power and gradually build and develop various power sources, other leaders gradually let their power bases erode and lose them. Why? Before we answer that question, managers need to understand the sources of position and personal power.

As we discussed earlier, position power can be thought of as the authority that is delegated down in an organization. Managers do, however, have some impact on how much position (coercive, connection, reward, and legitimate) power they get. The extent to which they develop rapport, confidence, and trust between themselves and senior management will determine how willing those above them will be to delegate power. In that sense, position power is something that a manager has to earn on a day-to-day basis.

The same can be said about personal power, except that the personal power (reward, information, and expert) that managers possess depends on the confidence and trust those managers generate from the people they are attempting to influence. For example, people might think that some leaders have charisma and other leaders do not. Leaders do not have charisma; followers give leaders charisma. We have all seen that phenomenon with elected officials. They are often carried into office because of their charisma, but when their actions do not gain general approval, they may lose their charisma overnight. Again, this is not to say that managers do not have some impact on how much personal power they get, but it is something that they have to earn on a day-to-day basis.

Position power and personal power bases together constitute an interaction-influence system. That is, power does not develop in a vacuum. Each power base tends to affect each of the other power bases. Thus, the extent to which people are willing to grant personal power to a manager depends a great deal on their perception of a leader's ability to provide rewards, punishment, or sanctions (position power). At the same time, the willingness of managers above a leader to delegate position power is often determined by the extent to which they perceive that leader as being liked and respected and having information and expertise (personal power) with their people. Keep in mind that we did not say how much personal power or position power affects whether leaders will be delegated authority or treated with respect. As we have noted before, it is the perception that others have of those power bases that is crucial.

Eroding Sources of Power

Since leaders have only a limited amount of power available to them, one would hope that they would hold on to whatever power bases they have. Yet some leaders who start off with significant power gradually lose their power bases and let them erode. The key to avoiding such erosion is to use your power bases. For example, a leader could have a significant amount of coercive power but gradually lose it by threatening followers with some kind of punishment and then not following through. In this context, people will start to think that the leader really does not have any coercive power. Similarly, leaders can lose their reward power if everyone gets the same reward whether they perform or not, or just because they have seniority in industry, or are older in the family. Some parents establish age requirements when kids can get to do things. "When you're 13, you'll be able to stay out past 10 o'clock. When you're 16, you'll be able to stay home alone." The problem with using age as a factor in determining when people can do things is that all they have to do is get older. When age is used as the determining factor, reward power as a parent or a leader is lost because what is happening is that people are getting rewards for being older, not for being more ready to take responsibility.

Connection power can be eroded when people begin to see that the sponsor or connection does not make any disciplinary interventions or provide any favors or sanctions. In other words, to be maintained, connection power needs occasional interventions from the sponsor. Similarly, managers can lose their legitimate power by not making decisions that people think they ought to make, given their position. Erosion of this power base can also occur if a manager continually makes decisions that are not fruitful. After a while, their staff members will no longer look to them to make decisions even if they have the title of senior research scientist or department manager.

This process also works with referent power. When you give praise or recognition to those who are performing and the same praise or recognition to those who are not performing, you begin to erode your referent power. If people do not have to earn praise and recognition then you no longer have referent power.

Leaders also have to be careful about eroding their information and expert power, particularly if they give away expertise and information to people whose goals are not organizational goals. If you give away too much information and knowledge, eventually those people will not need you. The only way you can get around this problem is to continually develop new information and new expertise so that they have to come back to the source.

If leaders let their power bases erode, they will also reduce the effectiveness of their leadership attempts. For example, an effective telling (S1) leadership style depends on having some coercive power. If leaders are not seen as being able to deliver punishments and sanctions, their use of that style is limited.

The same can be said about a selling (S2) style. Without some control over rewards, leaders are seen as not being able to reinforce or compensate for increased performance as people grow and develop their skills.

A participating (S3) style will not work if people do not like and respect a manager. In addition, if a manager has let reward power erode by not being particularly responsive to people, then a participative, high relationship style is going to be seen not as a reward, but as a punishment. Suppose a manager has ignored a staff member for a long time, then, suddenly, when that person's family life begins to deteriorate, the manager tries to comfort and console the staffer. Since the manager has eroded available referent power, these supportive leadership attempts are not seen as rewards, but as sanctions and punishments. Time with the boss is not seen as a positive experience.

A manager who is supervising highly competent and motivated people needs to have some expert power to make any kind of significant intervention. If the manager has eroded information and expert power, the possibility of influencing these people in any significant way will be very limited.

Do You Want Power?

Katherine Benzinger suggests, "If . . . you want to climb a career ladder or influence your organization significantly, you must not only understand power, you must seek it actively and skillfully." She also cautions that in order "to protect yourself from frustration and burn-out, you must therefore decide consciously whether you want power and are willing to do what it takes to acquire it."[30] She suggests two guidelines that are related to acquiring power:

1. Earning power requires a very substantial time commitment. If you are not willing to invest the time, perhaps gaining power is not right for you.
2. Gaining power in organizations requires confrontation. If you are not willing to play "King of the Mountain" to get on top and stay on top, then you may not wish to seek power.[31]

If you decide to seek more power, you may find options from Benzinger's 12-step strategy:

1. Learn and use your organization's language and symbols.
2. Learn and use your organization's priorities.
3. Learn the power lines.
4. Determine who has power and get to know those people.
5. Develop your professional knowledge.
6. Develop your power skills.
7. Be proactive.
8. Assume authority.
9. Take risks.
10. Beat your own drum.
11. Meet (your supervisor's) needs.
12. Take care of yourself.[32]

OTHER VIEWS ON DIFFERENCES BETWEEN MEN AND WOMEN MANAGERS

Other authors have commented on differences between male and female managers. Judy Rosener has noted that "men are more likely to use power that comes from their organizational position and formal authority, [whereas women] ascribed their power to personal characteristics like charisma, interpersonal skills, hard work, or personal contacts rather than to organizational stature."[33]

Gender-based stereotypes certainly still exist in the workplace Sue Shellenbarger, however, suggests that care must be taken not to stereotype men or women too rigidly in these roles.

She notes that a workforce study financed by 15 companies and foundations found that there are no differences existed in the way men and women managed, as viewed by those they managed. Women were sometimes seen as more sympathetic, which, in and of itself, might be a stereotype. With the workforce utilizing more women managers than ever, organizations should take note of this and other studies that identify few if any differences in the way men and women managers perform.[34] As Heilman, Wallen, Fuchs, and Tamkin found, women leaders face a double-bind: regardless of their actual qualities and behavior, they are more likely to have "feminine" traits ascribed to them, Since those traits are not highly associated with leadership or with managerial success, women can be subject to biases in leader selection and performance evaluations.[35]

What about Empowerment?

One of the most popular management themes in recent years is employee empowerment. The theme is an extension of delegation and suggests a high level of employee autonomy. The manager trusts the employee to decide how to accomplish his or her tasks. The results, in William J. Ransom's view, are "more rewarding than you can imagine when accomplished. You will gain more time to do the projects that only you can do. Your associates will become better at their tasks and operations will function more smoothly" as your "workers will become happier and more capable."[36]

Joy Day, managing principal in the consulting firm of Colby Day & Day, relates empowerment to developing an ownership attitude among a work group. The result? She has seen that attitude generate a productivity increase of 30 percent or more that is sustainable year after year. Her steps for creating such an attitude are:

- *Identify your starting point.* Who are true contributors and who are the slackers? It is important to get the right players on your team.
- *Educate.* Employees must have comprehensive knowledge of the organization, including finances, sales, and operations if they are to contribute.
- *Share the secrets.* Share what is really happening.
- *Create a daily score.* If employees know the score, they can make adjustments required to improve performance.
- *Ensure operational consistency.* Enforce operational standards to assure quality. Employees must meet customers' expectations.
- *Experiment with every element of the process/product over time in a methodical, documented way.* This is a proven approach to process improvement.
- *Tell stories about what your department and organization are doing and are about.* Stories give zest to the numbers and build a shared history.
- *Give more loyalty to your employees—after all they are your partners now.* If you expect loyalty, you must give loyalty *first*.
- *Expand decision-making responsibility of your staff.* You have established guidelines through the preceding steps; now is the time to trust your partners.
- *Party hearty.* Celebrate the successes and taste the vinegar of failure by learning from both.
- *Volunteer as a group.* Charity commitments add meaning to your mutual efforts.[37]

Oren Harari, a frequent contributor to the American Management Association's *Management Review*, has a somewhat different view of empowerment.

Your goal is not to empower, but to liberate. . . . Liberation involves freeing people from organizational constraints (including you) that inhibit their willingness to take proactive action and accountability. Power is a feeling, an experience, and the consequence of liberation.

All this empowerment stuff is a con because you cannot confer power on human beings. You cannot make anyone powerful. What you can do is create a condition where people will feel powerful, a condition where people choose to create power for themselves.[38]

We believe that these seemingly contradictory views of empowerment are correct in their context. If you consider delegating authority as setting freedom-of-action boundaries, then Harari's idea of liberation has value. Employees should be given freedom of decision-making action within prescribed, delegated boundaries. Delegation has always had limits; that is what differentiates it from abdication. If, on the other hand, you see authority as setting forth specific policies and guidelines, then the empowerment approach is more meaningful. You delegate authority to take specific actions.

We would be more inclined to support Harari's liberation view if the follower's Performance Readiness® Level is (R4), which suggests a delegating leadership style (S4). The follower, as we will see in our discussion of Contracting for Leadership Style in Chapter 11, determines what the area of freedom will be. For a follower at Performance Readiness® Level R1, the area would be very small; for a follower at Performance Readiness® Level R4, it would be rather large, but not infinite. This is what we mean when we say, "Let the individual or group run with the ball—*but within the playing field.*"

THE POWER PERCEPTION PROFILE

To provide leaders with feedback on their power bases so that they can determine which power bases they already have and which they need to develop, Hersey and Natemeyer developed the Power Perception Profile.[39] There are two versions of this instrument: One measures self-perception of power and the other determines perceptions of another's power.

Development of the Power Perception Profile

The power perception profile contains 21 forced-choice pairs of reasons often given by people when asked why they do things that a leader suggests or wants them to do.

After completing the power perception profile, respondents are able to obtain a score of the relative strength of each of the seven bases of power. This score represents the perception of influence for themselves or some other leader.

One of the shortcomings of most forced-choice instruments is that they provide comparisons only between items or categories but they do not offer any perspective on the overall scope of the concepts. In other words, a leader might score high or low on a certain power base when compared with each of the other power bases, but no indication is given on how that power base score compares with the score another leader might receive. For example, even if a leader's score on coercive power is low in relation to the other six power bases, the leader may be relatively high in coercive power when compared with other leaders the respondent has known. To correct this deficiency, the power perception profile goes one step further than most forced-choice questionnaires and asks respondents to compare the leader with other leaders they have known, in reference to each of the seven power bases.

Uses of the Power Perception Profile

The Power Perception Profile can be used to gather data in actual organizational settings or any learning environment—for example, student or training groups. In learning groups, the instrument is particularly helpful in groups that have developed some history—that is, they have spent a considerable amount of time interacting with each other analyzing or solving cases, participating in simulations or other training exercises. In this kind of situation, it is recommended that the group fill out one instrument together, using a particular member as the subject and arriving at a consensus on each of the items on the instrument. During each discussion, the person whose power bases are being examined should play a nonparticipant role. That person should not ask any questions or attempt to clarify, justify, or explain actions. An appropriate response might be, "Could you tell me more about that?" or "I'd like to hear more on that point." Then, at the end of the group's assessment, the person whose power bases were being examined is given an opportunity to respond to the group's discussion. This process is repeated until every participant has had a turn to get feedback from the group.

If the Power Perception Profile is being used to gather data in an organization, each organizational member from whom perceptions are desired should fill out a separate instrument. In this case, it is strongly suggested that the leaders not collect the data themselves. Instead, a third party who has the trust and confidence of all involved—such as a representative from human resources—should administer the questionnaire. It is also important to assure respondents that only generalized data will be shared with the leader, not the scores from any particular person. These suggestions are important because if leaders collect their own data, even if the instruments are anonymous, there is a tendency for some respondents to answer according to what they feel the leaders want or do not want to hear. Thus, to help establish a valid data base, leaders may want to have their data gathered by a third party.

Understanding power bases is important. If you understand which power bases tend to influence a group of people, you have some insight into who should be given a particular project assignment or responsibility. The person you assign to a particular task should have the power bases and be comfortable in using the appropriate leadership styles that are required in a particular setting. If someone really wants an assignment and does not have the appropriate power bases, it is a problem of self-development. You can work out a program to build that power base or appropriate style. What all this means is that we can increase the probability of success of a particular manager if we understand the territory—if we know what power bases and corresponding leadership styles are needed to influence the people involved effectively. That is the whole concept of team building. We will be talking about that subject in much greater depth in later chapters.

Notes

1. R. M. Stogdill, *Handbook of Leadership* (New York: Free Press, 1974).

2. Many of the concepts in this chapter were first published in Paul Hersey, Kenneth H. Blanchard, and Walter E. Natemeyer, "Situational Leadership®, Perception, and the Impact of Power," *Group and Organizational Studies 4*, no. 4 (December 1979): 418–428.

3. Pfeiffer, *Power Play.*

4. This section on defining power and other concepts originated with Walter E. Natemeyer, *An Empirical Investigation of the Relationships*

between Leader Behavior, Leader Power Bases, and Subordinate Performance and Satisfaction, a doctoral dissertation, University of Houston, August 1975.

5. James Hillman, *Kinds of Power* (New York: Currency-Doubleday, 1995), 97.

6. John B. Miner, *Organizational Behavior* (New York: Random House, 1988), 481.

7. Stephen B. Robbins, *Essentials of Organizational Behavior*, 4th ed. (Englewood Cliffs, NJ: Prentice Hall, 1994), 152.

8. M. F. Rogers, "Instrumental and Infra-Resources: The Bases of Power," *American Journal of Sociology* 79, no. 6 (1973): 1418–1433.

9. Amitai Etzioni, *A Comparative Analysis of Complex Organizations* (New York: Free Press, 1961).

10. David C. McClelland and David H. Burnham, *Power Is the Great Motivator, Harvard Business Review,* January-February 1995, 134.

11. Janet Hagberg, *Real Power: Stages of Personal Power in Organizations,* 3rd ed. (Salem, WI: Sheffield Publishing), 2003.

12. Niccolo Machiavelli, "Of Cruelty and Clemency, Whether It Is Better to Be Loved or Feared," *The Prince and the Discourses* (New York: Random House, 1950), Chapter 17.

13. Pfeiffer, 4.

14. Adapted from Paul Hersey, *Situational Selling* (Escondido, CA: Center for Leadership Studies, 1985), 14–15.

15. R. L. Peabody, "Perceptions of Organizational Authority: A Comparative Analysis," *Administrative Quarterly*, 6 (1962): 463–482.

16. A. C. Filley and A. J. Grimes, "The Bases of Power in Decision Processes," *Reprint Series 104* (Industrial Relations Research Institute, University of Wisconsin, 1967).

17. K. D. Beene, *A Conception of Authority* (New York: Teachers College, Columbia University, 1943).

18. John R. P. French and B. Raven, "The Bases of Social Power." in *Studies in Social Power*, ed. D. Cartright (Ann Arbor: University of Michigan, Institute for Social Research, 1959).

19. B. H. Raven and W. Kruglanski, "Conflict and Power." in *The Structure of Conflict*, ed. P. G. Swingle (New York: Academic Press, 1975), 177–219.

20. Paul Hersey and Marshall Goldsmith, "The Changing Role of Performance Management,"

Training and Development Journal (April 1980).

21. Steven Kerr, "On the Folly of Rewarding A, While Hoping for B," *Academy of Management Journal* 18 (1975): 769–783. Reprinted with commentary in *The Academy of Management Executive* 9, no. 1, (February 1995): 7–14 and an informal survey, "More on the Folly,"15–16.

22. Tom Peters, "Power: Get It and Use It with These 13 Secrets," *Star Tribune*, August 2, 1994, p. 2D.

23. K. R. Student, "Supervisory Influence and Work-Group Performance," *Journal of Applied Psychology* 52, no. 3 (1968): 188–194.

24. J. G. Bachman, C. G. Smith, and J. A. Slesinger, "Control, Performance, and Satisfaction: An Analysis of Structural and Individual Effects," *Journal of Personality and Social Psychology* 4, no. 2 (1966): 127–136.

25. J. G. Bachman, D. G. Bowers, and P. M. Marcus, "Bases of Supervisory Power: A Comparative Study in Five Organizational Settings." in *Control in Organizations*, Arnold S. Tannenbaum (New York: McGraw-Hill, 1968).

26. J. M. Ivancevich and J. H. Donnelly, "Leader Influence and Performance," *Personnel Psychology* 23, no. 4 (1970): 539–549.

27. R. J. Burke and D. S. Wilcox, "Bases of Supervisory Power and Subordinate Job Satisfactions," *Canadian Journal of Behavioral Science* (1971).

28. Natemeyer, *An Empirical Investigation of the Relationships between Leader Behavior, Leader Power Bases, and Subordinate Performance and Satisfaction.*

29. Hersey, Blanchard, and Natemeyer, "Situational Leadership®, Perception, and the Impact of Power."

30. Katherine Benzinger, "The Powerful Woman," *Hospital Forum* (May–June 1982): 15–20.

31. *Ibid.*, p. 15.

32. *Ibid.*, pp. 15–16.

33. Judy B. Rosener, "Ways Women Lead," *Harvard Business Review*, November–December 1990, 119–125.

34. Sue Shellenbarger, "Work-Force Study Finds Loyalty Is Weak, Divisions of Race and Gender Are Deep." *Wall Street Journal*, September 3, 1993, pp. B1, 9.

35. Madeline E. Heilman, Aaron S. Wallen, Daniella Fuchs, and Melinda M. Tamkins, "Penalties for Success: Reactions to Women Who Succeed at

Male Gender-Typed Tasks," *Journal of Applied Psychology 89* (2004): 416–427.

36. William J. Ransom, "There Is Profit in Empowerment," *Industrial Engineering,* February 1992.

37. Joy Day, "Getting The Edge: The Attitude of Ownership," *Supervision* 60, no. 6 (June 1999): 3–5, 8.

38. Oren Harari, "Stop Empowering Your People," *Management Review* 82, no. 11 (November 1993): 26–29.

39. This instrument was developed by Paul Hersey and Walter E. Natemeyer. Published by the Center for Leadership Studies, Escondido, CA 92025.

9

Situational Leadership®:

Training and Development

In Chapter 4 we stated that in evaluating performance, a manager ought to consider both output (productivity) and intervening variables (the condition of the human resources). We urged that both of these factors should be examined in light of short- and long-term organizational goals. If the importance of intervening variables is accepted, then one must assume that a key responsibility of managers, regardless of whether they are parents in the home or managers in a business, is developing the human resources for which they are responsible. Managers need to devote time to nurture the leadership potential, motivation, morale, climate, commitment to objectives, decision-making, communication, and problem-solving skills of their people. Thus, an important role for managers is the development of the task-relevant Performance Readiness® of their followers.

We think it is vital to emphasize this developmental aspect of Situational Leadership®. Failing to do so poses the danger that managers could use Situational Leadership® to justify the use of any behavior they wanted. Since the concept contends that there is no "best" leadership style, the use of any style could be supported merely by saying "the individual or group was at such-and-such Performance Readiness® Level." Thus, while close supervision and direction might be necessary initially when working with individuals who have had little experience in directing their own behavior, it should be recognized that this style is only a first step. In fact, managers should be rewarded for helping their people develop and be able to assume more and more responsibility. For example, in some progressive companies in which we have worked, we have been able to introduce a new policy which states: No managers will be promoted in this organization unless they do at least two things. First, they have to do a good job in what they are being asked to do—that is, good "bottom-line" results (output variables). Second, they have to have a ready replacement who can take over their job tomorrow (intervening variables).

This means that using a leadership style with a high probability of success for working with a given level of Performance Readiness® is not really enough. These managers may be accomplishing their goals, but their responsibilities should not stop there. Besides achieving goals, managers must develop their human resources (their followers).

How do effective leaders make this connection? It is through effective leadership, the primary topic of this and the next several chapters.

INCREASING EFFECTIVENESS

Rensis Likert found that employee-centered supervisors who use general supervision tend to have higher-producing sections than job-centered supervisors who use close supervision.[1] We emphasize the word *tend* because there are exceptions, which are evident even in Likert's data. What Likert found was that employees generally respond well to their supervisor's high expectations and genuine confidence in them and try to justify the supervisor's expectations of them. Employees with high performance will reinforce their supervisor's high trust for them; it is easy to trust and respect people who meet or exceed your expectations.

Cases and other evidence available from scientific research reveal:

- What a manager expects of his subordinates and the way he treats them largely determine their performance and career progress.
- A unique characteristic of superior managers is their ability to create high performance expectations that subordinates fulfill.
- Less effective managers fail to develop similar expectations, and, as a consequence, the productivity of their subordinates suffers.
- Subordinates, more often than not, appear to do what they believe they are expected to do.

When people respond to the high expectations of their managers with high performance, we call that the *effective cycle*, as illustrated in Figure 9–1.

Yet, as we pointed out earlier, the concentration on output variables as a means of evaluating effectiveness tends to lead to short-run-task-oriented leader behavior. This style, in some cases, does not allow much room for a trusting relationship with employees. Instead, employees are told what to do and how to do it with little consideration expressed for their ideas or feelings. After a while, the employees respond with minimal effort and resentment that lead to low performance. Reinforced by low expectations, it becomes a vicious cycle we call the ineffective cycle. Many other examples could be given of this all-too-common problem in organizations, as shown in Figure 9–2.

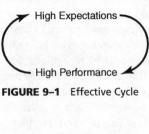

High Expectations

High Performance

FIGURE 9–1 Effective Cycle

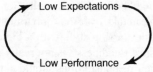

Low Expectations

Low Performance

FIGURE 9–2 Ineffective Cycle

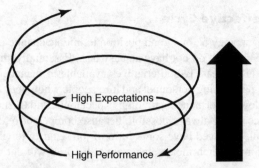

FIGURE 9–3   Upward-Spiraling Effect of the Effective Cycle

These cycles are depicted as static, but in reality they are dynamic. The situation tends to get better or worse. For example, high expectations result in high performance, which reinforces the high expectations and produces even higher productivity. It almost becomes an upward-spiraling effect, as illustrated in Figure 9–3. In many cases, this spiraling effect is caused by an increase in leverage created through the use of the motivators. As people perform, they are given more responsibility and opportunities for achievement, growth, and development.

This spiraling effect can also occur in a downward direction. Low expectations result in low performance that reinforces the low expectations and produces even lower productivity. It becomes a downward-spiraling effect, as shown in Figure 9–4. If this downward spiraling continues long enough, the cycle may reach a point where it cannot be turned around in a short period of time because of the large reservoir of negative experience that has built up in the organization. Much of the focus and energy are directed toward perceived problems in the environment such as interpersonal relations and respect for supervision rather than toward the work itself. Reaction to deteriorating hygiene factors takes such forms as hostility, undermining, and slowdown in work performance. When this happens, even if a manager changes behavior, the credibility gap based on long-term experience is such that the response is still distrust and skepticism rather than positive change.

One alternative that is sometimes necessary at this juncture is to bring in a new manager from the outside. The reason this has a high probability of success is that the sum of the past experience of the people involved with the new manager is likened to a "clean slate" and thus new manager behaviors are seen as more believable and change in employee behavior is more likely to occur.

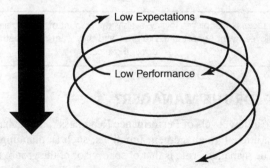

FIGURE 9–4   Downward-Spiraling Effect of the Ineffective Cycle

Breaking the Ineffective Cycle

Although new managers may be in a good position to initiate change in a situation that has been spiraling downward, they still do not have an easy task. Essentially, they have to break the ineffective cycle. There are at least two alternatives available to managers in this situation. Either they can fire the low-performing personnel and hire people whom they expect to perform well, or they can respond to low performance with high expectations and trust.

The first choice is not always possible because competent replacements are not readily available or the people involved have some form of job security (civil service, union tenure, or government regulations), which means they cannot be fired without considerable cost in time, energy, and trouble.

The latter choice for managers is also difficult. In effect, the attempt is to change the expectations or behavior of their people. It is especially difficult for managers to have high expectations and trust for people who have shown no indication that they deserve either. The key, then, is to change appropriately.

From our work with Situational Leadership®, we have identified two cycles that managers can use for changing or maximizing the task-relevant Performance Readiness® of their followers—the developmental cycle and the regressive cycle. In this chapter, we will discuss the developmental cycle. In Chapter 10, we will present the regressive cycle.

DEVELOPMENTAL CYCLE

The role managers play in developing the Performance Readiness® Level of their people is extremely important. Too often managers do not take responsibility for the performance of their people, especially if they are not doing well. If they are having problems, often managers will say, "I have an example of a Peter Principle," and not take responsibility for the poor performance. It has been our experience that managers who have to fire someone or find a place to hide them (this is what Peter called a "lateral arabesque"), or who are downright worried about someone's performance, should look in the mirror. In most cases, the biggest cause of the performance problem is looking back at them. Managers are responsible for making their people "winners," and this is what the developmental cycle is all about. Managers are involved in the developmental cycle any time they attempt to increase the present Performance Readiness® Level of an individual or group in some aspect of their work. In other words, the developmental cycle is a growth cycle.

> One of the biggest factors in employee loyalty levels is the amount of training and development companies provide . . . . Employees want opportunities to grow and they want career paths and opportunities to go down those paths.

WHAT IS IN IT FOR THE MANAGER?

When followers are at low levels of Performance Readiness®, the manager must take the responsibility for the "traditional" management functions, such as planning, organizing, motivating, and controlling.[2] The manager's role is that of supervisor of the group. However, when managers develop their people and have followers at high levels of Performance Readiness®, the followers can take over much of the responsibility for these day-to-day traditional management functions.

The manager's role can then change from supervisor to the group's representative in the next level of the organization.

> "Tell me and I'll forget; show me and I may remember; involve me and I'll understand."
> —Chinese Proverb

If they develop followers who can take responsibility for their own tasks on a day-to-day basis, managers can invest their time in the "high-payoff" management functions, the "linking-pin" (see Chapter 4) activities that enhance the group's performance. These functions include acquiring resources necessary for maximizing the group's productivity, communicating both horizontally and vertically, and coordinating the group's efforts with those of other departments to improve overall productivity. The manager, instead of getting trapped in minutiae, has time for long-range strategic planning and creativity.

Initially, close supervision and direction are helpful when working with individuals who have little experience in directing their own behavior. The manager recognizes that this style is only a first step. In order to maximize their potential in the high-payoff functions, managers must change their style and take an active role in helping others grow. The development of followers depends not only on the manager's behavior, but also on values and expectations.

What Do We Want to Influence?

The first question managers have to ask when they are thinking about developing their people is: What area of my employees' work do I want to influence? In other words, what are their responsibilities or goals and objectives? A foreman, for example, might want to influence productivity, quality, waste, absenteeism, accident rate, and so on. A university department chairman might want to affect the faculty's writing and research, teaching, and community service.

Once the objectives or responsibilities are identified and understood, managers must clearly specify what constitutes good performance in each area, so that both managers and employees know when performance is approaching the desired level. This is an important point. It is critical that both parties have clarity about what good performance looks like. For instance, what does a good sales record mean? Does it mean a certain number of sales made or dollar volume of sales? What is meant by "developing your people" or "being a good administrator"? Managers have to specify what good performance looks like or risk scenarios where employees think that they are doing just fine when in fact their performance is sub par. Just telling a person, "I want you to review credit histories" is not as helpful as saying, "I want you to review the credit histories of our 10 largest customers this week and give me a one page report on each by Friday afternoon." For managers and staff members to know how well someone is doing, good performance has to be clearly specified. Managers are likely to find it quite difficult to change and develop their followers' behavior in areas that are unclear.

How Is the Person Doing Now?

Before beginning the developmental cycle with an individual in a work situation, the manager must decide how well that person is currently doing. In other words, what is the person's Performance Readiness® Level right now in a specific aspect of the job? How able is the person to take responsibility for specific behavior? How willing or motivated is the person? As was discussed earlier, people do not have a degree of Performance Readiness® in any total sense; they may be higher in readiness for one task than for another. How then can we know what a person's Performance Readiness® Level is in a given situation?

Determining Performance Readiness®

In assessing the Performance Readiness® Level of an individual, we will have to make judgments about that person's ability and willingness. Where do we get the information to make these judgments? We can either ask the person or observe the person's behavior. We could ask a person such questions as, "How well do you think you are doing at such and such?" or "How do you feel about doing that?" or "Are you or are you not enthusiastic and excited about it?" Obviously, with some people, asking for their own assessment of their Performance Readiness® will not be productive. However, it has been surprising how even young children are able to share that kind of information. Phil and Jane learned that when they used to ask their two-year-old daughter, Lee, to do something, often Lee would reply, "I can't want to!" When translated, what Lee was really saying is, "I'm both unable and unwilling to do what you want me to do." If Lee's parents still wanted her to do it, they soon learned that they had to direct and closely supervise her behavior in this area (S1—"telling"). As children get older, they can play an even more significant role in determining their own Performance Readiness® Level. That process will be discussed in much more detail in Chapter 11.

You might be wondering whether people will always tell their managers the truth or just tell them what is necessary to keep the manager off their backs. Managers who doubt what their people tell them about their ability or willingness to do something can simply observe the staff members' behavior. Ability can be determined by examining past performance. Has the person done well in this area before or has performance been poor? Does the staff member have the necessary knowledge to perform well in the area, or does that person not know how to do what needs to be done?

Willingness can be determined by watching a person's behavior in a particular case. What is the person's interest level? Does the person seem enthusiastic or interested? What is the person's commitment to this area? Does the person appear to enjoy doing things in this area, or do they seem merely anxious to get them over with? Is the person self-confident and secure in this area, or does the person lack confidence and feel insecure? Remember that people can be at any of four levels of Performance Readiness® in each of their various areas of responsibility.

A person's Performance Readiness® Level gives us a good clue as to how to begin any further development of that individual. If a manager wants to influence a staff member in an area in which the person is both unable and unwilling (low Performance Readiness® Level), the manager must begin the developmental cycle by directing, controlling, and closely supervising (telling) the staff member's behavior. If, however, the person is willing (motivated) to do something, but not able to do it (low to moderate Performance Readiness®), the manager must begin the cycle by both directing and supporting (selling) the desired behavior. If the person is able to do something without direction, but is unwilling to do it or is insecure (moderate to high Performance Readiness®), the manager is faced with a motivational problem. Individuals reluctant to do what they are able to do are often insecure or lacking confidence. In this case, the manager should begin the developmental cycle by using a supportive style (participating) to help the individual become secure enough to do what the individual already knows how to do. Finally, if staff members are both able and willing to direct their own behavior (high Performance Readiness®), we can merely delegate responsibility to them and know that they will perform well. When that occurs, there is no need for beginning the developmental cycle. The person already has a high degree of Performance Readiness® in that area.

Increasing Performance Readiness®

Managers are engaged in the developmental cycle any time they attempt to increase the task-relevant Performance Readiness® of an individual or group beyond the level that individual or group has previously reached or is currently demonstrating. In other words, the developmental cycle is a growth cycle.

To explain fully how the developmental cycle works, let us look at an example. Suppose a manager has been able to diagnose the environment and finds that the task-relevant Performance Readiness® of a staff member is low (R1) in the area of developing a departmental budget. If the manager wants the staff member to perform well in this area without supervision, the manager must determine the appropriate leadership style for starting the developmental cycle. As can be seen in Figure 9–5, once this manager has diagnosed the Performance Readiness® Level of the follower as low, the appropriate style can be determined by drawing a straight line from a point on the Performance Readiness® continuum to where it meets the curved line in the style-of-leader portion of the model. In this case, it would be appropriate to start the developmental cycle by using a directive, telling style (S1). What then would a telling style look like in this situation?

It would involve a lot of who, what, when, and where guidance from the manager. First, the manager would have to tell the staff member exactly what was involved in developing a

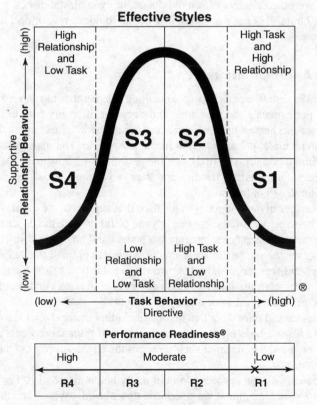

FIGURE 9–5   Determining an Appropriate Leadership Style

departmental budget—taking inventory, processing personnel and materials requests, comparing present costs with last year's budget, and so on. Second, the manager would begin to show the staff member how to do each of the tasks involved. Thus, telling in a teaching situation involves "show and tell"; the staff member must be told what to do and then shown how to do it. Although this telling style is high on direction and low on support, the manager is not necessarily being un-friendly to the staff member. Low supportive behavior in this situation merely means that the manager is not patting the staff member on the back before the individual has earned it. Until then, the manager emphasizes and focuses on explaining the what, when, where, and how of the job.

If the manager uses an S1 telling style in this situation, the departmental budget will prob-ably be done well, since the manager is working closely with the staff member. But if this same manager or leader assumes a responsibility to increase the task-relevant Performance Readiness® of the follower, then the manager has to be willing to take a risk at some point and begin to dele-gate some responsibility to the followers. This is particularly true when supervising an individual or group that has not assumed much responsibility in the past. Yet, if one is going to develop people—children in the home, employees on the job—one has to take that risk. Although tak-ing a risk is an inherent part of the developmental cycle, managers have to keep the degree of risk reasonable; it should not be too high. For example, suppose a mother wants to teach her eight-year-old daughter how to wash the dishes. The risk is a few broken dishes. It would be wise, then, to start the daughter off on old dishes, or even plastic dishes, rather than Grandma's priceless bone china. It is not a question of whether to take a risk or not; it is a matter of taking a calculated risk.

Successive Approximations

If a manager asks a staff member to do something the member has never been taught to do and expects good performance the first time, and does not offer any help to the staff member, the manager has set the person up for failure and punishment. Thus begins the widely used "tell, leave alone, and then 'zap'" approach to managing people. The manager tells the staff member what to do (without bothering to find out if the person knows how to do it), leaves the staff mem-ber alone (expecting immediate results), and then yells at and "zaps" the staff member when the desired behavior does not follow.

If the manager in our budget example used that approach, the events might look something like this. The manager might assume that anyone could prepare the departmental budget. So the manager tells the staff member to prepare the budget and have it within 10 days. Not bothering to analyze whether the staff member is able or willing to prepare the budget alone, the manager gives the order and then goes about his own responsibilities. When the staff member produces the budget 10 days later, the manager finds all kinds of mistakes and problems with it and yells at the staff member about the poor quality of the work.

Managers should remember that no one (including themselves!) learns how to do anything all at once. We learn a little bit at a time. As a result, if a manager wants someone to do some-thing completely new, the manager should reward the slightest progress the person makes in the desired direction.

Many parents use this process without really being aware of it. For example, how do we teach a child to walk? Imagine if we stood Eric up and said, "Walk," and then when he fell down we spanked him for not walking. Sound ridiculous? Of course. But it is not really any differ-ent from the manager's anger with the staff member about the poorly prepared budget. A child spanked for falling down will not try to walk because the child knows falling down leads to punishment. At this point, Eric is not even sure what his legs are for. Therefore, parents usually first teach children how to stand up. If the child stays up even for a second or two, his parents get excited and hug and kiss him, call his grandmother, and the like. Next, when the child can stand and hold onto a table, his parents again hug and kiss him. The same happens when he takes his first step, even if he falls down. Whether or not his parents know it, they are positively rewarding the child for small accomplishments as he moves closer and closer to the desired behavior—walking.

Thus, in attempting to help an individual or group develop—to get them to take more and more responsibility for performing a specific task—a leader must first delegate some responsibility (not too much or failure might result); and second, reward as soon as possible any behavior in the desired direction. This process should continue as the individual's behavior comes closer and closer to the leader's expectations of good performance. What would relationship behavior look like in this situation?

Relationship behavior would involve providing encouragement (positive strokes) and reinforcement. Positive reinforcement is anything that is desired or needed by an individual whose behavior is being reinforced. Whereas reducing task behavior precedes the desired behavior, relationship behavior, or positive reinforcement, follows the desired behavior and increases the likelihood of its recurring. It is important to remember that reinforcement must immediately follow any behavior in the desired direction. Reinforcement at a later time will be of less help in getting the individual or group to do something they have never done before on their own.

This two-step process of (1) reducing the amount of direction and supervision and (2) after adequate performance follows, increasing socioemotional support (relationship behavior) is known as *positively reinforcing successive approximations.*

Suppose a manager wanted to change leadership styles with an individual from point A to point C along the curvilinear function of Situational Leadership®, as illustrated in Figure 9–6. Step 1 would be to delegate some responsibility by decreasing task behavior to point B. This is a risky step because the manager is turning over the direction and the supervision of some of the tasks to the follower. If the follower responds well to the increased responsibility, it is then appropriate to engage in step 2—positively reinforcing this behavior by increasing socioemotional support (relationship behavior) to the higher level point C, as shown in Figure 9–6.

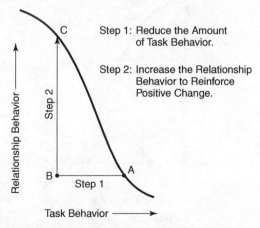

FIGURE 9–6 Two-Step Process of the Developmental Cycle

A leader must be careful not to delegate too much responsibility too rapidly. Doing so is a common error. Delegating responsibility before the follower can handle it may in fact set them up for failure and frustration that could prevent that person from wanting to take on additional responsibility in the future. The process is often started off by good intentions. For example, a manager provides direction and structure but then moves too quickly to a "leave-alone" leadership style. This abrupt movement from telling to delegating assumes that telling is learning when in fact impacting knowledge does not necessarily translate into demonstratable skill. Consequently, the manager is likely to return to style S1 rapidly in a punitive way if the job is not getting done.

In addition, a manager should not increase socioemotional support (relationship behavior) without first getting the desired performance; in other words, a manager should not positively reinforce nonperformance. A manager who does may be viewed as a soft touch. That is why the manager in our example does not immediately move from point A to point C along the curved line in Figure 9–6. If the manager moved from point A to point C without some evidence that the individual could assume responsibility at point B, it would be like giving the reward before the person had earned it. It would be like paying a person 20 dollars an hour right now who at present is worth only 5 dollars an hour. For many people, if you gave them 20 dollars an hour up front, there would be very little incentive to improve their performance. Thus, the leader should develop the Performance Readiness® of followers slowly on each task they must perform, using less task behavior and more relationship behavior as they become more willing and able to take responsibility. When an individual's performance is low on a specific task, one must not expect drastic changes overnight.

If the manager (in our example) finds that the follower is unable to handle that much added responsibility when task behavior is decreased to point B, the manager might have to return to a moderate level of direction (where the follower is able to take responsibility) somewhere between point A and point B. This new level of task behavior is indicated by point B′ in Figure 9–7. If the subordinate is now able to be effective at that level, then the manager can appropriately increase socioemotional support (relationship behavior) to point C′. Although this level of socioemotional support is less than depicted at point C, it is appropriate to the amount of task behavior that the follower, at that time, is able to assume.

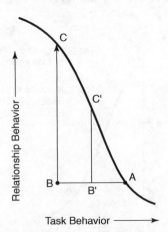

FIGURE 9–7 Adjustment When Growth Expectation Is Too High

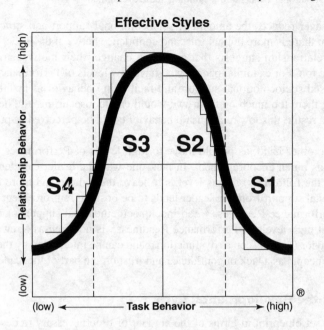

FIGURE 9–8   Developmental Cycle as People Develop over Time. "Steps" along the Curve Represent Successive Approximations

Source: Copyright © 1985, 2006, Leadership Studies, Inc. All Rights Reserved.

As shown in Figure 9–8, this two-step process—cutting back structure and then increasing socioemotional support if the follower can respond to the additional responsibility—tends to continue in small increments until the individual is assuming moderate levels of Performance Readiness®. This continual decreasing of task behavior, however, does not mean that the individual will have less structure but that the structure can now be internally provided by the follower instead of being externally imposed by the leader.

An interesting phenomenon occurs in the developmental cycle when the high point of the curvilinear function in the leadership style portion of the model is reached. This is where the function crosses the mean, or average, of task behavior. Past this point, a leader who is appropriately using leadership style S3 or style S4 is supervising people at moderate to high levels of Performance Readiness® (R3 and R4). At that time, the process changes and becomes one, whereby the leader not only reduces structure (task behavior), but, when the followers can handle their responsibility, reduces socioemotional support as well. This continuation of the successive approximation process is illustrated by the downward steps in Figure 9–8.

Sometimes the following question is raised: Does not the reduction of socioemotional support mean that there is a lack of confidence and trust between manager and follower? In reality, when a manager reduces the amount of socioemotional support and structure appropriately, it indicates that there is more mutual trust and confidence between the leader and the followers.

This relationship suggests that as people change, their motives and hierarchical needs often change too. For example, people who have low levels of Performance Readiness® tend to view increased socioemotional support and facilitating behavior as positive reinforcement. In fact, leaving them too much on their own would create insecurities and help reinforce fear and anxiety. As a result, this low relationship behavior could be perceived as punishment rather than reward.

On the other hand, as people move to high levels of Performance Readiness®, they do not require as much encouragement. In fact, one way the leader can demonstrate confidence and trust in the follower(s) at this level is to leave them more and more on their own. Just as socioemotional support from the leader tends to be positive reinforcement for persons with low levels of Performance Readiness®, too much socioemotional support or relationship behavior for people at high levels of Performance Readiness® is not seen as a reward. In fact, this supportive behavior is often seen as dysfunctional and can be interpreted by these high Performance Readiness® people as a lack of confidence and trust on the part of the leader.

Time and the Developmental Cycle

There is no set blueprint in terms of the amount of time necessary to develop an individual or group. A manager may be doing very well to move a group from Performance Readiness® Level 1 to Level 2 over a period of 18 months to 2 years. On the other hand, within that group there may be an individual or several individuals who will develop much more rapidly than the group as a whole. Thus, time is a function of the complexity of the job being performed and the performance potential of the individual or group. For example, one might take someone on a specific task through the total cycle—from low to high levels of Performance Readiness®—in a matter of minutes. And yet, in other tasks with that same individual, the Performance Readiness® development process may take a much greater amount of time. In fact, it could take weeks, months, or even years to move through the complete cycle in terms of appropriate leadership style from telling (S1) to delegating (S4). A short developmental process might be, for example, teaching a child to tie her shoes.

If the child has not made any attempt to learn to tie shoes, the parent needs to provide some high task behavior for the child. The child has low Performance Readiness® on this task, so the parent should explain what to do, how to do it, and where to do it. In essence, the parent must move into the early stages of coaching and counseling by holding the child's hands while guiding her through the motions of tying a shoelace. As the child begins to show the ability to do some shoe-tying functions, the parent reduces the amount of telling behavior and increases, to some extent, supportive behavior. "That's fine! Good! You're getting it!" And perhaps in a matter of minutes, the behavior of the parent may change from a highly structured style to just being nearby, providing a moderate amount of structure but also high levels of verbal and nonverbal supportive and facilitative behavior. In another few minutes, the parent may leave the child to practice alone while staying close enough to make an intervention if there should be some regression. Thus, in a matter of 10 to 15 minutes, the parent has taken the child in that specific task of shoe tying from style S1 through styles S2 and S3 to almost a complete delegation of that function to the child in a manner characteristic of style S4. This does not mean that the parent's style with that child should now always be style S4. It just means that in that specific task (shoe tying), the most appropriate style to use with that child is style S4.

Summary

The ultimate goal of the developmental process discussed in this chapter is to shift people toward self-management so that they can eventually assume responsibility for motivating their own behavior. This ultimate goal is mentioned to reassure people who have some real doubts about the use of reinforcement. Some readers may say, "People should be motivated by a desire to succeed or the desire to please people around them, not by a hoped-for reward," or "This sounds like bribery to me," or "If I use positive reinforcement with people, won't they always expect rewards for every little thing they do?"

Although we have shared similar concerns in the past, our experience in observing people in organizations has been reassuring. We have found that people who are reinforced when they are first learning new behaviors and performance areas and then are gradually allowed to be more and more on their own turn out to be self-motivated people who can be left alone with no significant drop in productivity.

Notes

1. Rensis Likert, *New Patterns of Management* (New York: McGraw-Hill, 1961), 7.

2. This section is adapted from Paul Hersey, *The Situational Leader* (Escondido, CA: Center for Leadership Studies, 1985), 92–94.

10

The Situational Leader and Constructive Discipline

I n the last chapter, we discussed how to develop Performance Readiness® and independence in people through the use of positive reinforcement and changing leadership styles. You should be aware, however, that for one reason or another, people's performance may begin to slip. And one of the most difficult challenges managers face is working with performance problems. That is because discipline is often viewed as a negative intervention. But the origin of the word *discipline* is "disciple"; *disciple* is a learner.

Unfortunately, in our culture many people interpret discipline as punishment. But it does not always have to be punishment. The problem-solving nature of *constructive discipline* differentiates it from punitive discipline. As such, constructive discipline is designed to be a learning process that provides an opportunity for positive growth. Effective managers use constructive discipline when people slip in Performance Readiness®.[1] In this chapter, we will attempt to help managers determine what needs to be done when this happens.

THE REGRESSIVE CYCLE

Managers may need to make a regressive intervention when their followers begin to behave less willingly than they have in the past. Thus, in a developmental cycle, managers are attempting to increase the task-relevant Performance Readiness® of an individual or group beyond where it has been in the past. The regressive cycle involves an intervention that leaders need to make when an individual or a group is becoming less effective. Thus, in a regressive cycle, managers must use a leadership style appropriate to the present level of Performance Readiness® rather than the style that might have been effective when the individual or group was at a higher level of Performance Readiness®.

Decreases in Performance Readiness® are often the result of what might be called "high-strength competing responses" in the environment. These responses are competing with the goals of the leader or the organization and, therefore, have become higher-strength needs to the followers in terms of their behavior.

> "Confidence is contagious. So is lack of confidence."
> —Vince Lombardi

Decreases in Performance Readiness® occur for a variety of reasons. Followers can have problems with the supervisor, problems with coworkers, suffer burnout, boredom, and have other problems on or off the job. These are just a few of the things that can have a negative impact on people's performance. Let us take an example of a performance problem.

While consulting with a large research and development laboratory, Dr. Hersey worked with a manager who was responsible for supervising John, one of the most motivated scientists on the staff. John was so committed to his job that it was not unusual to see a light under his laboratory door at eight o'clock in the evening. John often worked on weekends. He probably had more patents and made more contributions to the overall program than any person in the laboratory.

Observations indicated that John's manager was behaving appropriately in using a low relationship–low task style (S4) for John's high Performance Readiness® Level (R4). Thus, rather than operating as John's supervisor, the manager was behaving more as John's representative to higher levels in the organization. John's manager was attempting to maximize John's potential by engaging in such "linking-pin" activities as acquiring necessary resources and coordinating his activities with the activities of other staff members. Although John was at a high level of Performance Readiness® in this organizational setting, we learned that John's behavior was seen in a different light in his interactions in another organization—his family. In that organizational setting, his wife saw his behavior of working long hours and weekends as an indication that he no longer cared about her and their young daughter. So in his wife's eyes, John was behaving at a low Performance Readiness® Level. As a result, John went home one evening and found a note from his wife in which she told him that she had packed her bags and taken their daughter away to start a new life. John was shocked by his wife's action; he had perceived his own behavior quite differently from the way she did. He felt that he was excellent at providing for his wife and child.

With these family problems now on his mind, John's effectiveness on the job began to decrease. It has been said many times that you should leave your family problems at home and your job problems at work, but in reality we tend to carry problems both ways. Problems at home affect our behavior in the work environment, and problems at work affect our home environment. This was certainly true in John's case. As his concerns for his family began to take effect, his performance as a scientist began to shift from Performance Readiness® Level 4 into Level 3, as shown in Figure 10–1. Although his work emphasized technical competency, his declining psychological readiness was now affecting his performance. John did not seem to be able to cope with his problems at home. This meant that to maximize performance, John's manager had to shift his own leadership style from style 4 to style 3 to deal with this lowering Performance Readiness® Level (Figure 10–1). As a result, a moderate increase in direction and structure as well as significant increases in socioemotional support, two-way communication, and the willingness to listen actively and be supportive (relationship behavior) were necessary. At this point, the situation was still more of a problem to the follower than to the leader, but the high-relationship intervention by the manager seemed to help the situation.

Once John was able to cope with his problem and put it into perspective, it was possible for his manager to move directly back to style 4. This story illustrates one of the basic differences

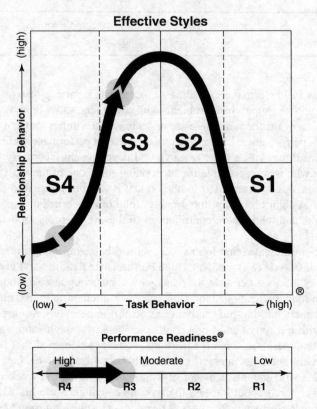

FIGURE 10–1 An Example of a Regressive Cycle Intervention

Source: Copyright © 1985, 2006, Leadership Studies, Inc. All Rights Reserved.

between a developmental cycle and a regressive cycle. In a regressive cycle, once an appropriate intervention has been made, the leader may often move back to the former leadership style without going through the process of positively reinforcing successive approximations. This is because the follower has previously demonstrated an ability to function at this level. If John's performance had continued to decline, however, the situation clearly would have become a problem to both the leader and the follower and would have demanded an eventual shift by the manager to a high task–high relationship style (S2).

In another example, Henry, a construction engineer, was operating as a project consultant; that is, he had a special expertise that was useful for a variety of projects. As a result, rather than being assigned to a specific project, he worked with a half-dozen projects at different construction sites. Since his Performance Readiness® Level was extremely high, his boss was also treating him appropriately in a style 4 manner. His supervisor was acting more as a linking pin with the rest of the organization than as his supervisor.

This style was effective until Henry began to take an active interest in golf. As a result of this new high-strength competing response, Henry could no longer be reached after two o'clock in the afternoon. It took several months for his supervisor to discover Henry's unavailability, because his coworkers just assumed that he was at one of the other construction sites. The supervisor finally became aware of Henry's behavior and discovered that his golfing was impeding progress at some of the construction sites. As a result, Henry's Performance Readiness® Level as a project consultant in terms of the accomplishment of organizational goals had moved from Performance Readiness® Level 4 to Performance Readiness® Level 1, particularly between two and five in the afternoon. More specifically, Henry would not respond to any calls or return messages at this time since he was out on the golf course. Occasionally he would rush to return what he felt were the "urgent" calls between five and six in the evening. His supervisor started receiving complaints about Henry's behavior. Things at several of the job sites were on hold, waiting for Henry's inspection. Thus, it became appropriate for the supervisor to shift his leadership style from S4 to S1 to deal with this drastic change in Performance Readiness®. What might be called a *disciplinary intervention* was necessary to redefine roles and expectations for Henry. His supervisor sat him down and clarified the various job site priorities. He also went so far as to remind Henry that his job performance impacted the whole organization and that Henry's recent lack of response was causing trouble for other workers. Once the manager "unfroze" Henry's new pattern, he could shift his style back to S4. Henry's return to his previous levels of Performance Readiness® made it appropriate for his boss to go back to the delegating and hands off style. This was possible, once again, because Henry had been at a high Performance Readiness® Level before. Thus, it may not be necessary for a manager to positively reinforce successive approximations before moving back to a previously appropriate style. Often in a disciplinary intervention, all managers have to do is get the attention of their followers to get them moving back in the right direction.

The regressive cycle should be taken one step at a time. If we are letting individuals operate on their own (by delegating that right to them) and performance declines, we should move toward a participating style and support their problem solving. If we are being supportive, but not directive (S3), and performance declines, we should move to a selling style by continuing to engage in two-way communication and by being more directive (S2). If we are providing both task and relationship behavior (S2) and performance still declines, we should move to a telling style (S1) and reduce some of our supportive behavior while increasing direction and supervision. In both the regressive and developmental cycles, we should be careful not to jump from delegating (S4) to selling (S2) or telling (S1), or from telling (S1) to participating (S3) or delegating (S4). Making a drastic shift backward in leadership styles is one of the common mistakes managers make. It sets up the leave-alone-and-zap style of management—an approach that is not only disruptive to the relationship a manager has with a staff member, but is also disruptive to that person's individual growth and development.

RELATIONSHIP BETWEEN ABILITY AND WILLINGNESS IN THE DEVELOPMENTAL AND REGRESSIVE CYCLES

Sometimes we are asked, "How can a person go from 'unable but willing or confident' (R2) to 'able but unwilling or insecure' (R3)?" Figure 10–2 answers that question. As people grow in their task-specific Performance Readiness®, the behaviors they need from the leader change. Followers who are performing at Performance Readiness Levels 1 and 2 need structure and guidance in order to perform well and grow. They also need increased supportive behavior as they move from R1 to R2 as reward and reinforcement for their efforts.

Often managers will observe followers moving from being unable and insecure, R1, to unable but confident, R2. They perform well as long as the leader is there providing direction. But as people grow and are given responsibility to accomplish tasks on their own, there is usually some apprehension with taking charge the first few times. Insecurity increases as the

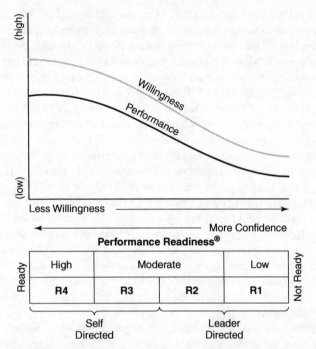

FIGURE 10–2 Relationship between Willingness and Performance in the Regressive Cycle; Confidence and Performance in the Development Cycle

Source: Copyright © 1985, 2006, Leadership Studies, Inc. All Rights Reserved.

follower moves from R2 to R3. This is the realm of *follower-directed behavior* versus *leader-directed behavior*.

Think about the first time you had to make a presentation in front of a group. Even though you may have practiced in front of a mirror and on videotape, you probably had some "butterflies" and insecurity right before the moment of truth. But after you had made a few successful presentations, you became both able and confident about performing on your own. Your insecurity came about, in part, because the leader was not right there to bail you out if you got into trouble.

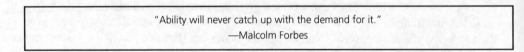

"Ability will never catch up with the demand for it."
—Malcolm Forbes

Figure 10–2 further clarifies the ability and willingness issues. Performance slippage in the short run is usually a willingness problem. It is not that an individual's or a group's ability has deteriorated significantly, but it is the use of ability that is causing the performance slippage. It is a motivation problem, not an ability problem. So if performance starts to slip, the person may be giving verbal and nonverbal clues about being upset with the boss, with a peer, with the organization about not getting an expected raise or promotion, or whatever it happens to be. The person's mental attitude is now focused on personal troubles rather than work requirements. If there are problems at home, the same things may occur.

As illustrated in Figure 10–2, first comes the decline in willingness, as shown by the top gray line, followed by a decline in performance, shown by the bottom darker line. There is a lead-lag relationship. There is another related point worthy of note: During the developmental cycle, issues of confidence or insecurity dominate psychological Performance Readiness®; during the regressive cycle, issues of willingness and commitment dominate.

SOME THINGS TO REMEMBER WHEN DISCIPLINING AN INDIVIDUAL

If a disciplinary intervention is called for, how can it be carried out effectively? As just discussed, it is important to use a leadership style appropriate for the follower's *present* level of Performance Readiness®; doing so may involve using different styles for the same person at different times. Here are a few other helpful guidelines.[2]

Making the Intervention Timely

Problem solving needs to be done in a timely manner. The sooner the intervention, the better the chance of stopping the performance slippage. The longer a manager waits, the more directive the intervention will have to be. Therefore, a manager may risk a follower becoming anxious, frustrated, or resentful. Even an appropriate directive intervention may lead to attempts to get out from under the manager or to get the manager out.

For example, Mary, the office manager, expects all employees to maintain good attendance records. For the last three months, however, Susan, a data entry clerk, has repeatedly arrived for work late and has failed to come to work twice. The other office staff members have been complaining among themselves about Susan's behavior and have mentioned their complaints to Mary. Mary knows that Susan has had problems with child care and has decided to wait and see if Susan's behavior will improve. As the weeks pass, Susan continues to arrive late for work. When Mary has finally had enough, she decides to let Susan really have it as soon as she finally gets into the office. Susan is likely to feel "zapped" by the interaction and maybe even a little bitter toward Mary if she did not see it coming. Susan may not even be able to focus on her real problem of poor attendance if she cannot get past her feelings of resentment and bitterness at being confronted in such a manner.

If Mary had intervened earlier, a participative style would probably have been enough to turn the problem around. But now, the highly structured style is necessary and will likely create resentment in Susan. This is a trap that managers fall into when making disciplinary interventions. First, they engage in "ostrich" leadership by sticking their heads in the sand and hoping the problem will go away. And then, when it does not, they get angry and zap the follower. By timing interventions appropriately and treating people according to the level at which they are *currently* performing, managers can begin to take a proactive approach to problem solving, as opposed to just reacting to each new crisis.

Unless discipline occurs close to the misbehavior or the poor performance, it will not be helpful in influencing future behavior. Some managers are "gunnysack" discipliners. That is, they store up observations of poor behavior, and then one day when the bag is full, they charge in and "dump everything on the table." Often, managers wait until the yearly performance review to take this action. They wait for this moment to tell their people all the bad things they have done over the last months or year. Manager and employee usually end up arguing about the "facts," and the employee does not really hear what is wrong. This is a version of the leave-alone-and-zap form of discipline. If managers would intervene early, they could calmly deal with one behavior at a time. The employees might even "hear" the feedback and take actions to change their behavior quickly.

Varying the Emotional Level

The emotional level of the intervention is different for constructive discipline than it is for developing people. When developing people, you are attempting to expand the present ability of the follower. Therefore, it helps to keep the emotional content of a development intervention at a low level. People often misinterpret Situational Leadership® because they think a telling style involves raising your voice or losing your temper. Actually, S1 can be a very soft and caring approach by providing the needed demonstration of how to do things. It would be inappropriate to shout or get angry at people who are developing. That approach would only make them feel insecure and would discourage them from learning.

But when followers choose not to use their present ability, and constructive discipline is appropriate, you can raise the emotional content to a moderate level. This helps to get people's attention, lets them know that you are aware of the performance problem, and tells them that you care. It also helps to "unfreeze" the inappropriate behavior so that change can take place.

Focusing on Performance

The next thing to consider in working with constructive discipline is the following admonition: *Don't attack personality—focus on performance.* If you attack personality and the person becomes angry, the probability of successfully working with the person will be much lower. Imagine a manager starting off a disciplinary intervention with, "I just told you that a week ago. Can't you remember to do anything, you dumb so and so?" Such an approach will only raise the emotional level of people; it will not get them to focus on the problem. If the focus is on performance, not on personality, both leader and follower can talk about the problem and solve it.

Be Specific, Do Your Homework

Being specific about performance problems is also important. When using constructive discipline, be careful of *glittering generalities*. Often managers perform all the other aspects of constructive discipline well. They use an appropriate leadership style for their people's current Performance Readiness® Level; they have good timing, they keep a moderate emotional profile, and they focus on performance. But their intervention sounds like this: "Look, you're just not doing the kind of job we both know you're capable of; now let's get back on track." Then the manager is bewildered or gets angry when the follower does not understand.

These kinds of glittering generalities do not solve the problem. You have to do your homework before the intervention and gather specific details that will be useful in problem solving. With specific information, the interventions might sound like, "Productivity is down fourteen and a half percent"; "Overtime is up six and a half percent"; or "Project Z is five days late and we've got three other departments depending on us for that component." Specificity allows the manager and followers to work together on developing a solution.

Harry Levinson, a well-known management consultant, agrees with this approach. He offers three general principles to follow when delivering bad news.

1. Don't be apologetic—expressing sorrow or sympathy is one thing, but you should never apologize for facing facts, calling the shots, and making tough decisions. (Not every decision you make is going to make people happy.)
2. Be honest. . . . sound the alarm early and lead people to redirect themselves voluntarily.
3. Be constructive and, when possible, get and follow suggestions from your employees to make them feel more a part of the process.[3]

Keep It Private

The last thing to remember is to keep disciplinary interventions private. As a guideline, it is a good idea to praise people in public and problem solve in private. If you address followers about problems when others are around, you run the risk of having them more concerned about being seen "catching hell" than with solving the problem. Discussing problems in private tends to make it easier to get your points across and to keep the other person focused on the problem-solving process.

> "If you want to give a man credit, put it in writing. If you want to give him hell, do it on the phone."
> —Charles Beacham

Leaders should also refrain from discussing the problems that they may be having with an employee with other employees. Discussing such problems may lead an employee to think, "What is the leader saying about me to other employees behind *my* back?"

Punishment and Negative Reinforcement

Punishment, as we discussed earlier, is a negative consequence. A negative consequence tends to weaken the action it immediately follows; that is, it prevents the recurrence of that behavior. It is a stimulus that an individual "will reject, if given a choice between the punishment and no stimulus at all."[4] As punishment suppresses the behavior that brought it on, *negative reinforcement* strengthens the response that eliminates the punishment.

An example of both punishment and negative reinforcement may be helpful. Suppose that whenever a manager brings the work group together to share some new information with them, Bill, one of the employees, pays little attention and talks to people around him. As a result, he is uninformed and his manager is irritated. The manager decides to punish Bill's whispering behavior by stopping in the middle of a sentence and looking at Bill whenever she sees him talk. The unexpected silence (a negative consequence, or punishment) causes the whole work group to focus on what stopped the manager's sharing of information (Bill's talking). The silence from the manager and all eyes on him are uncomfortable to Bill (punishment). He stops talking and starts listening to his manager, who resumes her discussion. His manager's use of a negative consequence, or punishment (silence and look), weakened and suppressed Bill's whispering behavior. At the same time, it operated as negative reinforcement in strengthening his listening, the behavior that took the punishment away (his manager stops looking at him and starts talking).

A manager must be careful in using punishment because one does not always know what a person will do when punished. For example, suppose a manager reprimands (punishes) Al, an employee, for sloppy work. If Al settles down, figures out what he has done wrong, and begins working carefully (negative reinforcement), the punishment has been helpful. After having this good experience, the manager might try the same technique with Mary, another employee who is doing sloppy work. But rather than making Mary behave more carefully, the punishment (reprimand) causes her to work even more sloppily, and she begins to become disruptive in other areas. Thus, whereas Al shaped up with a reprimand, Mary became more troublesome after the same intervention.

Another important point to keep in mind when using punishment is that punishment shows one what *not* to do, but it does not show one what *to* do. This distinction was vividly pointed out by John Huberman in a case study about a Douglas-fir plywood mill in which the management had continually used punitive measures to deal with sloppy workmanship and disciplinary problems.[5] Although punishment seemed to stop the inappropriate behavior for the moment, it had little long-term effect. Top management finally analyzed the system while preparing to double its capacity. They were amazed that:

> *Not a single desirable result could be detected.* The people who had been disciplined were generally still among the poorest workers; their attitude was sulky, if not openly hostile. And they seemed to be spreading this feeling among the rest of the crew.[6]

This reality and the findings that "85 percent of all those who entered the local prison returned there within three years of their release"[7] made management seriously question their use of punishment. Eventually they worked out a new and highly effective system, which Huberman called "discipline without punishment." One of the main ingredients of the new method was that rather than a punitive approach to unsatisfactory work or a discipline problem, a six-step process was initiated that clearly spelled out appropriate behavior, telling employees what to do, and placed "the onus on the employee" of deciding whether the employee wished (or was able) "to conform to the requirements of a particular work situation."[8]

In a disciplinary intervention, it is essential for task behavior to follow immediately. That is, once an intervention has been made, the manager must identify the new behavior that is to replace the undesired behavior. Only when that occurs can positive reinforcement be used to increase the likelihood that the new behavior will recur.

Extinction

When reinforcement is withheld after a behavior occurs, the behavior is said to be *on extinction*. Punishment tends only to suppress behavior; extinction tends to make it disappear. Extinguishing a response requires that there be *no* consequence of behavior. For example, suppose a child learns that he can get his parents' attention, and whatever else he wants, by stomping up and down and crying. If the parents do not want that kind of behavior, they can extinguish it by not responding to the child (in either a positive or a negative way). After a while, as the child sees that stomping and crying get him nothing, he will stop behaving that way to get what he wants. People seldom continue to do things that provide no negative or positive reinforcement.

Although extinction can help eliminate undesirable behavior, one should be careful not to use it unintentionally. Let us look at an example. Imagine that Emily who had been doing sloppy work is now working carefully and neatly because her manager has been praising (rewarding) her for everything she does right. But, suddenly, the manager stops rewarding Emily for neat work. Emily goes for perhaps a week or two working neatly with no reward. She may not be able to tell us what is different, but gradually her behavior gives us a clue. She soon begins to try other behaviors. She becomes less careful and neat, and if there are no negative consequences (punishment), within days she will most likely have reverted to her earlier behavior of doing sloppy work. In essence, neatness and carefulness will have been extinguished.

People seldom continue to do things that do not provide positive reinforcement, either through external reward or internal satisfaction. Emily did not find working carefully or neatly rewarding in itself. The intervention by her manager helped her task Performance Readiness® but Emily was not psychologically ready enough in this job (and she may never become so if it is a boring and unsatisfying job) to be left alone and not periodically reinforced for her neatness and carefulness.

In addition to its effect on the continuation of a particular behavior, extinction can also have an emotional impact. We could predict, for example, with an excellent chance of being correct, that Emily will become surly, will complain more than before, or will have problems getting along with her coworkers. Emotional behavior usually accompanies extinction when reinforcement or punishment is withheld.

Parents often extinguish behaviors unintentionally when they pay attention only when their children are behaving poorly. If parents pay little or no attention when the children are behaving appropriately, they, in a sense, put that behavior on extinction. A child who wants attention (a reward) from the parents may be willing to endure what the parents think is punishment to get it. So, in the long run, the parents might be reinforcing the very behavior they do not want and extinguishing more appropriate behavior.

Leaders in all kinds of settings must beware of positively reinforcing inappropriate behavior; yet it happens all the time. Have you ever given a crying child a piece of candy? The child may eat the candy and stop crying. But the next time the child wants a piece of candy (or your attention), he will know exactly how to get it—by crying. You made the mistake of positively reinforcing inappropriate behavior.[9]

This phenomenon is also very common in the world of work. For example, a manager's work group had responded well to a high task–low relationship style of always spelling out tasks specifically and dealing firmly with anyone who did not demonstrate appropriate behavior. Now suddenly this style is not achieving results, and followers are being disruptive and making unreasonable demands. What should the manager do? The first impulse of most managers is to think "Maybe I've been too hard on them" and begin to give in to their demands. Perhaps the manager should have increased relationship behavior earlier and moved to a high task–high relationship leadership style, but doing so now may be perceived as positively reinforcing inappropriate behavior—every time the work group wants something, they will become disruptive. Positively reinforcing inappropriate behavior generally results in more unwanted behavior.

When to Use Punishment or Extinction

In essence, what we are saying is that leaders must think before they behave because they never know what they may or may not be reinforcing. This is particularly true when it comes to using punishment and extinction. Yet these concepts can be useful in helping managers to effectively "unfreeze" inappropriate behavior so that they can begin to reinforce positively more desirable behavior. In using punishment or extinction, however, it is important to know what behavior you want to change and to communicate that in some way to the person(s) with whom you are working. To determine when to use punishment and when to ignore (extinguish by withholding reinforcement), managers need to estimate how long the undesirable behavior has been occurring. If the behavior is new, ignoring it (extinction) may get results and cause a person to abandon an inappropriate behavior. But if the behavior has been occurring for some time, it may be necessary to suppress this behavior through some form of punishment until some desirable behavior has a chance to become strong enough through positive reinforcement to replace the undesirable behavior. As we discussed in Chapter 2, the larger the reservoir of experience a person has in a particular behavior the more difficult the behavior will be to change, and, therefore, the harder the initial intervention may have to be before positive reinforcement can be used effectively to strengthen a new behavior.

An Example of Using Behavior Modification

Consider the behavior of Tony, a new employee right out of high school. Tony can be described as a very aggressive and competitive individual. During his first day on the job, he argues over tools with another young employee. To make certain that a manager would be sure of what to do about Tony's behavior and to summarize our discussion of behavior modification, we present some steps that managers can use to change employee behavior.[10]

- *Step 1.* Identify (for yourself and then with Tony) the behavior to be changed and the new behavior that is to replace it. Discover what Tony would consider to be positive reinforcement and punishment. Devise a strategy to get the new behavior, and determine the way you will positively reinforce it.
- *Step 2.* Attempt to find out whether the old behavior (arguing over tools) is such a strong behavior that you need to suppress it through punishment or whether it is a new enough behavior that a lack of any kind of reinforcement will extinguish it. If you decide to use punishment, determine what it will be. Remember, this punishment could operate as negative reinforcement and thus strengthen the behavior that removes the punishment. So be careful!
- *Step 3.* Develop a strategy to get Tony to practice the new behavior and positively reinforce it on a regular schedule. As soon as Tony has practiced the new behavior so that it is more likely to occur than the old behavior, change to an intermittent schedule of reinforcing the new behavior (make the intervals between reinforcement increasingly longer) so that new behavior will resist extinction.

In examining these steps, one could get the impression that the manager is dominating the process with little if any involvement from Tony. According to Situational Leadership®, this approach may be appropriate in working with people at low levels of Performance Readiness®, such as a new and inexperienced employee like Tony. But, as the Performance Readiness® Level of the people that a manager supervises begins to increase, this process of change becomes much more of a collaborative process. As we will discuss in Chapter 11, the extent of involvement of people in the change process will vary according to their Performance Readiness®.

PROBLEMS AND THEIR OWNERSHIP—WHO'S GOT THE PROBLEM?

As we have been suggesting in this chapter, effective managers are not only able to develop the Performance Readiness® of their people, they also are able to spot "slippage" in Performance Readiness® and intervene early enough to turn the situation around. How can managers know when to intervene? What should they look for?

As a simple guideline, whenever managers receive feedback—either verbal (one of their people tells them) or nonverbal (they observe the performance of one of their people)—indicating that a person is having a problem in some area, it is time to think about stepping in. A *problem* exists when there is a difference between what someone is doing and what that person's manager and that individual believe is really happening. Thus, detecting problems is all-important in determining what areas of a person's job require attention.

Thomas Gordon, in his book *P.E.T., Parent Effectiveness Training*, contends that one of the most important steps in becoming effective in rearing responsible self-motivated children is determining whether their behavior is acceptable or unacceptable to their parents as well as to themselves.[11] Once this question has been answered, then "who owns the problem" in terms of a child's behavior can be identified. Although the work of Gordon originated from observations of parents and teachers, the concepts behind the ownership of problems seem to apply to any organizational setting in which a leader is trying to influence the behavior of others.

Problem Ownership and Situational Leadership®

Let us look at problem ownership in the context of Situational Leadership®. If managers can identify who has the problem, then they are in a position to assess Performance Readiness® Level, determine the leadership style that has the best chance of success, and decide how to intervene with followers (see Figure 10–3). The four problem situations described next combine these elements.

1. *The manager has the problem.* In this situation, the follower's behavior is a problem to the manager but not to the follower. The follower's Performance Readiness® Level is R1 since

FIGURE 10–3 Four Problem Situations

Source: Copyright © 1985, 2006, Leadership Studies, Inc. All Rights Reserved.

the follower sees no problem. The appropriate leadership style for the manager is telling (S1). For managers to rid themselves of these problems, they must provide followers with structure in the form of direction regarding the task.

2. *The manager and the follower have the problem.* This situation involves the follower's behavior when it is a problem for both the manager and the follower. The follower's Performance Readiness® Level is R2 since the follower needs some direction. Furthermore, because the follower owns part of the problem, some relationship behavior in terms of two-way communication and facilitating behavior is also necessary. The appropriate leadership style is selling (S2) because the follower needs both direction and support to carry out the task.

3. *The follower has the problem.* Here, the follower's behavior is a problem for the follower but not for the manager. The follower's Performance Readiness® Level is R3 since the follower needs support and encouragement from the manager. The appropriate leadership style is S3, a participating style to facilitate two-way communication. The tragedy is that managers often treat this problem situation as if it were a problem to neither. If management intervention is not made soon, the problem could become a serious problem for the follower, the manager, and the organization.

4. *Neither the manager nor the follower has the problem.* In this situation, there are no problems requiring attention. Followers involved in this situation are R4, a high level of Performance Readiness®. The most appropriate leadership style is delegating (S4), since the manager's job is to monitor the situation so that no problems will form.

Let us look at some examples of how this concept might be used as a diagnostic tool. Veronica, a commodities trader in a large exchange, has always executed trades and recorded exchanges according to the high standards developed by her company. Since she is operating within guidelines, her behavior is not a problem to her manager or her company, but Veronica's behavior may be a problem to herself; her best friends on the exchange floor have been involved in some questionable practices and are pressuring her to take part. If Veronica's manager treats this situation as if it were a problem to neither and leaves Veronica alone, the situation could quickly become a problem for both. Because of the pressures from her peers on the exchange floor, a lack of active listening and support by her manager could move Veronica toward the same behavior her peers are practicing. Thus, by not making a high-relationship intervention at the appropriate time, Veronica's manager could create a problem for her company that did not exist before.

If the situation is one in which the behavior of the employee is a problem to the manager but not to the employee, the manager does not have to provide facilitating behaviors. For example, if the problem involves personal friends visiting the employee during working hours, the manager merely needs to provide the employee with an understanding of what the rules are (an S1 intervention). The employee, who does not see the situation as a problem, does not want to spend 15 or 20 minutes discussing it.

Another situation might be one in which no one has a problem. For example, a teacher assigns 15, 20, or 25 pages of reading for the next day. The students say nothing; the assignment does not strike them as a problem. All they want to know is what the teacher expects; they do not want to sit around and talk about it. But if the teacher says the assignment is 100 pages, the situation might quickly become a problem to both the students and the teacher. Now the teacher has to engage in selling behavior rather than telling. The teacher has to open up channels of communication and discussion and engage in facilitating behaviors. The teacher has to get the students to understand the "why" of the large assignment and have them "buy in" psychologically to the decision. The teacher might say, "A top lecturer is coming this week. That's why I'm making a heavy assignment for tomorrow. I want you to be prepared. Later in the week we'll have no reading assignment." In other words, the teacher attempts to make some trades to facilitate interaction but is still trying to get the students to buy into the decision.

As the discussion and examples suggest, the integration of Situational Leadership® with Thomas Gordon's problem ownership approach can be very helpful in determining the appropriate leadership style in various situations. Remember, even if the follower's behavior is acceptable to the leader, the leader may still have to take action if the follower needs support and encouragement to keep up the good work. If the follower's behavior is unacceptable to the leader, a more directive style of intervention is needed to turn the situation around. How direct the intervention must be (just telling or selling) depends on whether the follower also sees this behavior as a problem and "owns the problem" too. If leaders are going to help their people grow and develop into self-motivated individuals, they must gradually let them think for themselves and solve their own problems.

POSITIVE DISCIPLINE

Another model of dealing with employees who fail to meet performance goals or who violate organizational rules is called *positive discipline*.[12] Developed by Eric L. Harvey, this approach to employee discipline follows three simple and direct steps:

1. Warn the employee orally.
2. Warn the employee in writing.
3. If steps 1 and 2 fail to resolve the problem, give the employee a day off, *with pay.*

The model removes punishment from the disciplinary process and places responsibility for appropriate performance on the employee. In the first two steps, the manager focuses on the specific discrepancy between the employee's actual and expected performance and the business reasons why the performance expectation must be met. The manager describes why meeting the performance standard is important and works to gain the employee's agreement to change behavior and meet the standard. The employee is reminded that proper performance and behavior are the individual's responsibility, not the manager's. Hostile or defensive employee reactions are met with mature and adult explanations of the specific discrepancy and the standard that needs to be met.

If the employee fails to change after the first two steps are taken, the manager moves to step 3. During the day off with pay, which is referred to as a "decision-making leave," the employee is expected to be thinking about whether he or she wishes to remain in the organization. The leave communicates to the employee that, "Your job is on the line. What are you going to do about it?" The suspension from work highlights the seriousness of the situation; being paid for the day removes employee hostility and reinforces the organization's honest desire to help the individual take responsibility for his or her actions and meet organizational expectations. Upon returning to work, the employee tells the manager of his or her decision—to make the required changes and continue employment, or to quit. If the problems continue upon the employee's return, the employee is then terminated.

The model is based on the belief that an organization and its managers have the right to establish reasonable and appropriate standards, to point out discrepancies when they occur, and to let the individual decide whether or not to perform and meet those standards. Responsibility for performance is placed on the employee, not on the manager or the organization.

Summary

This chapter offered suggestions for developing strategies for disciplining followers constructively. Leaders must endeavor to remove themselves from the traditional job of directing, controlling, and supervising their followers and assist them in learning to stand on their own and achieve individual effectiveness in the demanding work environment.

The goal of constructive discipline is to make problem solving a positive growth-oriented opportunity instead of a punitive experience. It is important to:

• Use a leadership style appropriate for your follower's *present* level of Performance Readiness®

• Make the intervention in a timely manner
• Use an appropriate emotional level
• Focus on performance, not personality
• Do your homework and be specific
• Keep the intervention private

Managers who keep these factors in mind when making disciplinary interventions find that discipline can be constructive and supportive rather than destructive.

Notes

1. Adapted from Paul Hersey, *The Situational Leader* (Escondido, CA: Center for Leadership Studies, 1985), 114.
2. Adapted from Paul Hersey, *Situational Selling* (Escondido, CA: Center for Leadership Studies, 1985), 115–120.
3. Harry Levinson, "Getting Past the Bad News," *Management Review*, September 1993, p. 4.
4. R. L. Solomon, "Punishment," *American Psychologist* 19 (1964): 239.
5. John Huberman, "Discipline without Punishment," *Harvard Business Review*, May 1967, pp. 62–68.
6. *Ibid.*, pp. 64–65.
7. *Ibid.*, p. 65.
8. *Ibid.*
9. Taken from an enjoyable popular article on this subject by Alice Lake, "How to Teach Your Child Good Habits," *Redbook Magazine*, June 1971, pp. 74, 186, 188, 190.
10. These steps were adapted from seven steps identified by Madeline Hunter, *Reinforcement Theory for Teachers* (El Segundo, CA, TIP Publications, 1967), 47–48.
11. Thomas Gordon, *P.E.T., Parent Effectiveness Training* (New York: Peter H. Wyden, 1970).
12. Eric L. Harvey, "Discipline vs. Punishment," *Management Review*, March 1987, pp. 25–29.

CHAPTER

11

Self-Awareness and Leadership Style

I n the last two chapters, our emphasis was on helping leaders develop people to their fullest potential. This development process involves being able to shift your leadership style, to be able to adapt to various situations. But are most leaders able to be that flexible, or do they tend to be limited to only one or two leadership styles? Is your style the right style to use right now? How will people react to you using a variety of styles? How can you adapt your leadership style usage and yet still be genuine?

To address these questions, we must start to look at how clearly you see your own leadership style, how others see it, and what to do if there is a significant gap between those perceptions. Once you better understand your primary style, we will then consider how leaders can adapt and use a range of styles for greater effectiveness.

LEADERSHIP AND SELF-AWARENESS

By definition, effective leaders focus on others. They are keenly attuned to the strengths, needs, goals, and achievements of their people. We have already discussed how important the ability to accurately diagnose the Performance Readiness® of followers is to helping them grow and develop. As Daniel Goleman has described, such social competence is a critical aspect of demonstrating emotional intelligence as a leader. But he also asserts that leaders must manage themselves as well. They need to cultivate self-awareness, confidence, and self-control, and understand their own motivations.[1] After all, a manager who cannot see that he becomes defensive when offered suggestions is unlikely to invite honesty or inspire trust. Similarly, a supervisor who sets high standards for his people but makes questionable compromises can hardly be seen as a role model for integrity.

Self-awareness is a cornerstone of developing yourself as a leader.

Leaders need to look inward, recognize their thoughts and feelings, and evaluate their choices and the impact of their behavior. But how can you be sure that you are seeing yourself accurately? Robert S. Kaplan suggests that leaders and managers need to regularly ask themselves some basic questions—about their vision, priorities, and pressures—and try to answer them honestly.[2]

While reflection is helpful, it may not be enough to gain key insights because our self-perceptions can be distorted or inaccurate. That is why it is a best practice for leaders to intentionally seek out behavioral feedback from others about both their strengths and areas for improvement. Feedback, whether formal or informal, may confirm, confuse, or radically challenge the leader's self-perceptions. In any case, it offers a significant opportunity to improve self-awareness.

JOHARI WINDOW

A useful framework for thinking about how you perceive yourself as a leader compared to how others see you is the *Johari Window* (taken from the first names of its authors, Joseph Luft and Harry Ingham).[3]

The Johari Window comprises four areas that compare what is known and unknown to self, and what is known and unknown to others, as depicted in Figure 11–1. The area that is known to both self and others in any specific organizational setting is called the *public arena*. Note that the *known to self* area includes not only self-awareness but also knowledge of the way the leader is viewed by the people he or she is trying to influence.

The area that is unknown to self but known to others is referred to as the *blind spot*. It might be unknown to the leader because followers have been unwilling to share feedback with or communicate candidly with that leader. Or, perhaps the leader is unable or unwilling to recognize and accept the verbal and nonverbal cues from their followers.

In contrast, the *facade* is the area that is known to self but unknown to others. It may be private because the leader has been unwilling to share it with others in the organization or because others are not picking up any nonverbal and verbal cues provided by the leader.

The last area, called the *unknown*, is just that—unknown to self and to others. In Freudian psychology, this is referred to as the subconscious or unconscious.[4] As you may recall from Chapter 2, Freud likened personality to an iceberg. A certain portion of a leader's personality is above the surface—that is, it is visible. Anyone who looks in that direction can see the basic size, consistency, makeup, and configuration. But much of this iceberg exists beneath the surface, and unless we make conscious efforts to probe and understand, we will really never have any insight into it. Yet this unknown may be having an impact on the kinds of behaviors in which a leader engages when trying to influence others.

	Known to Self	Unknown to Self
Known to Others	Public	Blind
Unknown to Others	Facade	Unknown

FIGURE 11–1 The Johari Window

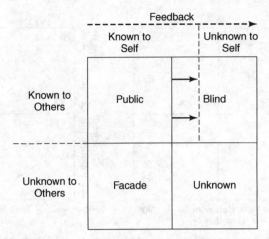

FIGURE 11–2   Effect of Feedback on the Johari Window

Feedback

Two processes affect the relative size of the four areas within the Johari Window. The first is *feedback*, which operates in the direction illustrated in Figure 11–2. When others are willing to openly share their views of the leader's behavior, that feedback can enlarge his or her self-awareness, expanding the public arena and diminishing the size of the blind spot.

Much has been written about the importance of becoming aware of the blind spot. Eichinger and Lombardo found that managers who overrated their own performance, compared to coworker ratings, were more likely to fail.[5]

As Max Bazerman and Ann Tenbrunsel have noted, significant research reveals the damaging impact of the blind spot at its worst, when leaders are unaware of the gap between how ethical they think they are and how ethical they truly are.[6] Sadly, there are too many now-familiar stories of leaders in business, government, and sports whose ethical blind spots were stopped only by very serious forms of feedback, such as whistle blowing testimony and criminal proceedings. Former executives Jeffrey Skilling and Ken Lay of the Enron Corporation, former Governor Eliot Spitzer of New York, and former Major League baseball player Barry Bonds all failed to either receive or respond to feedback about ethical boundaries that might have prevented the shameful actions that ruined their careers.

Ironically, as Kaplan has underscored, many leaders are reluctant to seek out unvarnished feedback from their people, particularly as they ascend in the organization. He recommends that leaders find a few trusted subordinates who are willing to tell them what they may not want to hear but need to know and improve the probability of uncovering blind spots.[7]

Disclosure

The other process that affects the shape of the Johari Window is *disclosure*. This is the extent to which leaders are willing to share information about themselves with others.

The way we use the term *disclosure* is different from the way many others in the field of behavioral science often use it. First, the most relevant disclosure is not what people say about themselves but rather how they behave. After all, people can say one thing but do something

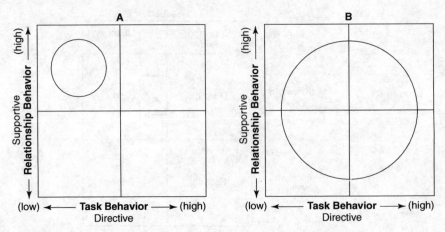

FIGURE 11–3 Style Range in Terms of Task Behavior and Relationship Behavior

else. So if you want to understand people better, you really have to look at their behavior to gain more relevant and reliable insights into their beliefs, values, and attitudes—what their behavior represents.

Second, we think disclosure is appropriate in organizations only when it is relevant to the organization. This is a different way of viewing disclosure than is urged by some people in the personal growth field, who think all disclosure is appropriate. In fact, some contend that it is appropriate for a leader or manager in an organizational setting to be open and disclose as much as possible and that the organization process that data. Our experience from numerous organizational development interventions suggests that two of the scarcest resources in any organizational setting are time and energy. If people disclosed almost everything about themselves at work and others took time to process all that information, there would not be much time left to get any work done. We feel disclosure is important and helpful in organizations as long as it contributes to the operation of the organization.

In the process of disclosure, the more organizationally relevant information that leaders disclose about the way they think or behave, the larger the public arena becomes and the smaller the facade gets (shown in Figure 11–3).

We use the Johari Window to focus on leadership personality, not overall personality, as it is sometimes used. What is the difference between leadership personality and leadership style? In this context, leadership personality includes self-perception and the perception of others, while style consists of the perceptions of others.

The Johari Window can help you organize and compare perceptions of your leadership from multiple points of view. Through feedback, your blind spots can be discovered and hopefully minimized. Disclosure helps enlarge and strengthen the public arena by peeling back your facade and improving transparency between leaders and followers (see Figure 11–4).

Building Self-Awareness through the LEAD Feedback

Like the Johari Window, the Leader Effectiveness and Adaptability Description (LEAD) Feedback assessment process, sometimes called a multi-source or multi-rater instrument, is frequently used in leadership development efforts to solicit and compare the perceptions of

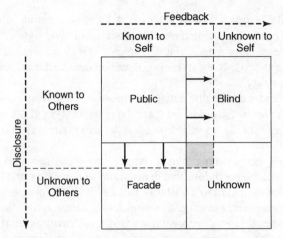

FIGURE 11–4 Effect of Feedback and Disclosure on the Johari Window

the leader, his or her followers, teammates, peers, clients or customers. In fact, "about 90% of Fortune 100 companies are estimated to use some form of multi-source evaluation."[8]

The Center for Leadership Studies developed the LEAD Feedback instrument, and has used it to develop leaders for more than five decades. The LEAD Self measures self-perception of how an individual behaves as a leader; the LEAD Other reflects the perceptions of a leader's followers, supervisors, and peers or associates.[9] The purpose of collecting and analyzing data from this instrument is to determine if there is any discrepancy between one's own view and the perception of others, and feed that information back to participating managers as an integrated profile.

The LEAD instrument was designed to measure three aspects of leader behavior:

1. style,
2. style range, or flexibility, and
3. style adaptability.

Leadership Style

Our extensive research over many years has revealed that all leaders have a *primary* leadership style with which they are most comfortable and most likely to use and may have a *secondary* leadership style. A leader's primary style is defined as the behavior pattern used most often when attempting to influence the activities of others, in other words, a favorite.

Interestingly, Spreier, Fontaine, and Malloy suggest that the preferred style the leader is an indicator of the person's dominant motive combined with the level of pressure in the workplace.[10]

The secondary style is what a leader tends to use occasionally, when the favorite style did not work, or in high-stress situations. However, an individual can range from having no secondary leadership style or several (up to three within the Situational Leadership® framework).

Style Range, or Flexibility

Style range is the extent to which people are able to vary their leadership styles. Leaders differ in their ability to vary their style in different situations. Some seem to be limited to one basic style and tend to be effective only in situations in which their styles are compatible with the situation or environment. Daniel Goleman has pointed out that this kind of style rigidity is, in fact, one of the two most common reasons for managerial derailment.[11] Other leaders are able to modify their behavior to use any of the four basic styles (as described in Situational Leadership®); still others can utilize two or three styles.

The style range of a leader can be illustrated in terms of task and relationship behavior, as shown in Figure 11–1. The area of the circle indicates the range of style. If the area is small, as in A, then the range of behavior of the leader is limited; if the area is large, as in B, the leader has a wide range of behavior.

Leadership situations vary in the extent to which they make demands on flexibility. William Reddin cited some of the conditions that demand, in his terms, low and high flexibility. For example, conditions that demand low flexibility include low-level managerial jobs, established tasks, and little environmental change. Conditions that demand high flexibility are the opposite—high-level managerial jobs, innovative tasks, and rapid environmental change. These conditions, as discussed in Chapter 1, are pervasive in the globalized markets and technology-driven work environments so common today.[12]

Style Adaptability

While style range is preferable to rigidity, it does not guarantee leadership effectiveness. *Style adaptability*, or the degree to which leaders are able to vary their style *appropriately* to the demands of a given situation, is what matters far more. Research has shown that adaptable leaders—those who have both a broad range of styles from which they strategically choose and use to suit the context—create high-performing and energizing climates that yield more lasting results.[13]

In comparison, style range has far greater limitations. People who have a narrow style range can be effective over a long period of time if they remain in situations in which their style has a high probability of success, but they cannot be said to have high style adaptability. Conversely, people who have a wide range of styles may be ineffective if they use a style that is not appropriate for the demands of the situation. These leaders, too, cannot be said to have high style adaptability.

For example, in Figure 11–1, **A**, the leader has a dominant relationship style with no flexibility (a narrow range); in **B**, the leader has a wide range of leadership styles because the leader is able to use all four leadership styles on various occasions. In this example, **A** may be effective in situations that demand a high relationship–low task style, such as in coaching or counseling situations. In **B**, the potential exists to be effective in a wide variety of instances, but the **B** style range will not guarantee effectiveness. **B**'s style will be effective only if the leader uses the style appropriate to the situation, that is, has style adaptability.

Flexibility: A Question of Willingness

The importance of a leader's *diagnostic ability* cannot be overemphasized. It is the key to adaptability. With that in mind, let us revisit a question raised at the beginning of this chapter: Are most leaders able to be that flexible, or do they tend to be limited to only one or two leadership styles?

It has been our experience that there are few, if any, leaders who cannot learn to use all four basic leadership styles. In fact, people use those behaviors almost every day. At least once a day you probably tell somebody what to do and watch the person closely (style S1), explain what you want somebody to do and permit the person to ask clarifying questions (style S2), share ideas with people and support their efforts (style S3), and turn over responsibility to someone to do it independently (style S4).

Learning to use the four basic styles is more an issue of willingness. If the person does not want to learn, then there is not much that you can do. When people are willing to learn to use all the leadership styles, we have found an interesting phenomenon. Once people learn to use an additional leadership style that previously was not a secondary style, it often becomes their most effective style. While this style may never become comfortable for the leader, it can become the most effective because it has been learned by choice and through conscious practice. People often use their comfortable or primary leadership style every day when they are influencing in a far more automatic, less conscious way. This is true not only in terms of leadership styles, but also in many other areas of their lives.

For example, suppose you are a golfer who enjoys and excels at hitting a drive but you need to improve your putting skill. So you decide to take lessons in putting. If you consciously make an effort, take lessons and practice to become a good putter, it very often is this part of the game that becomes your most potent weapon. You would still be more comfortable hitting the ball off the tee, but since you have practiced putting, it is now the strongest part of your game.

The same goes for leaders. Your primary style is often one that you do not have to think about using. But once you learn other styles through focused study and practice, these compensating styles can be your most effective style. Thus, we find that willingness—not ability—is the main issue in terms of style flexibility.

Is There Only One Appropriate Style?

Adaptability implies that the effective leader is able to use the right style at the right time. What if a leader makes a good diagnosis and then is unwilling or is unable to use the "best" style? Is that leader doomed to failure? Situational Leadership® not only suggests the high probability leadership styles for various Performance Readiness® Levels, but also indicates the probability of success of the other styles if the leader is unwilling or unable to use the "desired" style. The probability of success of each style for the four Performance Readiness® Levels is shown in Table 11–1.

As Table 11–1 indicates, the "desired" style always has a "second-best" style choice, that is, a style that would probably be effective if the highest probability style is not used. You will notice that at the low to moderate (R2) and moderate to high (R3) Performance Readiness® Levels there are two "second-best" style choices: Which one should be used depends on whether the Performance Readiness® of the individual is getting better, indicating that the leader should be involved in a developmental cycle (Chapter 9), or getting worse, revealing that a regressive cycle is occurring (Chapter 10). If the situation is improving, for instance, for a follower at R2, participating would be the best second choice style. Similarly, delegating would be the best second choice style to use with a follower at R3 who seems to be improving. If, however, things are deteriorating, a telling style for someone at R2 and a selling style for someone at R3 would be the most appropriate backup choices.

Table 11–1 also suggests that telling and delegating are the risky styles because one of the two is always the lowest probability style. Even so, later in this chapter we will discuss why it is important for leaders to learn to use these styles effectively.

Self-Perception versus Style

When we do an organizational diagnosis, the data from the LEAD Self, as we explained, denote self-perception. In terms of the Johari Window, the self-perception of leaders would represent what is known to them about their leadership style and would include both their public and private arenas. This self-perception of leadership style can be measured using the LEAD Self.

TABLE 11–1   Matching Performance Readiness® Level with the Leadership Style Most Likely to Work Well

Performance Readiness®	"Best" Style	"Second Best" Style	"Third Best" Style	Least Effective Style
R1	S1	S2	S3	S4
Low	Telling	Selling	Participating	Delegating
R2	S2	S1 Telling		S4
Low to moderate	Selling	or S3 Participating		Delegating
R3	S3	S2 Selling		S1
Moderate to high	Participating	or S4 Delegating		Telling
R4	S4	S3	S2	S1
High	Delegating	Participating	Selling	Telling

On the other hand, an individual's leadership style would represent what is known to others and would include both that person's public and blind areas on the Johari Window. Leadership style can be measured using the LEAD Other. The relationship between self-perception, leadership style, and the Johari Window is presented in Figure 11–5.

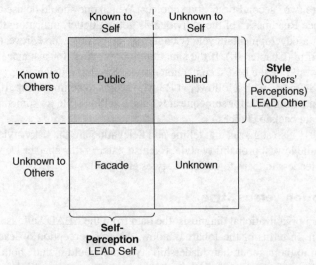

FIGURE 11–5   Self-Perception and Other Perception (Style)

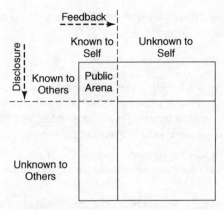

FIGURE 11–6   Public Arena When There is a Large Discrepancy in Perceptions

One of the interesting phenomena that we have discovered is that we can predict the shape of the public arena within the Johari framework based on LEAD results. For instance, if there is a great discrepancy between self-perception and the way others perceive a manager's style, the public arena in that manager's Johari Window will tend to be very small, as illustrated in Figure 11–6. But, if there is no significant difference between self-perception and the perception of others within a leader's organizational setting, the public arena in that person's leadership Johari Window would be large, as illustrated in Figure 11–7.

LEAD data can actually measure the shape of the arenas in an individual's leadership Johari Window for each of the organizational settings in which that person operates. For example, a manager responsible for three departments may find that in Department A, where there is good feedback and disclosure, the public arena is very large. In Department B, where there is very little contact, and thus infrequent feedback and disclosure, the public

 http://store.situational.com/products/LEAD-Self-Online.html

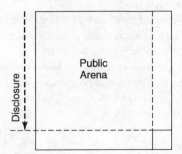

FIGURE 11–7   Public Arena When There is a Small Discrepancy in Perceptions

arena might be small. Finally, in Department C, where there is average interaction, the public arena might be moderate in size.

Is It Too Late?

In reading about effective leadership styles, managers might be feeling discouraged or even guilty. Maybe they have a problem employee or a difficult child and are thinking they have done a poor job as a manager or parent by using the wrong styles. Yet, as Wayne Dyer so aptly argued in his book *Your Erroneous Zones*, guilt is a useless feeling.[14]

> It is by far the greatest waste of emotional energy. Why? Because, by definition, you are feeling immobilized in the present over something that has already taken place, and no amount of guilt can ever change history.[15]

Managers can never redo what they should have done at an earlier time. Maybe you have made some mistakes. But that was yesterday. What are you going to do today? As the saying goes, today is the beginning of the rest of your life as a leader, manager, or parent. It is never too late to turn a situation around, as long as there is enough time.

Time is certainly a key factor that shapes our influence efforts, which is clear if we look at parenting over time. The earlier in a child's life a parent attempts to have an impact, the greater will be that parent's potential influence on the child's future behavior. During the early years, an intervention by a parent represents a substantial portion of the child's sum of experience in that area of the child's life; the same intervention later can never carry the same weight. In addition, the longer the behavior is reinforced, the more deeply ingrained it becomes, and the more difficult it is to change. That is why as a child gets older, it takes more time and more new experiences to bring about a change in behavior. Think of it this way: One drop of red food coloring in a half-pint bottle of clear liquid may be enough to change drastically the appearance of the total contents. But the same drop in a gallon jug may make little, if any, noticeable difference.

Yet even if our children are now teenagers or young adults, it is still possible, though difficult, to bring about some change in their behavior. At this juncture, though, it is worth a risk-benefit analysis. Let us take an extreme case. Suppose a teenage son is discovered by his parents to be taking drugs and in trouble with the law. What can his parents do now? One choice is to feel guilty and to try to make up for past mistakes by putting all kinds of time in with the son. But the son is likely to resent all this attention from his parents after having been left on his own for so long. If the son does not resent the sudden attention from his parents, then it becomes an economic question: Our children have unlimited needs, but we have limited time. Where can we put in the most effective time with the biggest payoff?

If the parents have plenty of time and decide to attempt to change their son's behavior (even though it is an old pattern), the concepts presented in this book should provide some helpful hints as to where and how to begin. Probably they will have to do some telling (S1) and selling (S2), both of which are time-consuming. However, with some concentrated effort, the parents can probably have an impact on this boy's behavior.

Before parents throw themselves into a change effort with one of their children, it is worth considering what impact this attention will have on the other children in the family. By devoting all of their time and energy to one problem, the parents may unwittingly create other problems. If all the parents' time is spent on this teenage son, the other children may get the impression that the only way to get time with mom and dad is by getting into trouble. Soon one problem child may have mushroomed into other problem children. Therefore, it is important to look at the big picture and allot time accordingly.

What is the lesson for managers to be learned from this example? The earlier you can diagnose and adapt your style, the better. Rescue and salvage work is tough, time-consuming and often comes too late to do much good.

Another point of importance concerns the types of stress placed on a manager. Elaina Zucker identified severe managerial stress as "that headache behind your left eye, the stiff neck, the quivering hands—these are the signs that stress is setting in."[16] Like guilt, stress does nothing to help a manager work effectively and is, in fact, often detrimental. Zucker suggests making a list of things that cause stress—for example, bad lighting, a certain employee, the commute to work—and reviewing the list periodically to evaluate whether these stressors can be either eliminated or somewhat alleviated. Just being aware that you are becoming stressed is helpful. Learning to cope with stress by altering your perspective and dealing with it in a positive manner are important weapons that a stressed manager can use to reduce tension.

Barbara Mackoff offered other strategies for reducing stress. Most involve friends and family outside of work. She suggests that managers conscientiously not bring work home, avoid "talking shop" at the dinner table and other social times, and seek out friends who will not be impressed with your business savvy. Rather, they should make life outside of work just as important, if not more important, than work itself.[17]

LEAD PROFILE RESULTS

Once a manager has learned that employees perceive that one style or another is used most of the time with them, what does it all mean?

Sample

In this section, we will examine and interpret some of the common profiles that we have found from analysis of LEAD Self and LEAD Other data accumulated at the Center for Leadership Studies.[18] The information was generated from a LEAD sample of over 80,000 leadership events from 14 cultures. A "leadership event" occurs when we have data not only in terms of self-perception (LEAD Self), but also the perception of others (LEAD Feedback) in that leadership environment. Of these respondents, we interviewed some 2,000 middle managers from industry and education; of that number, we conducted more than 500 in-depth interviews. The interviews included not only the leaders in terms of self-perception, but also a sample of the leaders' followers and their perceptions of the leaders' styles.

Two-Style Profile

In our in-depth interviews, the emphasis was on what we call "two-style profiles." A two-style profile includes either (1) a basic style that encompasses two of the four possible configuration styles or (2) a basic style and a supporting style.

It is suggested that as feedback is given on the specific two-style profiles, you keep in mind what you know about your own leadership style. If you think you have a one-style profile (you tend to use only one primary leadership style with little flexibility), then you need to remember that your profile represents only a portion of the two-style profile. If you think you have a three- or four-style profile (you have more than one supporting style in addition to your primary style), you may have to integrate the feedback that will be given to you into several of the two-style profiles. Remember that unless you have gathered specific data on how your leadership style is perceived by others, your perception of your own leadership style is only that—your perception.

Wide Flexibility

In working with people who have a wide range of styles, we have found that even though their effectiveness score may be low, a shorter period of time is needed to increase their effectiveness than is needed with people who have a smaller range of behavior. If people are engaging in a wide range of behavior, all you have to do to make a significant change in their effectiveness is teach them diagnostic skills. On the other hand, much more time is necessary for people who have had no experience in using a variety of styles to become comfortable in using different styles. They need to *learn* to use new behaviors, and that means taking the time to practice them.

Reference to Situational Leadership®

We will be referring to Situational Leadership® throughout the discussion of the two-style profiles. The basic framework is reproduced for your use in Figure 11–8.

Style Profile S1-S2

People who are perceived as using predominantly styles S1 and S2 (see Figure 11–9) tend to be able to raise and lower their socioemotional support or relationship behavior, but they often feel uncomfortable unless they are "calling the shots." They are most comfortable providing structure and direction. We found that this style profile tends to be characteristic of engineers who have become supervisors of other engineers but who tend to be reluctant to give up their engineering; salespersons who have become sales managers yet still love to sell; and teachers who have become administrators but still want to be directing the activities of students. In interviews, these leaders often project that "no one can do things as well as I can," which often becomes a self-fulfilling prophecy.

The style profile S1-S2 tends to be effective with low to moderate levels of Performance Readiness®. It is often an extremely effective style for people engaged in manufacturing and production where managers have real pressures to produce as well as with leaders in crisis situations where time is an extremely scarce resource. But when the crisis or time pressure is over, leaders with this style often are not able to develop people to their fullest potential. And this remains true until they learn to use styles S3 and S4 appropriately.

Style Profile S1-S3

People who are perceived as using predominately styles S1 and S3 (see Figure 11–10) fall into what is called the Theory X-Theory Y profile (based on McGregor's motivational theory discussed in Chapter 2). What we have found is that people who have a style profile S1-S3, with little flexibility to styles S2 and S4, generally view their followers with either Theory X or Theory Y assumptions about human nature. They see some people as lazy, unreliable, and irresponsible.

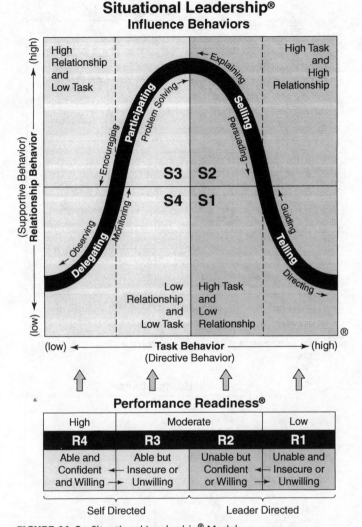

Situational Leadership®
Influence Behaviors

Performance Readiness®

High	Moderate		Low
R4	**R3**	**R2**	**R1**
Able and Confident and Willing	Able but Insecure or Unwilling	Unable but Confident or Willing	Unable and Insecure or Unwilling

Self Directed   Leader Directed

FIGURE 11–8   Situational Leadership® Model

Source: Situational Leadership® and Performance Readiness® are trademarks of Leadership Studies, Inc. Copyright © 1985, 2006, Leadership Studies, Inc. All Rights Reserved.

The only way to get anything out of these people is to coerce, reward and punish, and closely supervise them. Other people are seen very positively as creative and self-motivated; the only thing they have to do with these people is to provide socioemotional support. In fact, in interviewing managers with this profile, we have found that they talk about individuals they supervise as "good people" or "bad people" who are either "with me" or "against me." Their followers, when interviewed, tend to agree. They see their managers as labeling people, being very supportive (S3) with people they see in their "camp," but closely supervising, controlling (S1), and even punishing people whom they perceive as against them.

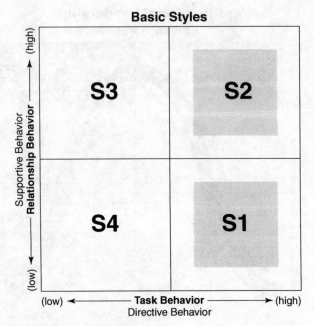

FIGURE 11–9   Style Profile S1-S2

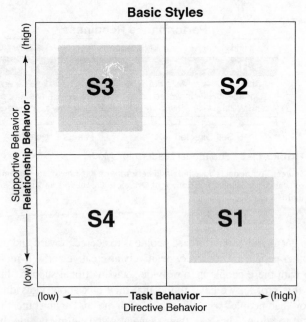

FIGURE 11–10   Style Profile S1-S3

One of the interesting things that occurs with this style profile is that it often becomes a self-fulfilling prophecy. A manager with this style takes people who are at moderate Performance Readiness Levels® (R2) and either moves them up to moderate to high (R3) or moves them down to low levels of Performance Readiness® (R1). Thus, this manager tends to be effective working with either low or moderate to high levels of Performance Readiness®.

A problem with this style is that the leaders who adopt it often are doing little to develop the potential of the people they do not like. They tend to keep them locked into low levels of Performance Readiness® by always relying on S1 (high task–low relationship behavior) with them. They lack the interim behaviors between style S1 and style S3 to operate effectively in the developmental cycle. At the same time, their style S3 (high relationship–low task behavior) with people of moderate levels of Performance Readiness® may keep these people psychologically dependent on them too long. These kinds of leaders do not seem to allow people to develop fully through delegation.

If there is any change in leaders with this style profile, it is usually a shift from style S3 to style S1. In other words, it is very difficult if you are being treated in a style S1 fashion by these leaders ever to receive style S3 types of behavior from them. But it is not too difficult to move from receiving style S3 behaviors to receiving style S1 behaviors. All you have to do is make some mistakes and these leaders tend to respond with highly structured behavior.

Style Profile S1-S4

People who are perceived as using mainly styles S1 and S4 (see Figure 11–11) have some similarity to the Theory X-Theory Y profile of style S1-S3 leaders. But rather than assessing people on whether they are "good" or "bad", the leader tends to view them as either competent or

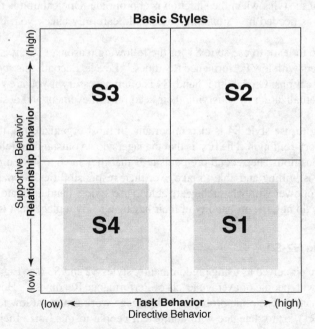

FIGURE 11–11   Style Profile S1-S4

incompetent. The interviews suggested that if you are competent you will be left alone, but that if you are incompetent, managers with this style profile will supervise your activities very closely.

This style profile is either telling or delegating. A leader with this style is effective at crisis interventions, and well-suited to intervene in an organization with severe problems and little time to solve them. This kind of leader is quite capable of making disciplinary interventions, going in and turning around a situation, and, hopefully, moving people back to a higher level of Performance Readiness®. Much like the style S1-S3 profile, this type of leader lacks the skill to develop people from low to higher levels of Performance Readiness®.

An interesting thing occurs when leaders with this type of profile are introduced into a group with a normal distribution of Performance Readiness®. What tends to happen is that the leader treats people in such a way that they either progress in their Performance Readiness® or they regress, so that now, rather than a normal distribution of Performance Readiness® Levels, followers are clustered at the high end (R4) and low end (R1) of the Performance Readiness® continuum. Once again, this style becomes a self-fulfilling prophecy.

Styles S1 and S4 are considered the "risky" styles. We say "risky" because if they are used inappropriately, they can result in a great deal of crisis. For instance, if someone is supervising a group at a very low level of Performance Readiness® and uses style S4, leaving people on their own, there is a high probability that the environment is going to deteriorate and serious problems will result. On the other hand, if you have an extremely high level of Performance Readiness® among your followers and you are attempting to use style S1 interventions, you are likely to generate much resentment, anxiety, and resistance, which may lead to what Machiavelli referred to as attempts to undermine, overthrow, or get out from under the leader, that is, hatred rather than fear. Even so, if you are going to maximize your role as leader, you have to be willing to take the risk and use these styles when the situation is appropriate. One caution is that if you feel either style S1 or S4 is needed in a situation, you should carefully check your diagnostic judgments before using it.

You need to learn to use style S1 for the following reasons. First, it is effective when people are beginners with low Performance Readiness® Levels. Second, this style is often necessary in disciplinary actions. On the other hand, S4 is often necessary if you are going to allow people to reach self-actualization by satisfying their need for achievement and desire to maximize their potential.

Learning to use style S4 is also important. In most organizations, there are at least two prerequisites for promotion. The first is that managers do an outstanding job delivering results in their present position. The second prerequisite is that they have to have a ready replacement—someone who is willing and able to take over their responsibilities. So managers must have at least one key follower with whom they are able to use style S4 and delegate significant responsibilities. If they do not, the probability of their having a ready replacement is very low.

Style Profile S2-S3

People who are perceived as using predominantly styles S2 and S3 (see Figure 11–12) tend to do well working with people of average levels of Performance Readiness®. However, they may find it difficult to handle discipline problems and manage work groups at low levels of Performance Readiness® (R1), or to delegate with competent people to maximize their development. This style tends to be the most frequently identified style in the United States and other countries that have a high level of education and extensive industrial experience. Managers in some of the emerging cultures tend to have a more structured style profile (S1 and S2).

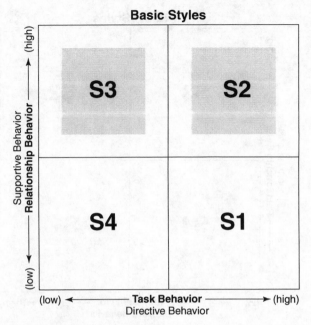

FIGURE 11–12   Style Profile S2-S3

Source: Copyright © 1985, 2006, Leadership Studies, Inc. All Rights Reserved.

The S2-S3 style leader tends to be effective more often than not, because most people in work settings usually fall into Performance Readiness® Levels R2 and R3. We find far fewer people, on the whole, at Performance Readiness® Levels R1 and R4.

If styles S1 and S4 are considered the "risky" styles, then S2 and S3 are considered the "safe" styles. Neither S2 nor S3 is ever likely to result in a crisis. But if leaders with this profile are going to maximize their potential as leaders, they need to learn to use styles S1 and S4 when necessary.

Style Profile S2-S4

People who are perceived as using mainly styles S2 and S4 (see Figure 11–13) usually have a primary style of S2 and a secondary style of S4. This style seems to be characteristic of managers who do not feel secure unless they are providing much of the direction, as well as developing a personal relationship with people in an environment characterized by two-way communication and emotional support (high-relationship behavior). These people feel comfortable delegating to someone occasionally. And when they do delegate, the person they choose may not be able to handle the project. The individual may not be able to complete the task or may come to the manager for help, being used to the leader's providing direction and emotional support. The reason that style profile S2-S4 leaders tend be unsuccessful in delegating is that they generally move from style S2 to style S4 without moving through style S3. Let us look at an example.

Suppose Mac, a supervisor, usually directs and closely supervises your activities (high-task behavior). You have good rapport and open communication with him, and you receive emotional support from these interactions (high-relationship behavior). One day Mac puts a couple

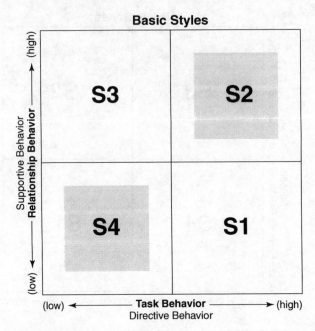

FIGURE 11–13   Style Profile S2-S4

of projects on your desk and tells you that they must be completed in two weeks. Then you do not see Mac again until the deadline approaches. You would probably respond to that behavior as if it were a punishment rather than a reward. You might say, "What's Mac giving me all this work for?" or "Mac must not care about me much anymore because I never see him now!" To be effective in delegating, managers with this style need to learn to move from selling (S2) through participating (S3) and then to delegating (S4) rather than suddenly shifting from S2 to S4.

Style Profile S3-S4

People who are perceived as using predominantly styles S3 and S4 (see Figure 11–14) tend to be able to raise and lower their relationship behaviors, but they often feel uncomfortable if they have to initiate structure or provide direction for people. Thus, while this style profile is appropriate for working with moderate to high levels of Performance Readiness®, it tends to create problems with people who are decreasing in Performance Readiness® and need more guidance. It also benefits inexperienced people who require more direction during the early phases of the developmental cycle.

Determining the Leadership Style of a Manager

In the beginning of this chapter, we raised the following question: How will changes in a leader's style affect followers' perceptions of the leader's intentions? From our experience, once managers begin to share Situational Leadership® with their key people and clarify what is expected of them, this question no longer becomes an issue. Managers no longer are the sole determiners of the

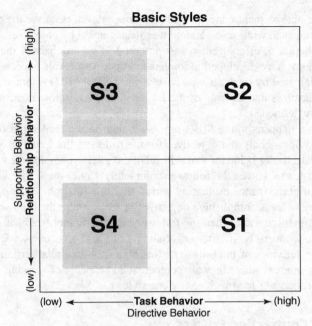

FIGURE 11–14   Style Profile S3-S4

style they use with their people. Their key people now play a vital role in shaping how they will work together. If the managers are practicing situational leaders, key staff start to realize that it is *their* behavior (not the manager's) that determines the leadership style to be used with them. So if everyone on a management team knows Situational Leadership®, all they have to do is perform in responsible ways—ways that everyone has agreed are appropriate—and their manager will be supportive (S3) or leave them alone (S4). But if they are at a low Performance Readiness® Level or they do not produce and perform in responsible ways, they know their manager will watch them more closely. They will know why they are getting more direct involvement from their manager, and they will know how they can get more support by either increasing their development level or getting back on track. But remember that this approach is effective only if managers are consistent in using the optimal styles even when it is inconvenient or unpopular with their people.

Thus, Situational Leadership® is a vehicle to help managers and their staff understand and share expectations in their organizational setting. If people know what is expected of them, they can gradually learn to supervise their own behavior and become responsible, self-motivated individuals.

CONTRACTING FOR LEADERSHIP STYLE

The process that was developed at the Center for Leadership Studies for sharing Situational Leadership® with key staff and helping to enlarge everyone's public arena (in Johari Window terms) is called "Contracting for Leadership Style." This process is a helpful addition to a management by objectives (MBO) effort.

Of all the management concepts and techniques developed over the past several decades, few have received such widespread attention as management by objectives. Theoretically, MBO, discussed in Chapter 6, offers tremendous potential as a participatory management approach. However, problems have developed in implementation. As a result, success stories do not occur as often as anticipated by theorists who have written about MBO or practitioners who have applied it. One reason is that the role of the leader in helping followers accomplish objectives is often not clearly defined.

What often happens in the MBO process is that once a leader and follower have negotiated and agreed upon goals and objectives for the follower, the leader may or may not engage in the appropriate leader behavior that will facilitate goal accomplishment for that person. For example, if the leader leaves the follower completely alone, the leader will be unaware until the next interim performance evaluation period that this low relationship–low task leadership style is appropriate for accomplishing objectives in areas where the follower has had significant experience, but inappropriate when the follower lacks sufficient technical skill and knowledge in another area. Conversely, if, after negotiating goals and objectives, a leader continually micromanages the activities of the followers, this high task–low relationship style might alienate people working in areas where they are competent and capable of working alone. Problems may occur when a leader uses too much of any one style.

Adding the Contracting Process

Adding Situational Leadership® to the MBO Process can increase its effectiveness. Once a leader and follower have agreed upon and contracted goals and objectives for the follower, the next logical step is for them to negotiate and agree upon the appropriate leadership style for helping the follower accomplish each one of the objectives. For example, an individual and the leader may agree on five objectives for the year. Here is what an effective leadership style contract might look like. In areas where the person is experienced and has been successful in accomplishing similar objectives over a period of time, the leader agrees to give the follower considerable freedom. Rather than directing and closely supervising behavior, the leader would be to make sure that the resources necessary for goal accomplishment are available and coordinate the results of this project with other projects being supervised. With another goal, the follower might be working on a new project with little prior experience, while the leader does have some expertise in this area. In this case, the follower and leader might negotiate significant structure, direction, and supervision from the leader until the follower is familiar with the task. Different leadership styles may be appropriate at different times, depending on the follower's Performance Readiness® in relation to the specific task involved.

There are two key criteria that should be included and discussed in negotiations of leadership style. First, it should be an open contract. Once a style has been negotiated for accomplishing a particular goal, it can be revisited for renegotiation by either party. For example, an individual may find on a particular task that working without supervision is not realistic. At this point, the follower may contact the leader and set up a meeting to negotiate for more direction. The leader, at the time, may gather some data that suggest that the style being used with an individual on a particular task is not producing desired results. The leader in this case can ask for a renegotiation of style.

Second, when a negotiation over leadership style occurs, it implies a shared responsibility if goals are not met. For example, if a follower has not accomplished the agreed-upon goals and the leader has not provided the contracted leadership style or support, that data then become part of the evaluation of both people. This means that if a leader has contracted for close supervision but does not provide it, the leader shares some of the responsibility for lack of goal accomplishment.

An Example—Contracting for Leadership Styles in a School

The Contracting for Leadership Style process used in an elementary school in eastern Massachusetts yielded some interesting results. In many school systems, the principal of a school is required by school policy to visit each classroom a certain number of times each year. This visitation policy is problematic for principals who recognize that their teachers vary in their experience and competence and so have varying needs for supervision from the principal. If a principal decides to schedule visitations according to perceptions of the teachers' competence, problems often occur with teachers at either end of the extreme. Left alone, a highly experienced teacher may be confused by the lack of contact with the principal and may even interpret it as a lack of interest. At the same time, an inexperienced teacher may interpret the frequent visits of the principal as a sign of lack of trust and confidence. In both cases, what the principal does may be interpreted negatively by the teachers.

These problems were eliminated in this elementary school when the principal shared Situational Leadership® with the staff and then attempted to negotiate what the principal's leadership style should be with each of the teachers. It was found that when low relationship–low task leadership style was negotiated between the principal and teachers because both agreed that these teachers were capable of working on their own, infrequent visits from the principal were perceived by the teachers as a reward rather than a punishment.

The same thing held true at the other end of the continuum. When negotiation for leadership style took place with inexperienced teachers (who realized that the system was designed to help teachers learn to work on their own), these teachers were less reluctant to share anxieties about certain aspects of their teaching. If the negotiation led to initial close supervision and direction, the teachers were able to view this interaction as positive, not punitive, because it was a temporary style and demonstrated the principal's interest in helping them learn to operate on their own.

Using the Performance Readiness® Style Match

A useful instrument, known as the Performance Readiness® Style Match, has been developed at the Center for Leadership Studies. This instrument formalizes the process of Contracting for Leadership Style[19]. As discussed in Chapter 7, the Performance Readiness® Style Match measures Performance Readiness® using two dimensions: (1) *ability*, or job Performance Readiness®, and (2) *willingness*, or psychological Performance Readiness®. The rating form also describes the four basic leadership styles.

As depicted in Figure 11–15, a person's ability (knowledge, experience, and skill) is relatively stable. Differences are a matter of degree; that is, an individual's ability does not change drastically from one moment to the next. At any given moment, an individual has a little, some, quite a bit, or a great deal of ability. Willingness (confidence, commitment, and motivation), however, is different. A person's psychological Performance Readiness® can, and often does, fluctuate from one moment to another. Willingness to take responsibility in a particular area could swing from seldom to often more quickly.

How can you combine the process of establishing objectives and agreeing on performance criteria with negotiating the appropriate leadership style a manager should use to

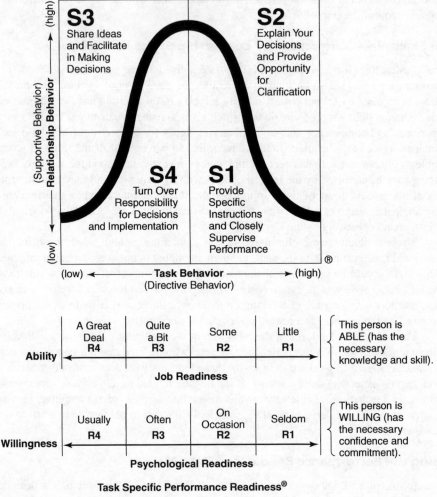

FIGURE 11–15   Defining Performance Readiness® and the Four Basic Leadership Styles

Source: Copyright © 1985, 2006, Leadership Studies, Inc. All Rights Reserved.

facilitate achievement of those objectives? The following steps outline how you can accomplish both.

1. **Establish objectives and performance criteria**. Manager and employee independently establish objectives and performance criteria for the employee.
2. **Reach agreement on objectives and performance criteria.** Manager and employee come together to discuss and reach agreement on objectives and performance criteria.
3. **Introduce Situational Leadership®**. Both manager and employee are introduced to Situational Leadership® (which can be accomplished by reading Chapter 7 of this book).

4. **Complete Performance Readiness® Style Match**. Manager and employee independently complete a Performance Readiness® Style Match rating form. The employee records the primary and secondary leadership styles that the manager has been using on each of the agreed-upon goals and objectives. The manager does the same, indicating what leadership style has been used with the employee on each of the agreed-upon goals and objectives. If the employee has never had a particular objective area before, no past leadership style can be diagnosed. After analyzing leadership style, both the employee and manager make judgments on the ability and the willingness of the employee to accomplish each of the goals and objectives established at the desired performance level without any supervision. In other words, the person participating in this process would analyze the leadership style that the manager has been using, as well as make self-assessment judgments of their Performance Readiness® Level. At the same time, the manager would be analyzing the Performance Readiness® Level of the employee as well as making leadership style self-assessment judgments.

5. **Meet to share data from Performance Readiness® Style Match**. Manager and employee meet and share the data from their Performance Readiness® Style Match rating forms, preferably by looking at one objective or responsibility at a time. The purpose of sharing data is to agree upon the Performance Readiness® Level and appropriate leadership style that can be utilized with the employee to maximize performance. During this process, the manager and employee should bring their calendars. Once they have determined the appropriate leadership style, they will schedule required meetings.

For example, in a particular objective area, any one of the four leadership styles may have been agreed upon as appropriate. If the employee is inexperienced and insecure about performing in a particular area, a telling (S1) style would be appropriate for the manager to use. If this is the case, they should schedule frequent meetings so that the manager can work closely with the employee.

If the employee is willing but inexperienced in a particular area, the manager should utilize a selling (S2) style. This would involve scheduling meetings to work with the employee, but not as frequently as under S1 supervision.

If the employee is able in a particular area, but is a little insecure about working completely alone, a participating (S3) leadership style would be appropriate. Meeting periodically over lunch may be helpful so that the employee can show the manager what has been accomplished and the proper support and encouragement can be given.

If the employee is able and willing to perform at the desired level in a particular objective area, no meetings are necessary unless requested by the employee. In this case, performance review can occur on an infrequent basis.

If the Contracting for Leadership Style process is utilized, the frequency of performance review will change depending on the ability and the willingness of the employee to perform at the desired level without supervision. A give-and-take process should occur between the leader and the follower.

The Performance Readiness® Style Match matrix is useful in providing insight into whether your manager is using "overleadership"—you have high levels of Performance Readiness®, but your manager is using telling and selling styles to a greater degree than necessary. It may also reveal "underleadership" is where you have low levels of Performance Readiness®, but your manager is using participating and delegating styles more than is appropriate. A high probability style match would be when the style(s) of your manager tends to correspond with the Performance Readiness® Level(s) you exhibit.

One warning should be given in using the Contracting for Leadership Style process and the Performance Readiness® Style Match rating forms. When managers go through that process, their public arena in the Johari Window becomes very large. Very little about what these managers think and feel about the employee is unknown to that employee, and vice versa. Feedback and disclosure become an ongoing process. If managers do not want their people to know what they think about them, they should be careful about using the described process. With some people they might want to remain less open. When managers make that choice, they must remember that with those people, the blind and private arenas in their Johari Window will be large.

Summary

This chapter has discussed the critical importance of leaders developing self-awareness. Soliciting feedback and discovering blind spots facilitate more accurate self-perceptions. The Johari Window was introduced as an approach to comparing the leader's self-perception and the perception of others. We also discussed three key aspects of leader behavior—(1) style, (2) style range or flexibility, and (3) style adaptability—and how LEAD instruments can be used to diagnose each of them. The relative effectiveness of several two-style profiles and steps for combining the management by objectives (MBO) process with contracting for leadership style were described.

Notes

1. Daniel Goleman, *Working with Emotional Intelligence*, (New York: Bantam Books, 1998), 26–27.

2. Robert S. Kaplan, "What to Ask the Person in the Mirror," *Harvard Business Review*, January 2007, 86–95.

3. Joseph Luft and Harry Ingham, "The Johari Window, A Graphic Model of Interpersonal Awareness," *Proceedings of the Western Training Laboratory in Group Development* (Los Angeles: UCLA, Extension Office, 1955). A more up-to-date version of the framework is presented in Joseph Luft, *Group Process: An Introduction to Group Dynamics*, 2nd ed. (Palo Alto, CA: National Press Book, 1970).

4. Sigmund Freud, *The Ego and the Id* (London: Hogarth Press, 1927).

5. Eichinger, R. W. and Lombardo, M. M., "Knowledge Summary Series: 360-Degree Assessment," *Human Resources Planning* 26 (2003): 34–44.

6. Max H. Bazerman and Ann E. Tenbrunsel, *Blind Spots: Why We Fail to Do What's Right and What to Do about It* (Princeton and Oxford: Princeton, 2011), 5.

7. Kaplan, "What to Ask the Person in the Mirror," p. 89.

8. Leanne Atwater and David Waldman. "Accountability in 360 Degree Feedback," *HR Magazine*, May 1998, 96.

9. LEAD (formerly known as the Leader Adaptability and Style Inventory, LASI) is based on the Situational Leadership® Model. The first publication on this LEAD instrument appeared as Paul Hersey and Kenneth H. Blanchard, "So You Want to Know Your Leadership Style?" *Training and Development Journal* (February 1974). The LEAD Other is the same instrument as the LEAD Self but written so that a subordinate, superior, or peer could fill it out on a leader. Copies of the LEAD Self and LEAD Other instruments can be ordered from the Center for Leadership Studies, Escondido, CA 92025.

10. Scott W. Spreier, Mary H. Fontaine, and Ruth L. Malloy, "Leadership Run Amok," *Harvard Business Review*, June 2006, 72–82.

11. Daniel Goleman, *Working with Emotional Intelligence* (New York: Bantam Books, 1998), 40.

12. William J. Reddin, *The 3-D Management Style Theory, Theory Paper #6—Style Flex* (Fredericton, N.B., Canada: Social Science Systems, 1967), p. 6.

13. Spreier, Fontaine, and Malloy, p. 77.

14. Wayne W. Dyer, *Your Erroneous Zones* (New York: Funk & Wagnalls, 1976).

15. This statement is adapted from a quotation by Dorothy Canfield Fisher that Dyer referred to in *Your Erroneous Zones*, p. 195.

16. Elaina Zucker, "5 Tips for Managing a Stressful Job," *Nursing* (May 1993).

17. Barbara L. Mackoff, "Leave the Office Behind," *Public Management* (June 1992).

18. The analysis of LEAD data was first presented in Paul Hersey, *Situational Leadership: Some Aspects of Its Influence on Organizational Development,* Ph.D. dissertation, University of Massachusetts, 1975.

19. This contracting process first appeared as Paul Hersey and Kenneth H. Blanchard, "What's Missing in MBO?" *Management Review* (October 1974). Much of the discussion that follows was taken from that article.

12

Effective Communication

W hen we think of leaders who are great communicators, we often picture them at a podium giving prepared speeches and briefings, reviewing PowerPoint slide decks, or taking the stage for a webcast. Their written statements are carefully crafted, with key phrases that may be repeated by thousands. While these kinds of "one-to-many" communications are often important, they probably take place far less often than the informal one-to-one or team interactions that fill most managers' days. As Google's study of effective manager behaviors suggests, the concept is a simple one: "Be a good communicator and listen to your team."[1] Doing it well is another matter.

So much depends on your communication as a leader: your credibility, negotiation outcomes, buy-in to change, collaboration in virtual teams. As Malcolm Gladwell has revealed in his book *Blink*, people make emotional "snap judgments" about you within a mere seven seconds.[2] Your smile can convey warmth or coolness, your questions may seem curious or defensive, and your posture could appear confident or tentative. It all matters when it comes to influencing others.

In this chapter, we will explore this critical competency through three basic communication models, including the functions and types of nonverbal communication. We will then look at what happens and what to do when communication falters, with special attention to gender and cross-cultural differences.

HOW IMPORTANT IS EFFECTIVE COMMUNICATION?

The evidence clearly shows that written and oral communication skills are critical not only in getting a job, but also in performing effectively on the job. For example, in a study of hiring factors among graduating business students, written and oral communication skills were the two most important factors or skills rated.[3] This finding was confirmed in a recent study of MBAs by Kimberly F. Kane:

Nearly two-thirds (of recruiters surveyed) thought MBAs have fully satisfactory skills and knowledge in their specialty areas. However, fully half thought MBAs were lacking to some degree in both interpersonal and written communications skills—the very skills reported to be the most important hiring criteria. One-third reported that MBAs were lacking in some degree in oral communication skills.[4]

But what is the relationship between oral and written communication skills and performance on the job?

Most executives see employee communication skills as vital, as seen in statements such as "there is a direct correlation between employee communication and profitability" and "I find that making good profits goes hand in hand with having good communication."[5] Perhaps the importance of good communication is best summarized by a senior executive who noted:

> The best business plan is meaningless unless everyone is aware of it and pulling together to achieve its objectives. Good communications are the lifeblood of any enterprise, large or small. Communications are essential to keep our entire organization functioning at maximum levels and to make the most of our greatest management resource—our people.[6]

With this level of importance, how can we, as leaders and potential leaders, improve our communication skills? Let us look first at some of the fundamentals captured by three basic communication models: linear, interactional, and transactional, with the last being most relevant to leadership situations.

COMMUNICATION MODELS

Components of Communication

Any communication begins when people **encode** their thoughts into **symbols**. Symbols are things that represent something else. The words on this page, for example, are symbolic of thoughts and ideas. The same is true of corporate logos and computer icons. In and of themselves they do not mean anything, yet represent the corporation or a computer application. For example, a person seeing an older gentleman with a goatee and a shock of white hair in an oval on the top of a red and white striped container realizes that this person is not alive on the cardboard, but represents the fast-food restaurant KFC.

Once the symbols are created, they are then formed into a **message,** which can be one symbol or a set of symbols. The message is then placed into a **channel** for distribution, through either verbal or nonverbal communication or a combination of both. Channels could include your speaking, your gestures, e-mail or instant messages, signs or advertisements.

Verbal communication refers only to spoken words. Leaders should be aware that their words could be perceived as powerful or powerless. Powerless language choices include hedges ("I *think* it will work"), gap-filling sounds (the use of "ums" and "ers"), tag questions ("We need your help, *don't you think so?"),* and disclaimers ("I would do that, *but I am not the boss.").* Bradac, Wiemann, and Schafer point out that numerous studies have shown that a person who uses power*ful* language is perceived as competent, dynamic, and attractive while a person who uses hedges and other power*less* language choices uncertain.[7] Regardless of the time and attention we devote to fine-tuning the words we use, their contribution to the total message is actually quite small relative to that of the nonverbal communication that accompanies our language choices.

The Weight of Words: A Classic Study

Consider the following percentages when you consider how much the content—the actual words you say—contribute to effective communication:

Words	7%
Tone (pitch, timbre, tempo, volume, emotion)	38%
Physical/visual (gestures, posture, facial expressions)	55%

Source: Alton Barbour and Mele Koneya, *Louder Than Words: Nonverbal Communication*, Merrill, 1976.

Nonverbal cues include all other aspects of physical communication, such as gestures, tone of voice, eye contact, facial expressions, posture, movement, and physical proximity to others. Nonverbal cues have four basic functions: (1) They supplement the verbal by accenting or adding emphasis to certain words (making a powerful gesture); (2) they can substitute for verbal cues (smile or frown); (3) they can contradict the verbal cues (saying, "This will work" while sweating, twisting a foot back and forth while looking for an emergency exit); and (4) they regulate verbal cues (increasing the pitch at the end of a sentence as you ask a question, pausing to await a response, holding up a hand to stop someone speaking).

How you enter an office, how you support your message through gestures and facial expressions, and how you imply interest and vitality through eye contact and other nonverbal behaviors affect other people's reaction to you. In turn, the nonverbal cues of followers serve as windows to their emotions, desires, and attitudes. Changes in a follower's body posture and gestures often signal a change in readiness. Movement toward the front of a chair may indicate interest. Relaxation of the body may reflect acceptance. Mirroring of your nods, smiles, and gestures suggests rapport and engagement.

As a leader, you should also understand how followers view space and its relationship to you. It is important to monitor how you position yourself in relation to followers. People have levels of comfort when it comes to how close they want you to be, depending on variables such as whether you are standing, sitting, meeting in a neutral location or in the boss's office. The general rule is, if you are making them uncomfortable, then change, either by moving closer or by moving farther away.

When you first encounter a prospective follower, before you say your first word you have already made a statement about yourself. Part of this statement involves how you move—the way you walk as your approach, the grip of your handshake, the choice of where you sit or stand. On the other hand, how you look—your clothing and accessories, grooming, neatness, hairstyle, and other personal features—also enters into the equation.

Many of these "nonverbals" are under your direct control and, like our word choices, have tremendous power to influence interactions with followers. Carol Kinsey Goman has identified numerous ways that nonverbals can create a language of inclusion and enhance collaboration. She notes that direct eye contact, a genuine smile, and nodding are behaviors that tend to encourage others to speak up and participate.[8]

However, like verbal behavior, nonverbal cues are subject to wide cultural and gender differences. For example, in Japan, immediate and sustained direct eye contact is uncomfortable and may be seen as disrespectful between the follower and the leader. When it comes to physical proximity, men and women demonstrate some very different nonverbal habits. According to Deborah Tannen's research, women tend to sit more squarely and closer to each other in conversations, while men tend to sit angled, almost side-by-side, glancing over their shoulders toward the other person. She is careful to point out that this does not mean that men are any less engaged in their conversations.[9]

There are also many variables and different norms when it comes to attire and general appearance. While your clothing can reflect a sense of personal style, it should always remain professional and match or slightly exceed the current organizational norms and values. With the advent of "business casual" and "casual Friday" in many workplaces, it can be confusing to understand what that means from one setting to another. So it is even more important to be clear about expectations. Jeans may be acceptable attire in one organization, culture, or country, but not in another. While first impressions do matter, you can be sure that each and every time you interact with a follower you cannot make a neutral statement with your appearance.[10]

In recent years, increasing attention has been paid to how communication slights, whether they are intentional or not, can hinder your leadership effectiveness. Such subtle messages, sometimes known as "microinequities," can damage relationships and performance in the workplace.[11] These messages may be based on what is said, but they can also take the shape of looks, gestures, tones, proximity, or position in the physical environment. Imagine entering an interview and being seated in a chair slightly lower than the interviewer with a table or a large desk positioned between you. Or, you may notice that an executive directs more of his eye contact to men in the room than women. Regardless of what is said in the interview or happens in the meeting, an individual's perception of these subtle aspects of an interaction can diminish trust and impede influence opportunities.

Paralanguage is a specific type of nonverbal cue based on the ability of the voice to affect how something is said. The voice is a highly versatile instrument through which you can convey enthusiasm, confidence, anxiety, urgency, serenity, and other states of mind and intent. The pace of your speech, increasing or decreasing your voice intensity, pausing, varying pitch, and other aspects of speech patterns can increase your ability to influence. By closely attending to the followers' paralanguage, you can pick up clues about your progress in influencing them.

The Linear Model

Now that we have covered the fundamental components of communication, let us look at the first and simplest model we will review. The **linear model** (Figure 12–1) shows communication as a one-sided activity from the leader on the left to the follower on the right.

The main problem with the linear model is that the follower is not involved. This model does not explain face-to-face communication but does represent other one-way communicative activity, such as e-mail, billboards, television, flyers, and signs. But how many employees actually read the many items on the organization's Web homepage? Do the employees fully understand the latest quarterly report or strategy statement? The linear model is based on the hope that the follower actually receives, opens, reads, and understands the barrage of communications sent daily.

The Interactional Model

By comparison, the interactional model describes the follower must be involved in some response to the message (Figure 12–2). After receiving the message, the follower then **decodes** the message to ascertain some form of meaning for the message. The follower translates the symbols

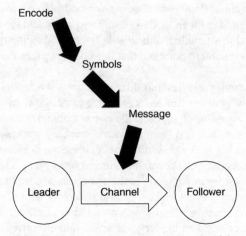

FIGURE 12–1 Linear Communication Model

(Quality Is Job One; Be All That You Can Be), and has an opportunity to create a message to return to the leader. After decoding, the follower can encode symbols that can be placed in the form of a message and give **feedback** to the leader. Feedback may involve verbal and/or nonverbal cues and, with the examples given above, the responses could include: "I believe in quality—I'll buy a Ford"; "I'll be at the recruiting station in the morning." The leader can then reshape or change a return message and send another to the follower.

This turn-taking is similar to what Galanes, Adams, and Brilhart call "a tennis game." The server sends the message, the receiver lobs a response back. This is misleading because communication is a multidirectional transactional process.[12]

What does this model represent with respect to communication in the workplace? E-mail? Telephone calls? Instant messaging? Even if there is no response from the follower, the lack of a response is **feedback** to the leader. The key to creating a model that best explains face-to-face human communication is to show that the responses of the other person involved are continual. This process is known as the **transactional communication model**.

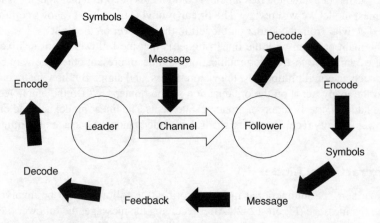

FIGURE 12–2 Interactional Communication Model

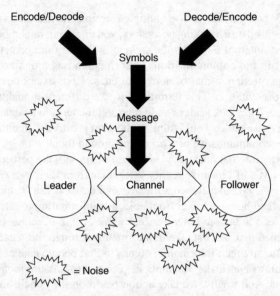

FIGURE 12–3 Transactional Communication Model

The Transactional Communication Model

This model gives us our best understanding of face-to-face human communication. As shown in Figure 12–3, the channel is now a two-headed arrow representing an ongoing process between the leader and the follower and adds three new elements not seen in the previous two models. The first of these is **noise**.

External noise occurs outside the brain of the decoder, distracting from the communication. Examples might include your stomach growling during a meeting, watching a news break on television, or being interrupted by the sound of an incoming phone call. Effective leaders must be aware of possible external factors that could interfere with their communication and try to minimize them. For example, instead of checking the cell phone to see who called, you could set it to silence or vibration instead so that you can sustain focus to your followers.

Internal noise can be created in at least four different ways. First, internal noise occurs because of our brain's processing capacity. Because we think faster than we can hear or speak, your brain decides to use the spaces of "free time" to fill in with other thoughts, which may begin to compete with what is actually being said or heard.

Paul Cameron, a professor at Wayne State University in Detroit, conducted a study with 85 college sophomores. An associate made a loud noise 21 times during Professor Cameron's lectures over the length of the course. The students had been told that they needed to encode their thoughts at that time. The results reported to the American Psychological Association showed that 20% of the students were reminiscing about something; 20% were pursing romantic thoughts; 20% were actually paying attention; 12% were actively listening; and the rest were worrying, daydreaming, thinking about lunch, or thinking about religion. In other words, 88% of this population was not actively involved in the lecture due to internal noise. Just imagine what occurs during a project meeting!

Second, external noise can also cause internal noise. A stomach growling may produce thoughts that cry out for lunch rather than paying attention to the discussion. The overwhelming smell of perfume or cologne may cause multiple reactions in your brain from romance to revulsion. If you were focused on a breaking news story, you might not remember a phone conversation.

The third way internal noise can be created is through the perception process of the individuals involved in the communication. Every person has a distinct method for selecting, organizing, and interpreting verbal or nonverbal cues.[13] For example, a person hears the term "leader" during a presentation. This term may invoke different thoughts in different people. A person who disliked a previous leader would interpret the term in a negative way, while a person who admired a previous leader would think of the term positively. In either case, **neither** paying any attention to the communicative acts occurring around them.

The fourth way internal noise can be created is through the perceptual process. People do not behave on the basis of objective reality, but rather from their *perception* and *interpretation* of that reality. Chris Argyris developed a framework known as the "ladder of inference" that can help people understand how we travel from objective information to arrive at subjective conclusions, which then lead to action. Peter Senge, in *The Fifth Discipline*, elaborated on the ladder concept. He explained that we first take in information through the senses: sight, hearing, smell, taste, and touch. But so much information comes in that people cannot attend to it all. We then add our own meanings and make assumptions. From those assumptions, we draw conclusions and make decisions. And finally, we take action based on the conclusions and assumptions we made about the limited sensory data we took in initially.

Communication effectiveness is enhanced if you, as a leader, understand the way people move up and down their particular ladders, knowing that perceptions differ from person to person.[14]

Here is an example of how perception affects behavior. Some friends made a reservation at a seaside restaurant that has a world famous view of the ocean and the crashing surf. Their reservations were for 7:00 P.M., but they arrived a little early. To their dismay, they watched as other groups entered the restaurant and were seated. Time passed, and it was now 7:10 P.M. Convinced that they had been snubbed or ignored by the management of the restaurant, they were about to make an angry complaint to the maitre d' when he approached. "May I seat you now?" he asked, as he led them to one of the best tables, where they had a spectacular view. "I am sorry for the delay, but the previous party just wouldn't leave!" The friends' perception was the opposite of what was really happening. Instead of snubbing them, the restaurant management was doing their best to seat them at a table with an excellent view. Had the situation been explained earlier, they would not have been so impatient and they would have perceived the situation entirely differently.

In the context of communication, the perceptual process creates **semantic** noise, also known as word noise. As Ogden and Richards explain in their classic text, *The Meaning of Meaning*:

> When we speak, the symbolism we employ is caused partly by the reference we are making and partly by social and psychological factor—the purpose for which we are making the reference, the proposed effect of our symbols on other persons, and our own attitude.[15]

When we hear what is said, the symbols both cause us to perform an act of reference and to assume an attitude which will, according to the circumstances, be more or less similar to that of the speaker. We see or hear an object and then think about how to categorize or define the symbol or object, and we name that symbol or object. All of this occurs while we study the context of the situation, including who or what transmitted the symbol or object, deciding our relationship with the person or thing involved, and checking our past experiences with the symbol or object. All of this goes on within the brain in a split second.

Problems occur when one of two conditions is present. If there are multiple referents for a symbol or object, a follower may use one that the speaker did not intend to be used. An executive may urge the organization to become more efficient. What does efficient mean? Faster? Better output? Less time off? More cost-effective? Followers may interpret the executive's remarks as a signal for future layoffs, while the executive may simply have been urging watching the expenses to avoid future layoffs—one simple word, two opposite interpretations.

A classic example of too many referents was experienced some years ago by automaker Chevrolet when it marketed the Nova model in Spanish-speaking countries. Nova in Spanish means, "No go," which not only shows semantic noise, but also shows a direct relationship to sales.

The second way that semantic noise may occur is when there is no referent for a symbol or object. The music associated with, "Intel Inside" is widely known. However, if a person is not computer literate, the music has no referent. Similarly, when a person joins a new company, the slang, terms, and acronyms used in the company must be taught to the new employee or semantic noise will occur.

Jay A. Conger of McGill University reinforces the need for careful word selection, use of paralanguage, and nonverbal behavior to inspire others. Leadership, as we noted in Chapter 1, is more than having technical and conceptual skills; leadership involves capturing the hearts and minds of followers.

Conger cites the well-known story of two stone masons to support his view of the motivational aspect of leadership. When one of the stone masons was asked what he was doing, the reply was: "I am cutting stone." When the other mason was asked, his reply was: "I am building a great cathedral." Leaders must build "great cathedrals" with their communications. Conger's guidelines for more expressive, inspirational leadership include:

1. Craft your organization's mission statement around the basic deeply held values, beliefs, and societal purposes of the organization.
2. Use key elements of the organization's culture, for example, stories, analogies, metaphors, when you are communicating the mission into action.
3. Use rhetorical techniques such as paralanguage and nonverbal behavior.
4. Show your emotions to reflect your personal feelings and concern.[16]

Conger summarizes his views of the leader as a communicator: "It is important that . . . leaders see their role as 'meaning makers.' They must pick from the rough materials of reality to construct pictures of great possibilities," and "If you, as a leader, can make an appealing dream seem like tomorrow's reality, your [employees] will freely choose to follow you."[17]

Leaders need to understand that they cannot influence others if the message they are sending is interrupted or disregarded due to these common factors. By diminishing external noise and clarifying terminology to decrease internal noise, leaders can enhance their influence and the effectiveness of the communication process. Effectiveness depends to a large extent on how large or small the gap is between your intended message and the received message. The bigger the communication gap, the bigger the potential for misunderstanding, lack of trust, or inaction. Kouzes and Posner have pointed out how critical it is for leaders to follow up their words with actions because your followers may hear your intended message as a promise. And if you do not act on what you say, your credibility will be diminished. They suggest simply asking yourself: Am I communicating clearly or carelessly?[18] Would your followers answer the same way you did?

TABLE 12–1 Communication Skills Training (Average Person)		
Skill	**Years of Training**	**Extent Used in Adult Life**
Writing	14	Little
Reading	8	Some
Speaking	1	Quite a bit
Listening	0	A great deal

Active Listening

Leaders spend more time communicating than doing any other single activity. Yet studies summarized in Table 12–1 show that many have not had a great deal of training in developing their ability to communicate effectively. Research also shows that people spend about 45 percent of their communication time listening. Even so, the average listener understands and retains only about half of what is said immediately after a presentation. And within 48 hours, this level drops off to 22 percent. Active listening can allow a leader to become a more effective communicator. Communication is not only a process of sending messages; the leader must also be skilled in receiving, or listening to, messages. Human physiology influences our ability to listen accurately and actively. We speak at an average pace of 125 words per minute, but our brain is able to listen at a speed of 400 to 600 words per minute. Because the brain can listen faster than we can speak, a "listening gap" occurs for the average person. The gap allows the mind to wander to thoughts unrelated to those being expressed by the speaker and influences the ability of the receiver to accurately hear the message being sent.

Anthony Alessandra identified four types of listeners: the nonlistener, the marginal listener, the evaluative listener, and the active listener.[19] The nonlistener and the marginal listener hear the words being spoken but are preoccupied, uninterested, or busy preparing their next statement. These listeners are concerned with neither the message nor the context in which it is being presented. The evaluative listener makes a sincere attempt to listen by paying attention to the speaker but makes no effort to understand the intent of the speaker's message. This listener hears the words but not the feelings and meaning of what is being said.

The active listener, on the other hand, hears and understands the message. The active listener's full attention is on the content of the message and the intention of the speaker. Active listening is a skill that can be learned through daily practice and use. Carl Rogers, who popularized the term *active listening*, proposed five guidelines you can use to perfect your technique.

1. *Listen for the content of the message.* Make an effort to hear precisely what is being said.
2. *Listen for the feelings of the speaker.* Try to perceive the speaker's feelings about what is being said through the way that the message is delivered.
3. *Validate the feelings of the speaker.* Demonstrate to the speaker that you recognize and understand the feelings being expressed.
4. *Note the speaker's cues, both verbal and nonverbal.* Attempt to identify mixed messages and contradicting messages the speaker may be expressing.
5. *Reflect back to the speaker what you think you are hearing.* Restate to the speaker in your own words what you think the speaker said. Allow the speaker to respond to further clarify the message being sent.[20]

C. Glenn Pearce reinforces the importance of effective listening. "The ability to listen effectively is a predictor of managerial success."[21] This was also the conclusion of researchers at Cornell University, who also found a correlation between effective listening and position within an organization, especially that of "top-level" management.[22] Through effective, active listening, the leader can develop better relationships between management and staff, can increase the establishment of clear and concise goals that are understood by all, and can decrease the chance of communication misunderstandings that could progress into complex and costly problems.

> "One friend, one person who is truly understanding, who takes the trouble to listen to us as we consider our problems, can change our whole outlook on the work."
> —Elton Mayo

Developing these skills is not easy. Becoming an effective, active listener requires considerable skill. Most participants in listening skills seminars do not improve in these skills until the second or third course, indicating that effective listening, as is true of almost any skill, comes only with practice and a determination to learn.

Pacing, Then Leading

Leaders, as we have seen, influence from both personal power and position power. You can begin building personal power by establishing rapport, a level of comfort and conversational ease, with the people you are attempting to influence. In order to understand how to establish rapport, you should keep some key concepts in mind:

- *Rapport*. Being attuned to other people verbally or nonverbally so that they are comfortable and have trust and confidence in you.
- *Pacing*. Establishing rapport by reflecting what others do, know, or assume to be true (doing something similar, matching some part of their ongoing experience) and getting in alignment with their words, their voice characteristics, and their nonverbals.
- *Leading*. Getting other people to pace with you (attempting to influence them to consider other possibilities).
- *Having behavioral adaptability*. Having enough range in your own behavior to pace with others during interactions.[23]

When you have established rapport with people, they are more apt to follow your conversational lead. The general pattern can be thought of in this way:

> When you're interacting with other people, you're either pacing—doing something similar—or leading—having them pace with you. If your primary objective is to gain acceptance, then pacing may be enough. But if your objective is to influence them to consider other alternatives, then you must also lead. Managers can sometimes lead first and then pace to get results, since they often have position power.[24]

How to Test for Rapport

Sometimes, it is useful to test the level of rapport you have established. In the following example, the salesperson attempts to lead the customer to a buying decision after pacing with the customer through the early part of the sales process.

SALESPERSON: [attempting to lead customer: leaning forward and showing interest] Tom, we've agreed that increasing sales is important. Our program has demonstrated a significant impact on that objective. You viewed turnover as the major problem your marketing group is presently facing. Our training program, through its emphasis on professionalism, can impact that directly.

CUSTOMER: [accepting lead: leaning forward, partially mirroring the salesperson's posture] Yes, cutting down on our turnover would be a positive step in cost containment.

SALESPERSON: [continuing to lead: sensing that they now have rapport and are in agreement and alignment at both the verbal and nonverbal levels] You might consider conducting some pilot programs. Although our minimum order is 200 units, training 100 new hires with the five-day design and 100 experienced representatives with a combination of the other designs would give you a chance to evaluate actual results.

If the customer continues to pace, then the salesperson can keep leading.

In the following example, the customer does not respond on a verbal or nonverbal basis. The key here is to return to pacing to re-establish comfort and rapport.

SALESPERSON: [attempting to lead: leaning forward and showing interest] Are we in agreement that turnover is the major problem your marketing group is presently facing?

CUSTOMER: [resisting lead: remaining in the same posture] I'm not so sure. The real issue might be our advertising program.

SALESPERSON: [returning to pacing: mirroring customer's posture] I can understand how advertising can impact your sales.

In summary, the general rules of pacing, as shown in Figure 12–4 are: (1) If those you are attempting to influence go with your lead, continue to lead; (2) if they resist your lead, go back to pacing, match their behavior to re-establish rapport, and then look for new opportunities to lead.

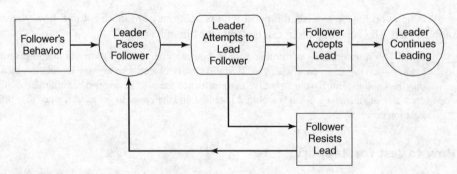

FIGURE 12–4 Influencing from Personal Power: The Pace-Lead Process

Source: Adapted from Pawlttersey, Situational Selling, (Escondido CA: Leadership Studies, Inc. 1985.) Reprinted with Permission.

ORGANIZATIONAL COMMUNICATION

Organizations have unique communication systems that a leader can use to communicate effectively and efficiently. All members of an organization have an inherent desire to know what is occurring in their workplace; information is gained through communication with others.

Organizations communicate externally with their environment and internally through specific systems. Researchers have identified five basic internal organizational communication systems: downward communication, upward communication, horizontal communication, the grapevine, and networks.[25] These five systems can be grouped into informal and formal channels of communication. Informal channels allow information to be carried outside of the formal communication channels. The grapevine and networks are informal communication channels. The other three systems are formal communication channels. They are planned and established by the organization.

Downward communication is a common and necessary type of communication between managers and followers. It may take the form of:

1. *Specific task directives*. Describes the best way to complete a task.
2. *Job rationale*. Defines a job and relates it to organizational goals and objectives.
3. *Organizational policies and objectives*. Changes in policies and objectives need to be communicated to employees.
4. *Performance feedback*. Rates an employee's performance and ways to improve.
5. *Information of an ideological nature*. Explains organizational goals.

Distortion of communication in this system can occur if a manager attempts to restrict or monitor the amount and type of information passed to employees.

Upward communication is characterized by communication from the subordinate to the manager and can be verbal, nonverbal, or written. Upward communication provides management with feedback about current issues and problems, with day-to-day information about progress toward meeting organizational goals, and with information about the effectiveness of downward communication. A sincere and trusting relationship and active listening between a manager and employees increase the accuracy of information passed in this system. Encouraging followers to discuss bad as well as good news will help build trust and confidence in the manager's ability.

Communication between a manager and peers or between coworkers is called *horizontal communication*. This system is less formal than the two vertical types of systems and usually involves problem solving and the coordination of workflow between peers or groups. Horizontal communication also forms a useful link in decision making for task coordination and provides emotional and social support to individual organizational members. As Marshall Goldsmith has pointed out, since there is no direct line authority between peer managers, influence efforts depend on ideas and information rather than position power to elicit cooperation. Peer managers also need to be sensitive to the impact of their communications and requests, since they may have shared and limited resources.[26]

The *grapevine* communication system is often neglected by managers but can be found in any organization. Grapevines grow primarily to meet organizational members' innate need for information. Although information is often incomplete, it is 70 percent to 90 percent accurate in content, and travels at an extremely rapid pace. The grapevine acts without conscious direction or thought; it will carry any information at any time, anywhere in the organization. Both managers and followers have links into the grapevine system.

Effective leaders can see the positive and negative value of the grapevine system. It can allow a manager to gain insights into employee attitudes, provide a release valve for employee emotions, and help spread useful information. Negative aspects of the grapevine system include rumors, false information, and irresponsible sharing of confidential matters. The grapevine grows most vigorously in organizations where secrecy, poor communication by management, and autocratic leadership styles are found. Adopting a proactive communication policy and integrating the grapevine into more formal communication systems can help decrease negative aspects of the grapevine system.[27]

Networks are patterned after regular interactions of organizational members and are composed of various groups of people. Networks link the other organizational communication systems. Network characteristics and actions are reflective of small groups, with members serving as opinion leaders, gatekeepers, and bridges to other networks. Members who take work breaks together and socialize outside of work may also form strong networks. Networks can encourage strong identification with work and serve as essential socializing units.

The influential leader understands these various communication systems inherent in an organization and uses them for different reasons, depending on the goal, timing, and opportunity.

PATTERNS OF COMMUNICATION

One of the most important considerations in determining whether to use a participative or directive change strategy, or some combination of the two, is how communication patterns are structured within a group or organization prior to implementing a change.[28] Two of the most widely used ways of structuring communications are the star and the circle (illustrated in Figure 12–5).

The arrowhead lines represent two-way communication channels. In the circle, each person can send messages to a colleague on either side, and, thus, the group is free to communicate all around the circle. In other words, nothing in the structure of the communication pattern favors one group member over another as leader. In essence, this depicts an open, democratic organization in which there is participation in decision making by all members. In the star communication pattern, however, one individual (C) is definitely in a leadership position; C can communicate with the other four members of the group, and they can communicate with C but not with each other. This group represents an autocratic structure, with C acting as the manager. Either of these groups might be analogous to groups of department heads, each having a department, but all reporting eventually to the same manager. In both patterns, A, B, D, and E are department heads and C is the manager.

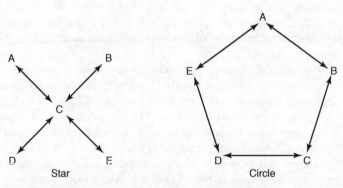

Star   Circle

FIGURE 12–5   Two Ways of Structuring Communications

IS THERE A "BEST" PATTERN OF COMMUNICATION?

Once these two patterns of communication have been identified, the usual question arises about which is the best pattern. Some classic experiments conducted by Alex Bavelas attempted to answer that question.[29] He was particularly interested in determining how each of these communication patterns affected the efficiency of a group's performance as well as the group's morale.

In one experiment, two groups were put to work in the star and circle patterns. Sets of five marbles were given to each of the five group members. The marbles of each set had different colors, but one color was common to all sets. The two groups were to discover the common color. When that had been accomplished, the task was completed. In essence, it was the star, or autocratic, pattern against the circle, or democratic, pattern.

The autocratic star pattern was much faster. Its four followers simply had to describe their marbles to the leader. After noting the common color, the designated leader sent correct information back. In trial after trial, the star group arrived at correct answers in an average of about 30 to 40 seconds. The circle group took 60 to 90 seconds. The star group was not only faster but also used fewer messages and developed more efficient ways of solving problems. In addition, group members respected their communication pattern.

The star pattern, although fast, tended to have a negative effect on morale. While group members had a high opinion of their communication pattern or organization, they had a low opinion of themselves except for the leader (C). With each ensuing trial, they felt less important and more dissatisfied. In fact, on one occasion the leader received a message, "Enough of this game; let's play tic-tac-toe." On other occasions, messages were torn up or written in French or Spanish; yet, on the whole, the group still was faster and more productive than the circle group.

The circle could be described as slow, inaccurate, but happy. It developed no system for working on problems, and no one leader seemed to emerge. Although members were openly critical of the organization's productivity, they seemed to enjoy the tasks. No one attempted sabotage, by, for example, sending messages in a foreign language.

In terms of performance, everything seemed to be in favor of the autocratic groups, until Bavelas created a so-called emergency. He changed the marbles. Instead of simple solid colors, each group was given odd-colored marbles that were difficult to describe. The task, as before, was to find out which marble all members of the group had in common. The new marbles required close observation to tell one from another. In fact, two group members could be looking at identical marbles and describe them quite differently.

Since morale was good in the circle group, members pulled together in the "emergency" and were able to solve the problem. On the other hand, the star pattern group members looked to the leader to solve the problem with little commitment from them.

The new task confused both groups. Errors mounted, and it took 10 minutes or more to solve the problem. Yet, eventually, the circle seemed to adapt to the crisis, and after a number of trials had restored its efficiency completely. On the other hand, the star could not seem to cope with it, taking two times as much time and committing three to four times as many errors as the circle.

Why was the star communication pattern normally faster? Essentially, because it was a one-way communication system dominated by a single leader. With this communication pattern, a process was imposed on the group that eliminated extra messages. In the circle, no such clear organization existed. Each group member could communicate with two people. Since they had this kind of mobility, they seemed to get around more and thus spend more time. Since the members of a circle group sent more messages, however, they could take advantage of more checkpoints and, thus, could locate and correct more of their errors.

Members of the circle group had more chance to participate and take responsibility. They were less dependent on one person since they could check with another member. Thus, they were more satisfied and happy. The leader (C) in the star also felt quite happy and satisfied, probably for the same reasons as the members of the circle pattern—C was given responsibility and had several sources of information and checkpoints. In essence, C was independent and powerful.

In summary, these experiments suggest that the mere structure of communication patterns can influence how people feel and act in terms of independence, security, and responsibility. This same structure also can influence the total operational efficiency of a group in terms of speed, accuracy, and adaptability. In essence, the structure seems to influence the way people feel in one direction and their speed and accuracy in another. Although the two communication patterns discussed have been described as if they were either/or structures, in reality the design for an effective organization may need to incorporate both. For example, with an experienced staff, a manager might find it most appropriate to structure the communication pattern in a democratic, freewheeling manner, as in the circle. However, with inexperienced personnel, the manager might find it appropriate to operate in a more autocratic manner, as in the star pattern. These groups may be at different levels of commitment, motivation, and ability to take responsibility, and therefore different kinds of communication patterns are needed.

GENDER AND GENERATIONAL COMMUNICATION DIFFERENCES

There are many sources of potential differences and conflict, and gender is certainly one that has been apparent for some time, at work and at home. Research has shown that men and women exhibit some key communication differences, both verbal and nonverbal. Take for example, a typical question-and-answer period following a public presentation. Men tend to ask the first question, more and longer questions. Why? Tannen has documented that women have a preference for "rapport talk" that takes place one-on-one or in small groups, while men are more likely to engage in "report talk" that preserves their independence and status.[30]

Yet another trend that presents leaders with numerous communication challenges is the fact that there are now at least four different generations of employees working together. They are usually described as the Traditionalists, (born prior to 1946), Baby Boomers (born between 1946 and 1964), Gen X, born between 1965 and 1976), and Gen Y (also known as Millennials, born between 1977 and 1997). Workers from these different generations vary in values, motivation, communication preferences, and more. As a leader, you will need both the skills and tools to communicate with the Gen Y hyper-connected, who are used to rating everything and everyone in their lives, while managing the frustration of Boomers who find the constant texting annoying, even disrespectful.

COMMUNICATING ACROSS CULTURES

Now that so many companies see the world, not just their market or nation, as the competitive arena, leaders also need to develop their cultural competence All the key leadership activities—exchanging ideas and information, leading, motivating, negotiating, and decision-making—are subject to differences from one culture to another, and impact what comprises effective communication. Now that employees come from numerous cultures with varied and often differing management styles, a manager today will not only have to make difficult decisions but also have to use various communication techniques and platforms.

Attribution, the judgments we make about the characteristics and behavior of others, plays an important role in cross-cultural communication. Three factors affect the attributions or judgments we make: perception, stereotyping, and ethnocentrism. *Perception* is the mental process we use to select, organize, and evaluate stimuli from the external environment to mold them into a meaningful experience. We have more difficulty perceiving a person's behavior when we are unfamiliar with their language or their culture. *Stereotyping* is a mental form of organizing information about behavioral norms for members of a particular group. Effective stereotyping can assist you in understanding, communicating, and acting appropriately in new situations, but stereotyping can lead to poor communication if the stereotypes we have are inaccurate. *Ethnocentrism* occurs when members of a particular group believe that their cultural values, habits, and beliefs are superior to those of all other groups. Ethnocentrism can lead to complete communication breakdowns. Awareness of these three factors and active work to eliminate cultural biases facilitate effective international communication.

As mentioned earlier in this chapter, nonverbal communication—gestures, eye contact, and facial expressions—also vary across cultures. For example, the American "OK" gesture with thumb and forefinger touching in a circle means money to the Japanese, zero to the French, and an obscenity to Brazilians.[31] Cultures have unwritten rules regarding, for example, the distance one stands or sits from another in a face-to-face interaction and how waiting lines are formed and maintained.[32] The use of time also varies among cultures. For example, Americans are clock watchers and value punctuality. Indonesians do not place the same value on time; an Indonesian businessperson could arrive 30 minutes after an agreed-upon appointment time and still not be considered late.

Chinese and U.S. companies are becoming more frequent business partners and, as a result, executives from the two countries must often work together. The Chinese culture has many traditions and beliefs that a U.S. company should follow when working with Chinese organizations. For example, some unique aspects of conducting a meeting that should be recognized are:

- Forms of address
- Greetings
- Gestures
- Personal contact
- Negotiation protocol
- Gifts[33]

Differences in sentence structure, word meaning, and tense also create communication difficulties when translating messages from one language to another. Even within the same language, words can have different meanings; for example, what belongs on the head of an American (a "bonnet") is a term for a car part in England.

Awareness of attributions we make about a person from another culture, understanding of cultural norms and behaviors, and the use of resources to bridge cultural and language gaps will help leaders facilitate the development of an overall company culture of inclusion. Katz and Carroll have identified both mindsets and specific inclusive behaviors that leaders can model and encourage toward that end.[34] But we need not look across oceans to realize that the differences in cultures among people must be acknowledged and addressed. The culturally diverse workforce we see everywhere today makes the need apparent.

WHEN COMMUNICATION FALTERS

Communication is much more difficult when there is a difference of opinion between employee and supervisor, or between any colleagues at work, than when they agree. Laura Carrol has outlined a series of steps for employees to use when they wish to communicate a problem to an employer or coworker or to get a negative situation resolved. The central idea is the idea of creating a thought process that fosters an understanding of what the problem is and how it can best be resolved. She suggests that the employee see the problem from the other person's point of view and make certain that the "facts" of the situation are true from both viewpoints. If this can be done, then there exists a level, nonjudgmental, playing field from which solutions can arise without hurt feelings and misgivings. This is what the communication process is all about: respect for yourself, your ideas, and those of the other person.[35]

Under the stress of differences, however, it is all too easy for empathy to disappear and judgment to take the center stage. As Stone, Patton, and Heen have described, any difficult conversation is really three conversations in one, all operating at the same time. The first is the "What Happened?" conversation in which you describe "my story" and the other person defends theirs, instead of exploring each other's stories and acknowledging what each party contributed to the issue. Second is the "feelings" conversation—which is often regarded as unprofessional and may be discouraged in the workplace. However, emotions are always present, they are normal, and they are data that can more fully inform the nature of the conflict. Finally, there is the "identity" conversation, in which those involved may feel that some part of their identity (e.g., subject matter expert, good person, reliable source) is threatened.[36] Leaders with social competence (one aspect of emotional intelligence) can navigate these three conversations and transform them into one learning conversation at a time.

Summary

Many studies have demonstrated that interpersonal skills and written and oral communication skills are requisites of effective leaders. These skills are vital in gaining meaningful jobs and performing well in these jobs. In the words of Irving S. Shapiro:

> One important day-to-day task for the CEO [Chief Executive Officer] is communication— digesting information and shaping ideas, yes, but even more centrally, the business of listening and explaining. Decisions and policies have no effect nor any real existence unless they are recognized and understood by those who must put them into effect. . . . It sounds banal to say that a CEO is first and foremost in the human relations and communication business—what else could the job be?—but the point is too important to leave to inference. No other item on the chief executive's duty list has more leverage on the organization's prospects.[37]

The transactional model of communication presented in this chapter best explains the type of communication needed in today's workplace with its emphasis on teams, the central topic of the next chapter.

Notes

1. Adam Bryant, "Google's Quest to Build a Better Boss," *New York Times*, March 12, 2011.

2. Malcolm Gladwell, *Blink* (New York, Little Brown and Company, 2005), 9.

3. Gary L. Benson, "On the Campus: How Well Do Business Schools Prepare Graduates for the Business World?" *Personnel*, July–August 1983, 63–65. See also "Can We Talk? Can We Ever?" *Fortune*, July 11, 1994, 54.

4. Kimberly F. Kane, "MBAs: A Recruiter's-Eye View," *Business Horizons* (January/February 1993): 69.

5. Frederick Moss, "Perceptions of Communication in the Corporate Community," *Journal of Business and Technical Communication* (January 1, 1995): 63; Deborah Britt Roebuck, Kevin W. Sightler, and Christina Christenson Brush, "Organizational Size, Company Type, and Position Effects on the Perceived Importance of Oral and Written Communication Skills," *Journal of Managerial Issues*, (Spring 1995): 97–116.

6. Robert Powell and Mary Jane Collier, "Public Speaking Instruction and Cultural Bias," *American Behavioral Scientist* 34, no. 2 (November/December 1990): 245–246.

7. James, J. Bradac, John M. Wiemann, and Kathleen Schaefer, "The Language of Control in Interpersonal Communication." In *Strategic interpersonal communication,* eds. J.A. Daly and J.M. Wiemann (Hillsdale, NJ: Erlbaum, 1994), 91–108.

8. Carol Kinsey Goman, *The Silent Language of Leaders: How Body Language Can Help—or Hurt—How You Lead* (San Francisco, CA: Jossey-Bass, 2011), 57–65.

9. Deborah Tannen, *You Just Don't Understand: Women and Men in Conversation* (New York: Harper, 2001), 246, 268–270.

10. Sherry Maysonave, *Casual Power: How to Power Up Your Nonverbal Communication & Dress Down for Success* (Austin, TX: Bright Books, 1999), 55–56.

11. Eric L. Hinton, "Microinequities: When Small Slights Lead to Huge Problems in the Workplace," *DiversityInc*, 2004. See also Mary Rowe, "Micro-Affirmations and Micro-inequities," *Journal of the International Ombudsman Association* (March 2008).

12. G. J. Galanes, K. Adams, and J. K. Brilhart, *Communicating in Groups,* 4th ed. (Boston: McGraw Hill, 2000).

13. Coon, D. *Psychology: A Modular Approach to Mind and Behavior,* 6th ed. (St Paul, MN: West Publishing, 1992).

14. Peter Senge, *The Fifth Discipline* (New York: Doubleday, 1994).

15. C. K. Ogden and I. A. Richards. *The Meaning of Meaning: A Study of the Influence of Language Upon Thought and of the Science of Symbolism* (London: Routledge and Kegan Paul, 1949), 10.

16. Jay A. Conger, "Inspiring Others: The Language of Leadership," *Academy of Management Executive* 5, no. 1 (1991): 31–45.

17. *Ibid.,* p. 44.

18. James M. Kouzes and Barry Z. Posner. *Credibility: How Leaders Gain and Lose It, Why People Demand It* (San Francisco, CA: Jossey-Bass. 1993), 109.

19. Anthony J. Alessandra, "How Do You Rate as a Listener?" *Data Management* (February 1986): 20–21.

20. Carl Rogers, *Client–Centered Therapy: Its Current Practice, Implications, and Theory* (Boston: Houghton Mifflin, 1951).

21. C. Glenn Pearce, "How Effective Are We as Listeners?" *Training & Development* (April 1993): 15.

22. Judi Brownell, "Research Capsules," *Training and Development,* (April 1993): 79.

23. Jerry Richardson and Joel Margulis, *The Magic of Rapport* (San Francisco: Harbor Publishing, 1981), 19–59.

24. John Grinder and Richard Bandler, *The Structure of Magic II* (Palto Alto: Science and Behavior Books, 1976), 4–6.

25. Marshall Goldsmith, Cathy Greenberg, Alastair Robertson, and Maya Hu-Chan, *Global Leadership: The Next Generation* (Upper Saddles River, NJ: Financial Times Prentice Hall, 2003), 111.

26. J. L. DiGaetani, ed., *The Handbook of Executive Communication* (Homewood, IL: Dow-Jones Irwin, 1986). See also P. V. Lewis, *Organizational Communication: The Essence of Effective Management* (New York: John Wiley, 1987).

27. A. Zaremba, "Working with the Organizational Grapevine," *Personnel Journal* (July 1988): 38–42.

28. Kenneth H. Blanchard and Paul Hersey, "The Importance of Communication Patterns in Implementing Change Strategies," *Journal of Research and Development in Education* 6, no. 4 (Summer 1973): 66–75.

29. Alex Bavelas, "Communication Patterns in Task-Oriented Groups." In *Group Dynamics:*

Research and Theory, eds. Dorwin Cartwright and Alvin Zander (Evanston, IL: Row, Peterson, 1953).

30. Tannen, *You Just Don't Understand: Women and Men in Conversation*, 76–77.

31. Joseph H. Singer, "How to Work with Foreign Clients," *Public Relations Journal* (October 1987): 35–37.

32. Richard G. Linowes, "The Japanese Manager's Traumatic Entry into the United States: Understanding the American-Japanese Cultural Divide," *Academy of Management Executive* 7, no. 4 (November 1993): 21–37.

33. Anne Stewart, "Communication Protocols," *CIO*, July 1994, 100–102.

34. Judith H. Katz and Frederick A. Miller, "Inclusion: The *HOW* for the Next Organizational Breakthrough" in *Practicing Organization Development—Third Edition*, eds., W. Rothwell, J. Stavros, A. Sullivan, and R. Sullivan (Jossey-Bass/Pfeiffer, 2009).

35. Laura Carrol, "A 10-Step Strategy for Issue Resolution," *HR Focus*, December 1993, 19.

36. Douglas Stone, Sheila Heen, and Bruce Patton, *Difficult Conversations: How to Discuss What Matters Most* (New York, Penguin, 1999), 9–17.

37. Irving S. Shapiro, "Executive Forum: Managerial Communication: The View from Inside," *California Management Review*, Fall 1984, 157.

13

Leading Effective Teams

O ne of the undeniable realities of organizational life today is that we must work with others to accomplish our aspirations. No matter how much we value our individuality and autonomy, many of our goals can only be achieved through teamwork. Although the following description was written 50 years ago, it is probably even truer today.

> The paradox of modern man is that only as the individual joins with his fellows in groups and organizations can he hope to control the political, economic, and social forces which threaten his individual freedom. This is especially true now that massive social groupings—in nations and combinations of nations—are the order of the day. Only as the individual in society struggles to preserve his individuality in common cause with his fellows can he hope to remain an individual.[1]

While teams can achieve certain synergies, promote collective commitment, and deliver on complex projects, they also pose some real challenges for team leaders. How can you reward team members fairly when company compensation may be based on individual effort? How can you minimize the potentially toxic effect of one team member who is not pulling his or her weight? How can you help the team work through its inevitable conflicts? Behavioral science principles and concepts help both team leaders and members become more effective. In this chapter, we will describe how you can apply Situational Leadership® within the teams you manage.

TEAMS AS A COMPETITIVE STRATEGY

Organizations today are under tremendous pressure to survive in a competitive environment. As discussed in Chapter 1, the problems we now have to solve in a fast-paced, global market are more complex than ever. Collaboration is a must, and companies need productive virtual teams, project teams, and cross-functional teams that can be rapidly assembled to take advantage of the many perspectives and approaches involved, and manage progress across multiple time zones.

But the advantages of teams far outweigh the challenges. Many companies have found that effective teamwork has increased productivity and revenues, and decreased absenteeism and turnover. In addition to increasing corporate performance, membership in a team benefits the individual. Employees who work in teams report that they experience greater job satisfaction, collaborate better with others, have increased pride and ownership in their job, and experience higher self esteem.[2] According to Jon Katzenbach and Douglas Smith, teams benefit the organization and team members because:

- Projects assigned to a team are more likely to be accomplished than those assigned to an individual.
- Teams can and do make practical and reasonable decisions provided there are concrete measurable goals by which to judge their performance, and the teams are given timely, meaningful feedback.
- Rewards and punishment are more effective in swaying individual performance when given by a team rather than a single superior.
- Working as a team member is preferred by many employees, particularly those who resent being bossed.
- Work teams can effectively handle inventory, scheduling, quality assurance, and other disciplines typically reserved for members of management.
- Management costs are often lower when teams are used in a business because employee-to-supervisor ratios can be reduced to as much as 50 to 1.[3]

"Coming together is a beginning. Keeping together is progress. Working together is success!"
—Henry Ford

DEFINITIONS AND DISTINCTIONS

Group

Let us begin by defining some key terms. "Group" is a very broad term that has perhaps as many definitions as "leadership." This lack of common definition creates problems in terms of communicating, diagnosing, and being able to think through strategies for change. We also often see that "groups" and "teams" are used interchangeably. To help reduce this confusion, we will use the following working definition: a *group* is two or more individuals interacting, in which the existence of the group is necessary for the individual group members' needs to be satisfied. And individual needs satisfaction may be quite different for each member of the group.

One of the principal problems with most definitions of a group is the assumption that its members have common goals and purposes. There are many examples of groups devoid of common goals or purposes. For example, imagine that three teenage boys form a group—in this case, a rock and roll band. They plan to play at local clubs. But they join the band with very different individual. One boy has a need for power (he clearly sees himself as lead singer). Another boy agreed to play drums because of the need for social interaction (he likes being with his friends). Yet another joined because of his need for status or esteem (he will be seen as "cool" and maybe even meet girls more easily). These individual band members do not necessarily have a common purpose of playing great music together. But the satisfaction, at least in part, of their individual needs is dependent on the existence of the band. Without it, there is no lead, no hanging out in long practice sessions, no girls.

Individual needs satisfaction is the missing ingredient from most definitions of groups, and differentiates effective from ineffective ones. Common, or at least harmonious, goals or purposes are not criteria of all groups, but of *effective* groups. The band may well be effective if they learn to play music together well enough to get some bookings. But that goal is secondary to their individual needs.

Case in Point: The Beginning of the End for the Beatles

John Lennon meets and falls in love with avant-garde artist Yoko Ono. They planned art projects together. John tried to get the other Beatles to join in, but they had little enthusiasm for these projects. Eventually John worked with Yoko on their artwork without them. Meanwhile, the members of the group began moving in different directions, each recording their own solo album. Within a year, The Beatles had broken up.

They became an ineffective group when their individual needs were no longer being satisfied by creating and performing music together.

Source: Bob Spitz: *The Beatles: The Biography*, Little, Brown and Company, 2005.

Any group without clear-cut objectives is likely to have difficulty developing behavioral guidelines (show up on time for practice), defining roles and responsibilities (lead singer), and ensuring accountability among its members (everybody learns their part of the song). For a group to be productive, it must have goals that are understood by all the members and provide them with a way to measure progress. Research has consistently shown that group productivity is highest when the attainment of group goals also brings fulfillment of the needs of individual group members.

Organization

What is the difference between groups and organizations? Again, it is not common goals or purposes. Do owners, managers, first-line supervisors, and line workers have the same goals? Not in all organizations.

Our definition of an *organization* is a group that has stated and formal goals. Organizations exist for various reasons and have different organizational goals. *Organizational goals* are targets toward which input, process, and output are directed; for example, make a 10 percent return on investment, reduce toxic emissions by 7% to fight global warning, or increase sales 20 percent during the current fiscal year.[4]

Collection

Yet another formation of people is a *collection*. Which of these three entities has the best chance of having common goals—a group, organization, or collection? A collection. Twenty-seven people standing on a corner waiting for a bus have a common goal—to get on the next bus. Interdependence is not necessary. Suppose you are swimming across the bay from Oakland to San Francisco. Another swimmer comes alongside. Are the two of you a group? No, you are a *collection* because you only have a common goal—to get to San Francisco. There is no interdependence. If, however, you start to interact, give encouragement, and support each other so that you both meet your individual needs by swimming together, then you have a group. Now suppose that you decide to meet three times a week at Oakland to swim to San Francisco to get in shape. Now you are an organization because you have stated or formal goals. Do you necessarily share the same goal? No, but you both agree on the formal stated goals.

> "Teamwork is like a salad: Individually, each ingredient may be tasty and fresh, but they will certainly not add up to a gourmet experience. Put together in the right way, the ingredients enhance one another to produce startling results. Each ingredient retains its character and strengths, but contributes to a more exciting and effective overall result."
> —John Cunniff

Team

When might these swimmers be considered a team? If they establish a common goal to set a world record for the longest distance swimming in relay in open water, they would be a team. They share the goal, which can only be achieved together, and both hold each other responsible for beating the record.

People may gather for a moment on a street corner until the light changes or pause with others at the scene of an accident. They may join a sorority, a choir, a book club. Or they may arrive at the base of a mountain, fully equipped to scale it. At the foot of Mt. Everest, your best chance of survival is with a team. Are you clear about what you are leading?

- *Collection*. Two or more individuals with at least one common goal.
- *Organization*. Two or more individuals who have stated and formal goals.
- *Group*. Two or more individuals in which the existence and interdependence of all is necessary for the satisfaction of individual needs.
- *Team*. A small number of people with complementary skills who are equally committed to a common purpose, goals, and working approach for which they hold themselves mutually accountable, and who must work interdependently to achieve them.[5]

We often hear managers refer to the employees who work for them as a "my team." It is useful to recognize how a work group differs from a team in an organizational setting, where the nature of objectives, membership, and evaluation are shaped by the reporting relationships and business goals.

We will focus on *teams* for the balance of this chapter for three reasons: (1) The major emphasis will be on teams in the workplace, (2) the term is used frequently in settings other than work (e.g., athletic *teams*), and (3) *team* is often used to describe a motivational state ("Let's work as a *team*").

TEAM BASICS

Organizations that can match the right type of team to the right situation are positioned for high return on their investment. Why is a team needed? Will it recommend an action, make or do something, or manage a specific function?[6] With clarity about why the team will exist, the team may be one of the following types:

- Problem-solving teams: They attack a problem than disband.
- Management teams: They coordinate work from different functions.
- Work teams, including self-managed: They do the daily work.

- Project teams: They work on specific projects.
- Virtual teams: They are not co-located, so they use various technical tools and platforms to exchange ideas and make decisions.

Once the team is formed, Dumaine offers four guidelines for the most effective use of teams:

1. *Use the right team for the job.* For example, problem-solving teams should be disbanded once the job is done.
2. *Create a hierarchy of teams.* There must be an organizational structure of teams to facilitate coordination and communication.
3. *Build trust.* For example, you cannot build team spirit if the team's task is to eliminate team member jobs.
4. *Address "people" issues.* A significant investment must be made in building and maintaining teams if they are going to work.[7]

Some Problems Are Timeless

We trained hard, but it seemed every time we were beginning to form into teams we would be reorganized. We tend to meet any new situation by reorganizing and a wonderful method it can be for creating the illusion of progress while producing confusion, inefficiency and demoralization.

—Petronious, 210 B.C.

OBSTACLES TO EFFECTIVE TEAM PERFORMANCE

Lack of Emotional Intelligence

The diverse membership and skills within a team, as well as its mutual accountability for results, provides plenty of opportunity for clashes as well as collaboration. Patrick Lencioni has described five dysfunctions that can often undermine teams: absence of trust, fear of conflict, lack of commitment, avoidance of accountability, and inattention to results.[8]

Trust is first on this list because it is so critical to creating an experience of interpersonal safety and inclusion for all the members. When people first become part of a team, there is a subtext, rarely shared, to the initial formative conversations: Will my ideas really be accepted? Do we have the right people? Is it okay to confront others if they do not deliver?

If building trust is so important, should team building be the first activity that takes place? Adam Bryant recommends that managers start even sooner by proactively helping people get to know each other as much as possible before they are ever put on project teams, even it is through social networking tools at a distance. That way some familiarity and seeds of trust are already established and the team can start working effectively more quickly.[9]

In a classic model of group development first proposed by Bruce Tuckman, he proposed that that teams grow and change across four predictable stages over time, memorably called Forming, Storming, Norming, and Performing.[10] There are key tasks and relationship issues for the team to address at each of these stages. When teams first form, they need to define their purpose, goals, roles, and process guidelines. Some do this through a formal chartering process. Once a team begins the actual work, conflict, or storming, is inevitable. The team then needs to develop and practice effective norms, or best practices, to improve their processes and performance. Effective teams that attend to these tasks may end up performing optimally.

The relationship issues at each stage present a different kind of demand on the team. The emotional terrain of a team can be rocky indeed. How can conflict and competition, mistrust and misalignment be avoided, or at least minimized? Druskat and Wolff contend that a team needs to create emotionally intelligent behavioral norms that support building trust, group identity, and group efficacy. This is more complex and challenging than it is for individuals. Why? Teams must pay attention to the emotions of its members, its own emotional currents, and the emotions of other relevant groups and individuals outside its boundaries. Even a team that seems to have everything going for it—talented, competent people, sufficient resources, clear purpose—could still fail because it lacks group emotional intelligence.[11]

Norms would both describe and encourage specific behaviors that both create awareness of emotions and help manage emotions that merge through teamwork. For example, when a team member becomes dominant or disruptive, the team must be willing to call that behavior out. Feedback between team members is as important to its performance as it is to any individual. If the team cannot address its emotional life with courage and candor, it can endanger milestones and lose precious time and energy. Marshall Goldsmith and Howard Morgan have developed an efficient way to take the team's temperature using simple mini-survey with just a couple of questions. The responses provide clues to problems and potential norms that are being compromised.[12]

Small Acts of Emotional Intelligence That Make a Big Difference

It is not about a team member working all night to meet a deadline;
it is about saying thank you for doing so.
It is not about in-depth discussion of ideas;
it is about asking a quiet member for his thoughts.
It is not about harmony, lack of tension, and all members liking each other;
it is about acknowledging when harmony is false, tension is unexpressed, and treating others
with respect.

—Vanessa Urch Druskat and Steven B. Wolff

Lack of Leadership Skill

Another important impediment to achieving team effectiveness is a lack of leadership skill. Drucker recognized that the essential task and inherent of the team leader is "to make people capable of *joint performance*, to make their strengths effective and their weaknesses irrelevant."[13] This is easier said than done.

The role of a team leader is paradoxically both simple and complex. It is simple because effectively functioning groups tend to harness a natural synergy that gives them momentum, allowing you to step aside and let the group work on its own. It is complex because your relationships with group members are dynamic and constantly changing, depending on the situation, goals, and the environment. Remember that a team, by definition, should develop shared leadership, but that does not happen right away. They must learn how to share it.

Managers often think that by simply applying leadership concepts that work well with individuals, they can effectively manage a team. But the leader must now pay attention to and manage team members as individuals, collectively as a team, and in relation to their stakeholders. Teams may be productivity engines, but, as Dumaine suggests, like engines, they require care and maintenance.[14]

LEADERSHIP IN A TEAM ENVIRONMENT

Now that we have defined some important terms, we can extend the Situational Leadership® Model to the team environment. Whether you are working with individuals or teams, the three basic competencies of influence—diagnosing, adapting, and communicating—apply.

Diagnosis centers around five well-designed and interrelated questions:

1. What objective do we want to accomplish?
2. What is the team's Performance Readiness® in the situation?
3. What intervention should the leader make?
4. What was the result of this leadership intervention?
5. What follow-up, if any, is required?

Let us address each of these questions as it applies to team leadership.

What Objective Do We Want to Accomplish?   The manager must first determine the task-specific outcome the team is to accomplish. Without creating clarity on outcomes, objectives, subtasks, milestones, and so on, the manager has no basis for determining team Performance Readiness® or the specific behavioral style to use for that level of Performance Readiness®.

Objectives are just parts of the desired road to goal achievement. They must be integrated with the organization's vision, mission, and business objectives, as we discussed in Chapter 4. One illustration of a task-specific objective for a team is: "To make specific recommendations on how to reduce paper waste by 2% through our recycling program."

What Is the Team's Performance Readiness® in the Situation?   Once an objective has been stated, the manager must then diagnose the team's Performance Readiness® to accomplish the objective. Some clues may be found using Figure 13–1.

Performance Readiness® Level R1   This team resembles "Pick-up Sticks" in terms of their orientation toward the specific objective. In this "forming" stage, uncertainty and lack of goal and role clarity are evidenced by a strong need for definition of the objective. The entire team is unable and unwilling or insecure in reference to the specific objective.

Performance Readiness® Level R2   This team is "coming around," but teams at this "storming" stage are often divided with intrateam dissonance and competition for recognition and influence. The team as a whole is unable, but willing and confident, in reference to the specific objective.

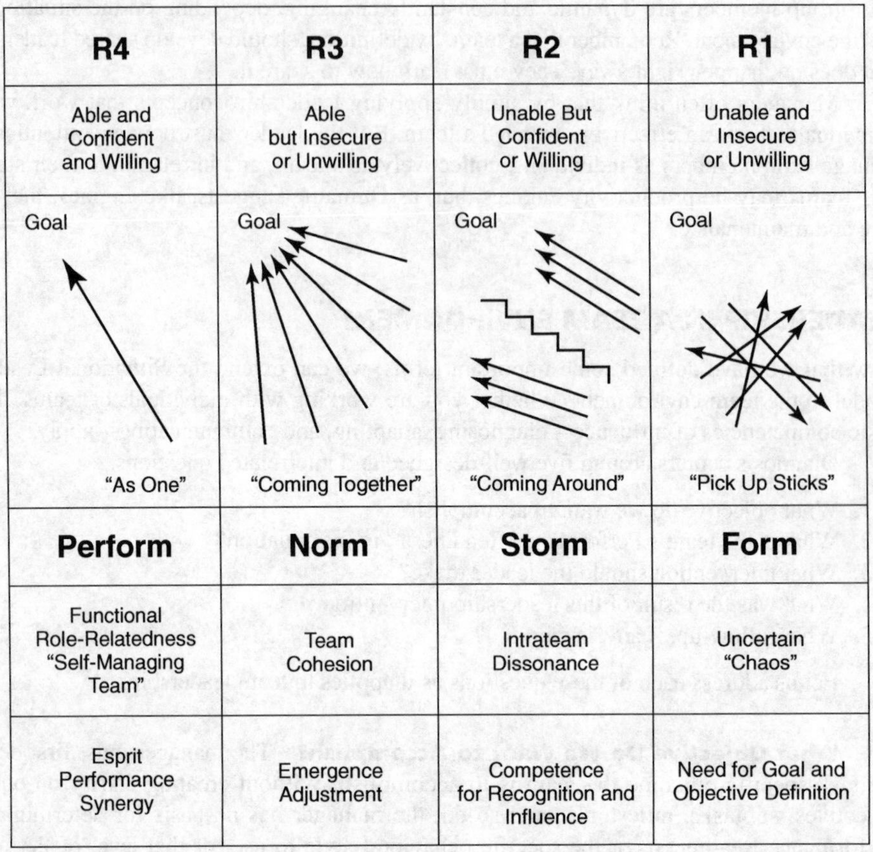

R4	R3	R2	R1
Able and Confident and Willing	Able but Insecure or Unwilling	Unable But Confident or Willing	Unable and Insecure or Unwilling
Goal	Goal	Goal	Goal
"As One"	"Coming Together"	"Coming Around"	"Pick Up Sticks"
Perform	**Norm**	**Storm**	**Form**
Functional Role-Relatedness "Self-Managing Team"	Team Cohesion	Intrateam Dissonance	Uncertain "Chaos"
Esprit Performance Synergy	Emergence Adjustment	Competence for Recognition and Influence	Need for Goal and Objective Definition

FIGURE 13–1 Indicators of Team Performance Readiness®

Source: Copyright © 1985, 2006, Leadership Studies, Inc. All Rights Reserved.

Performance Readiness® Level R3   This team is "coming together," with team cohesion very important at this "norming" stage. Adjustments are made between individuals and factions, and informal leaders and experts emerge. The team itself is now demonstrating ability with modest accomplishments, but it is still unwilling or insecure in its efforts toward accomplishing the objective.

Performance Readiness® Level R4   This team acts "as one" and shows strong evidence of functional role-relatedness, esprit, synergy, and high levels of performance. The team is now a team: able, willing, and confident in relation to the objective.

It is almost certain that, even in teams at an R4 level, there will be some individual team members at a lower level. The team leader as well as other members of the team needs to increase these members' Performance Readiness®.

How else can a manager measure Performance Readiness®? A convenient way is to assess a team's ability and willingness. Ability includes knowledge, experience, and skill; willingness includes confidence, commitment, and motivation. The manager can use a Likert-type scale ranging from very high (+ +) to very low (− −). For example, a team's knowledge could range from very high to very low.

What should the Leader Do?   After the team's Performance Readiness® has been diagnosed, the leader is now prepared to use the appropriate style (see Figure 13–2). But what style, and how central or peripheral does the leader need to be in guiding and supporting the

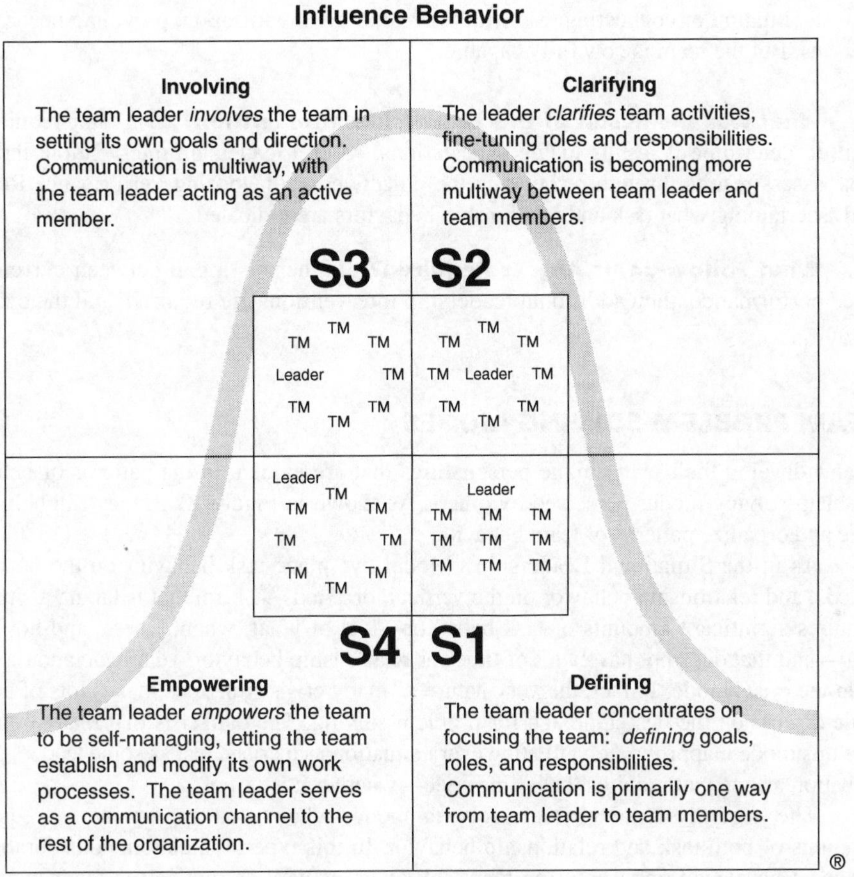

Influence Behavior

Involving	Clarifying
The team leader *involves* the team in setting its own goals and direction. Communication is multiway, with the team leader acting as an active member.	The leader *clarifies* team activities, fine-tuning roles and responsibilities. Communication is becoming more multiway between team leader and team members.

S3   S2

TM TM TM Leader TM TM TM TM	TM TM TM TM Leader TM TM TM TM
Leader TM TM TM TM TM TM TM TM	Leader TM TM TM TM TM TM TM TM TM

S4   S1

Empowering	Defining
The team leader *empowers* the team to be self-managing, letting the team establish and modify its own work processes. The team leader serves as a communication channel to the rest of the organization.	The team leader concentrates on focusing the team: *defining* goals, roles, and responsibilities. Communication is primarily one way from team leader to team members.

®

Team Performance Readiness®

R4	R3	R2	R1
Able and Confident and Willing	Able But Insecure or Unwilling	Unable But Confident or Willing	Unable and Insecure or Unwilling

FIGURE 13–2   Leadership in a Team Environment

Source: Copyright © 1985, 2006, Leadership Studies, Inc. All Rights Reserved.

team? The following descriptions of the leader role may help you adapt as the team develops over the course of its work:

- *Style S1—Defining.* This is a "front-and-center" position. Defining goals and objectives is of primary importance in this role.
- *Style S2—Clarifying.* This role makes the leader the "indispensable hub" of the team.
- *Style S3—Involving.* The leader is an unequal member of the team (contributing and the formal leader), but with a lessening role in day-to-day operations.
- *Style S4—Empowering.* The leader is away from the daily "spin" of the team, and plays a facilitating or connecting role with the rest of the organization, providing needed resources. But the team is now fully capable.

What was the Result of this Leadership Intervention?   This step requires assessment to determine if results match expectations. After a leadership intervention, the manager must assess results through rechecking the objectives, rediagnosing Performance Readiness®, and ascertaining what task and relationship behaviors are indicated.

What Follow-up, If Any, Is Required?   If there is a gap between current and desired performance, then additional leadership interventions are required, and the cycle begins again.

TEAM PROBLEM-SOLVING MODES

Teams develop their own unique personalities that are evident in the patterns of behavior and problem-solving modes perceived by others. As shown in Figure 13–3, they can help us recognize and organize patterns of team behavior.

As in the Situational Leadership® Model, we place task behavior on the horizontal, or *X*-axis, and relationship behavior on the vertical, or *Y*-axis. A team that is facing a situation that requires significant amounts of task behavior—lots of what, when, where, and how information—and that does not have a lot of time for relationship behavior—dialogue and discussion—is in the crisis mode. In fact, the very nature of many crisis situations makes lots of action with little discussion the best approach for problem solving. The danger is that many organizations use this mode inappropriately, treating every situation as a crisis, just as some leaders treat every situation as one that requires the telling style—whether it is or not.

The organizational problem-solving mode, when used appropriately, requires high amounts of both task and relationship behavior. In this type of situation, considerable emphasis must be placed on structuring team activities, as well as motivating team members. For example, eight teachers met with the principal and the superintendent of a school district. The job at hand was to revise the general curriculum. The curriculum had been neglected in the past because energies had been directed toward student disciplinary problems. At the meeting, the superintendent and principal both spelled out what needed to be done. The principal then elicited ideas from each team member and encouraged dialogue among the team members. By giving the team content, structure, and a motivating process, the principal assured a productive team meeting.

In the interpersonal problem-solving mode, a high relationship–low task approach is appropriate. For example, if disruptive cliques form within the team, relationship behaviors need to be used to increase interaction to include all the team members.

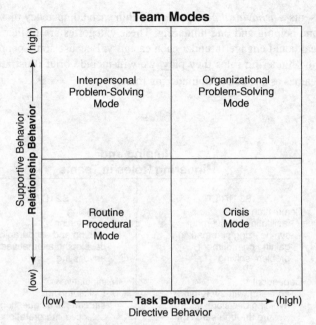

FIGURE 13–3 Team Problem Solving Modes

Source: Copyright © 1985, 2006, Leadership Studies, Inc. All Rights Reserved.

When appropriately used, the routine procedural mode requires low task and low relationship behaviors. For example, a team of managers finds that they need to revise an important report before an early meeting the next day. The clerical staff has gone home. They quickly decide who is going to do what task and play what role. The emphasis is on getting the job done through performing the assigned roles with few structuring activities and socioemotional support.

A characteristic of effective teams is that they can move rapidly and easily from one mode to another. We enrich the ability of the team to respond to different situations and face different problems if we help them develop the adaptive ability to move from one mode to another.[15]

HELPING AND HINDERING ROLES

Individuals within teams play different roles that may be defined by their expertise (e.g., technical analyst) or by a process (facilitator, change agent). Roles may either help or hinder team performance depending on the situation.

In our extensive work with organizations, the *taxonomy of influence* shown in Figure 13–4 has been particularly useful in giving people insights into roles they are and should be exhibiting in team settings. You will note that it is organized in much the same way as the Situational Leadership® Model, with the dimensions of task behavior and relationship behavior. Each style,

S1 to S4, represents a *behavioral competency*. Within each competency there are two categories of behavior—one helping and one hindering. These categories are further divided into behaviors an individual could engage in under each category. Because some people seem to be fairly predictable in the hindering roles they play, we will include brief illustrations of some of the psychological games associated with hindering roles.

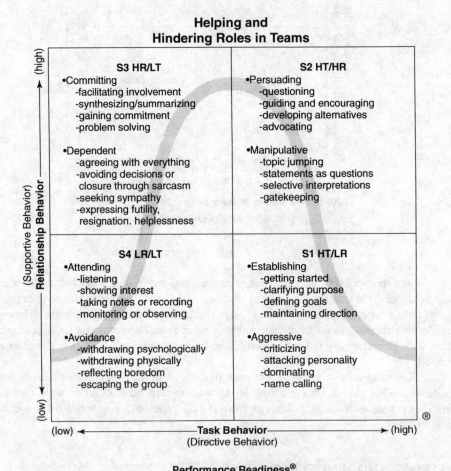

Helping and Hindering Roles in Teams

S3 HR/LT
- Committing
  - facilitating involvement
  - synthesizing/summarizing
  - gaining commitment
  - problem solving

- Dependent
  - agreeing with everything
  - avoiding decisions or closure through sarcasm
  - seeking sympathy
  - expressing futility, resignation. helplessness

S2 HT/HR
- Persuading
  - questioning
  - guiding and encouraging
  - developing alternatives
  - advocating

- Manipulative
  - topic jumping
  - statements as questions
  - selective interpretations
  - gatekeeping

S4 LR/LT
- Attending
  - listening
  - showing interest
  - taking notes or recording
  - monitoring or observing

- Avoidance
  - withdrawing psychologically
  - withdrawing physically
  - reflecting boredom
  - escaping the group

S1 HT/LR
- Establishing
  - getting started
  - clarifying purpose
  - defining goals
  - maintaining direction

- Aggressive
  - criticizing
  - attacking personality
  - dominating
  - name calling

(Supportive Behavior) **Relationship Behavior** (high) / (low)

(low) ←——— **Task Behavior** ———→ (high)
(Directive Behavior)

Performance Readiness®

High	Moderate		Low
R4	**R3**	**R2**	**R1**
Able and Confident and Willing	Able but Insecure or Unwilling	Unable but Confident or Willing	Unable and Insecure or Unwilling

FIGURE 13–4 Helping and Hindering Roles in Teams

Source: Copyright © 1985, 2006, Leadership Studies, Inc. All Rights Reserved.

S1 (HT/LR) COMPETENCY

Helping Role Category: Establishing

S1 influence behavior helps start the team along new paths. It proposes tasks and goals, defines problems, helps set rules, and contributes ideas. S1 may suggest a plan of attack to handle a problem. It can also interpret issues and helps clear up ambiguous ideas or suggestions. It helps focus attention on the alternatives and issues before the team.

Establishing Behaviors

Getting started is about initiating action and suggesting roles, structure, or procedures for the team to use. For example, "I suggest we go once around the table. Each of us will have an opportunity to give input."

    Clarifying purpose involves stating why the team has been called together, which ensures a common view of the intended result. "We have a responsibility to develop a realistic strategic plan for our company."

    Defining goals takes place to specify what is needed to fulfill the team's purpose. For example, "To meet budget guidelines, we must submit our plan by December first and within the target of two and a half million. The first step is to agree on the line items."

    Maintaining direction is about keeping the team on track with a laser focus on the stated goals and purpose. For example, "I think we're missing the point. We are not here to redefine the company's mission, we are here to agree on funding for each of the line items."

Hindering Role Category: Aggressive

The person in this role asserts personal dominance and attempts to get their own way, regardless of the impact on others. He or she may react with hostility toward aspects of the problem or toward individuals who appear to be blocking progress. They may criticize either directly or through sarcasm and innuendo. They may refuse to cooperate by rejecting all ideas or by interrupting, monopolizing the conversation or by acting as an authority. They may also engage in other aggressive behaviors, such as bullying, ridiculing ideas, and boasting.

Aggressive Behaviors

    Criticizing Downgrading, putting down, or otherwise finding fault with the suggestions or input of others. For example, "These trite sayings of yours don't tell me anything about how you really see the situation."

    Attacking Focusing on someone's personal attributes instead of the performance issue or problem the team is facing. For example, "It's that kind of attitude that keeps holding us back."

    Dominating Taking "air time" and blocking other team members' opportunity to make suggestions. For example, "I will not be quiet. I've got something to say that you need to hear."

    Name Calling Stereotyping or using labels that generalize about a person or team in a demeaning manner. For example, "You support staff types wouldn't know about this strategic roadmap."

Games Played by Aggressive People

Creating Uproar   Often begins with some form of critical statement that triggers an attack-defense series of transactions, and ends with loud arguments among team members.

Blame Games   Used to transfer ownership or accountability for an error to another person, usually in a forceful, attacking manner. The message is: "My lack of influence [or the team's ineptness] is your fault."

S2 (HT/HR) COMPETENCY

Helping Role Category: Persuading

Requesting facts and relevant information on the problem. Seeks out expressions of feelings and values. Asks for suggestions, estimates, and ideas. Responds openly and freely to others. Encourages and accepts contributions of others, whether expressed verbally or nonverbally.

Persuading Behaviors

Questioning   Asking questions for the sake of clarity and shared understanding of a point. Productive questioning enhances team process and quality of content. For example, "Of your training objectives, which one do you consider to be the most important?"

Guiding and Encouraging Responses   It is not sufficient to ask good questions. It is also people's willingness to respond that helps bring out information and insights into their feelings and values. For example, "That is an excellent idea. Please tell us more about it."

Developing Alternatives   Creating options. Coming up with various interpretations or multiple conclusions or strategies for consideration. For example, "Perhaps we should look at the financial plan from a 'best case–worst case' set of scenarios."

Advocating   Suggesting that the team pursue one alternative over another. For example, "Since we seem to be stuck, I'd like to suggest that we talk about the acquisition next."

Hindering Role Category: Manipulative

Responds to a problem rigidly and persists in using stereotypical responses. Makes repeated attempts to use solutions that are ineffective in achieving team goals. Selectively interprets data so as to validate personal opinions and censures input perceived as unsupportive. Responds to personal motives, desires, and aspirations to the exclusion of the public agenda. Attempts to lure others into joining position. Evaluates communication context. Judges remarks before they are understood and cross-examines others on their input.

Manipulative Behaviors

Topic Jumping   Getting off course, such as in discussion about X, suddenly bringing up Y. Or, "hairsplitting"—focusing on and debating one detail so much that it is taken out of context and becomes a topic of its own. For example, "I agree that a business plan is important, but I think we should talk about raising capital first."

Statements as Questions   Saying something in question form or a one-liner that is actually a statement of justification or criticism. For example, "Don't you think it's time you got this meeting started again? We're not getting anything accomplished here."

Selective Interpretations   Twisting what was said to discredit someone's point or taking a point out of context. For example, "That may be true, but we have never been successful in introducing a product without television advertising."

Gatekeeping   Hearing what one wants to hear. Attempting to control the input to match your own assessment of significance and responding accordingly. For example, says "Thank you for your suggestion," And writes it down, but does not write down another one while saying, "That is interesting."

Games Played by Manipulative People

Blemish   Becoming the team's nitpicker. Sifting through positive contributions looking for the chink in the armor and focusing on existing weak points.

Corner   Maneuvering other people through a series of seemingly plausible questions into a situation in that, no matter what they do, they never come out right.

Now I've Got You   Listening carefully to what is said, even questioning to get information, then pouncing on whoever makes a mistake or steps into the trap.

S3 (HR/LT) COMPETENCY

Helping Role Category: Committing

Helps to ensure that all members are part of the decision-making process. Shows relationships between ideas. May restate suggestions to pull them together. Summarizes and offers potential decisions for the team to accept or reject. Asks to see if the team is nearing a decision. Attempts to reconcile disagreements and facilitate the participation of everyone in the decision. Helps keep communication channels open by reducing tension and getting people to explore differences.

Committing Behaviors

Facilitating Involvement   Making sure that people are getting enough time to provide input. Making efforts to tap into the resources that are available in the team. For example, "I'm sure others would like to hear what you have to say."

Synthesizing/Summarizing   Taking a variety of inputs and putting them into a new idea. Integrating what people say into a holistic framework. Summarizing existing ideas. For example, "If we take Joe's idea for a redesigned package and Mary's suggestion for in-store promotion, we may be able to launch the product two months ahead of schedule."

Gaining Commitment   Tapping into the team to ensure members are on board and buying into the team's progress or results. Securing a shared sense of ownership. For example, "How many of you are willing to sign on to our commitment to ship fifty thousand units by November first?"

Problem Solving   Dealing with problems affecting team commitment near the point of implementation. If there is skepticism, offering proof; if there is misunderstanding, clarifying; if there is a drawback, being creative; procrastination, creating a sense of urgency; if there is a solution not within the team's scope of authority, identifying who is in authority, ask for support, and make suggestions. For example, "We have not been making very good progress. If we are going to wind this up today, we have to reach agreement before lunch on this evaluation system."

Hindering Role Category: Dependent

Reacts to people as authority figures. May acquiesce to anyone who is seen as an overt leader. Abdicates problem solving to others and expects someone else to lead to the solution. Unwilling to use leadership resources available within self or others. Attempts to escape tension through diversions or the inappropriate use of humor. Easily embarrassed and vulnerable to criticism. Often apologizes for given input. Requires constant encouragement to participate. Seeks sympathy.

Dependency Behaviors

Agreeing with Everything   Deferring to others. Suppressing one's feelings. Appears to agree with all members on all issues. For example, "No, I guess you're right. I'm out of ideas."

Avoiding Decisions or Closure Through Sarcasm   Making an inappropriate attempt at humor that keeps issues open when the team could be making a decision. For example, "Did you hear the story about the . . ."

Seeking Sympathy   Attempting to gain attention or concessions from other team members through sulking, looking dejected, or similar behaviors. Using such behaviors as manipulative ploys to gain influence. For example, "You always make my department take more than our share of the cuts. Why do we always have to give in? Why do we have to be punished?"

Expressing Futility, Resignation, or Helplessness   Snapping your gum, drawing, playing paper-and-pencil games, and doing things that distract team members and demonstrate noninvolvement. Announcing all the reasons why something is wrong or will not work. The aim is to convince others that the team is powerless and lacks control. For example, "Management is never going to listen to our ideas anyway. It's just a waste of time."

Games Played by Dependent People

Ain't It Awful   Presenting superficial concern for and commitment to the team's efforts when really attempting to thwart those efforts through statements, such as: "It will take too much work" or "There'll be no support" or "No one ever listens to us."

Wooden Leg   Trying to avoid accomplishment, accountability, work, or to gain sympathy. Using some contrived or exaggerated handicap as an excuse for not being able to fulfill good intentions.

Poor Me   Behaving in a way that reinforces some form of self-pity and self-negation. The game is played to gain sympathy. Griping continues, but the person makes no real effort to change or improve the situation.

S4 (LR/LT) COMPETENCY

Helping Role Category: Attending

Listens as well as speaks. Easy to talk to. Encourages input from team members and tries to understand as well as be understood. Records input for use later. Demonstrates a willingness to become involved with other people. Takes time to listen and avoids interrupting.

Attending Behaviors

Listening   Remaining silent, maintaining eye contact, and paying attention to what is being said with the purpose of understanding, not of agreeing. For example, "I've been listening very carefully and it seems Tom has some very good points."

Showing Interest   Communicating in a way that shows one is involved in the team's process and concerned with its workings. The communication is usually nonverbal and is a type of emotionally neutral reinforcement. For example, leaning forward, visibly concentrating on discussions.

Taking Notes (for oneself) or Recording (for the team)   Keeping some form of registered evidence of the team's inputs, activities, and decisions that will make them accessible at a later point. For example, "I've made some notes and I'd like to say something."

Monitoring or Observing   Auditing or examining the team. Paying special attention to the impact things have on the team's progress or performance. For example, showing alertness during discussions.

Hindering Role Category: Avoidance

Retreats emotionally in thought or physically. Daydreams, avoids the topics, or remains indifferent. Engages in individualistic activity that has little or nothing to do with team activity. May withdraw from the team. Scoffs at team effort, rolls eyes in disgust, or demonstrates aloofness nonverbally. Will occasionally preplan a means to leave the team early.

Avoidance Behaviors

Withdrawing Psychologically   Being unresponsive, withdrawn, seemingly checked out from the team's activities—preoccupied with thoughts other than the issues before the team. For example, trying not to be involved in the team's activities—looking intently at pictures and so on.

Withdrawing Physically   Stationing oneself away from the team. Creating a physical distance between oneself and the team's activities. For example, getting up from the team discussion area and walking over to the windows, a few feet away.

Reflecting Boredom   Pouting, physically conveying the message "I'd rather not be here." Being an active competing response for the team. For example, slouching in the chair and appearing uninterested.

Escaping the Team   Physically leaving the environment, planning to be late, intentionally absenting oneself from the team. For example, phone rings as secretary makes prearranged call. "Sorry, folks, but I have to leave to take care of some important business."

Games Played by Avoidance People

Harried   Appearing too overworked or busy to meet deadlines and commitments. To sustain the game and maintain this image, the player will take on and even solicit added responsibilities. This overload provides the basis for permission to be late, to leave meetings before the team comes to closure, and to turn over unfinished work with incomplete instructions to other team members—guilt-free and with justification.

Kick Me   Making a mistake, that is, coming to work late or unprepared and hoping that someone in the team will provide the desired kick—criticism or questions. This kick provides the payoff the player seeks. An eventual result is that the person will probably withhold contributions or withdraw psychologically or physically from the team. Although this may give the hinderer some short-term satisfaction, it undermines the team process.

These are some of the behaviors that contribute to or detract from functional and constructive team problem solving. We want to emphasize again that these roles are not by themselves helping or hindering; it depends on the situation. Your awareness and management of these roles will make a very real contribution toward increasing your effectiveness in teams.

Summary

This chapter has shown that the management of teams requires the special challenges of leading individuals to become something more than their individual selves. As Katzenbach and Smith suggest, "In the end, the wisdom of teams is within the team itself. It is not in creating the high-performance organization, managing transformational change, enforcing corporate performance ethics, or inspiring new dimensions of leadership. It is in a small team of people so committed to something larger than themselves that they will not be denied."[16]

Notes

1. David Krech, Richard S. Crutchfield, and Egerton L. Ballachey, *Individual in Society* (New York: McGraw-Hill, 1962), 529.
2. Charles L. Parnell, "Teamwork," *Vital Speeches of The Day,* September 14, 1996, 46–49.
3. Jon R. Katzenbach and Douglas K. Smith, quoted in W. H. Weiss, "Teams and Teamwork," *Supervision* 59, no. 7 (July 1998): 9.
4. Sam Certo, *Principles of Modern Management: Functions and Systems* (Dubuque, IA: Brown, 1983).
5. Jon R. Katzenbach and Douglas K. Smith, *The Wisdom of Teams* (New York: Harper Collins, 1994), 259.
6. W. H. Weiss, p. 9.
7. Brian Dumaine, "The Trouble with Teams," *Fortune,* September 5, 1994, 86–92.
8. Patrick Lencioni, Five Dysfunctions of a Team: A Leadership Fable (San Francisco: Jossey-Bass, 2002), 195–220.
9. Adam Bryant, "Collaboration Is a Team Sport, and You Need to Warm Up," *HBR Insight Center: Making Collaboration Work,* Blog, May 31, 2011. Online.
10. Bruce Tuckman, "Developmental Sequence in Small Groups." *Psychological Bulletin* 63, no. 6 (1965): 384–399.
11. Vanessa Urch Druskat and Steven B. Wolff, "Building the Emotional Intelligence of Groups," *Harvard Business Review*, March 1, 2001.
12. Brian Dumaine, "The Trouble with Teams," *Fortune*, September 5, 1994, 86–92.
13. Marshall Goldsmith and Howard Morgan, "Team Building without Time Wasting," *Harvard Business Review* blog, October 2007. Online.
14. Dumaine, 88.
15. *Ibid.*
16. Jon R. Katzenbach and Douglas K. Smith, *The Wisdom of Teams* (New York: Harper Collins, 1994), 259.

CHAPTER

14

Implementing Situational Leadership®:
Managing Performance

Our approach in these final chapters is to review some of the most significant contributions to effective management in recent years, using Situational Leadership® as a focal point. In this chapter, we will look at bottom-line approaches to performance management— how to get the most from your people. We will begin at the 50,000-foot level with a strategic model of organizational performance, then drill down to a close-up, tactical view of planning, coaching, and evaluating the performance of the individuals you manage. By doing so, you will be able to see the platinum thread that connects strategy to individual performance, and you will be able to help your people make that connection too.

DEFINING ORGANIZATIONAL PERFORMANCE

Organizational performance is the collective outcome of many factors, such as organizational structure, knowledge, nonhuman resources, strategic positioning, and human process (see Figure 14–1).[1] A *strategy* is a broad integrated plan of action to accomplish organizational goals within a specific context—the industry, market or country, economic and environmental climate. Because a strategy is an integrated plan, all of these factors or variables are interrelated. And they all contribute to *performance,* which is defined as achieving or surpassing business objectives and social responsibilities from the perspective of the judging party (e.g., owners, shareholders, regulatory agencies). Integration is essential to meeting current business and social needs, but also to meeting future ones through an intentional process of change (as shown in Figure 14–2).[2] For example, if a chemical company decides to "go green" (social policy) and use more environmentally friendly containers (equipment), people will need to know how to purchase and dispose of them differently (knowledge) and are likely to feel proud of this new practice (attitude).

Although all of these factors are important and are certainly worthy of study, our primary emphasis in this book is on people, the vital human resources who have a significant shaping

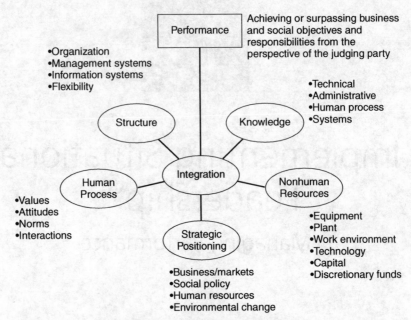

FIGURE 14–1 Satellite Model of Organizational Performance

Source: Reprinted by permission of the publisher, from Alan A. Yelsey, "Strategies and Actions for Improving Organizational Performance," *Academy of Management Review,* June 1984, pp. 45, 46, © 1984, Academy of Management, New York. All rights reserved.

influence on all the other key performance factors.[3] As Ian MacMillan and Randall Schuler have suggested, "Focusing on a firm's human resources could provide a significant opportunity to secure a sustained edge over competitors."[4] That edge is about being able to hire and retain talent in an era where employees have learned not to trust their employers. It is also about recognizing gaps in key skills and developing learning strategies for not only individuals, but for the company overall. They recommend asking these questions:

1. Which human resources in the company are unequivocally excellent?
2. How can best practices in people management be applied to motivate the employees who possess the key skills?
3. What strategic targets could be pursued?
4. What strategic thrusts will be critical in the industry chain in the future?[5]

Leaders, business managers, and human resource managers will need to genuinely partner in order to answer them, and to use their people for strategic competitive advantage.

Similarly, Ken Blanchard has reinforced the central importance of what he calls the "leadership-profit chain," comprising strategic and operational leadership, for driving organizational vitality and long-term sustainability. He asserts that too many leaders act as if they must make an "either-or" choice between people and profits. Not only is this a false proposition, it misses the key linkage between profit and creating a motivating environment for employees. Instead, companies that take care of their people spark passion, which inspires customer devotion, which in turn predicts organizational success.[6]

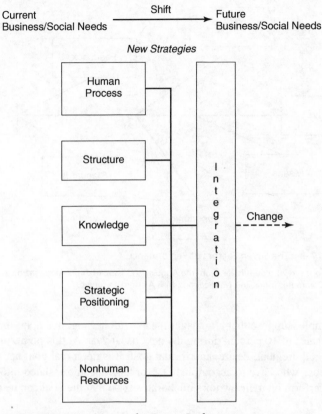

FIGURE 14–2 Positioning for Future Performance

Source: Reprinted by permission of the publisher, from Alan A. Yelsey,
"Strategies and Actions for Improving Organizational Performance,"
Academy of Management Review, June 1984, pp. 45, 46, © 1984, Academy
of Management, New York. All rights reserved.

Another useful model, developed by Clay Carr, positions the two most critical elements in organizational performance as motive and goal (see Figure 14–3). In Carr's terms, "This is based on a straightforward assumption about human action in general and organizational performance in particular; individuals who set goals and are motivated to achieve those goals will attempt to achieve them regardless of any other factors. . . . All performance factors are not created equal. An individual's goal and motives for accomplishing that goal dominate the other factors."[7] This approach is fully consistent with the conclusions of many significant findings in behavioral science, as discussed in Chapters 2 and 3.

Goals

Carr defines a goal as "a different state of affairs that the individual [or organization] actively seeks to achieve."[8] He notes that this definition implies three important distinctions:

1. A goal is not a requirement.
2. A goal is not a desire.
3. Formal goals and real goals are different entities.

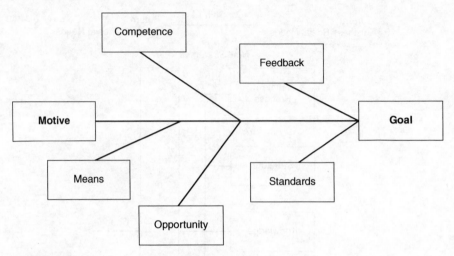

FIGURE 14–3 The Seven Factors of Performance

Source: Reprinted with permission from the August 1993 issue of *Training* magazine. Copyright © 1993. Bill Communications, Inc. Minneapolis, MN. All rights reserved.

For example, suppose that a manager meets with her regional team to announce a goal of an increase in sales of 10 percent during the next fiscal year. At this point, this statement is only the manager's requirement, desire, and formal goal. It is not a real goal because it has not been accepted by those who have to accomplish it. Nor has it been translated into the tasks that individuals must perform on their own or collaboratively so that the goal can be reached.

Standards

Standards are important because they tell whether the goal was accomplished. A specific standard answers the question, "How and when will I know I am successful"? Companies increasingly rely on metrics to establish standards in order to avoid more subjective judgments about goal achievement.

Two Opposing Views on Metrics

"If you can't measure something, you can't manage it."
—A meme of uncertain origin; attributed to Edward Deming, Peter Drucker, and others

"Everything that can be counted does not necessarily count; everything that counts cannot necessarily be counted."
—Albert Einstein

Feedback

Goals, standards, and feedback are intertwined. Feedback reports both the quality and quantity of progress toward reaching a goal that has been defined by standards. Feedback is particularly important when we consider "real" goals—goals that are accepted by employees as meaningful and worthwhile.

Katie, the district manager, observed Mac, a store manager, using a new iPad application. When she asked him what he was doing, Mac replied, "I am checking to see how many of my customers have responded to a survey I sent to their mobile devices." It was not Katie's goal or the owner's goal, it was Mac's goal. Mac had combined goal, standard, and feedback because it was a real goal.

Means

"What resources do I have to help me accomplish this goal successfully?" If your machine cannot be calibrated, if your computer program is flawed, if you cannot hire the people you need, or if you do not have access to critical information, you cannot do your job. These resources are quite literally means to an end.

Competence

Competence is a key ingredient in performance. How can we know if someone truly has the necessary skills, knowledge, and experience to perform the job-related tasks? We have to see them do it. Of course, we also seek indirect evidence (a report, a design) or trust other stakeholders to attest to it from their own experience.

Motive

From our discussion of motivation in Chapters 2 and 3, we know managers can facilitate performance motivation in many ways, through recognition, challenging goals, achievable standards, feedback, freedom to do the job, time to do it, the necessary resources, money, and removal of disincentives. We purposely listed money—an extrinsic motivator—last, since there is a noticeable trend away from the importance of compensation when compared to the potential to grow, develop, and take on new responsibilities or flexible schedules on the job.

Opportunity

Two factors contribute to the lack of opportunity to perform: time and eligibility. Higher priority tasks get more attention and consume available time. If employees are hindered from performing because supervisors do not believe in quality or customer satisfaction, they will be effectively blocked from *eligibility* to perform.

These eight factors are closely related and yet in a delicate balance. If one or more of the factors are missing, organizational performance can easily be compromised. The result? Goals are not accomplished and standards are not met.

Improving Productivity

Productivity is the ratio of the output of goods and services divided by the input or resources used to produce them. Like all ratios, it can be improved by increasing the output, decreasing the input, or both. Joel Ross makes the point that improvement has focused on technology and capital equipment to reduce the input of labor cost while using industrial engineering techniques to improve output. He goes on to make the important observation that "both of these approaches are still appropriate, *but the current trend is toward better use of the potential available through human resources* [emphasis added]."[9]

We can see that any one factor on the productivity wheel ultimately impacts the achievement of business objectives, for better or worse. On the output side, for example, better service adds value, which translates to more units sold or dollars of revenue gained, and more output. On the input side, improved communication can retain people, leading to less resource loss, which requires less input. Almost every action and technique for improving productivity can drive or diminish organizational performance.

Balanced Scorecard

Many organizations now use the balanced scorecard (BSC) to define what management means by "performance" and to measure whether management is achieving desired results. Developed by Robert S. Kaplan and David P. Norton, the balanced scorecard framework translates a company's mission and vision into a comprehensive set of objectives and performance measures that can be quantified and evaluated.[10] These measures typically include organizational performance categories, such as:

- Financial performance (revenues, earnings, return on capital, cash flow);
- Customer value performance (market share, customer satisfaction measures, customer loyalty);
- Internal business process performance (productivity rates, quality measures, timeliness);
- Innovation performance (percentage of revenue from new products, employee suggestions, rate of improvement index);
- Employee performance (morale, knowledge, turnover, use of best demonstrated practices).

Recent research shows that, according to a survey of more than 1,200 international executives, the balanced scorecard is currently the most widely adopted performance management tool in use within their organizations, providing critical measures of how strategy is being executed.[11]

MANAGING INDIVIDUAL PERFORMANCE

Does organizational performance equal the sum of all individual employee performance? No, but managing individual and team performance is the most powerful lever a people manager can use to influence it. Most companies have a performance management process to help define and structure what is expected of people on the job, to measure progress against those expectations, and to evaluate their contributions. If you pay close attention in this chapter, you will discover that Lewis Carroll's *Alice in Wonderland* has relevance to each part of the process.

The three major steps in implementing performance management are performance planning, coaching to reinforce performance plans and develop followers, and conducting the formal performance review.

1. *Performance Planning*: Setting objectives and directions with followers at the beginning of a planning period and developing plans for achieving those objectives.
2. *Performance Coaching*: Day-to-day feedback and development activities aimed at enhancing performance.
3. *Performance Review*: Overall evaluation of performance for the specific planning period, usually a single business year.

> "If you don't know where you are going, any road will get you there."
> —Lewis Carroll

Performance Planning

Individual objectives need to cascade down from the highest-level business goals so that the employee has a clear line of sight between their accomplishments and overall business performance. Much has been written about how to create performance objectives that clearly describe what the person will do, how and when they intend to accomplish them, and the expected results. Paul J. Meyer, an early proponent of goal setting, defined five memorable criteria using the "SMART" acronym, that have been widely adopted in the corporate world:

     S—Specific

     M—Measurable

     A—Achievable

     R—Results-Oriented

     T—Timely.[12]

In today's competitive environments, in which organizations are continually "raising the bar" on what they need to deliver, employees are often encouraged to challenge themselves on what achievable by setting stretch objectives that are ambitious without being overwhelming. Ken Blanchard and Garry Ridge suggest an approach that is both positive and practical: use the 80/20 rule (also known as the Pareto Principle) for goal setting. In other words, establish objectives only for the 20% of activities that are likely to yield 80% of the results and value added, and help the employee stay focused on achieving those.[13]

Yet with the trend toward granting employees more autonomy and flexibility, some companies are freeing their employees to spend as much as 10% to 20% of their time working on anything they choose to. In so doing, they have overturned the commitment to SMART, highly defined objectives (at least in part), and are seeing positive outcomes in innovation, empowerment, and higher employee engagement.

> "Sometimes I've believed as many as six impossible things before breakfast."
> —Lewis Carroll

Performance Coaching

Too often managers invest significant energy at the beginning and end of the performance management cycle, and overlook the "long highway" to be traveled between setting objectives and year-end appraisal. Managers who invest in ongoing coaching all along the way can help develop the capabilities of your people, both in their current job and for their longer-term career aspirations. Think of yourself as the GPS of your employees' performance. You navigate them toward excellence until they can find the way themselves.

Coaching provides an opportunity for quality dialogue and feedback about current performance against objectives. It also allows for earlier course correction if an individual is struggling or failing to meet expectations. Managers may meet and conduct regular meetings, in person or virtually, for informal feedback, but organizations may also use more formal, structured feedback processes and tools, such as the 360° assessment, for development or evaluation purposes.

FEEDBACK AND THE 360° ASSESSMENT PROCESS

The 360° assessment process, sometimes called a multi-source or multi-rater tool, is being used with increasing frequency for evaluating employee performance. The 360° feedback is a full-circle evaluation of an employee's performance by evaluating an ". . . employee's skills, abilities, styles, and job-related competencies."[14]

A common practice in 360° feedback is to have the employee complete a self-assessment, as well as having several peers, subordinates, supervisors, and customers complete instruments. Traditionally, a typical evaluation was completed by one person who assessed an employee's performance, but the use of 360° feedback can help eliminate some of the common rater biases that may occur during performance evaluations (see Table 14–1).

However, there are also pros and cons to using 360° feedback:

Pros

- Feedback lessens discrimination
- Bias in evaluations is decreased

TABLE 14–1 Common Rater Biases	
Type of Bias	**Description**
Halo	Rating an employee highly on all aspects of performance based on a general, positive impression, rather than rating on each objective
Horns	Rating an employee poorly overall because of performance problems in one or two areas
Central Tendency	Rating most employees as average overall
Leniency	Rating an employee higher than is justified
Opportunity	Failing to factor opportunity (factor beyond their control) into an employee's performance evaluation
Similar-to-Me	Rating an employee highly because of similarities to the manager in background, experience, or style
Self-Serving	Attributing an employee's high performance to one's own management, but taking no ownership for an employee's poor performance

Source: Adapted by permission of the publisher, from The Complete Guide to Performance Appraisal by Dick Grote. © 1996 Richard Charles Grote, AMACOM, division of American Management Association, New York, NY. All rights reserved. www.amanet.org

- People are able to identify areas that need improvement
- Information is gathered from different organizational levels
- An in-depth look is offered at the raters behavior patterns and the difference between their perceptions and the organization's view
- Employee's strengths and development needs are presented

Cons

- Feedback can hurt
- People can be malicious with criticism
- There may be conflicting opinions (Who's right and who's wrong?)
- The employee may choose friends to give feedback
- People may not be truthful in their responses
- Too many surveys in a short period of time can lead to burnout and inaccurate feedback.[15]

Consultants typically analyze the data and present it to the employee in writing or face-to-face. The purpose is to discuss and clarify information to help the employee develop strategies and goals to help change targeted behavior(s) or develop in a particular skill area.

A follow-up assessment should be done after six months to determine whether the behavior changing strategies worked and the goals were achieved.

Mary Vinson has suggested several recommendations that will improve the likelihood that feedback will produce real, lasting, and meaningful change.

- Feedback must be anonymous and confidential
- Employee must have been in a position for at least six months prior to feedback
- A feedback expert should interpret the feedback
- Feedback should not be used to determine salaries or promotion
- Feedback providers should be given the chance to provide written descriptions as well as numerical data
- The instrument should be reliable, valid, and based on sound statistical methods
- Feedback should not be used with two employees in one area at a time because it may cause "survey burn-out."[16]

Stephen R. Covey has related 360° feedback to empowerment:

Within a culture of high trust, the entire organization can participate in a system of regular written and verbal 360 degree feedback. If the desired results have been clearly defined and other elements of a win-win agreement are in place, trustworthy people know better than anyone else how they are performing. People don't need their supervisors to judge their performance; they can judge themselves.

When employees have no system of feedback except annual performance appraisals, the information comes too late, too general and from the wrong source to be truly empowering. "How am I doing in meeting your needs?" should be a question to all stakeholders that every employee and organization should be able to answer regularly.[17]

However, in an interesting twist on conventional corporate wisdom, Marshall Goldsmith has pointed out a fundamental problem with feedback: "It focuses on a *past*, on what has already occurred—not on the infinite variety of opportunities that can happen in the future. As such, feedback can be limited and static, as opposed to expansive and dynamic." He advocates that managers and employees alike try "feedforward" by soliciting suggestions for the future that might help them achieve a positive change in their selected behavior.[18]

> "I can't go back to yesterday because I was a different person then."
> —Lewis Carroll

Performance Review

In the final performance appraisal meeting between the manager and the follower, there should be no surprises. If the manager has done a thorough job of performance planning and day-to-day coaching, both parties should see this meeting as a review of what happened during the planning and coaching periods.

PERFORMANCE MANAGEMENT USING THE ACHIEVE MODEL

By integrating the Situational Leadership® concept and the ACHIEVE model introduced in Chapter 4, managers can individualize performance planning, coaching, and review by choosing managerial techniques that fit the unique situation faced by each of their followers.

Recap of the ACHIEVE Model

The ACHIEVE model was designed to help managers do more than just identify what performance problems exist; most people are quite capable of finding faults and deficiencies in others. As you may recall though, the model is intended to help followers figure out not only *why* those problems exist but also how to develop change strategies to solve them.[19]

The key factors Hersey and Goldsmith isolated that can influence the effectiveness of a follower's performance are: (1) ability; (2) understanding; (3) organizational support; (4) motivation; (5) performance feedback; (6) validity; and (7) environment, summarized by the acronym ACHIEVE:

Ability (Knowledge and Skills)

Clarity (Understanding or Role Perception)

Help (Organizational Support)

Incentive (Motivation or Willingness)

Evaluation (Coaching and Performance Feedback)

Validity (Procedures, Practices, Rules, and Regulations)

Environment (Environmental Fit)

The ACHIEVE model equips a manager to evaluate how each of these factors will affect the current or potential performance of followers for a given task. The manager can then identify the unique cause(s) of the performance problem and generate problem-solving alternatives.

Readiness for Performance Planning

Many traditional management-by-objectives (MBO) approaches indicate that managers and followers should develop objectives in a joint decision-making process. Not surprisingly, Situational Leadership® suggests that participation in objective setting may be appropriate for followers at moderate Performance Readiness® Levels (R2 or R3), but not as appropriate with followers who have very high or very low Performance Readiness® Levels (R4 or R1).

In cases where followers have low Performance Readiness® Levels, managers may be better off setting the goals and communicating them to the follower. If the follower is at a very high Performance Readiness® Level, it may be acceptable (and even desirable) for the follower to take the major leadership responsibility in setting more-specific objectives. In summary, Situational Leadership® suggests that managers should involve followers in the performance-planning process at a level consistent with the follower's Performance Readiness® for the task under discussion.

Another use of Situational Leadership® in the performance-planning process involves the idea of Contracting for Leadership Style (see Chapter 11). In setting objectives, it is not enough for the manager and follower to determine what objectives should be achieved. It is also useful for them to agree upon their respective roles in the achievement of those objectives. Managers and followers should agree up front on the degree of managerial involvement expected for each specific task. Managers should let followers know where structure and direction can be expected and where delegation may be appropriate. By clarifying their roles in the performance-planning process, both managers and followers can help avoid unnecessary stress and surprises as work goes forward.

One weakness of many MBO-type systems is that the manager and follower negotiate only for what the follower is going to contribute. The ACHIEVE model suggests that the manager and follower also need to get a clear idea of what support the organization is going to contribute. Using the ACHIEVE model in performance planning, the manager can deal with questions, such as "Does the follower have the ability to do the job? Does the follower clearly understand what to do and how to do it? What degree of support is needed from the organization? Is there a process for ongoing coaching and feedback?"

The ACHIEVE model gives the manager a clear analysis of performance potential. If any problems appear to exist, the manager should address those problems before the individual is assigned specific objectives. For example, if the manager feels that the follower lacks ability, necessary training should occur before the follower starts unsuccessfully trying to achieve the objective.

If an analysis of each performance factor in the ACHIEVE model is conducted before the follower starts to do the work, it increases the probability of setting challenging but realistic objectives.

Note that special attention should be paid to the validity factor. If performance objectives have been set in a way that may unfairly discriminate against any individual or group, human resources may be contacted and the objectives changed.

Diagnosis before Coaching

Managers can develop a situational approach to coaching by actually using the leadership styles contracted for during the performance-planning process. In coaching, Situational Leadership® helps managers make clear connections between their leadership styles, the objectives set in the performance-planning process, and the follower's Performance Readiness® Level for achieving each specific objective.

One serious problem managers have in coaching is the lack of sufficient analysis before making a coaching intervention.[20] The ACHIEVE model can serve as a quick mental checklist managers can use to analyze performance problems quickly and decide what remedial actions to take.

Follower Involvement in the Performance Review

The manager can use Situational Leadership® to determine the degree of follower involvement in the formal review process.

Managers may want followers at high Performance Readiness® Levels for the majority of task being reviewed to complete self-evaluations, which can be discussed before final managerial ratings. Followers at moderate Performance Readiness® Levels for the majority of task being reviewed may require a joint decision-making process, with the degree of follower direction depending on Performance Readiness® Level for each specific goal. Followers at low Performance Readiness® Levels for the majority of tasks being reviewed may require a directive review, with most of the information going from the manager to the follower.

In the final performance review, managers can use the ACHIEVE model to analyze why performance results did or did not meet the standards set in the performance-planning process. After the causes of performance problems have been determined by the manager and follower, developmental strategies can be designed to fit the specific performance problems that have occurred. The ACHIEVE model can help the manager attain specific performance-related data that can be used in future training, transfer, and personnel decisions. The ACHIEVE model also helps managers decide whether failure to meet performance standards was due to a lack of follower performance or to managerial, organizational, or environmental problems.

Summary

Performance management builds upon the basic philosophy of Situational Leadership® by providing managers with easy-to-use guidelines for analyzing work situations, determining why performance problems may exist, and identifying strategies for providing guidance and support to their followers. Another significant benefit of the situational approach to performance management is that it provides an effective framework that trainers can use for developing managers in performance planning, coaching, and performance review.

Notes

1. Alan A. Yelsey, "Strategies and Actions for Improving Organizational Performance," *Academy of Management Review* 9 (June 1984): 25.

2. *Ibid.*, p. 26.

3. See, for example, the increasing importance of human resources in "Human Resources Managers Aren't Corporate Nobodies Anymore," *Business Week*, December 2, 1987, 58–59. See also William A. Medlin, "Managing People to Perform," *The Bureaucrat*, Spring 1985, 52–55; Jac Fritz Enz, "Human Resource: Formulas for Success," *Personnel Journal* 64, no. 10 (October 1985): 52–60; Philip H. Mirvis, "Formulating and Implementing Human Resource Strategy," *Human Resource Management* 24, no. 4 (Winter 1985): 385–412.

4. Ian C. MacMillan and Randall S. Schuler, "Gaining a Competitive Edge through Human Resources," *Personnel* 62 (April 1985): 24. See also Dave Ulrich, "Human Resource Planning as a Competitive Edge," *Human Resource Planning* 9, no. 2 (1986): 41–49.

5. *Ibid,* p. 28.

6. Ken Blanchard, "Performance Management: Focus on People…and Profit" *Training Industry Quarterly* (Summer 2011): 17–22.

7. Clay Carr, "The Ingredients of Good Performance," *Training*, (August 1993): 528.

8. *Ibid.*

9. Joel E. Ross, *Principles of Total Quality* (Delray Beach, FL: St. Lucie Press, 1999), 335.

10. Robert S., Kaplan and David P. Norton. "The Balanced Scorecard: Measures That Drive

Performance." *Harvard Business Review*, February 1992, 71–79. See also *The Balanced Scorecard: Translating Strategy into Action* (Boston, MA: Harvard Business School Press), 1996.

11. Darrell K. Rigby, *Management Tools 2011: An Executive's Guide,* (Boston, MA: Bain & Company, Inc., 2010), 12–13.

12. Paul J. Meyer, *Attitude Is Everything!* The Peoples Network, 1997.

13. Ken Blanchard and Garry Ridge, *Helping People Win at Work* (Upper Saddle River, NJ: FT Press, 2009), 96–97.

14. Mary N. Vinson, "The Pros and Cons of 360-degree Feedback: Making It Work," *Training & Development* (April 1996): 11.

15. *Ibid.*

16. *Ibid.*

17. Stephen R. Covey, *Principle-Centered Leadership* (New York: Fireside Press, 1990), 196–198.

18. Marshall Goldsmith, "Try Feedforward Instead of Feedback," adapted from *Leader to Leader,* Summer 2002.

19. This has been a primary research objective at the Center for Leadership Studies. This section on the ACHIEVE model is adapted from Paul Hersey and Marshall Goldsmith, "A Situational Approach to Performance Planning," *Training and Development*, 34 (November 1980): 38–40.

20. John W. Atkinson, *An Introduction to Motivation* (New York: Van Nostrand, 1958).

15

Implementing Situational Leadership®:

Making Decisions, Building Commitments

M aking effective decisions and building commitments are two of the most important activities a manager can perform. In this chapter, we will consider perspectives from neuroscience, complexity science, and behavioral science as they relate to decision making. We will then look at how Situational Leadership® applies to not only making good decisions but to building commitments, as seen in the approach used by the management consulting firm of Keilty, Goldsmith, and Boone.[1]

HOW YOUR BRAIN MAKES DECISIONS

Decision making has long been framed as either rational or emotional in nature, intellectual or intuitive. Well-known psychological instruments, such as the Myers-Briggs Type Indicator (MBTI), validate these dichotomies by describing decisions as based on a significant preference for either thinking or feeling. With the advent of interest in emotional intelligence and its relevance for leadership, we now understand more fully how brain structure and function shape our decisions. So let us first look briefly at the polarities of raw emotions and pure intellect.

Our emotions originate in the limbic system, the more primitive part of the brain that we share with all mammals. It triggers our emotional reactions, particularly impulses toward aggression, sex, and survival. But humans alone evolved to have a neocortex, the seat of reason and morality. This capability for rational, "higher-order thinking" has long been regarded as what separates us from the animals and seen as the superior way to approach our world and each other. For many in the scientific and business communities, logical analysis has been hailed as a far more reliable process than going on "gut feelings" when presented with important choices.

But Daniel Goleman has described how the "emotional brain" can act faster than and, in some cases, independently of the neocortex, or "thinking brain" in response to strong stimuli, whether they are real crises or perceived threats.[2] As we discussed in Chapter 12, our gut instinct registers rapidly (in seven seconds or less), but that speed leads some people to distrust and override it, sometimes to the point of "paralysis by analysis." By comparison, the prefrontal cortex can only hold about seven pieces of information at a time, so it is relatively limited and easily overwhelmed.[3] Should our feeling brain then take the reins in guiding our decisions? Can others count on our instincts to know the right path?

Case in Point: A Tragic Intersection in the Mann Gulch

A group of fire jumpers and their leader, Wag Dodge, quickly realized they were facing a "blow-up": The fire would chase them at a very rapid speed. Dodge directed his men to run for the ridge, but it was quickly apparent that most of them couldn't get there fast enough. In an instant, he came up with a strategy never used before in fire fighting. He lit a match and tossed it into an open grassy area. Dodge called his team to come lay down with him in the freshly burned out area. Thinking he had gone crazy, none of them listened. Moments later the fire roared toward the ridge and rolled right over Dodge, leaving him untouched. The burned out area had deprived the fire of any fuel. Sadly, 13 of the 15 men who tried to outrun the fire died.

Dodge had made a brilliant intuitive decision, one based on an instantaneous and novel synthesis of experiences and conditions he had experienced before. So why didn't his team follow him? Dodge didn't know them very well, had not yet built a lot of trust, and had no time to explain the thinking behind his decision.

Intuitive decisions are not transparent. People can't see or hear the rationale behind them. So it can be harder and slower to gain their buy-in and build their commitment. In this case, the outcome was tragic.

Source: Based on Norman Maclean, *Young Men and Fire* (Chicago: University of Chicago Press, 1993).

The latest findings in neuroscience suggest that longstanding "either-or" views of decision processes are inaccurate. Jonah Lehrer has explained that the "old" and "new" parts of brain are actually in constant communication. Our best decisions are a finely tuned blend of both feeling and reason, shaped by the specific situation.[4]

Consider the 2009 story of the "Miracle on the Hudson," when pilot "Sully" Sullenberger safely water landed a passenger plane less than five minutes after both engines were knocked out by a bird strike. How did the Captain make that perfect decision? He admitted to having "the worst sickening, pit-of-your-stomach, falling-through-the-floor feeling" that he had ever experienced.[5] Sullenberger's limbic system knew full well that 155 lives, including his own, were at risk. But on high alert, his neocortex cooperated: "One way of looking at this might be that for 42 years, I've been making small, regular deposits in this bank of experience: education and training. And on January 15 the balance was sufficient so that I could make a very large withdrawal."[6]

DECISION MAKING IN CONTEXT

Effective leaders will need to recognize and rely on their emotions as well as their reasoned thinking if they are to make decisions that can hold up under the weight of complexity in today's diverse, unpredictable business contexts. They increasingly face inadequate input, conflicting information, budget constraints, time pressures, scarce resources, and many other elements that cloud the issues and threaten the quality of decisions. Snowden and Boone have recently explored the relevance of "complexity science" for decision making. Their framework describes the characteristics of four different contexts—simple, complicated, complex, and chaotic—and how the leader can best involve their people in decisions within each one.[7]

Many managers rely on a straightforward, rational process for making decisions. In simple, relatively stable contexts, the conventional steps for collecting and analyzing data, weighing alternatives, testing possible solutions, and arriving at a course of action work well enough.

But simplicity is diminishing and fact-based management is proving inadequate. Managers are more likely to struggle between several "right" answers, than between simple right or wrong choices. With more complex circumstances, filled with "known unknowns," Snowden and Boone see the need for leaders to engage more pattern-based thinking, to encourage competing ideas, to inquire and empathize more than ever. They acknowledge that "a deep understanding of context, the ability to embrace complexity and paradox, and a willingness to flexibly change leadership style will be required for leaders who want to make things happen in a time of increasing uncertainty."[8]

Even so, poor decision making is not likely to be excused because of the complexities inherent in the manager's role. Your chances for success in your current role as well as future career advancement are helped if you can (1) make effective decisions in areas you control and (2) submit sound recommendations when requested by your manager.[9] Situational Leadership® provides you with a framework for flexibility in your leadership style, and also indicate which style of decision making is most optimal in a given situation.

> "Nothing is more difficult, and therefore more precious, than to be able to decide."
> —Napoleon Bonaparte

Figure 15–1 not only describes four problem-solving situations, but also suggests four basic decision-making styles—authoritative, consultative, facilitative, and delegative. Each decision-making style has a high probability of getting results as long as it corresponds with the readiness of the followers and the situation.

DECISION STYLE

Authoritative decision making applies in situations where the manager has the necessary experience and information to reach a conclusion but followers do not possess the ability, willingness, or confidence to help. In this case, the manager should make the decision without seeking assistance from the follower.[10] Input from other knowledgeable people may be useful, however.

The authoritative style requires directive leader behavior. Followers are usually not actively involved in determining the course of action. Therefore, they hear little about the decision until the manager announces it. Authoritative decisions are commonly communicated with phrases, such as "I've decided that . . ." and "Here's what we're going to do."

What kinds of circumstances require the leader to make authoritative decisions? Suppose that your background in product development is all that is needed to set the budget for the next year's research program. You have managed your department for four years. You know the goals set for your work group. You are aware of all budgeting policies governing staff, supplies, and travel. Furthermore, your followers know little about budgeting and are new to your department (R1 for most tasks). They are still learning the basics and are not ready to assist you in making this decision. Therefore, you need to make this decision yourself. Your experience in this area

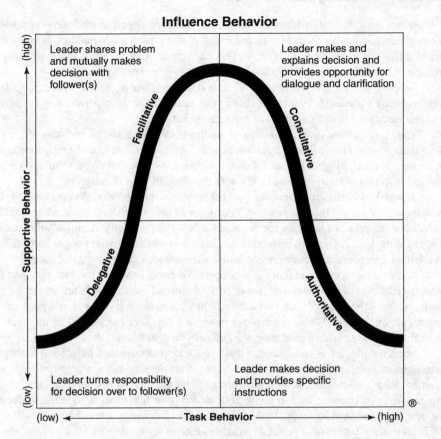

FIGURE 15–1 Problem-Solving and Decision-Making Styles

assures you that (1) your conclusion has a high probability of being correct and (2) your proposed budget has a high probability of being accepted by your supervisor.

Authoritative decisions are also required in cases where you are the only source of information or expertise. If a coworker suddenly begins choking—even though your knowledge of first aid is limited—you may be the *only* available resource. Your experience may not provide all the answers you need, but there are no alternatives.

Consultative decision making is a valuable strategy when the manager recognizes that the followers also possess some experience or knowledge of the subject and are willing, but not yet able to help. In this case, the best strategy is to obtain their input before making the decision.

When using the consultative approach, the manager selects those followers who can help to reach a decision and asks their assistance with phrases, such as "What do you know about . . ." and "I'd like some information on . . ." The manager may or may not share all aspects of the problem. After hearing from the followers, *the manager makes the final decision.*

Suppose you are a marketing manager and are considering a new ad campaign for one of your company's products. Two members of your staff have some experience in this area, so you ask their assistance in determining the product market strategy.

Your consultative strategy has two immediate benefits. First, by enlisting the cooperation of your somewhat knowledgeable resources, you increase the likelihood that your decision will be correct. Second, by giving your followers a chance to contribute, you reinforce their motivation and help them identify more closely with the goals of your department.

A word of caution: Whenever you bring others into the decision-making process, you must make the ground rules very clear. Followers of low to moderate in readiness (R2) can be included in the process, but they are not ready to act independently. A consultative decision still belongs to the leader. To avoid misunderstandings, you should let your people know that you will weigh their input carefully but may not follow their advice in reaching a decision.[11]

Facilitative decision making is a cooperative effort in which the manager and followers work together to reach a shared decision. In situations where followers are moderate to high in readiness (R3), the manager can enlist their help with phrases, such as "Let's pool our thoughts and decide on . . ." or "We've got a problem and I'd like your opinion." The implication is that these followers are capable of sharing the authority to decide what should be done.

For example, let us assume that both you and your assistant have been through project management situations before. You know how the scheduling and work assignments should be handled. Your assistant can administer "process" items, such as communications, record keeping, reporting procedures, and so forth. Your best approach is to work together in deciding how the new project should be set up. In this case, you are effectively committing yourself to a shared decision-making process—a perfectly good leadership style when dealing with an able, but not yet confident, follower.[12]

Finally, *delegative* decision making is used with followers high in readiness (R4) who have the experience and information needed to make the proper decision or recommendation. In situations where delegation is appropriate, the manager can look forward to a high level of performance simply by saying: "You know this subject. Work on it and let me know what you come up with."

For example, your plant supervisors are seasoned employees who know how to schedule their swing shifts so that all your requirements are met. Although you could accomplish this task yourself, you recognize that your people are self-motivated and capable of self-direction in this specific situation. Therefore, your high probability strategy is to delegate this task to them and await their decision.[13]

As a general rule, you can select the appropriate decision-making style by using Situational Leadership® to determine "who owns the decision."

- If none of your followers have experience or information in the specific area, they cannot own any part of the decision. You should make the *authoritative* decision by yourself and tell them what to do.
- If your followers have some knowledge of the subject, they may be capable of contributing to but not making the final decision. You should seek their help in a *consultative* manner and make your decision after considering their input.

- If your followers have quite a bit of experience, they can take some of the responsibility for making the decisions. You should use a *facilitative* strategy to share the decision-making process with them.
- If your followers have a thorough understanding of the subject and a willingness to deal with it, you should use a *delegative* style. Give them the full permission to make and execute the decision.

It is important to remember that, although you may choose to give others a degree of authority in making decisions, the ultimate responsibility remains with you.

Critical Thinking Challenge

How would you relate the decision-making styles in Situational Leadership® (authoritative, consultative, facilitative, and delegative) to the various contexts in which you might need to use them (simple, complicated, complex, and chaotic)?

Tip: Learn more about Snowden and Boone's Cynefin Framework for Decision Making and Tools for Managing in a Complex Environment (see Notes for source).

DECISION MAKING AND LEADER LATITUDE

The LaJolla-based management consulting firm of Keilty, Goldsmith, and Boone has adapted the Situational Leadership® Model to an approach to decision making that combines the leader's decision-making latitude with follower readiness. As illustrated in Figure 15–2, the basic

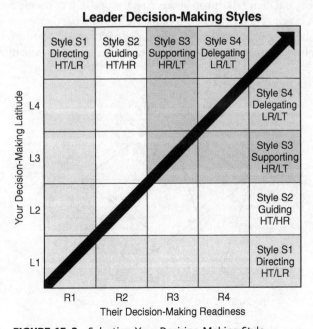

FIGURE 15–2 Selecting Your Decision-Making Style

decision-making styles of *directing* (high task–low relationship), *guiding* (high task–high relationship), *supporting* (high relationship–low task), and *delegating* (low relationship–low task) are the results of the various combinations of leader latitude and follower readiness dimensions. The four degrees of leader decision-making latitude are L1 (little or no latitude), L2 (low to moderate latitude), L3 (moderate to high latitude), and L4 (high latitude). The four degrees of follower decision-making readiness are R1 (low), R2 and R3 (moderate), and R4 (high), as in Figure 15–1.

Keilty, Goldsmith, and Boone illustrate the relationships in Table 15–1. This table integrates decision-making style, characteristics of the decision, decision-making latitude, follower decision-making readiness, and the characteristics of effective design makers. Working through this table in much the same way you would work through a decision-logic table will help you improve your decision-making skills.

BUILDING COMMITMENTS

Keilty, Goldsmith, and Boone have performed extensive research in identifying and defining the qualities that make managers successful and helping their clients apply those qualities within their own corporation or organization. As frequently happens, some individuals are admired and respected for the way they manage others, but the reasons for their success are not always apparent. Building on the work of McKinsey and Company, the internationally respected management consulting firm, and through its experience with many excellent companies and managers, it has developed valuable insights and a very useful model concerning managerial excellence, the Five Key Commitments model, shown in Figure 15–3. The essential qualities and relationships necessary for successful management can be explained and understood in terms of commitment, a characteristic common to all individuals recognized for managerial excellence.

Managers carry out their tasks in an interpersonal world. Other people continually view the manager's manner, bearing, and conduct. From their observations, they form impressions of the manager's values, beliefs, and attitudes. Excellent managers make a powerful and positive impression on others because they blend a set of positive beliefs with an equally appropriate set of

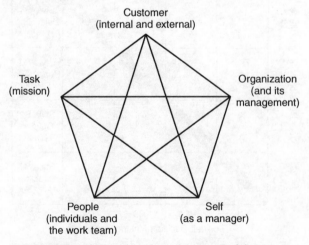

FIGURE 15–3 The Five Key Commitments Model

TABLE 15–1 Decision-Making Characteristics

Your Decision-Making Style	Characteristics of the Decision	Your Decision-Making Latitude	Their Decision-Making Readiness	Characteristics of Effective Decision Makers
Style S1, Directing		**L₁, Little or None**	**R₁, Low**	
High task and low relationship (HT/LR)	The decision is made by you or from top down with little input from them	Decision is already made Decision is nonnegotiable Examples: rules, regulations, clearly defined procedures	They lack the motivation, ability, or understanding to make the decision	Makes the rules clearly understood Levels with people on what is not negotiable Gives specific direction when it is needed Maintains light controls when necessary
Style S2, Guiding		**L₂, Low to Moderate**	**R₂, Moderate**	
High task and high relationship (HT/HR)	The decision is primarily made by you or with high input from them	Decision can be changed but will be made from top down Examples: decisions on strategy implementation	They want to be involved, but lack the ability and understanding to make the decision	Gives orientation to people in new assignments Build's people's understanding and ability Takes time to answer questions and explain decisions Provides coaching and guidance when needed
Style S3, Supporting		**L₃, Moderate to High**	**R₃, Moderate**	
High Relationship and low task (HR/LT)	The decision is primarily their responsibility with high input from you	Decision must involve you but need not be controlled by you Examples: decisions requiring your feedback to higher management	They have the ability and understanding to make the decision with high input from you	Collaborates appropriately in setting objectives Encourages participation in decision making when appropriate Provides support when needed Builds and maintains people's confidence
Style S4, Delegating		**L₄, High**	**R₄, High**	
Low relationship and low task (LR/LT)	The decision is their responsibility with little input from you	Decision can legitimately be made by them Examples: their defined job responsibilities	They are willing and have the ability to make the decision with little input from you	Delegates when possible Lets others make decisions when appropriate Encourages others to take as much responsibility as they can handle Gives people the freedom to do their job well

positive behaviors. These beliefs and actions form "commitments." The most effective managers share a fundamentally similar set of five commitments. These are:

- Commitment to the customer
- Commitment to the organization
- Commitment to self
- Commitment to people
- Commitment to task

Separately, each commitment is extremely important to effective management. Together, these commitments form the essential framework for long-term achievement of managerial excellence. True excellence seems to result from genuine dedication and positive service in all five areas of commitment. Figure 15–3 shows the five key commitments and their interrelationships.

Commitment to the Customer

The first and probably most important management commitment focuses on the customer. Excellent managers strive to provide useful service to customers. A customer is defined as anyone who should rightly benefit from the work of a manager's unit. For some managers, their work directly affects the external customer. For other managers, the essential customer is internal. For example, employees in one unit often serve members of another unit in the same organization. Whether the customer is primarily external or internal, the key to this commitment is service. The two primary ways in which an excellent manager demonstrates strong commitment to the customer are serving the customer and building customer importance.

Serving the customer boils down to consistent, conscientious dedication to customer needs. This requires responsiveness to customers through continually encouraging and listening to input from the people who use the manager's services or products. Clear, current identification of customer needs is necessary to genuinely serve the customer. In addition to knowing the customer and the needs of the customer, the excellent manager acts to solve customer problems in a timely manner. "Research has estimated that four out of five quality improvement efforts initiated by North American companies have either failed or experienced false starts," according to Tom Keiser, former president of the Forum Corporation. He and many others point the finger of responsibility at upper management. "Why do so many companies stumble? . . . Top management is often under-involved in the effort. When they delegate the effort to lower levels of the organization, it inevitably fails."[14]

Building customer importance means presenting the customer in a positive manner to those who actually provide service to the customer. The customer is not always appreciated by others within an organization. In fact, some employees view the customer as a necessary evil. To these employees, the customer is the source of most problems and often is viewed as someone to be tolerated. Excellent managers build customer importance by (1) clearly communicating the importance of the customer to employees, (2) treating the customer as a top priority, and (3) prohibiting destructive comments about the people who use their work group's products or services.

Robert Wayland and Paul Cole offer the following examples of principles an organization should adopt to acquire and retain loyal customers:

- Customers are assets. Understand, nurture, and protect their lifetime value.
- Products come and go; customers are forever (you hope!).
- Know what you are really selling. Focus on the total customer experience, not just the sale.
- Customers relate to people, not companies. Empowered employees excite customers.

- Expectations are more important than explanations. Point your customer information system forward, not backward.
- Customers are known by the company they keep. Build a strong brand.[15]

Jeffrey Gitomer believes that understanding and providing true value establishes commitment to customers:

> The word "value" has a difficult time being defined and understood. Giving value and adding value are words that many salespeople and sales executives have a difficult time in understanding, let alone providing. Most people think that value is all about something the company adds. Some small additional service, something tacked onto the product, a slight reduction in price, even something "free". Wrong. These things are promotions not values. Value is something done for the customer, in favor of the customer.[16]

Gary Neilson, senior vice president in Booz Allen Hamilton, suggests that the commitment to customer include: "Put yourself in the customer's shoes and evaluate performance in customer terms. The best process profiles are prepared from the customer's perspective."[17]

Eisuke Toyama, former president of Nissan Canada, also explains customer commitment:

> Customer Satisfaction is the new buzzword for business success. And with good reason . . . [The] ability to satisfy customers in a global marketplace will separate the winners from the losers.
>
> . . . Leadership in customer satisfaction became the guiding principle behind all of Nissan's business strategies. Nissan would never again distance itself from customers. Instead, our corporation would differentiate itself on customer satisfaction and establish itself as the leader in meeting customer needs and wants. Our research clearly shows that dealers with the highest customer satisfaction rating are also the most profitable. More than any other, this single point illustrates the importance of our global commitment to customer satisfaction. Long term customer loyalty is the key to profitability.
>
> In its purest form, customer satisfaction is an unbroken chain of events that stretches from one end of the organization to the other. Your organization's definition of a customer should be expanded to include internal customers—such as staff, colleagues, dealers and suppliers . . .
>
> To enhance customer satisfaction, you must serve both internal and external customers well. Successful organizations will focus on constantly improving the level of service they provide to both.[18]

Commitment to the Organization

The second management commitment focuses on the organization. Effective managers personally project pride in their organizations. They also instill the same pride in others. A manager positively demonstrates this commitment in three ways: building the organization, supporting higher management, and operating by the basic organizational values.

Building the organization is achieved by constantly presenting the organization in a positive way. Most people lose their motivation if they are ashamed of where they work or are embarrassed by what they do. They want to be part of something positive. The excellent manager builds support for what the organization does and effectively prevents destructive comments.

Supporting higher management is essential to the loyalty any organization needs in order to function. Excellent managers add value to the organization by showing and inspiring this necessary loyalty. These managers view their position in the organization as involving a dual responsibility (see Figure 15–4). The first responsibility is to actively challenge and lead "up" in the organization. The excellent manager takes decisions from above in the organization, makes them work, and expects others to do likewise. This manager does not blame higher management

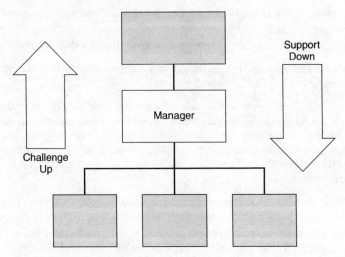

FIGURE 15–4 The Roles of the Manager

or pass the buck. The excellent manager's behavior strengthens the organization's ability to implement decisions and achieve objectives.

Operating by the basic organizational values clearly communicates the importance of what the organization stands for. A difficult aspect of managerial excellence is living the values of the organization, especially when those values are challenged during trying times. If an organization has a clearly defined and communicated set of basic beliefs, it is the manager's responsibility to function in a manner consistent with those fundamental beliefs. Managers are the clearest models of what the organization stands for. The excellent manager lives up to this challenge and this commitment.[19]

Commitment to Self

The third management commitment focuses on the manager personally.[20] Excellent managers present a strong, positive image of others. They act as a positive force in all situations. This attitude is not to be mistaken as engaging in self-serving or selfish behaviors. Excellent managers are seen as individuals who combine strength with a sense of humility. Commitment to self is evidenced in three specific activities: demonstrating autonomy, building self as a manager, and accepting constructive criticism.

Demonstrating autonomy is an important dimension for an effective manager. Within their own organizational units, excellent managers act as though they are running their own business. They take responsibility and ownership for decisions. They stand up for personal beliefs. When taking risks, they are reasonable and more concerned with achieving excellence than with "playing it safe."

Building self as a manager deals with the self-image a manager projects to others. Excellent managers appear confident and self-assured. They act on the basis of total integrity. They do not belittle or overplay their own accomplishments. It becomes obvious to others that these managers belong in their jobs. Excellent managers live up to the faith others place in them. They act on the basis of honesty and expressly behave with exceptional integrity.

Accepting constructive criticism forms a balance with the first two aspects of a positive commitment to self. Many people act autonomously and as if they are worthy of their positions. It is the truly excellent manager who remains receptive to criticism or comment in order to become even better. Excellent managers demonstrate long-term ability to admit mistakes, encourage and accept constructive criticism, and avoid recrimination and adverse reaction. In other words, after receiving personal feedback, excellent managers do not "shoot the messenger" or discount the message. It is not easy to graciously accept criticism. However, the ability to listen and act positively to improve oneself is essential to sustain personal excellence over time.

Commitment to People

The fourth management commitment focuses on the work of team and individual group members. Excellent managers display a dedication to the people who work for them. This commitment denotes the manager's use of the proper style of leadership to help individuals succeed in their tasks. Figure 15–5 reinforces the developmental process of matching leadership style to the ability and motivation of individuals. Positive commitment to people is demonstrated daily by a manager's willingness to spend the necessary time and energy working with people. Specifically, three vital activities constitute this commitment: showing positive concern and recognition, giving developmental feedback, and encouraging innovative ideas.

Showing positive concern and recognition focuses on the positive aspects of making people feel and act like winners by rewarding and reinforcing their performance. It also involves the creation of an environment in which people treat each other with courtesy and respect. For example, destructive comments concerning other people are not acceptable.

Giving developmental feedback is a realistic method of dealing with individual performance failure or setback. People sometimes fail to live up to positive expectations. The excellent manager is willing to intervene when performance does not meet established standards. Using honest feedback, the excellent manager works with the individual to reestablish realistic performance goals. Also, the manager is willing to take the time to guide and coach the individual to improve performance.

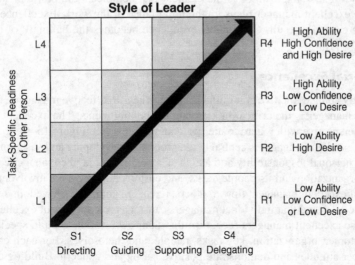

FIGURE 15–5 Using the Leadership Style That Fits

Encouraging innovative ideas demonstrates interest in others and stimulates individual and group progress. This positive action is often the difference between successful work teams and those that stagnate or disintegrate. The excellent manager taps into the full capacity of people through such commonsense actions as listening to others' ideas, providing opportunities to test ideas, and directing the credit for a successful idea to its originator. These actions tend to create a desirable atmosphere of confidence, accomplishment, and trust.

Part of this commitment to people includes recognizing diversity within your workforce and addressing its issues openly and with compassion.

Commitment to the Task

The fifth management commitment concentrates on the tasks that need to be done. Successful managers give meaning and relevance to the tasks people perform. They provide focus and direction, assuring successful completion of tasks. The durability of a manager's excellence is demonstrated through the sustained high performance of the organizational unit managed. This commitment is achieved by keeping the right focus, keeping it simple, being action-oriented, and building task importance.

Keeping the right focus refers to maintaining the proper perspective on tasks. The excellent manager concentrates everyone's attention on what is most important. This is determined through knowledge and support of the organization's overall mission. The manager consistently ties individual objectives into larger organizational goals.

Keeping it simple entails breaking work down into achievable components while avoiding unnecessary complications and procedures. The excellent manager fully considers objectives, tasks, and human capabilities, thus restraining the natural tendency to try to accomplish too much. Focus is clearly centered on major objectives within organizational priorities.

Being action-oriented is simply described as accomplishing. Excellent managers get things done. They execute. They maintain positive momentum. Realistic deadlines are set and met. People are encouraged to take action, and a sense of positive direction and accomplishment results.

Building task importance is the element that completes the fabric of managerial excellence. The excellent manager plays up the importance of the work. Excellence in task achievement is an expected result. Continuous excellence becomes the hallmark of the manager and the group.

Managerial Excellence

Consistently applied, the five commitments are the keys to effective management. And as importantly, the manager is the critical link among the commitments. The excellent manager takes a personal perspective with regard to the five commitments (see Figure 15–6).

The excellent manager is central to the process of developing and sustaining commitments. By taking personal responsibility and acting as a positive force, the manager can strongly influence the organization and its people, tasks, and customers. The active involvement and personal integrity of excellent managers flow to others. Excellent companies have long realized that "they are their people" and that individual managers can act as role models of excellence.

These excellent managers recognize that their own task is to build specific commitments to the customer, organization, key tasks, people, and themselves. For each commitment, they build proper attitudes and demonstrate positive caring and concern. Building commitments becomes the responsibility of every employee, not just the manager. The excellent manager lives

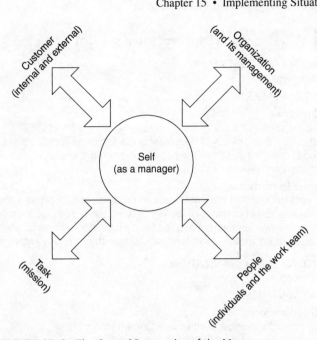

FIGURE 15–6 The Central Perspective of the Manager

by the five commitments and works in concert with others to build commitments. Table 15–2 outlines specific behaviors characteristic of the excellent manager in each of the five commitments. Sustaining and replicating excellence is a reinforcing cyclical process based on the five key commitments (see Figure 15–7).

Fundamentally, these commitments are built through dedication and service. When the excellent manager demonstrates genuine dedication and service to employees, they demonstrate

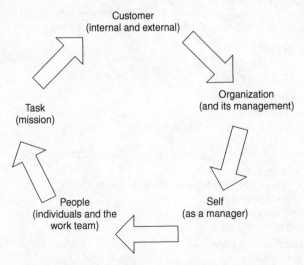

FIGURE 15–7 The Commitments As a Reinforcing Cycle

TABLE 15–2	What Does the Excellent Manager Do?

COMMITMENT TO THE CUSTOMER
(internal and external)

THE EXCELLENT MANAGER:

Serves the Customer
Knows who the customers are
Is dedicated to meeting the needs of people who use the organization's services or products
Encourages and listens to input from the people who use the organization's services or products
Acts to solve customers' problems in a timely manner

Builds Customer Importance
Consistently treats the users of the organization's products or services as a top priority
Clearly communicates the importance of the people who use the organization's products or services
Does not allow destructive comments about the people who use the organization's products or services
Is more committed to customers' long-term satisfaction than the organization's short-term gain

COMMITMENT TO THE ORGANIZATION
(and its management)

THE EXCELLENT MANAGER:

Builds the Organization
Knows and supports the mission of the overall organization
Discourages destructive comments about the organization
Is honest and positive in describing organizational benefits
Inspires pride in organization

Supports Higher Management
Describes higher-level managers in a positive way
Avoids destructive comments about higher-level managers
Personally supports higher-level management decisions
Does not pass the buck or blame higher level management
Operates by the basic values
Understands the basic values of the organization
Manages using the basic values of the organization
Encourages others to operate using the basic values of the organization
Takes corrective action when basic organizational values are compromised

COMMITMENT TO SELF
(as a manager)

THE EXCELLENT MANAGER:

Demonstrates Autonomy
Stands up for personal beliefs
Takes responsibility and ownership for decisions
Takes reasonable risks in trying out new ideas
Is more concerned with achieving excellence than playing it safe

Builds Self as a Manager
Shows a high degree of personal integrity in dealing with others
Presents self in a positive manner
Demonstrates confidence as a manager
Avoids destructive self-criticism

Accepts Constructive Criticism
Is willing to admit mistakes
Encourages and accepts constructive criticism

TABLE 15–2 *(continued)*

Acts on constructive advice in a timely manner
Does not discourage people from giving constructive criticism

COMMITMENT TO PEOPLE
(individuals and the work team)

THE EXCELLENT MANAGER:

Shows Positive Concern and Recognition
Consistently shows respect and concern for people as individuals
Gives positive recognition for achievement without discomfort to either party
Adequately rewards and reinforces top performance
Makes people feel like winners
Avoids destructive comments about people at work
Gives developmental feedback
Effectively analyzes performance
Develops specific plans when performance needs improving
Strives to improve people's performance from acceptable to excellent
Gives developmental performance feedback in a timely manner

Encourages Innovative Ideas
Encourages suggestions for improving productivity
Provides opportunities for others to try out new ideas
Acts on ideas and suggestions from others in a timely manner
Avoids taking credit for the ideas of others

COMMITMENT TO THE TASK
(mission)

THE EXCELLENT MANAGER:

Keeps the Right Focus
Knows and supports the mission of the overall organization
Ties individual objectives to larger organizational goals
Concentrates on achieving what is most important
Places greater emphasis on accomplishing the mission than following procedures

Keeps It Simple
Keeps the work simple enough to be understood and implemented
Breaks work into achievable components
Encourages efforts to simplify procedures
Avoids unnecessary complications

Is Action-Oriented
Communicates a positive sense of urgency about getting the job done
Emphasizes the importance of day-to-day progress
Encourages taking action to get things done
Concentrates on meeting deadlines

Builds Task Importance
Is committed to excellence in task achievement
Makes the task meaningful and relevant
Encourages suggestions for improving productivity
Does not downplay the importance of the work

a dedication and commitment to their tasks. This dedication to task excellence forms the basis for a strong dedication and service to the customer. The net result is that the customer benefits. As the customer profits, so does the organization. Customers maintain the organization's health and vitality through the same kind of dedication and loyalty to the organization. An organization experiencing continued customer loyalty is then in a position to build loyalty and dedication to its management by providing the tools for management's continued success. Long-term excellence is not a mystery. It is the result of building commitments.

Notes

1. C. Patrick Fleenor, David L. Kurtz, and Louis E. Boone, "The Changing Profile of Business Leadership," *Business Horizons* 26, no. 4 (July/August 1983): 43–46.

2. Daniel Goleman, *Emotional Intelligence: Why It Can Matter More Than IQ* (New York: Bantam Books, 1995), 17–21.

3. Jonah Lehrer, *How We Make Decisions* (New York: Houghton Mifflin Harcourt, 2009), 17–21.

4. *Ibid.*

5. "Miracle on the Hudson," *CBS 60 Minutes,* February 8, 2009. Television.

6. *Ibid.*

7. David J. Snowden and Mary E. Boone, "A Leader's Framework for Decision Making," *Harvard Business Review*, November 2007. Online.

8. *Ibid.*

9. Mohammad A. Yaghi, "The Behavioral Model: A New Approach to Decision Making," *Pakistan Management Review* 23, no. 2 (Fall 1982): 39–49.

10. Joseph Steger, George Manners, and Thomas Zimmerer, "Following the Leader: How to Link Management Styles to Subordinate Personality," *Management Review* 71, no. 10 (October 1982): 22–28.

11. Waldon Berry, "Group Problem Solving: How to Be Efficient Participants," *Supervisory Management* 28, no. 6 (June 1983): 13–19. See also Edwin A. Locke, David M. Schweiger, and Gary P. Latham, "Participation in Decision Making," *Organizational Dynamics* 14, no. 3 (Winter 1986): 65–79.

12. Colin Eden and John Harris, *Management Decision and Decision Analysis* (New York:

Wiley, 1975). See also Robert Hollmann and Maureen F. Ulrich, "Participative and Flexible Decision Making," *Journal of Small Business Management* 21, no. 1 (January 1983): 1–7.

13. Patrick J. Montana and Deborah F. Nash, "Delegation: The Art of Managing," *Personnel Journal* 60, no. 10 (October 1981): 784–787. See also Charles D. Pringle, "Seven Reasons Why Managers Don't Delegate," *Management Solutions* 31, no. 11 (November 1986): 26–30.

14. Thomas C. Keiser and Douglas A. Smith, "Customer-Driven Strategies: Moving from Talk to Action," *Planning Review* 21, no. 5 (1993), 25–28, 32.

15. Robert E. Wayland and Paul M. Cole, "Turn Customer Service into Customer Profitability," *Management Review* (July 1994): 22–24.

16. Jeffrey Gitomer, *Jeffrey Gitomer's Little Red Book of Selling: 12.5 Principles of Sales Greatness, How to make sales FOREVER* (Austin: Bard Press, 2004), 65.

17. Gary Neilson, "Delivering Quality through Business Processes," *The Planning Forum Network* 5, no. 4 (April 1992): 2, 9.

18. Eisuke Toyama, "Customer Service Turns Nissan Fortunes Around," *The Planning Forum Network* 4, no. 12 (December 1991): 2–3, 6.

19. Andrew M. McCosh, *Management Decision Support Systems* (New York: Wiley, 1978).

20. This section is based on J. Keith Murnighan, "Group Decision Making: What Strategies Should You Use?" *Management Review* 70, no. 2 (February 1981): 55–62.

CHAPTER

16

Planning and Implementing Change

M ark Twain once said, "The only person who likes change is a baby with a wet diaper!" Like it or not, in the dynamic society surrounding today's organizations, the question of whether change will occur is no longer relevant. Change will occur. It is no longer a choice. Instead, the issue is: How do managers and leaders cope with the inevitable barrage of changes that confront them daily in attempting to keep their organizations viable and current? Although change is a fact of life, if managers are to be effective, they can no longer be content to let change occur as it will. They must be able to develop strategies to plan, direct, and control change.

In a survey of 400 executives from Fortune 1000 companies, 79 percent of the executives interviewed reported "the pace of change at their companies as 'rapid' or 'extremely rapid' and 61 percent believed the pace will pick up in the future."[1] In contrast, most executives reported that they did not have formal plans for dealing with change. In addition, "62 percent believed they have a conservative or reluctant approach to change," and "more than 75 percent said that American managers resist change because they are 'too short-term oriented,' they 'don't like to lose control of people or events,' they have 'a vested interest in the status quo,' and they 'do not know what to do about change.'"[2]

This resistance to change is contradictory to the manager's primary role as a leader. You will recall that in Chapter 1 we defined leadership as influencing the behavior of others, individually and in groups. Influencing means moving from one behavior to another; in other words, change. In Chapter 4, we shared Warren Bennis' definition of leadership as the process of creating and implementing a vision. To be a leader, therefore, implies that you must learn to love change because it is intrinsic to the leadership process. Leaders must overcome their resistance to change and become *change managers*.

To be effective managers of change, leaders must have more than good diagnostic skills. Once they have analyzed the demands of their environment, they must be able to adapt their leadership style to fit these demands and develop the means to *change* some or all of the other situational variables.

GENERAL FRAMEWORK FOR UNDERSTANDING CHANGE

Managers who are interested in implementing some change in their group or organization need a road map for change. The road map developed by Beckhard and Harris shown in Figure 16–1 is regarded as being among the best by prominent behavioral scientists such as Edgar Schein, professor emeritus at the Sloan School of Management, MIT.[3] Furthermore, it is supported strongly by research. Let us take a journey using this road map to understand the change process.

Diagnosis (Why Change?)

The first, and in some ways the most important, stage of any change effort is diagnosis. The central issue is identifying the *need* to change. Broadly defined, the skills of diagnosis involve techniques for asking the right questions, sensing the environment of the organization, establishing effective patterns of observation and data collection, and developing ways to process and interpret data. In diagnosing for change, managers should attempt to find out (a) what is *actually* happening now in a particular situation; (b) what is *likely* to be happening in the future if no change effort is made; (c) what would people *ideally* like to be happening in this situation; and (d) what are the *blocks,* or restraints, stopping movement from the actual to the ideal?

There are at least three steps in the diagnostic process: point of view, identification of problem(s), and analysis.

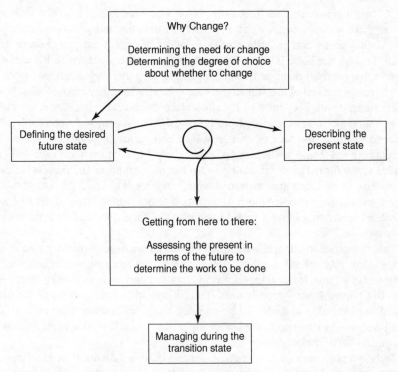

FIGURE 16–1 A Map of the Change Process

Source: R. Beckhard and R. Harris, Organizational Transitions: Managing Complex Change, © 1987, P. 31. Reprinted by permission of Pearson Education, Inc., Upper Saddle River, New Jersey.

POINT OF VIEW   Before beginning to diagnose in an organization, you should know through whose eyes you will be observing the situation—your own, those of your boss, your associates, your followers, an outside consultant, or others.

Ideally, to get the full picture you should look at the situation from the points of view of the people who will be affected by any changes. Reality, however, sometimes restricts such a broad perspective. At any rate, you should be clear about your frame of reference from the start.

IDENTIFICATION OF PROBLEM(S)   Any change effort begins with the identification of the problem(s). A problem in a situation exists when there is a discrepancy between what is actually happening (the *real*) and what you or someone who hired you (point of view) would like to be happening (the *ideal*). For example, in a given situation, there might be tremendous conflict among individuals in a work group. If this kind of conflict is not detrimental, there may be no problem. Until you can explain precisely what you would like to be occurring and unless that set of conditions is different from the current situation, no problem exists. On the other hand, if you would ideally like this work group to be harmonious and cooperative, then you have a problem—there is a discrepancy between the real and the ideal. *Change efforts involve attempting to reduce discrepancies between the real (actual) and the ideal.* It should be pointed out that change efforts may not always involve attempting to move the real closer to the ideal. Sometimes, after diagnosis you might realize that your ideal is unrealistic and should be brought more in line with what is actually happening.

It is in problem identification that the concepts and theoretical frameworks presented in this book begin to come into play. For example, two important potential areas for discrepancy are, in Rensis Likert's terms, end-result variables and intervening variables. These were discussed in Chapter 6.

In an examination of *end-result variables,* the question becomes: Is the organization, work group, or individual doing an effective job in what it was asked to do; that is, production, sales, teaching the three Rs, and so on? Are short-term goals being accomplished? How does the long-term picture look? If performance is not what it should be, there is an obvious discrepancy.

If performance is a problem, you might want to look for discrepancies in the *intervening variables,* or condition of the human resources. For example, is there much turnover, absenteeism, or tardiness? How about grievances, accident rate, and such? The concepts that you have been studying in this book can generate diagnostic questions for the change situation you are examining, such as:

- What leadership, decision-making, and problem-solving skills are available? What is the motivation, communication, commitment to objectives, and climate (morale)? (Likert, Chapter 4)
- What is the readiness level of the people involved? Are they willing and able to take significant responsibility for their own performance? (Hersey and Blanchard, Chapter 8)
- What need level seems to be most important for people right now? (Maslow, Chapter 2)
- What are the hygiene factors and motivators? Are people getting paid enough? What are the working conditions? Is job security an issue? How are interpersonal relations? Do people complain about the manager? Are people able to get recognition for their accomplishments? Is there much challenge in the work? Are there opportunities for growth and development? Are people given much responsibility? (Herzberg, Chapter 3)

Good theory is just organized common sense. Therefore, use the theories and questions presented here to help you sort out what is happening in your situation, what might need to be changed, and the degree of choice about whether to change.

ANALYSIS—AN OUTGROWTH OF PROBLEM IDENTIFICATION   Problem identification flows almost immediately into analysis. Once a discrepancy (problem) has been identified, the goal of analysis is to determine why the problem exists. The separation between problem identification and analysis is not always that clear, however, because identifying areas of discrepancy is often a part of analysis.

Once a discrepancy has been identified in the end-result variables or intervening variables, the most natural strategy is to begin to examine what Likert calls causal variables—the independent variables that can be altered or changed by the organization and its management, such as leadership or management style, organizational structure, and organizational objectives. In other words, can you identify what in the environment might have caused the discrepancy? Again, different theorists come to mind and stimulate various questions.

- What is the dominant leadership style being used? How does it fit with the Performance Readiness® Level of the people involved? (Hersey and Blanchard, Chapter 8)
- What are the prevailing assumptions about human nature adhered to by management? How well do those assumptions match the capabilities and potential of the people involved? (McGregor, Chapter 3)
- Are people able to satisfy a variety of needs in this environment? How do the opportunities for need satisfaction compare with the high-strength needs of the people involved? (Maslow, Chapter 2)
- How do the expectations of the various situational variables compare with the leadership style being used by management? (Hersey and Blanchard, Chapter 7)

Implementation—Getting from Here to There

The implementation process involves the following: identifying alternative solutions and appropriate implementation strategies, anticipating the probable consequences of each of the alternative strategies, and choosing a specific strategy and implementing it.

This stage of the change process involves the translation of diagnostic data into change goals and plans, strategies, and procedures. Questions such as the following must be asked: How can change be effected in a work group or organization, and how will it be received? What is adaptive, and what is resistant to change within the environment?

Once your analysis is completed, the next step is to determine alternative solutions to the problem(s). Hand in hand with developing alternative solutions is determining appropriate implementation strategies. Three approaches are helpful in the implementation process: Lewin's change process and force field analysis and Schein's idea of psychological safety.

Lewin's Change Process

In examining change, Kurt Lewin identified three phases of the change process—unfreezing, changing, and refreezing.[4]

UNFREEZING   The aim of *unfreezing* is to motivate and make the individual or the group ready to change. It is a thawing-out process in which the forces acting on individuals are rearranged so that now they see the need for change. According to Schein, when drastic unfreezing is necessary, the following common elements seem to be present: (1) The individuals being changed are physically removed from the accustomed routines, sources of information, and social relationships; (2) all social supports are undermined and destroyed; (3) the individuals being changed are demeaned and humiliated so that they will see their old attitudes or behavior as unworthy and thus be motivated to change; (4) reward is consistently linked with willingness to change and punishment with unwillingness to change.[5]

In brief, unfreezing is the breaking down of folkways, customs, and traditions—the old ways of doing things—so that individuals are ready to accept new alternatives. In terms of force field analysis, unfreezing may occur when either the driving forces are increased or the restraining forces are reduced.

CHANGING   Once individuals have become motivated to change, they are ready to be provided with new patterns of behavior. This process is most likely to occur by one of two mechanisms: identification or internalization.[6] *Identification* occurs when one or more models are provided in the environment—models from whom individuals can learn new behavior patterns by identifying with them and trying to become like them. *Internalization* occurs when individuals are placed in a situation in which new behaviors are demanded of them. They learn these new behavior patterns not only because they are necessary for survival, but also because new high-strength needs are induced by coping behavior.

> Internalization is a more common outcome in those influence settings where the direction of change is left more to the individual. The influence that occurs in programs such as Alcoholics Anonymous, in psychotherapy or counseling for hospitalized or incarcerated populations, in religious retreats, in [some kinds of] human relations training, . . . and in certain kinds of progressive education programs is more likely to occur through internalization or, at least, to lead ultimately to more internalization.[7]

Identification and internalization are not either/or courses of action. Rather, effective change is often the result of combining the two into a strategy for change.

Compliance is sometimes discussed as another mechanism for inducing change.[8] It occurs when an individual is forced to change by the direct manipulation of rewards and punishment by someone in a power position. In this case, behavior appears to have changed when the change agent is present, but it is often dropped when supervision is removed. Thus, rather than discussing force or compliance as a mechanism of changing, we should think of it as a tool for unfreezing.

REFREEZING   The process by which the newly acquired behavior comes to be integrated as patterned behavior into the individual's personality or ongoing significant emotional relationships is referred to as *refreezing.* According to Schein, if the new behavior has been internalized while being learned, "this has automatically facilitated refreezing because it has been fitted naturally into the individual's personality. If it has been learned through identification, it will persist only so long as the target's relationship with the original influence model persists, unless new surrogate models are found or social support and reinforcement are obtained for expressions of the new attitudes."[9]

This statement highlights how important it is for an individual engaged in a change process to be in an environment that continually reinforces the desired change. The effect of many training programs has been short-lived when the person returns to an environment that does not reinforce the new patterns or, even worse, is hostile toward them.

Force Field Analysis

Force field analysis, a technique developed by Kurt Lewin, assumes that in any situation there are both driving and restraining forces that influence any change that may occur.[10] *Driving forces* are those forces affecting a situation that are pushing in a particular direction; they tend to initiate a change and keep it going. In terms of improving productivity in a work group, encouragement from a supervisor, incentive earnings, and competition may be examples of driving forces. *Restraining forces* are forces acting to restrain or decrease the driving forces. Apathy, hostility, and poor maintenance of equipment may be examples of restraining forces against increased production. *Equilibrium* is reached when the sum of the driving forces equals the sum of the restraining forces. In our example, equilibrium represents the current level of productivity, as shown in Figure 16–2.

This equilibrium, or current level of productivity, can be raised or lowered by changes in the relationship between the driving and the restraining forces. For illustration, let us look at the dilemma of the new manager who takes over a work group in which productivity is high, but whose predecessor drained the human resources (intervening variables). The former manager had upset the equilibrium by increasing the driving forces (i.e., being autocratic and keeping continual pressure on workers) and thus achieving increases in output in the short run. By doing this, however, the manager fostered new restraining forces, such as increased hostility and antagonism. At the time of the former manager's departure, the restraining forces were beginning to increase, and the results manifested themselves in turnover, absenteeism, and other restraining forces, which lowered productivity shortly after the new manager arrived. Now, a new equilibrium at a significantly lower productivity is faced by the new manager.

Now just assume that our new manager decides not to increase the driving forces but to reduce the restraining forces. The manager may do this by taking time away from the usual production operation and engaging in problem solving and in training and development. In the short run, output will tend to be lowered still further. However, if commitment to objectives and technical know-how of the group are increased in the long run, they may become new driving forces, and, along with the elimination of the hostility and apathy that were restraining forces, will now tend to move the balance to a higher level of output.

Managers are often in a position in which they must consider not only output but also intervening variables, not only short-term but also long-term goals in diagnosing these interrelationships. Force field analysis is also useful in analyzing the various change strategies that can be used in a particular situation.[11]

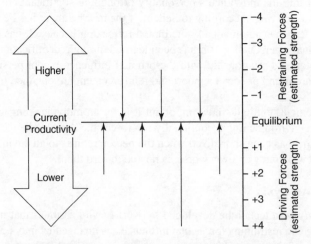

FIGURE 16–2 Driving and Restraining Forces in Equilibrium

Once you have determined that there is a discrepancy between what is actually happening and what you would like to be happening in a situation—and have done some analysis on why that discrepancy exists—then force field analysis becomes a helpful tool. Before embarking on any change strategy, it seems appropriate to determine what you have going for you in this change effort (driving forces) and what you have going against you (restraining forces). We have found that if managers start implementing a change strategy without doing that kind of analysis, they can get blown out of the water and not know why. An example might help.

In August, an enthusiastic superintendent of schools and his assistant took over a suburban school district outside a large urban area in the Midwest. Both were committed to changing the predominant teaching approach used in the system from a teacher-centered approach in which the teachers always tell the students what to do, how to do it, when to do it, and where to do it (high task–low relationship style) to a child-centered approach in which students play a significant role in determining what they are to do (low relationship–low task style).

To implement the changes they wanted, the two administrators hired a business manager to handle the office and the paperwork. They themselves essentially had no office. They put telephones in their cars and spent most of their time out in the schools with teachers and students. They spent 15 to 18 hours a day working with and supporting teachers and administrators who wanted to engage in new behavior. Then suddenly, in January, only six months after they had been hired, the school board called a special meeting and fired both administrators by a seven-to-two vote.

They could not believe what had happened. They immediately started a court suit against the school board for due process. They charged that the board had served as both judge and jury. In addition to the court actions, the administrators became educational martyrs and hit the lecture tour to talk about the evils of schools. During one of their trips, the assistant superintendent was asked to participate in a graduate seminar on the management of change. The class at that time was discussing the usefulness of force field analysis. The administrator, who did not know Lewin's theory, was asked to think about the driving and restraining forces that had been present in the change situation. In thinking about the driving forces that were pushing for the change they wanted, the administrator was quick to name the enthusiasm and commitment of the top administrators, some teachers, and some students, but really could not think of any other driving forces. When asked about the number of teachers and students involved, the administrator suggested that they were a small but growing group.

In thinking about restraining forces, the assistant superintendent began to mention one thing after another. The assistant said that they had never really had a good relationship with the mayor, chief of police, or editor of the town paper. These people felt that the two administrators were encouraging permissiveness in the schools. In fact, the town paper printed several editorials against their efforts. In addition, the teachers' association had expressed concern that the programs being pushed were asking the teachers to assume responsibilities outside their contract. Even the parent-teachers association (PTA) had held several meetings because of parent concerns about discipline in the schools. The administrator also reported the fact that the superintendent had been hired by a five-to-four vote of the board and that some supporters had been defeated in the November election. In general, the assistant superintendent implied that the town had been traditionally very conservative in educational matters, and on and on.

Figure 16–3 suggests the relationship between driving and restraining forces in this change situation. As can be seen, even with adding some board members as driving forces and not mentioning some teachers and students as restraining forces, the restraining forces for

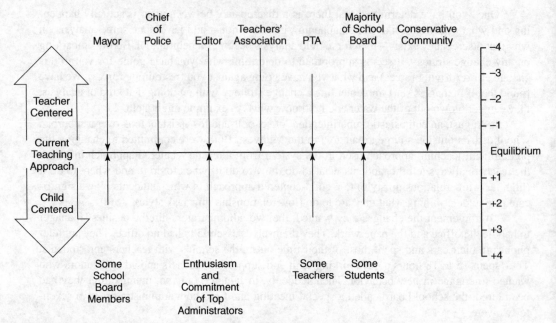

FIGURE 16–3 Driving and Restraining Forces in an Educational Change Example

changing this school system from a teacher-centered approach to a child-centered approach not only outnumbered but easily outweighed the driving forces. As a result, the restraining forces eventually overpowered the driving forces and pushed the equilibrium even more in the direction of a teacher-centered approach.

Here are a few guidelines for using force field analysis to develop a change strategy.

1. If the driving forces far outweigh the restraining forces in power and frequency in a change situation, managers interested in driving for change can often push on and overpower the restraining forces.

2. If the restraining forces are much stronger than the driving forces, managers interested in driving for change have two choices. First, they can give up the change effort, realizing that it will be too difficult to implement. Second, they can pursue the change effort, but concentrate on maintaining the driving forces in the situation while attempting, one by one, to change each of the restraining forces into driving forces or somehow to immobilize each of the restraining forces so that they are no longer factors in the situation. The second choice is possible, but very time-consuming.

3. If the driving forces and restraining forces are fairly equal in a change situation, managers probably will have to begin pushing the driving forces, while at the same time attempting to convert or immobilize some or all of the restraining forces.

In this school example, the situation obviously represented an imbalance in favor of restraining forces, yet the administrators acted as if the driving forces were clearly on their side. If they had used force field analysis to diagnose their situation, they would have seen that their change strategy was doomed until they took some time to try to work on the restraining forces.

Schein's Psychological Safety

Edgar Schein's idea of psychological safety is a major contribution to the understanding of the change process. We know that significant change means the casting off old rules and procedures and the putting on of new ones. It means, for each organization undergoing change, a complete rethinking of its plans from vision to specific tasks. However, as an organization "unfreezes," in Lewin's term, from the old ways of doing business, it faces two types of anxiety, suggested by Schein:

> [**Anxiety 1**] . . . is associated with inability or unwillingness to learn something new because it appears too difficult or disruptive.
> [**Anxiety 2**] . . . is the induced anxiety of continuing to do something that will lead to failure.[12]

Anxiety 1 is caused by fear of changing; anxiety 2 is caused by fear of not changing. For change to occur, anxiety 2 must be greater than anxiety 1; that is, the fear of doing something new (anxiety 1) must be reduced, and the fear of *not* doing something new (anxiety 2) must be increased. Top management must create psychological safety in making the transition to a new course of action.

How can psychological safety be accomplished? One method is to use a powerful vision to *reduce* the fear of changing and *increase* the fear of not changing. This vision can be enhanced through portrayals of the change's potential and feasibility. What might appear nebulous and indistinct can be given life and meaning through such portrayals, simulations, or scenarios.

Because our purpose is to focus on anxieties 1 and 2, the approach must *build confidence* in the new direction while *increasing anxiety* about the *current,* business as usual, way of operating. In addition, the approach must be easy to use to avoid anxiety resulting from using the method itself. In summary, the two phases in the process are:

- **Phase 1.** Increase anxiety 2 (fear of *not changing*).
- **Phase 2.** Decrease anxiety 1 (fear of *changing*).

For example, a firm that has been using traditional technology for two decades has sales, market share, and a pretax cash flow near the industry average. In the past three years, sales growth has slowed as competitors have adopted new technology. This competitive pressure has resulted in drastically reduced pretax cash flow. When the bank notified it that its line of credit might not be renewed, the firm undertook a searching review of its business operations.

Complicating the decision process was the issue of environmental concerns. The new technology it needed would not only require the purchase of new manufacturing equipment, but also would require the purchase of air-purification equipment to reduce undesirable emissions. How could this firm address these issues using the anxiety 1–anxiety 2 approach?

Phase 1 was to take another look at its cash flow projections. These projections confirmed its bank's analysis. Business as usual would lead to bankruptcy. *This phase increased the fear of not changing (anxiety 2).*

The next phase included examining the impact of installing the new technology, again using cash flow projections. The projections showed that the new technology plus needed environmental equipment would pay for themselves, and *the fear of change (anxiety 1) was reduced.*

Options for change must be developed in such a way that, if found feasible, they can add confidence to the change decision. At the very least, a firm may be faced with the fact that given the analysis in phase 1, there is just no other alternative but to adopt new business strategies.

Force field analysis can also be employed to increase or decrease each of the anxieties. An analysis of factors that might help lead to increased sales—e.g., new markets, higher margins, developing an expanded sales force, creating new advertising approaches, and opening new distribution channels—might serve to reduce the fear of change, that is, reduce anxiety 1.

We can make the following conclusions about the change process:

1. In order for an organization to change, it must go through an "unfreezing" step.
2. This unfreezing involves two anxieties: Anxiety 1 is the fear of changing; anxiety 2 is the fear of not changing.
3. For an organization to unfreeze, anxiety 1 must be decreased and anxiety 2 must be increased.
4. Anxiety 2 issues should be addressed before anxiety 1 issues.
5. Anxieties can be further analyzed using established techniques such as force field analysis.

FIRST-ORDER AND SECOND-ORDER CHANGE

One way of approaching change for the purpose of diagnosis is to look at it from the perspective of two different frameworks. This approach is important because change does not always occur in a stable environment. Organizations have experienced revolutionary changes in technology, competition, and socioeconomic conditions; some changes have destroyed old industries and created new ones. Leaders need to recognize and understand the two frameworks in which change can occur.

The change process most managers are familiar with is continuous, or *first-order change*—change that occurs in a stable system that itself remains unchanged. The change processes previously discussed in this chapter focus on managing first-order change. These changes are necessary for a business to grow and thrive in a competitive environment.

Discontinuous, or *second-order change* occurs when fundamental properties or states of the system are changed.[13] The fall of communism and the introduction of democratic and free market principles in Eastern Europe and the former Soviet Union are examples of the cataclysmic upheaval of second-order change. Some industries currently experiencing the magnitude of second-order change include telecommunications, financial services, and health care, as discontinuous changes restructure the industry, relocate its boundaries, and change the bases of competition.

Adaptation change theories maintain that individual firms monitor their environments continuously and make purposeful adjustments to them. *Incrementalism* refers to organizational changes in new products, structures, and processes; resource dependence mechanisms see organizational change as a response to external dependencies, such as suppliers, markets, or governmental policies.

Evolution change theories describe the first-order changes that industries experience. *Natural selection* mechanisms view the entry and exit of firms in an industry as the primary method of evolution. *Institutional isomorphism* occurs when organizations change to conform to the norms of the industry environment.

As firms experience various stages of the organizational life cycle, they experience *metamorphosis,* second-order change. Metamorphosis differs from adaptation in that the entire firm goes through a transformation and emerges with a different configuration and strategic intent. An example of this type of change can be seen when a visionary inventor with a small business brings in a professional management team, and the small business metamorphoses into a growing firm with a different organizational structure and competitive focus. The change is transforming for the members of the small business.

Revolutionary change occurs when an entire industry is restructured and reconstituted during a brief period of quantum change that is preceded and followed by a long period of stability. *Quantum speciation,* a term from biology, has been proposed as a mechanism through which new organizational forms emerge during a revolution. The breakup of AT&T into "baby bells" and the introduction of new competitors into long-distance telecommunications companies is an example of second-order revolutionary change in an industry.

Most organizational changes you initiate as a leader will occur on a level of first-order change. You should also understand the opportunities presented by second-order change and work to meet the challenges this type of change can create.

CHANGE CYCLES

Levels of Change

There are four levels of change: knowledge changes, attitudinal changes, individual behavior changes, and group or organizational performance changes.

Changes in *knowledge* tend to be the easiest to make; they can occur as a result of reading a book or an article or hearing something new from a respected person. *Attitudes* differ from knowledge in that they are emotionally charged in a positive or negative way. The addition of emotion often makes attitudes more difficult to change than knowledge.

Changes in *individual behavior* seem to be significantly more difficult and time-consuming than either of the two previous levels. For example, managers may have knowledge about the advantages of increased follower involvement and participation in decision making and may even feel that such participation would improve their performance; however, they may be unable to delegate or share decision-making responsibilities significantly with followers. This discrepancy between knowledge, attitude, and behavior may be a result of their own authoritarian leader-follower past. This experience has led to a habit pattern that feels comfortable.

Individual behavior is difficult enough to change, but implementing change within *groups* or *organizations* is even more complicated. The leadership styles of one or two managers might be effectively altered, but drastically changing the level of follower participation throughout an entire organization might be a very time-consuming process. At this level, you are trying to alter customs, mores, and traditions that have developed over many years.

Levels of change become very significant when you examine two different change cycles—the participative change cycle and the directive change cycle.[14]

Participative Change

A participative change cycle is implemented when new knowledge is made available to the individual or group. It is hoped that the group will accept the data and will develop a positive attitude and commitment in the direction of the desired change. At this level, an effective strategy may be to involve the individual or group directly in helping to select or formalize the new methods for obtaining the desired goals. This step is group participation in problem solving.

The next step will be to attempt to translate this commitment into actual behavior. This step is significantly more difficult to achieve. For example, it is one thing to be concerned about increased follower participation in decision making (attitude), but another thing to be willing actually to get involved in doing something (behavior) about the issue. An effective strategy may be to identify the informal and formal leaders among the work group(s) and concentrate on gaining their behavioral support for the desired change. Once the behavior of the group leaders has been

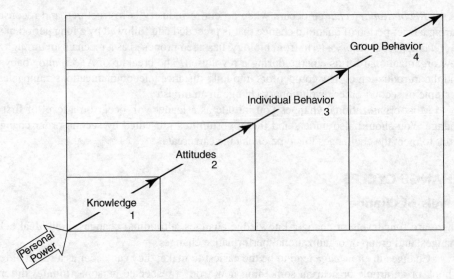

FIGURE 16–4   Participative Change Cycle

Source: Adapted from *Strategic Management Journal,* Meyer, Brooks, and Goes, 1990. © Wiley and Sons Limited. Reproduced with permission.

changed, organizational change may be effected as other people begin to pattern their behavior after those persons whom they respect and perceive in leadership roles. This participative change cycle is illustrated in Figure 16–4.

Directive Change

We have all probably been faced with a situation similar to the one in which there is an announcement on Monday morning that "as of today all members of this organization will begin to operate in accordance with Form 10125." This is an example of a directive change cycle. It is through this change cycle that many managers in the past have attempted to implement such innovative ideas as management by objectives, job enrichment, and the like.

This change cycle begins when change is imposed on the total organization by some external force, such as higher management, the community, or new laws. In turn, the change will affect individual behavior. The new contacts and modes of behavior create new knowledge, which tends to develop predispositions toward or against the change. The directive change cycle is illustrated in Figure 16–5.

In cases in which change is forced, the new behavior sometimes creates the kind of knowledge that develops commitment to the change, and the change begins to resemble participative change as it reinforces individual and group behavior. The hope is that "if people will only have a chance to see how the new system works, they will support it." This is illustrated in Figure 16–5 by the dashed line. The sequence goes from group behavior, individual behavior, to knowledge and then back to attitudes.

Is There a "Best" Strategy for Change?

Given a choice between the polarities of directive and participative change, most people would tend to prefer the participative change cycle. But, just as we have argued that there is no best

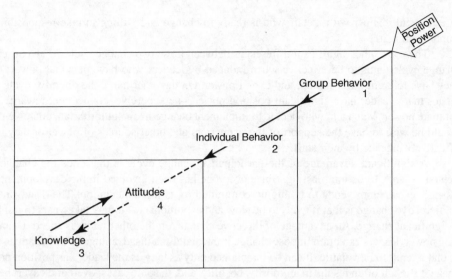

FIGURE 16–5   Directive Change Cycle

leadership style, there also is no best strategy for implementing change. Effective change agents are identified as those who can adapt their strategies to the demands of their unique environment. Thus, the participative change cycle is not a better change strategy than the directive change cycle, and vice versa. The appropriate strategy depends on the situation, and there are advantages and disadvantages to each.

Advantages and Disadvantages of Change Cycles

The participative change cycle tends to be more appropriate for working with individuals and groups who are achievement-motivated, seek responsibility, and have a degree of knowledge and experience that may be useful in developing new ways of operating—in other words, people with moderate to high task-relevant readiness. Once the change starts, these people are highly capable of assuming responsibilities for implementation of the desired change. Although these people may welcome change and the need to improve, they may become very rigid and opposed to change if it is implemented in a directive (high task–low relationship) manner. A directive change style is inconsistent with their perceptions of themselves as responsible, self-motivated people who should be consulted throughout the change process. When they are not consulted and change is implemented in an authoritarian manner, conflict often results. Examples occur frequently in organizations in which a manager recruits or inherits a competent, creative staff who is willing to work hard to implement new programs and then proceeds to bypass the staff completely in the change process. This style results in resistance and is inappropriate to the situation.

A directive change style might be appropriate and productive with individuals and groups who are not ambitious, are dependent, and are unwilling to take on new responsibilities unless forced to do so. In fact, these people might prefer direction and structure from their leader to being faced with decisions they are not willing or experienced enough to make. Once again, diagnosis is all-important. It is just as inappropriate for a manager to attempt to implement change in a participative manner with a staff who has never been given the opportunity to take responsibility and has become dependent on its manager for direction as it is to implement change in a forceful manner with a staff who is ready to change and willing to take responsibility for implementing it.

There are other significant differences between these two change cycles. The participative change cycle tends to be effective when induced by leaders who have personal power; that is, they have referent, information, and expert power. On the other hand, the directive cycle necessitates that a leader have significant position power—i.e., coercive, connection, reward, and legitimate power. Managers who decide to implement change in an authoritarian, coercive manner would be wise to have the support of their superiors and other sources of power or they may be effectively blocked by their staff.

A significant advantage of the participative change cycle is that once the change is accepted, it tends to be long-lasting. Since everyone has been involved in the development of the change, each person tends to be highly committed to its implementation. The disadvantage of participative change is that it tends to be slow and evolutionary—it may take years to implement a significant change. An advantage of directive change, on the other hand, is speed. Using position power, leaders can often impose change immediately. A disadvantage of this change strategy is that it tends to be volatile. It can be maintained only as long as the leader has position power to make it stick. It often results in animosity, hostility, and, in some cases, overt and covert behavior to undermine and overthrow.

In terms of force field analysis, the directive change cycle could be utilized if the power of the driving forces pushing for change far outweighed the restraining forces resisting change. On the other hand, a directive change cycle would be doomed to failure if the power of the restraining forces working against the change was greater than the power of the driving forces pushing for the change.

A participative change cycle that depends on personal power could be appropriate in either of the cases just described. With frequent and powerful driving forces pushing for change in a situation, a leader might not have to use a high task, directive change cycle because the driving forces are ready to effect the change and do not have to be forced to engage in the new desired behavior. At the same time, when the restraining forces could easily overpower the driving forces, managers would be advised to begin with participative change techniques designed gradually to turn some of the restraining forces into driving forces or at least immobilize their influence in the situation. In other words, when the odds are against you and you have little power, your best bet would be to try to moderate the forces against the change rather than to try to force change.

These two change cycles have been described as if they were either/or positions. The use of only one of these change cycles exclusively, however, could lead to problems. For example, if managers introduce change only in a directive, high task–low relationship manner without any movement toward participative change, members of their staff—if they decide to remain—may react in one of two ways. Some may fight the managers tooth and nail and organize efforts to undermine them. Others may buckle under to their authority and become very passive, dependent staff members, always needing the manager to tell them what to do and when to do it before doing anything. These kinds of people say yes to anything the manager wants and then moan and groan and drag their feet later. Neither of these responses makes for a very healthy organization. At the other extreme, managers who will not make a move without checking with their staff and getting full approval also can immobilize themselves. They may establish such a complicated network of "participative" committees that significant change becomes almost impossible. Thus, in reality, the question is "What is the proper blend of the directive and participative change cycles in this situation?" rather than "Which one should I use?"

Change Process—Some Examples

To see the change process in operation, consider these examples:

A college basketball coach recruited Bob Anderson, a 6 foot 9 inch center, from a small town in a rural area where 6 feet 6 inches was a good height for a center. This fact, combined with his deadly turnaround jump shot, made Anderson the rage of his league and enabled him to average close to 30 points a game.

Recognizing that Anderson was a bit short for a college center, the coach hoped that he could make him a forward, moving him inside only when they were playing a double pivot. One of the things the coach was concerned about, however, was how Anderson, when used in the pivot, could get his jump shot off when he came up against other players ranging in height from 6 feet 11 inches to more than 7 feet. He felt that Anderson would have to learn to shoot a hook shot, which is much harder to block, if he were going to have scoring potential against this kind of competition. The approach that many coaches would use to solve this problem would probably be as follows: On the first day of practice, the coach would welcome Anderson and then explain the problem to him as he had analyzed it. As a solution, he would probably ask Anderson to start to work with the varsity center, Steve Cram, who was 6 feet 11 inches and had an excellent hook. "Steve can help you start working on that new shot, Bob," the coach would say. Anderson's reaction to this interchange might be one of resentment, and he would go over and work with Cram only because of the coach's position power. After all, he might think to himself, "Who does he think he is? I've been averaging close to 30 points a game for 3 years now, and the first day I show up here the coach wants me to learn a new shot."

So he may start to work with Cram reluctantly, concentrating on the hook shot only when the coach is looking but taking his favorite jump shot when not being observed. Anderson is by no means unfrozen, or ready to learn to shoot another way.

Let us look at another approach the coach might use to solve this problem. Suppose that on the first day of practice he sets up a scrimmage between the varsity and the freshmen. Before he starts the scrimmage, he takes big Steve Cram, the varsity center, aside and tells him, "Steve, we have this new freshman named Anderson who has real potential to be a fine ball player. What I'd like you to do today, though, is not to worry about scoring or rebounding—just make sure every time Anderson goes up for a shot, you make him eat it. I want him to see that he will have to learn to shoot some other shots if he is to survive against guys like you." So when the scrimmage starts, the first time Anderson gets the ball and turns around to shoot, Cram leaps up and stuffs the ball right down his throat. Time after time this occurs. Soon, Anderson starts to engage in some coping behavior, trying to fall away from the basket, shooting from the side of his head rather than from the front in an attempt to get his shot off. After the scrimmage, Anderson comes off the court dejected. The coach says, "What's wrong, Bob?" Bob replies, "I don't know, coach, I just can't seem to get my shot off against a man as big as Cram. What do you think I should do?" "Well, Bob," says the coach, "Why don't you go over and start working with Steve on a hook shot. I think you'll find it much harder to block. And, with your shooting eye, I don't think it will take long for you to learn." How do you think Anderson would feel about working with Cram now? He'd probably be enthusiastic and ready to learn. Being placed in a situation in which he learns for himself that he has a problem will go a long way in unfreezing Anderson from his past patterns of behavior and preparing him for making the attempt at identification. Now he will be ready for identification. He has had an opportunity to internalize his problem and is ready to work with Steve Cram.

Often the leader who has knowledge of an existing problem forgets that until the people involved recognize the problem as their own, it is going to be difficult to change their behavior.

Internalization and identification are not either/or alternatives, but they can be parts of developing specific change strategies appropriate to the situation.

Another example of the change process in operation can be seen in the military, particularly in the induction phase. In a few short months, the military is able to mold inductees into an effective combat team. This feat is not an accident. Let us look at some of the processes that help accomplish this change.

The most dramatic and harsh aspect of the training is the unfreezing phase. All of Schein's four elements of drastic unfreezing are present. Let us look at some specific examples of these elements in operation.

1. The soldiers are *physically removed from their accustomed routines, sources of information, and social relationships.*
2. The DI (drill instructor) *undermines and destroys all social supports.* "Using their voices and the threat of extra PT [physical training], the DI . . . must shock the recruit out of the emotional stability of home, girlfriend/boyfriend, or school."[15]
3. *Demeaning and humiliating experiences* are commonplace during the first two weeks of the training as the DIs teach inductees to *see themselves as unworthy and thus be motivated to change* into what the DIs want a soldier to be.
4. Throughout the training, *reward* is consistently *linked with willingness to change and punishment with unwillingness to change.*

Although the soldiers go through a severe unfreezing process, they quickly move to the changing phase, first identifying with the DI and then emulating informal leaders as they develop. "Toward the end of the third week, a break occurs. What one DI calls 'that five percent—the slow, fat, dumb, or difficult' have been dropped. The remaining [soldiers] have emerged from their first week vacuum with one passionate desire—to stay with their platoon at all costs."[16]

Internalization takes place when the recruits, through their forced interactions, develop different high-strength needs. "Fear of the DI gives way to respect, and survival evolves into achievement toward the end of training. 'I learned I had more guts than I imagined' is a typical comment."[17]

Because the group tends to stay together throughout the entire program, it serves as a positive reinforcer, which can help to refreeze the new behavior.

BRINGING CHANGE THEORIES TOGETHER

The preceding theories should help a manager determine some alternative solutions to the identified problem(s) and suggest appropriate implementation strategies. For example, let us reexamine the case of our enthusiastic school administrators who wanted to humanize the schools in their system and change the predominant teaching approach from teacher-centered to child-centered. As we suggested, if they had done a force field analysis, they would have realized that the restraining forces working against this change far outweighed the driving forces in power and frequency. The analysis would have suggested that a directive, coercive change strategy would have been ineffective for implementing change, because significant unfreezing had to occur before the restraining forces against the change could have been immobilized or turned into driving forces. Thus, a participative change effort probably would have been appropriately aimed at reeducating the restraining forces by exposing them in a nonthreatening way (through two-way communication patterns) to new knowledge directed at changing their attitudes and eventually their behavior.

Although this approach might be appropriate, it also must be recognized that it will be time-consuming (4 to 7 years). The superintendent and his assistant just might not be willing to devote that kind of time and effort to this change project. If they are not, then they could decide not to enter that school system or to charge on in a coercive, directive manner and be ready for the consequences. Or, they could choose their action from a number of other alternatives that may have been generated.

CHANGE PROCESS—RECOMMENDED ACTION

After suggesting various alternative solutions and appropriate implementation strategies, a leader or manager interested in change should anticipate the probable consequences (both positive and negative) of taking each of the alternative actions. Remember:

1. Unless there is a high probability that a desired consequence will occur and that the consequence will be the same as the conditions that would exist if the problem were not present, then you have not solved the problem or changed the situation.
2. The ultimate solution to a problem (the change effort) may not be possible overnight, and, therefore, interim goals must be set along the path to the final goal (the solving of the problem).

The end result of analysis (which includes determining alternative solutions) should be some recommended action that will decrease the discrepancy between the actual and the ideal. Although action is the end result, you must remember that action based on superficial analysis may be worse than no action at all. Too frequently, people want to hurry on to the action phase of a problem before they have adequately analyzed the situation. The importance of the analysis part cannot be given too much emphasis—a good analysis frequently makes the action obvious.

Summary

The focus in this book has been on the management of human resources, and, as a result, we have spent little time on how technical change can have an impact on the total system. Our attempt in this example was to reiterate that an organization is an "open social system"; that is, all aspects of an organization are interrelated; a change in any part of an organization may have an impact on other parts or on the organization itself. Thus, a proposed change in any part of an organization must be carefully assessed in terms of its likely impact on the rest of the organization.

Notes

1. The survey was conducted by the Gallup Organization and commissioned by Proudfoot Change Management, a division of an international consulting firm. It was reported in Barbara Ettorre, "Buddy, Can You Spare Some Change!" *Management Review* 83, no. 1 (January 1994): 5.
2. *Ibid.*
3. Edgar H. Schein, *The Corporate Culture Survival Guide* (San Francisco: Jossey-Bass, Inc., 1999), 132.
4. Kurt Lewin, "Frontiers in Group Dynamics: Concept, Method, and Reality in Social Science; Social Equilibria and Social Change," *Human Relations* 1, no. 1 (June 1974): 5–41.

5. Edgar H. Schein, "Management Development As a Process of Influence." in *Behavioral Concepts in Management,* ed. David R. Hampton (Belmont, CA: Dickinson Publishing, 1968), 110. Reprinted in *Industrial Management Review* 2, no. 2 (May 1961): 59–77.

6. The mechanisms are taken from Herbert C. Kelman, "Compliance, Identification and Internalization: Three Processes of Attitude Change," *Journal of Conflict Resolution* II, no. 1 (1958): 51–60.

7. Schein, "Management Development As a Process of Influence," p. 112.

8. See Kelman, "Compliance, Identification and Internalization."

9. Schein, "Management Development As a Process of Influence," p. 112.

10. Kurt Lewin, "Frontiers in Group Dynamics: Concept, Method, and Reality in Social Science; Social Equilibria and Social Change," *Human Relations* 1, no. 1 (June 1947): 5–41.

11. *Ibid.*

12. Edgar H. Schein, in an invited address to the World Economic Forum, February 6, 1992, Davos, Switzerland.

13. Paul Watzlawick, John Weakland, and Richard Fisch, *Change: Principles of Problem Formation and Problem Resolution* (New York: Norton, 1974).

14. Paul Hersey and Kenneth H. Blanchard, "Change and the Use of Power," *Training and Development Journal* (January 1972). See also Chris Argyris, *Strategy, Change and Defensive Routines* (Cambridge, MA: Ballenger Publishing, 1985).

15. "Marine Machine," *Look Magazine,* August 12, 1969.

16. *Ibid.*

17. *Ibid.*

17

Leadership Strategies for Organizational Transformation

W hy is organizational transformation important? You will recall that in Chapter 1 we described a world in transformation. In all spheres of activity, we have entered a period of rapid, large-scale, and discontinuous change. Geopolitically, a new mosaic of nations, countries, and political systems is forming and reforming. Socially, the human race has been subjected to forces of cataclysmic proportions in areas such as health, welfare, and even physical safety. The technological explosion seems to be sweeping everybody along on a surprise-a-minute roller-coaster ride. The whole world has become one business arena, forcing all of us into new and qualitatively different ways of thinking and doing.

In such a dynamic environment, it is inevitable that organizations of all shapes, sizes, and types will also undergo major change and upheaval. Organizational transformations have become the order of the day, and with them has come the potential for crises and chaos—or for new freedoms and better ways of living. The scope and the scale of change require leadership at a level and of a quality never experienced before. How are we as leaders to respond? One important response in the face of these great challenges and threatening periods of uncertainty is *transformational leadership*. This chapter was contributed by Gustav Pansegrouw.

CHARACTERISTICS OF ORGANIZATIONAL TRANSFORMATION

According to Richard Beckhard, one of the pioneering practitioners and researchers in the field of organizational development, a transformation represents a vital organizational change.[1] Transformation is characterized by certain features that clearly differentiate it from other types of change. First, according to Beckhard, it involves substantial and discontinuous change to the shape, structure, and nature of the organization, rather than incremental adjustments and fine-tuning of the current situation. One example of a discontinuous change would be when a firm changes from being production-driven to being customer-driven. Another would be a merger of two organizations. In both instances, the shape of the organization can be expected to change radically. An organization transforming from a production orientation to a customer orientation will need to drastically decentralize and delegate authority. In a merger, entirely new roles and working relationships will be created.

A second characteristic of transformation is that the need for change is caused by forces external to the organization rather than forces inside the organization. A typical example would be when an organization changes from a functional to a divisional structure in response to market forces or industry pressures in the form of competitor actions or regulatory changes. Currently, globalization is one of the most powerful external forces for organizational transformation.

A third distinguishing feature of transformation is that the change is deep and pervasive, rather than shallow and contained. The change affects all parts of the organization and involves many levels. Decentralization, downsizing, and the geographic relocation of functions and activities exemplify changes that transform structural relationships deeply and pervasively.

Finally, transformation requires significantly different, and even entirely new, sets of actions by the members of the organization, rather than more or less of existing behavior patterns. Examples are changes to the norms and core values of an organization that are brought about through acquisition, deregulation, and privatization or through a drastic strategic repositioning such as shifting from a production-efficiency focus to a customer-service strategy. An organizational transformation is thus characterized by the fact that the organization as a whole has to do substantially new and different things rather than only some people having to do more or less of the same thing.

A transformation starts beyond the current organization in that it deals with changes in the external environment; it includes realignment of the mission, strategy, structure, and systems; and it requires re-creation of the culture and behavioral processes of the organization as a whole.[2]

TRANSFORMATIONAL LEADERSHIP

Studies of successful and unsuccessful organizational transformations have emphasized the decisive role of leadership in these situations and have given rise to the concept of *transformational leadership,* which is also termed *visionary leadership, strategic leadership,* or *charismatic leadership.* This new leadership arena involves specific leadership styles, actions, and strategies that are required to bring about organizational transformation. Table 17–1 summarizes the characteristics of transformational leadership that have been proposed by various authors. These studies spanning more than a decade show that the concept of transformational leadership does not alter the basic definition of leadership presented in Chapter 1—i.e., the process of influencing the activities of an individual or a group in efforts toward goal achievement in a given situation. It does, however, highlight the specific actions that the leader should perform in a transformation. On the basis of the strategies and characteristics presented in Table 17–1, let us summarize the key leadership actions for bringing about organizational transformation. It should be noted that these summary statements do not necessarily depict a sequential flow of events or a sequential process. Rather, we have attempted to emphasize *critical leadership incidents* for organizational transformation as reported by the cited authors in a brief, easy-to-use format. A sequential process model appears in a recent work of Nadler.[3]

Personal Commitment to the Transformation by the Leadership

The leadership of the organization must be fully committed to the transformation, and the commitment must be visible to other organizational members and external stakeholders (key players).

TABLE 17–1 Transformational Leadership Strategies and Characteristics

Bennis and Nanus (1985)	Tichy and Devanna (1986)	Kouzes and Posner (1987)	Nadler and Tushman (1989)	Conger (1989)	Nevis ET AL. (1996)
Attention through vision	Recognizing the need for revitalization	Challenging the process	Envisioning	Detecting unexploited opportunities and deficiencies in the current situation	Persuasive communication
Meaning through communication	Creating a new vision	Inspiring a shared vision	Energizing		Participation
Trust through positioning	Institutionalizing change	Enabling others to act	Enabling	Communicating the vision	Expectancy
Deployment of self		Modeling the way	Structuring	Building trust	Role modeling
		Encouraging the heart	Controlling	Demonstrating the means to achieve the vision	Structural rearrangement
			Rewarding		Extrinsic rewards
					Coercion

Sources: Edwin C. Nevis, Joan Lancourt, and Helen G. Vasallo, *International Revolutions* (San Francisco: Jossey Bass, 1996); Warren Bennis and Burt Nanus, *Leaders: The Strategies for Taking Charge* (New York: Harper & Row, 1985); Noel M. Tichy and Mary Anne Devanna, *The Transformational Leader* (New York: John Wiley and Sons, 1986); James M. Kouzes and Barry Z. Posner, *The Leadership Challenge* (San Francisco: Jossey Bass, 1987); Jay Conger, *The Charismatic Leader* (San Francisco: Jossey Bass, 1989); David A. Nadler and Michael Tushman, "Leadership for Organizational Change." In *Large Scale Organizational Change*, ed. Allen M. Mohrman, Jr., Susan Albers Mohrman, Gerald E. Ledford, Jr., Thomas G. Cummings, Edward E. Lawler III and Associates (San Francisco: Jossey Bass, 1989).

Firm, Relentless, and Indisputable Communication of the Impossibility of Maintaining the Status Quo

The leadership must forcefully communicate the *failure* of the status quo. This must be done in such a way that a critical mass of members will want to change. You will recall the Schein model in Chapter 16 that emphasized the importance of increasing the anxiety of not changing and decreasing the anxiety of changing. This process requires:

- Firm statements backed by credible evidence that the status quo is untenable because of circumstances and trends external to the organization.
- Clear indications that the failure of the status quo is final and irreversible.

Clear and Enthusiastic Communication of an Inspiring Vision of What the Organization Could Become

The leadership must persistently communicate a clear picture of the future state of the organization in a way that this vision is shared and supported by the members of the organization, individually and collectively. This communication requires:

- A clear and vivid value-based vision created by an appropriate mix of rational analysis, intuition, and emotional involvement.
- Repeated communication of the vision, beliefs, and values to the members of the organization in a way that inspires and excites them and touches their hearts and minds with a sense of urgency.

Timely Establishment of a Critical Mass of Support for the Transformation

The leadership must identify the key players and power holders in the organization and in its operating environment and obtain their support for the change. Obtaining support requires:

- Acknowledging the power that key players in and outside the organization have.
- Discussing with them the failure of the status quo, presenting them with the vision of the future and the values accompanying it, and convincing them of the need to change.
- Showing personal and organizational benefits to be achieved and involving them in decisions and implementation.

Acknowledging, Honoring, and Dealing with Resistance to the Transformation

The leadership must acknowledge resistance to the change and deal with it as a necessary stage in the process of abandoning the status quo and embracing the new vision with its beliefs and values. Dealing with resistance requires:

- A willingness to listen.
- Some tolerance and patience.
- Clarification and repetition of the need to change and the benefits of the transformation.

Defining and Setting Up an Organization That Can Implement the Vision

The leadership must design and put into action an organization that will be congruent with the new beliefs and values. Leadership must be willing to risk the introduction of structural changes and the acquisition and allocation of resources that will secure the competence and commitment to make the transformation work and that will put into place appropriate systems of organization for the transformation, including:

- Modeling and anchoring the required beliefs and values in appropriate new roles and actions.
- Implementing strategies, structures, and systems, including a power network that is clearly aligned to, and supportive of, the actions that need to be accomplished in order to realize the vision and enact the new beliefs and values.
- Replacing key staff, or staff in key positions, who are not suited to the change.
- Introducing education, training, and retraining in the actions required by the transformation and specifically by the new beliefs and values.
- Implementing a reward system that will reinforce actions that are congruent with the new set of beliefs and values.

Regular Communication of Information about Progress and Giving Recognition and Reward for Achievements

The leadership must communicate to the organization how the transformation is progressing, announce and celebrate achievements, openly share setbacks, and encourage the risk-taking behavior required to implement the vision. This step requires:

- Regular publication of achievements and face-to-face feedback sessions.
- Emphasizing, recognizing, and consistently rewarding the gains made toward the implementation of the vision, the beliefs, and the values.

Transformational leadership thus includes both the dramatic, courageous, and emotionally stirring actions and the mundane, ongoing day-to-day transactions that are integral to life in organizations. Putting all of this together, we define transformational leadership as:

> A deliberate influence process on the part of an individual or group to bring about a discontinuous change in the current state and functioning of an organization as a whole. The change is driven by a vision based on a set of beliefs and values that require the members of the organization to urgently perceive and think differently and to perform new actions and organizational roles.

Let us examine this definition in some detail.

A DELIBERATE INFLUENCE PROCESS   The leadership is very conscious of what they want to bring about, and they have a specific plan, at least initially, of how they want to bring about the transformation. Their actions are premeditated rather than spontaneous.

ON THE PART OF AN INDIVIDUAL OR GROUP   This phrase specifies that the leadership may be an individual or a group within the organization.

TO BRING ABOUT A DISCONTINUOUS CHANGE   The term *discontinuous* is used in deliberate contrast to the term *incremental*. A transformation is a clear break from the past and the present. The acid test for a discontinuous change is analysis of future critical success factors. If these factors are not qualitatively different from the current critical success factors, the change is probably only incremental.

IN THE CURRENT STATE AND FUNCTIONING   *State* refers to the *performance* of the organization, such as the health of the organization. *Functioning* includes the internal and external *interactive patterns* as reflected in organizational structures and systems.

OF AN ORGANIZATION AS A WHOLE   Transformational leadership is pervasive in terms of both the horizontal and vertical dimensions of the organization, and it is also systemic in that it sees the organization as a system to be changed.

THE CHANGE IS DRIVEN BY A VISION BASED ON A SET OF BELIEFS AND VALUES   The development and pursuit of a belief- and value-anchored vision is the distinguishing feature of transformational leadership. The vision, in terms of being a belief- and value-infused picture or representation of what the organization as an entity could become, is also the clearest signal that the change to come is discontinuous. The vision, and particularly the set of underlying beliefs and values, is, in effect, a control mechanism for ensuring the type of activities required to achieve the future state.

THAT REQUIRES THE MEMBERS OF THE ORGANIZATION TO URGENTLY PERCEIVE AND THINK DIFFERENTLY AND TO PERFORM NEW ACTIONS AND ORGANIZATIONAL ROLES   Transformational leadership aims at instilling new behaviors in most members of the organization and without exception requires new role sets and role behaviors in the classic interpretation of the concept of role, as used in the behavioral sciences. Although we have put the emphasis on new actions as the observable result, we also include in the concept new ways of perceiving and thinking as the precursors toward observable behavior. Transformational leadership is also invariably characterized by an urgency; time is important, and because a transformation more often than not is a response to an organizational crisis, the new actions are urgently required.

NO ONE "IDEAL" WAY FOR ORGANIZATIONAL TRANSFORMATION

The caution for leaders who wish to transform their organizations is not to idealize a given set of key actions as the one best way of bringing about transformations.[4] A cookbook approach tends to disregard the differences that exist from one situation to another. What may have worked well in one transformation situation may not work at all in another. There is always the danger that leadership recipes, collected from a variety of successful "meals," may be put together in a list that then becomes touted as the one best way, or best recipe, for attempting all organizational transformations irrespective of situational differences.

The Situational Leadership® for Transformation model states that any combination of or all of the preceding leadership actions may be appropriate or inappropriate for bringing about a transformation, depending on the situation in which they are used. The most important situational factor is the "fit" between the leadership actions and the organization in terms of the organization's readiness for transformation. This view is consistent with our discussion in Chapter 8. Of the many important situational factors the leader may consider, the relationship between the leader and the follower is the most critical. In this context, the relationship is between the leader and the organizational entity.

ORGANIZATIONAL READINESS FOR TRANSFORMATION

The inherent complexity of organizational behavior on the one hand and the scale of change involved in transformation on the other warn against an oversimplification of the concept of *readiness for transformation*—a concept that has not received sufficient attention in the field of organizational change and transformation.[5]

In our view, organizational readiness for transformation is a function of, or is determined by, the *culture* of the organization. Although organizational culture is itself a complex phenomenon with many interpretations, there is some agreement in the literature that the primary element of organizational culture is shared basic assumptions, or beliefs, about how to cope with the two fundamental problems that all groups and organizations face: survival and adaptation to the external environment, and the internal integration and coordination of organizational functioning.[6] A shared basic assumption, or belief, consists of cognitive, emotional, motivational, and behavioral components that are so taken for granted that as a rule they are seldom confronted or challenged by organizational members. When a shared assumption is held in an organization, it defines for the members what they should pay attention to, what meaning they should attach to environmental trends and organizational events, what action preferences and motivations they should have, and how they should react emotionally to issues inside and outside the organization.

In one sense, basic assumptions are the analytic, interpretive, decision-making, and coping frameworks, or models, that members of the organization share. They play a major role in providing meaning to events in and around the organization. Basic assumptions function as *coping mechanisms* in that they determine what information and events the organization will pay attention to, how they will be interpreted, and how they will be acted on. As such, basic assumptions are *ability factors* of organizational culture—they make the organization more or less able to cope with events. However, basic assumptions also reflect the preferences and motivational orientations, or models that the members of the organization share. They play a major role in determining priorities and guidelines for selection and choice with regard to ends and means. Basic assumptions thus also function as *motivational mechanisms* in that they determine what the organization will strive for and how it will be achieved. As such, basic assumptions are also *willingness* factors of organizational culture—they make the organization more or less willing to pursue certain ends (and means to ends) rather than others.

Basic assumptions, or beliefs, often operate outside of awareness, and they may be viewed as a collective mindset that guides the organizational processes of interpretation, action preferences, and emotional reactions. The need for congruence created by shared assumptions is often so powerful that it may even bring about denial, projection, and other forms of distortion of events in and around the organization.[7]

We suggest that the more the basic assumptions, or belief systems, reflect a *learning culture,* the higher the organizational readiness for transformation will be. The past decade has witnessed an ever-increasing emphasis on the need for organizations to develop a learning culture as the only way to sustain a competitive advantage over the long term in an increasingly complex and turbulent environment. A learning culture is characterized by continuous learning from experiences and by learning how to learn.[8]

The basic assumptions, or beliefs, that characterize a learning culture can be described along two dimensions: flexibility with regard to the external environment ability and organizational commitment willingness.[9]

Flexibility with regard to the external environment includes the following organizational characteristics:

- Risk-seeking behavior
- Tolerance of ambiguity
- Ease in uncertain situations
- Inquisitiveness, scientific interest, experimentation
- High frequency of interaction with external environment
- Active customer information gathering
- Entrepreneurial orientation, innovation alertness
- Functional orientation

Organizational commitment consists of organizational characteristics, such as:

- Sharing of goals, responsibilities, and information, supportive and "we" feelings, participative mindset
- Mission and goal orientation, results orientation
- Congruence and internal consistency, systemic integration
- Opportunities for creativity, freedom of ideas, individualism

The shared basic assumption that contrasts with, or is opposite to, flexibility with regard to the external environment is *rigidity with regard to the status quo*. The shared basic assumption that contrasts with organizational commitment is a *parochial orientation*. Integrating the concepts discussed so far allows us to develop the model of organizational readiness for transformation shown in Figure 17–1. This model presents four types of culture, each representing a different level of organizational readiness for transformation.

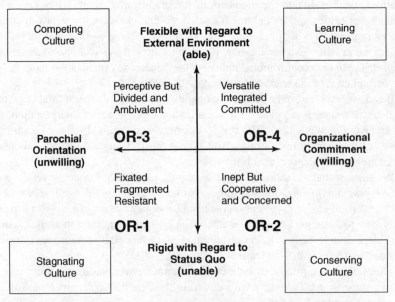

FIGURE 17–1 Organizational Readiness (OR) for Transformation Model

OR-4: THE LEARNING CULTURE   Basic assumptions reflect flexibility with regard to the external environment and organizational commitment. This culture is able and willing to deal with organizational transformation. The ability is reflected in a versatility to effectively cope with any demands presented by the external environment. The willingness is demonstrated by the integrated way in which the organization functions and by high levels of commitment to the organization as a whole and its continued well being.

OR-3: THE COMPETING CULTURE   Basic assumptions reflect flexibility with regard to the external environment, but the organization has a parochial, or vested-interest, orientation. This culture is able, but unwilling to deal with organizational transformation. The ability is expressed as perceptiveness with regard to the demands of the external environment. The unwillingness is manifested as the divided way in which the organization functions and an ambivalence about the benefits that the transformation may bring about for the various vested-interest groups and role players in the organization.

OR-2: THE CONSERVING CULTURE   Basic assumptions reflect a rigidity with regard to the status quo but also show an organizational commitment. This culture is unable, but willing to deal with organizational transformation. The inability is displayed by an ineptness in dealing with the demands of the external environment. The willingness is demonstrated by the cooperative way in which the organization functions and by a concern for the viability of the organization as a whole.

OR-1: THE STAGNATING CULTURE   Basic assumptions reflect a rigidity with regard to the status quo and parochialism. This culture is both unable and unwilling to deal with organizational transformation. The inability is expressed as a fixation on the status quo and apathy toward the demands of the external environment. The unwillingness is reflected in the fragmented functioning of the organization and in a resistance to any actions that may jeopardize vested interests and parochial preferences.

TRANSFORMATIONAL LEADERSHIP ACTIONS

Earlier in this chapter, we summarized the key leadership actions and models for bringing about organizational transformation, as reported by various authors. An analysis of these models and actions leads us to conclude that the leadership actions that leaders can use to bring about transformation can be divided into two types: structuring actions and inspiring actions.

Operationally, the leadership actions are defined as follows:

Structuring actions. The extent to which the leader engages in shaping new beliefs and value-based actions by providing information about the status quo, specifying the desired future state, defining and forming the required organization, and providing appropriate human and material resources. When using structuring actions, the leader is attempting to influence by creating a physical and psychological environment that reduces the choice of possible organizational behaviors to those required by the transformation.

It is important to remember that structuring actions may be viewed as a continuum, ranging from low amounts to high amounts of structuring behavior. A leader who presents only information on the inadequate functioning of the organization is providing a low amount of structuring behavior. Conversely, a leader who not only communicates the failure of the status quo but also restructures the organization, replaces key people, introduces new management systems, and develops different criteria for organizational effectiveness is engaging in high amounts of structuring behavior. Structuring actions, to be successful, require sufficient position power.

> *Inspiring actions.* The extent to which the leader engages in exciting organizational members by persuading and encouraging; discussing and clarifying; facilitating, processing, developing, and reinforcing the beliefs and new value-based actions that are required by the transformation. A leader uses inspiring actions to attempt to influence by persuasive and motivational communications that activate and induce the organizational actions required by the transformation.

Inspiring actions also fall on a continuum of low to high amounts. A leader who matter-of-factly tries to communicate a vision to the whole organization during an annual convention speech is demonstrating a low amount of inspiring behavior. On the other hand, a leader who passionately and frequently communicates the vision and values, discusses and clarifies the benefits of a new order, and also models, facilitates, encourages, and reinforces the new ways of doing things as required by the transformation is providing high amounts of inspiring actions. Inspiring actions, to be successful, require sufficient personal power.

In summary, structuring actions aim at limiting the range of new actions and constrain choice to those roles and actions required by the intended transformation. Inspiring actions aim at motivating organizational members, building their desire for the intended transformation, and inducing the behavior and roles it requires.

Transformational Leadership Strategies

The relative amounts of structuring and inspiring actions combine in an interactive influencing system to form four basic leadership strategies.

- *Enforcing strategies (S1).* Destroy the status quo and implement the new structure. Moderate to high amounts of structuring actions (HS) and moderate to low amounts of inspiring actions (LI).
- *Enabling strategies (S2).* Envision the future and develop the required actions and roles. Moderate to high amounts of structuring actions (HS) and moderate to high amounts of inspiring actions (HI).
- *Enlisting strategies (S3).* Facilitate commitment and participate in decisions and implementation. Moderate to low amounts of structuring actions (LS) and moderate to high amounts of inspiring actions (HI).
- *Endorsing strategies (S4).* Sponsor the transformation and monitor progress. Moderate to low amounts of structuring actions (LS) and moderate to low amounts of inspiring actions (LI).

THE SITUATIONAL LEADERSHIP® FOR TRANSFORMATION MODEL

The Situational Leadership® for Transformation model (SLT) is presented in Figure 17–2. In this model, the four quadrants, S1, S2, S3, and S4, represent the four basic transformational leadership strategies as derived from the relative amounts of structuring and inspiring actions. The structuring and inspiring actions are represented on two interacting dimensions. The four levels of readiness, OR-1, OR-2, OR-3, and OR-4, together with the descriptors for each level, are shown below the transformational leadership strategies. The curved line through the four transformational leadership strategies represents the high probability combination of structuring

FIGURE 17–2 Situational Leadership for Transformation Model (SLT)

Source: Copyright © the Center for Leadership Studies.

behavior and inspiring behavior. To use the model, identify a point on the organizational readiness continuum that represents organizational readiness to perform a specific transformation. Then draw a perpendicular line from that point to a point where it intersects with the curved line representing transformational leader behavior. This point indicates the most appropriate amount of structuring behavior and inspiring behavior for that specific level of organizational readiness.

We suggest that you use the same five-step implementation process described in Chapter 8 when you implement the Situational Leadership® for Transformation model. You should first determine whether the change being considered qualifies as a transformation. It must be a discontinuous change as defined earlier in this chapter. For instance, you may be considering changing from a production-efficiency to a customer-satisfaction paradigm. The next step is to determine the readiness level of your organization by assessing the organizational ability and organizational willingness for transformation. Third, the Situational Leadership® for Transformation model should be used to select and implement the appropriate transformational leadership strategy in terms of the mix of structuring and inspiring actions for the diagnosed level of organizational readiness. Fourth, the result of the transformational leadership strategy should be assessed. And fifth, depending upon the assessment, the cycle should begin again, or no further action should be taken at this time.

The appropriate transformational leadership strategies for each level of organizational readiness are as follows:

OR-1, FIXATED, FRAGMENTED, AND RESISTANT/S1, ENFORCING STRATEGY   "Destroy the status quo and implement new structure." The leader needs to engage in moderate to high amounts of structuring actions with below-average amounts of inspiring actions. Essential actions will include:

- Relentlessly, firmly, and repetitively presenting factual information that clearly and indisputably shows the impossibility of maintaining the status quo.
- Disconfirming all attempts to deny, rationalize, or refute the negative information about the status quo.
- Specifying and asserting the desired future state in terms of required performance criteria and critical success factors, modeling the belief systems, values, and actions required by the transformation.
- Replacing people who do not have the potential to develop the skills, insights, experience, and values required by the transformation with individuals from inside and outside the organization who are more suited to the change.
- Acquiring and reallocating the resources such as money, time, power, and rewards that will be required and shaping those roles and management systems that need to be aligned to, and that will support, the future state.

OR-2, INEPT BUT COOPERATIVE AND CONCERNED/S2, ENABLING STRATEGY   "Envision the future and develop the required actions and roles." The leader needs to engage in moderate to high amounts of both structuring and inspiring actions. Essential actions will include:

- Persuasive, enthusiastic, and inspiring communication of the vision, including the new beliefs and values to all parts of the organization; advocating the vision, beliefs, and values in discussions with individuals and groups; and explaining and reinforcing the benefits of the transformation and expressing confidence in accomplishing the vision.
- Modeling, clarifying, and reinforcing the beliefs, values, and actions that will fit the transformation.
- Interacting with, encouraging, and supporting those members and groups that show understanding and concern.
- Instituting performance enhancement systems built on the required beliefs and values (e.g., customer service, total quality).
- Educating and training the future key players specifically, and the organization in general, in the insights, understanding, and skills needed to implement and achieve the vision and enact the values.
- Replacing people who do not have the skills, beliefs, insights, experience, and values required by the change with individuals from inside and outside the organization who are more suited to the change.

- Acquiring the physical resources such as money and materials that will be required.
- Restructuring and reorganizing those parts and systems of the organization that need to be realigned to the future state.

OR-3, PERCEPTIVE BUT DIVIDED AND AMBIVALENT/S3, ENLISTING STRATEGY "Facilitate commitment and participate in decisions and implementation." The leadership needs to engage in moderate to high amounts of inspiring actions and below-average amounts of structuring actions. Essential actions will include:

- Expressing confidence and placing trust in the skills, insights, experience, and values of the organization and its overall capability to cope effectively with the change.
- Involving individuals and groups in the creation and communication of a clear vision and shared beliefs and values and the benefits they will offer the organization.
- Repeated and enthusiastic processing of the vision, the beliefs, and the value set with individuals and groups; clarifying and reinforcing the benefits of the transformation; and dealing with uncertainties and doubts.
- Interacting with individuals and groups to facilitate self-management and joint restructuring of elements such as roles, objectives, structures, and systems that will effectively implement the transformation, accomplish the vision, and enact the values.
- Providing assistance in allocating and utilizing the resources needed by individuals and specific groups to implement the actions that are required.

OR-4, VERSATILE, INTEGRATED, AND COMMITTED/S4, ENDORSING STRATEGY "Sponsor the transformation and monitor progress." The leadership needs to engage in below-average amounts of both structuring and inspiring actions. Essential actions will include:

- Trusting and inviting individuals and groups to contribute significantly to the creation of the vision, beliefs, and values for the future.
- Monitoring the decisions and plans for the design and implementation of the strategies, structures, and systems required.
- Being available for advice, opinion, support, and sanction.
- Linking with the external environment and stakeholders to facilitate the achievement of the transformation.

POWER BASES FOR TRANSFORMATIONAL LEADERSHIP

In Chapter 9, we discussed the importance of power and the integral relationship between leadership and power. Where leadership is defined as an attempt to influence the activities of others, individually and in groups, power may be defined as the leader's influence potential. Leaders must thus not only assess their leader behavior, or style, to understand and improve their influence with or over the members of their organization, but they must also assess their possession and use of power, especially in transformational leadership. The task of bringing about discontinuous change and getting organizational members to enact a new set of values in their work actions and organizational roles demands, above all, the skillful use of leadership and power.

In recent years, many academics, writers, and practicing managers have emphasized both the reality of power in organizational life and the fundamental need for power in leadership and change management.[10] Nevertheless, the concept of power has a negative connotation for some leaders, probably because of an unwarranted narrow association of the term with images of coercion and suppression. Coercive power is only one of several kinds of power that may be used by a leader in bringing about organizational transformation (see Chapter 9).

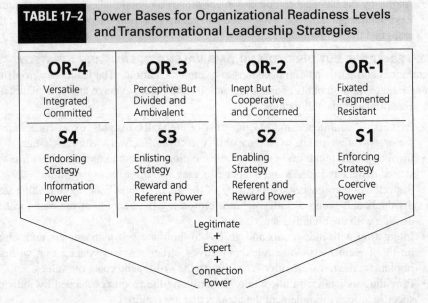

TABLE 17–2   Power Bases for Organizational Readiness Levels and Transformational Leadership Strategies

OR-4	OR-3	OR-2	OR-1
Versatile Integrated Committed	Perceptive But Divided and Ambivalent	Inept But Cooperative and Concerned	Fixated Fragmented Resistant
S4	**S3**	**S2**	**S1**
Endorsing Strategy	Enlisting Strategy	Enabling Strategy	Enforcing Strategy
Information Power	Reward and Referent Power	Referent and Reward Power	Coercive Power

Legitimate
+
Expert
+
Connection
Power

The appropriate power bases for specific organizational readiness levels and leadership strategies are shown in Table 17–2. Notice that in transformational leadership situations, all four of the transformational leadership strategies need a foundation of legitimate, expert, and connection power. These power bases may be seen as the general power bases that underpin the effectiveness of all leadership strategies throughout, and at any stage of, a transformation.

Legitimate power is probably the most critical. If the leaders who are initiating and attempting the transformation are not seen as legitimate, as not having the right to lead the transformation, their efforts will come to nothing. The condition that most often precipitates the need for a transformation is a crisis of poor organizational performance, and the current leadership is inevitably associated with the development of the crisis. Their consequent loss of legitimate power is the main reason why, in most transformations, the leaders who are charged to bring it about are newly recruited from outside the organization or the existing power network of the institution.

Expert power provides the leadership with credibility in terms of being perceived as having relevant knowledge and experience and knowing what needs to be done and how to do it—throughout the entire process.

Connection power provides the leadership with a network of additional reserves, or sources, of power on which to draw if required. Connection power can augment and strengthen any or all of the other power bases and is often the reason why outside consultants are called in to assist with the transformational process.

With the general power bases in place, it is appropriate now to look at the specific power bases that individually, or in combinations, serve to facilitate the implementation of a specific leadership strategy for a given organizational readiness level.

OR-1, FIXATED, FRAGMENTED, AND RESISTANT/S1, ENFORCING STRATEGY: COERCIVE POWER   Given the characteristic behavior patterns associated with OR-1, the leadership, through structuring actions, will need to institute high amounts of radical physical and perceptual change in a relatively short period of time to enforce the required new ways of perceiving, thinking, and acting. To achieve these changes in the face of apathy, fragmented organizational functioning, and resistance, the leader needs coercive power as the base from which to execute the enforcing strategies.

OR-2, INEPT BUT COOPERATIVE AND CONCERNED/S2, ENABLING STRATEGIES: REFERENT AND REWARD POWER The unfreezing achieved through the proper use of the enforcing strategies sets the scene for the enabling strategies. The OR-2 characteristics of ineptness coupled with cooperative organizational functioning and a concern for the viability of the organization call for the strong emphasis on high amounts of both structuring and inspiring actions of the enabling strategy.

This strategy, especially the communication of the vision, beliefs, and values for the future, is greatly enhanced by a referent power base. Referent power, otherwise known as *charisma,* is the critical power base for high amounts of inspiring actions. The leadership will also need reward power with which to encourage and reinforce the demonstrated new ways of perceiving and thinking and the new behavior patterns that will develop as a result of the enabling programs. Because the willingness element at OR-2 is characterized by anxiousness and receptiveness, the high amounts of structuring actions can be enhanced by reward power rather than coercive power.

OR-3, PERCEPTIVE BUT DIVIDED AND AMBIVALENT/S3, ENLISTING STRATEGY: REWARD AND REFERENT POWER At OR-3, the organization and key staff are characterized by perceptiveness, but they also exhibit divided organizational functioning and ambivalence toward the transformation. The need for the change is accepted, but there is doubt or skepticism about the viability and benefits of the transformation. The enlisting strategy utilizes the learning ability of the organization to facilitate commitment and to develop a participatory implementation of the vision for the future. These strategies create opportunities to overcome the ambivalence and skepticism through high amounts of inspiring actions. The inspiring actions now consist of clarifying, advocating, and involving, rather than the compelling leadership communication of vision, beliefs, and values. Reward power enables the leadership to show and clarify individual and organizational benefits stemming from the transformation and to commit to providing those benefits. Reward power is the critical power base of the enlisting strategy. Referent power, in the form of identification with the leadership, remains a very important additional power base.

OR-4, VERSATILE, INTEGRATED, AND COMMITTED/S4, ENDORSING STRATEGY: INFORMATION POWER At OR-4, the organization and key staff are versatile and function as an integrated and committed system. The role of the leadership is really that of letting the organization get on with the transformation through the use of an endorsing strategy with emphasis on low amounts of both structuring and inspiring actions. Because the organization at OR-4 will be taking charge of the structuring and inspiring actions in a self-leading fashion, the leadership's role will shift to one of being available for advice, acting as a sounding board from time to time, and fulfilling a linking-pin function with the stakeholders. Endorsing strategies are enhanced by information power; that is, the leadership either is a source of or is an access channel to information that may be required during the planning and execution of the transformation.

Summary

The Transformational Leadership strategies presented in Figure 17–2 can be used to assist leaders in diagnosing organizational readiness. Change strategies can then be designed that more correctly reflect the leaders role in implementing successful change that last. It is probable that the earlier phases will require more structuring strategies and the later phases will require more inspiring strategies. The appropriate strategy, however, will be determined by the organization's readiness to implement that phase. Each phase is, likely, in reality, a "situation."

Notes

1. Richard Beckhard, "The Executive Management of Transformational Change," in *Corporate Transformation,* eds. Ralph H. Kilman, Teresa Joyce Couin and Associates (San Francisco: Jossey Bass, 1989), 89–90.

2. See also Chapter 16: First-Order and Second-Order Change, pp. 290–291.

3. David A. Nadler, *Champions of Change* (San Francisco: Jossey Bass, 1998), 74.

4. Edwin C. Nevis, Joan Lancourt, and Helen G. Vassallo, *International Revolutions* (San Francisco: Jossey Bass, 1996), 42–43.

5. Beckhard and Harris use the concept of readiness to describe a system's or subsystem's attitudes toward the intended change. These authors identify capability as a second, apparently independent, factor to consider. See Richard Beckhard and Rueben T. Harris, *Organizational Transitions: Managing Complex Change* (Reading, MA: Addison-Wesley, 1977), 24–25. See also Anton J. Cozijnsen and William J. Vrakking, *Organisatie—diagnose en Organizatie verandering* (Alphen aan den Rijn: Samson Bedrijfs Informatie, 1992), 76–82. These authors use innovation capacity as their central concept. It is clear, however, that the term *innovation* is used in the context of a large-scale organizational change rather than in the sense of introducing a single innovation. See also Vrakking and Cozijnsen, *Management—Technieken bij Effectief Innovering* (Deventer Kluwer Bedrijfswetenskappen, 1992).

6. Edgar H. Schein, *Organizational Culture and Leadership* (San Francisco: Jossey Bass, 1992), 17–26. See also Edward J. Dwyer, "More Lessons in Leadership for Organizational Managers: From Tempest to Transformation," *Training and Development* 48 (March 1994): 41.

7. Schein, *Organizational Culture and Leadership.*

8. Dave Ulrich, Mary Ann Von Glinow, and Todd Jick, "High Impact Learning: Building and Diffusing Learning Capability," *Organizational Dynamics* (Autumn 1993): 53–54. See also Chris Argyris and D. Schon, *Organizational Learning: A Theory of Action* (Reading, MA: Addison-Wesley, 1978); Peter Senge, *The Fifth Discipline: The Art and Practice of the Learning Organization* (New York: Doubleday, 1991); Anne Perkins, "The Learning Mind-Set," *Harvard Business Review,* March–April 1994, pp. 11–12.

9. These characteristics are adopted from a checklist for assessing organizational culture or innovativeness by Vrakking and Cozijnsen. See Vrakking and Cozijnsen, *Management,* p. 73. See also Robert Clement, "Culture, Leadership, and Power: The Keys to Organizational Change," *American Demographics,* January 1994, pp. 42–45. For a similar list of characteristics of a learning organization culture, see also Schein, *Organizational Culture and Leadership,* pp. 364–366.

10. Jeffrey Pfeffer, *Power in Organizations* (Marshfield, MA: Pitman, 1981). See also Henry Mintzberg, *Power in and around Organizations* (Upper Saddle River, NJ: Prentice Hall, 1983); John P. Kotter, *Power and Influence—Beyond Formal Authority* (New York: The Free Press, 1985); Ronald G. Harrison and Douglas C. Pitt, "Organizational Development: A Missing Political Dimension," in *Power, Politics, and Organizations,* eds. Andrew Kakabadse and Christopher Parker (London: John Wiley and Sons, 1984), 65–85.

CHAPTER

18

Synthesizing Management Theory

Integrating Situational Leadership®
with the Classics

We have introduced a number of theories, concepts, and empirical research throughout the text. While introducing these theories, we have contended that there is no one best theory to utilize. In fact, all have had merit in lending to our collective knowledge of attitudes, behaviors, and personality. Rather than argue for one best approach or theory, we have attempted to create threads between them. It is important to understand how these theories weave together not only to support each other, but also to ultimately impact successful diagnoses and prediction of Performance Readiness®. In this chapter, we will synthesize these more clearly for you by weaving these independent theories and viewpoints into a holistic fabric with the Situational Leadership® Model at its core holding it all together.

While weaving these concepts together, we will not hold to a chronological order. We will begin to weave this leadership tapestry starting with a major contribution to the field—the Managerial Grid®.

MANAGERIAL GRID®

As mentioned in Chapter 4, the Managerial Grid by Blake and Mouton is an attitudinal model. The grid was based on two axes: high to low concern for production and high to low concern for people (see Figure 18–1). The model focuses on "concern," which is the values and attitudes that we carry within ourselves. While our attitudes may influence our feelings, they do not necessarily predict behavior. We cannot look at someone and see what his or her attitudes and values are, but we can make judgments based on behavior. It is important to recognize what this model is and what it is not. It is an attitudinal model, not a behavioral one.

To recall, the Managerial Grid is built up of nine axis points, which create the grid of 81 potential management styles (see Figure 18–2). Some of these were named. For instance, a 9 on production and a 1 on people would be called a "task leader." A 9 on production and a 9 on people would be called a "team leader/manager." A 1 on people and a 9 on production would

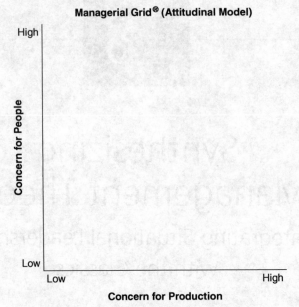

FIGURE 18–1   Managerial Grid®

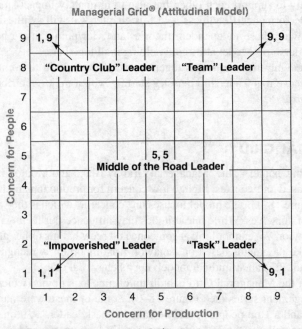

FIGURE 18–2   Management Styles

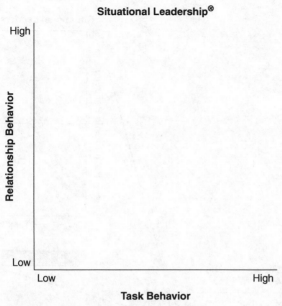

FIGURE 18–3   Situational Leadership®

be called a "country club manager," and a 1 on people and a 1 on production would be called an "impoverished leader." In a subsequent publishing, Blake and Mouton contended that a pendulum exists on this grid from a 9,9 to a 1,1 and in the middle falls a 5,5, which they named a "middle-of-the-road manager." These descriptors were later ranked by people and were assigned a value. As was expected, the respondents indicated that a "team leader" was valued much more than a "task leader" and definitely more so than an "impoverished leader." Trainings based on this model were created to take people from wherever they were on the grid to a 9,9. We believe that all leaders should have a high concern for results and a high concern for people.

While the Managerial Grid may at first appear to be different from Situational Leadership®, they actually fit together very well. Notice that in the Situational Leadership® Model, the axes are high to low task behavior and high to low relationship behavior (see Figure 18–3). Situational Leadership® makes the assumption that if you are going to be effective as a manager, you need to have a high concern for both production and people. The issue that arises from the Managerial Grid is that people were drawing behavioral conclusions from an attitudinal model. We cannot predict behavior from the basis of an attitudinal model. Leader behavior—not feelings, attitudes, and values—impacts follower behavior and performance. For example, many people have the same attitude about poverty yet behave differently under similar circumstances. One person may take action and volunteer at a soup kitchen or donate money, while another person with the exact same value and attitude regarding poverty may do nothing at all. Having the right values and attitudes is not enough. Having a high concern for results and people, though, is reflected in Situational Leaders who endeavor to use the most appropriate leadership style to match the follower's Performance Readiness® in any given situation. Figure 18–4 shows how Situational Leadership® carries out high concern for results and people through a variety of leadership styles. Thus, by viewing the Managerial Grid as an attitudinal model and Situational Leadership® as a behavioral model, the two models are complementary.

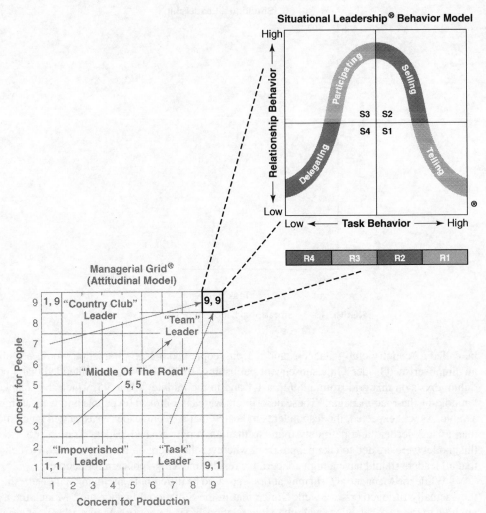

FIGURE 18–4 The Managerial Grid® and Situational Leadership®

Source: Copyright © 1985, 2006, Leadership Studies, Inc. All Rights Reserved.

Now that we have established a weave between the Managerial Grid and Situational Leadership®, let us begin to weave other theories into our holistic fabric.

LIKERT'S CAUSAL, INTERVENING, AND OUTPUT VARIABLES, AND SKINNER'S THEORY

You may remember that Likert (see Chapter 6) classified leadership strategies, skills, and styles as causal variables.[1] Likert also classified the condition of human resources as intervening variables. The interaction of causal variables and intervening variables leads to an end result variable

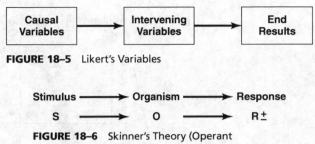

FIGURE 18–5 Likert's Variables

FIGURE 18–6 Skinner's Theory (Operant
Conditioning and Behavioral Modification)

(see Figure 18–5). This model is very similar to that of Skinner's theory, where a Stimulus on an Organism creates a Response (see Figure 18–6). We can shape that response by rewarding it, punishing it, or putting it on extinction. Both of these theories can be woven into the Managerial Grid, where intervening variables or the Organisms are similar to the concern-for-people axis; the end result variables or the Response are similar to the concern-for-production axis (see Figure 18–7). What, then, are we missing here? The causal variables are missing. The causal variables are the behaviors! This is where Situational Leadership® now comes into play, which ideally would be based on a value set of 9,9 in the Managerial Grid (see Figure 18–7). Situational Leadership® creates the necessary behavior by determining which style (S1, S2, S3, or S4) is needed to match the Performance Readiness® Level (R1, R2, R3, or R4) that is supported by the leader's values and attitude.

THEORIES OF MCGREGOR, LIKERT, MCCLELLAND, ARGYRIS, AND OTHERS

There are other theories that help us to understand attitudes or dispositions that deserve honorable mention. Several favorites are Mindset Y, 7 Habits, and Servant Leadership (see Figure 18–8). McGregor's Theory X and Theory Y, Likert's Management Systems, and Argyris's Immaturity-Maturity Continuum also weave easily into the holistic fabric.[2]

In essence, Likert's system 1 (Chapter 4) describes behaviors that have often been associated with Theory X assumptions about the nature of man. According to these assumptions, most people prefer to be directed, are not interested in assuming responsibility, and want security above all. Managers who hold Theory X assumptions think that people are basically lazy. They think that if they are going to get people to do anything, they are going to have to use the lower levels of Maslow's hierarchy of needs; they are going to have to use deprivation and fear. They believe that most people are not capable of leadership, that leaders are born not made. They think things, such as "The only leaders here are me and you, and I'm not sure about you." Theory X assumptions about the nature of man and Likert's corresponding system 1 behaviors seem to be consistent with the immature end of Argyris's continuum. System 4 illustrates behaviors that have often been associated with Theory Y assumptions. A Theory Y manager assumes that people are not lazy and unreliable by nature and, thus, can be self-directed and creative at work if properly motivated. They believe that most people can become leaders. These Theory Y assumptions about the nature of man and Likert's corresponding system 4 behaviors seem to be compatible with the mature end of Argyris's continuum. System 1 is a task-oriented, highly structured, authoritarian management style. System 4 is based on teamwork, mutual trust, and confidence.

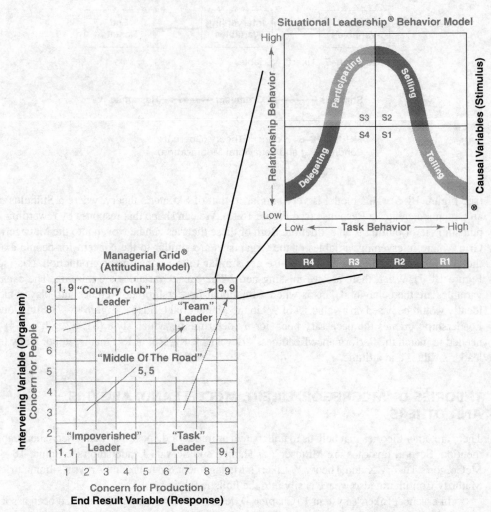

FIGURE 18–7   Likert's Variables, Skinner's Theory, and Situational Leadership®

Source: Copyright © 1985, 2006, Leadership Studies, Inc. All Rights Reserved.

In general, the tendency among people is to consider Theory X managers as emphasizing task behaviors in highly structured ways and Theory Y managers primarily using relationship behaviors. This is not always accurate. Theory X and Theory Y are managers' *assumptions* about the nature of people and do not necessarily translate directly into leader *behaviors*. There are numerous examples of both Theory X and Theory Y managers who use all four of the leadership styles. The assumptions underlying rational-economic people are very similar to those depicted by McGregor's Theory X. In essence, people are seen as primarily motivated by economic incentives: passive beings to be manipulated, motivated, and controlled by the organization and irrational beings whose feelings must be neutralized and controlled.

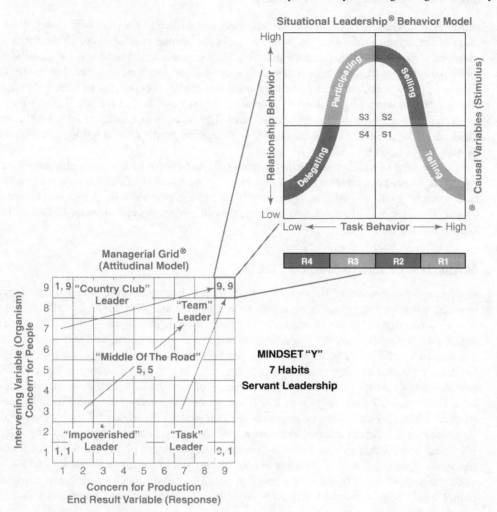

FIGURE 18–8 Other Theories

Source: Copyright © 1985, 2006, Leadership Studies, Inc. All Rights Reserved.

With social people come the assumptions that human beings are basically motivated by social needs; they seek meaning in the social relationships on the job and are more responsive to these than to the incentives and controls of the organization. The managerial strategy implied for social people suggests that managers should not limit their attention to the task to be performed, but should give more attention to the needs of their people. Managers should be concerned with the feelings of their people and, in doing so, must often act as the communication link between the employees and higher management. In this situation, the initiative for work begins to shift from leader to follower, with the leader tending to engage in behaviors related to Situational Leadership® Styles S2 and S3.

Self-actualizing people are seen as seeking meaning and accomplishment in their work as their other needs become fairly well satisfied. As a result, these people tend to be primarily self-motivated, capable of being very self-directed, and willing to integrate their own goals with those of the organization. With self-actualizing people, managers need to enrich their jobs and make them more challenging and meaningful. Managers attempt to determine what will challenge particular workers; managers become catalysts and facilitators rather than motivators and controllers. They delegate as much responsibility as they feel people can handle. Managers are now able to leave people alone to structure their own jobs and to provide their own socio-emotional support through task accomplishment. This strategy is consistent with a Situational Leadership® Style S4 that is appropriate for working with people of high levels of Performance Readiness® (R4).

According to McClelland, achievement-motivated people have certain characteristics in common.[3] They like to set their own goals, especially moderately difficult but potentially achievable "stretch" goals. In addition, they seem to be more concerned with personal achievement than with the rewards of success. As a result, they like concrete, task-relevant feedback. They want to know the score.

MASLOW'S HIERARCHY OF NEEDS

In developing the model of the motivating situation (Chapter 2), we contended that motives directed toward goals result in behavior. One way of classifying high-strength motives is Maslow's hierarchy of needs (Chapter 2).[4] As mentioned earlier, Maslow's hierarchy of needs model consists of five needs: physiological, safety, social, esteem, and self-actualization. The hierarchy of needs can be woven into the holistic fabric by knitting it into Situational Leadership® Styles and Performance Readiness® Levels to match. Looking at Figure 18–9, a person trying to satisfy physiological needs (matter of survival such as starvation) will tend to be at Performance Readiness® Level R1. If the person were attempting to fulfill safety needs (the fear of being killed, hurt, or maimed), the Performance Readiness® Level would tend to be around an R2. Social needs (acceptance, belongingness, and association) of the R2 and R3 would be best matched with the high-relationship behavior of S2 and S3. Esteem needs (recognition, status, power, and ability to lead others) would correspond with R3 and R4, and self-actualization needs (need to maximize potential and to do the best job one is capable of doing) would be best matched with an S4 style to correspond with the individual's R4 needs for autonomy.

It should be stressed that the relationship of Maslow's theory to the readiness levels in Situational Leadership® is not necessarily a direct correlation; it is an integrative benchmark to use in attempting to make better decisions for managing human resources. As a result, styles suggested as appropriate for one need level might not be exclusively for that level; other styles may also satisfy those needs to some degree. This caution holds true throughout our discussions in this chapter.

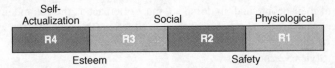

FIGURE 18–9 Maslow's Hierarchy of Needs and Situational Leadership®

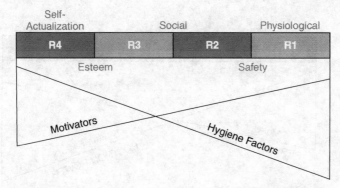

FIGURE 18–10 Herzberg's Theory and Situational Leadership®

HERZBERG'S THEORY OF MOTIVATION

Goals that tend to satisfy needs can be described by Herzberg's hygiene factors and motivators (Chapter 3).[5] Remember that the hygiene factors (environmental) included variables, such as company policies and administration, supervision, working conditions, interpersonal relationships, money, status, and security. Motivators (having to do with the work itself) included variables, such as achievement, recognition, challenging work, increased responsibility, growth, and development. They are not ends of a continuum; they are separate and distinct. Similar to Maslow's hierarchy of needs theory discussed above, hygiene and motivators can be woven into the holistic fabric with Situational Leadership® by matching them with the appropriate leadership styles and Performance Readiness® Levels. Looking at Figure 18–10, those who are currently more influenced by hygiene factors would fit better with lower levels of Performance Readiness®. Individuals who are more influenced by motivators will match up more closely with Performance Readiness® Levels R4 and R3.

SITUATIONAL LEADERSHIP® AND POWER BASES

In Chapter 8 we discussed two types of power: personal power and position power. *Position power* is the extent to which those people to whom managers report are willing to delegate authority and responsibility down to them. *Personal power* is the extent to which followers respect, feel good about, and are committed to their leader and to which they see their own goals as being satisfied by the goals of their leader. Also discussed in Chapter 8 were the seven power bases that are types of personal power (referent, information, and expert) or position power (coercive, connection, reward, and legitimate). As is illustrated in Figure 18–11 and supported by the work of Hersey, Blanchard, and Natemeyer, Situational Leadership® can provide the basis for understanding the potential impact of each power base.[6] In fact, in Chapter 8 it was established that the readiness of the follower not only dictates which style of leadership will have the highest probability of success, but also the power base that the leader should have in order to influence behavior.

As is suggested in Figure 18–11, a follower low in readiness (R1) generally needs directive behavior in order to become productive. Effective use of this S1 style may require position power. As a follower begins to move from Performance Readiness® Level R1 to R2, directive behavior is still needed (still requiring position power), and increases in supportive behavior are also

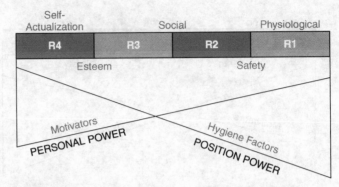

FIGURE 18–11 Situational Leadership® and Power Bases

important. S3 leadership styles tend to influence moderate levels of Performance Readiness® (R2 and R3) where combinations of both position and personal power become necessary. Personal power supports S3 and S4 styles that tend to motivate followers effectively at above-average Performance Readiness® Levels (R3 and R4).

PERSONALITY THEORIES

Along with all of these theories and viewpoints creating our holistic fabric, personality theories can also be woven into the mix. Personality is composed of not solely values, but also recurring modes of behavior. Personality theories such as DISC and Social Styles can be combined to help form a comprehensive view of human behavior. Although not originally intended to do so, DISC and Social Styles complement each other quite well.

DISC	Social Styles
Dominate	Driver
Influence	Expressive
Steadiness	Amiable
Conscientiousness	Analytical

These two theories can be laid out on a grid, with the axes on the grid representing the level or degree of assertiveness and the level or degree of responsiveness (see Figure 18–12). David McNally provides a good summary of the Social Styles personality styles.[7] People who have a "driver" personality style are often assertive and take charge of situations. These people tend to withhold emotions until they feel safe to express them. When influencing a person who is primarily a "driver," or D-type, personality, the leader should deliver messages with conviction. An "expressive" personality style is described as "spontaneous and demonstrative with opinions and feelings." People with expressive personalities will happily shake your hand and introduce you to others. When influencing a person who is primarily an "expressive," or I-type, personality, the leader should deliver messages with flair. The personality style of "amiable" is described as friendly, approachable, attentive, respectful, and sensitive. When influencing a person who is an "amiable," or S-type, personality, the leader should deliver messages with warmth. The personality style "analytical" is characterized as formal and reserved. When influencing a person who is primarily an "analytical," or C-type, personality, the leader should deliver messages with data.

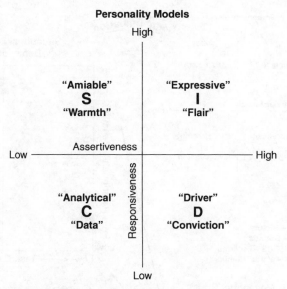

FIGURE 18–12   Personality Theories

What these models give you is insight into how to put the message you are trying to convey in a way that the person can best understand and, therefore, accept. Personality models provide the communication link.

Neuro Linguistic Programming (NLP) is another personality theory. It suggests that people tend to map their psychological world based on their favored representational system. Basically, this means that we perceive the world through our senses. Some people are kinesthetics, or feelings people, and prefer to touch their world. Some people are visuals, or picture people, and need to see the message we are trying to convey. Some people are tonals, or auditory people, and have to hear the message. Others are digitals, or data people, with a preference for numbers and facts. How we perceive the world gets filtered through our favored representational system and creates understanding. This does not tie in directly to the Situational Leadership® Model per se, but understanding somebody's representational system can help us in our attempts to influence others. Effective communication is about crafting a message that others are more likely to receive, accept, and understand.

Summary

Figure 18–13 integrates the summary material presented in this chapter. (Figure 18–14 is Dr. Hersey's original hand drawn illustration.) The table indicates how many of the theories discussed throughout this book are related to the various Performance Readiness® levels and their corresponding appropriate leadership style.

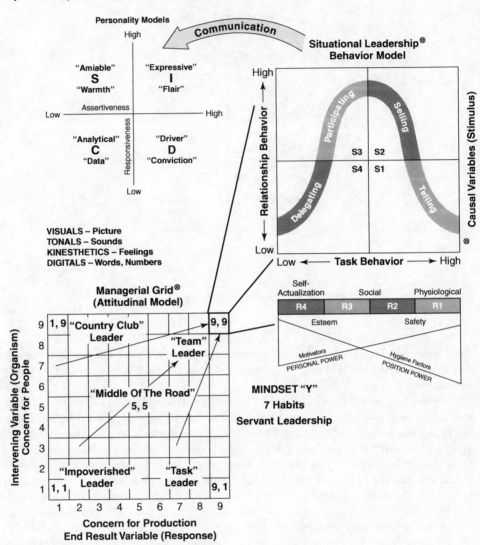

FIGURE 18–13 Forty Years of Behavioral Science

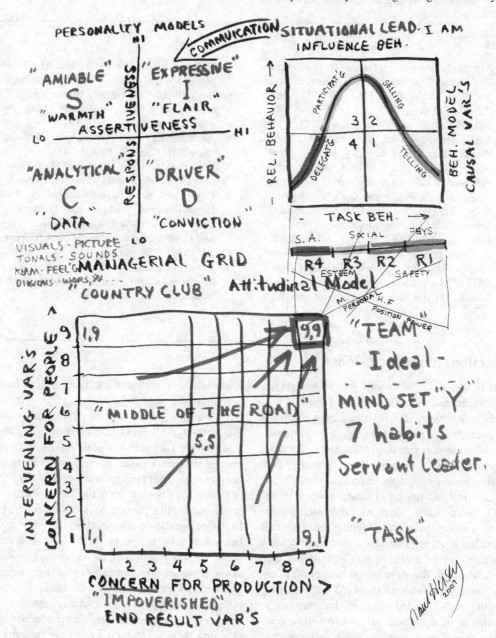

FIGURE 18–14 Integrating Situational Leadership® with the Classics

Source: Copyright © 1985, 2006, Leadership Studies, Inc. All Rights Reserved

Notes

1. Rensis Likert, *The Human Organization Managerial Grid® III*, 3rd ed. (Houston, TX: New York: McGraw-Hill, 1967), 197–211. (Gulf Publishing, 1984).

2. Douglas McGregor, *The Human Side of Enterprise* (New York: McGraw-Hill, 1960); Rensis Likert, *The Human Organization* (New York: McGraw-Hill, 1967); Chris Argyris, *Personality and Organization* (New York: Harper & Row, 1957). See also Chris Argyris, Robert Putnam, and Diana M. Smith, *Action Science* (San Francisco: Jossey-Bass, 1985).

3. David C. McClelland, John W. Atkinson, R. A. Clark, and E. L. Lowell, *The Achievement Motive* (New York: Appleton-Century-Crofts, 1953); McClelland Atkinson, Clark, and Lowell, *The Achieving Society* (Princeton, NJ:

D. Van Nostrand, 1961). See also McClelland, *Motivation and Society* (San Francisco: Jossey-Bass, 1982); McClelland, *Motives, Personality, and Society: Selected Papers* (New York: Praeger, 1984).

4. Abraham Maslow, *Motivation and Personality* (New York: Harper & Row, 1954).

5. Frederick Herzberg, *Work and the Nature of Man* (New York: World Publishing, 1966).

6. Paul Hersey, Kenneth H. Blanchard, and Walter E. Natemeyer, "Situational Leadership®, Perception, and the Impact of Power," *Group and Organizational Studies* 4, no. 4 (December 1979): 418–428.

7. David McNally, *The Eagles Secret: Success Strategies for Thriving at Work and in Life* (New York: Delacorte Press, 1998).

Reflections and Conclusions

Much is still unknown about human behavior. Unanswered questions remain, and further research is necessary. Knowledge about motivation, leader behavior, and change will continue to be of great concern to practitioners of management for several reasons: It can help improve the effective use of human resources. It can help in preventing resistance to change, restriction to output, and personnel disputes. And often it can lead to a more productive organization. Our intention has been to provide a conceptual framework that may be useful to you in applying the conclusions of the behavioral sciences. The value that a framework of this kind has is not in changing one's knowledge, but in changing one's behavior in working with people. We have discussed three basic competencies in influencing: diagnosing—being able to understand and interpret the situation you are attempting to influence, adapting—being able to adapt your behavior and the resources you control to the contingencies of the situation, and communicating—being able to convey the message in such a way that people can easily understand and accept it. Each of these competencies is different and requires a different developmental approach.

We have provided many examples and illustrations throughout this book showing how the behavioral sciences can make a positive difference in the performance of both individuals and organizations. But perhaps our primary objective in writing this book is to make a contribution to mankind, one that paves the way to peace. We believe that significant contributions to human well-being will not come primarily through economic, social, military, political, or technological decisions. If we are going to achieve our long-sought goal of world peace, it must come through a more effective leading of our human resources—toward helping people become more productive and allowing them a greater share of the benefits of that effort. Our viewpoint is a world outlook for practical, applied behavioral science—a point of view that sees all peoples sharing in the benefits that informed leadership brings, a world where people live and work in a way that contributes to their personal well-being, a world of peace. We invite you to join us in working toward this goal.

INDEX